Suleiman The Magnificent Sultan Of The East

Harold Lamb

Suleiman

THE MAGNIFICENT

by Harold Lamb

BIOGRAPHICAL NARRATIVES

Suleiman the Magnificent
Genghis Khan
Tamerlane
Nur Mahal
Omar Khayyam: A Life
Alexander of Macedon: The Journey to World's End

NOVEL

A Garden to the Eastward

HISTORICAL NARRATIVES

*The March of the Barbarians: The Mongol Dominion to the
    Death of Kubilai Khan*
The Crusades: Iron Men and Saints
The Crusades: The Flame of Islam
*The March of Muscovy: Ivan the Terrible and the Growth of the
    Russian Empire*
*The City and the Tsar: Peter the Great and the Move to the
    West (1648–1762)*

FOR OLDER CHILDREN

Durandal
White Falcon
Kirdy: The Road Out of the World

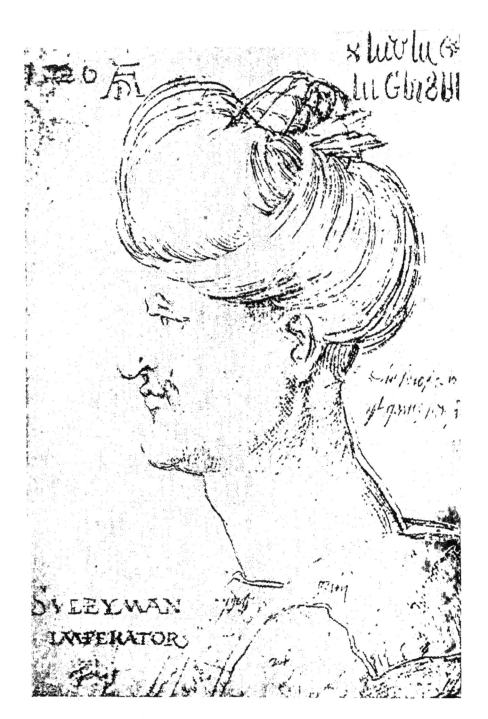

SULEIMAN AT THIRTY YEARS OF AGE

Sketched by Durer from contemporary description

Suleiman

THE MAGNIFICENT

Sultan of the East

HAROLD LAMB

Garden City, N.Y.

DOUBLEDAY & COMPANY, INC.

1951

To

MAJOR GENERAL EARL S. HOAG

U. S. Air Force

a friend of the Turks and my friend

Contents

I THE SUMMONS   1

   The Messengers   1
   Voices of the City   9
   Seclusion of the Family   18
   Sheepskins in the Treasury   27
   The Rose Garden between Two Worlds   33
   The White City   40

II LANDS OF WAR   45

   The Bastard of the Magnifica Comunita   45
   School of the Tribute Children   48
   Rhodes   56
   The Surrender   63
   The Cost of the Capture of Rhodes   67
   Mainstays of the Organization   75
   Appearance of the Laughing One   79
   The First Show at the Hippodrome   82
   Janizaris Overturn Their Kettles   88
   The Warning of Mohács   92
   Opening of the Corridor   99
   Appeal of the Queen Mother of France   105
   Europe's Kaleidoscope Changes   109

CONTENTS

Laws and Human Needs 114
Challenge of the First Embassies 119
Road to Vienna 123
The Kärtnertor 125
Retreat 130
Evidence of the Hippodrome 136
End of the Three Gentle Souls 140
The Utopia of 1531 144
March of the Phantom Army 150
Truce on the Danube 156

III   THE SEA 161
The Impelling Forces 161
Khair ad-Din Barbarossa 164
Charles Sails to Africa 170
Barbarossa Sells Himself 176
The Instructions of Monsieur de la Forêt 181
Foray into Italy 183
The Lost Army and the Holy League 187
The Duel off Prevesa 193
The Wind of Charles 198

IV   THE QUEST IN ASIA 207
The Secret in the Poem 207
What Ogier Busbecq Saw 209
The Enemy in Asia 211
Journey into the Past 213
The Case of Iskander Chelebi 217
The Power and the Glory 220
On the Steppes of Asia 222
Barbarossa's Last Jest 227
Dragut 232

CONTENTS

A Peace Is Won 238

The First Conspiracy of the Harem 241

The Three Mutes of the Bowstring 247

The Refuge on the Hill 253

The Danger of Peace and Wealth 257

The Approach of Ivan the Terrible 262

The Lost Admiral 265

The Ride to the Last Judgment 271

V MALTA, AND THE LAST MARCH OUT 277

The Impossible Task 277

Death of Bayazid 281

Refuge on the Black Mountain 288

The Dead Men of St. Elmo 292

Change of the Leaders 301

The Anniversary at Sziget 305

VI EBB OF THE TURKISH TIDE 311

The Lawgiver 311

The Accusers 315

When the Women Ruled 318

The Impelling Forces 325

The Destructive Forces 326

The Legend of the Warrior 329

The Legend of the Pirates, and Lepanto 332

The Barbary Coast 337

Suleiman and Ivan the Terrible 340

The Turks Hold to the Black Sea 342

"The Russians Stand Firm without Their Heads" 345

ACKNOWLEDGMENT 350

INDEX 357

ix

Suleiman
THE MAGNIFICENT

I

The Summons

The Messengers

WHEN the two foreign physicians consulted together and agreed that life had left the cancer-eaten body of Yavuz Sultan Selim, they told the Vizir they were certain.

They helped the Vizir carry the brazier of glowing charcoal farther away from the body stretched on the mattress under its brocade coverlet. Then they stretched out themselves to sleep on the rug. For nine days, they knew, they could not leave the sleeping compartment of the great tent. The death of the Sultan must not be revealed outside the tent for that many days. So the Vizir had decided.

Piri Pasha, the Vizir, was an old man, and he had not expected to live that long himself. Selim had been ailing for years; an indomitable will had driven his pain-racked body upon ceaseless campaigns for the eight years of his rule. A gnawing anger had made him merciless to those nearest him. Piri Pasha had been nearest of all—the minister who had shouldered the duties of an empire. The Bearer of the Burden, Selim had called him.

With the care of an alchemist leaving his crucibles and fires for a time Piri Pasha surveyed the sleeping quarters of his master, trying to think what might appear amiss to other eyes looking in through a slit in the cloth walls. Putting out all the flames but one in the oil lamps, he gathered up a pen case and

1

some scrolls of paper. These he placed by the mattress, as if
Selim had been writing. It had been the Sultan's habit to do so
in the hours of a night when he could not sleep. Glancing at a
paper to make certain it was in Selim's hand, Piri Pasha read
two lines of verse.

Those who ride to the hunt, do they ask——
In truth who are the hunters and who may the hunted be?

Yavuz, the Grim, had also been a poet.

In the reception quarter, Piri Pasha told the watching servants that the Sultan slept and he himself was going to rest. Outside by the standard pole he warned the household guards to
allow no one to leave the tent after him. But he did not rest.

Casually, as if refreshing himself in the cold mountain air,
he moved toward the horse-lines where two men waited. They
had been waiting at their post for several days.

As he went on alone the pasha sensed the muted stirring of a
great encampment—the creaking of water carts, the scurrying
of sheep driven toward the butchers. Through the night mist
drifted the smoke of damp fir wood. Around him the campfires
traced their orderly pattern into the hills. Nothing seemed to
be changed this night. But the old minister knew that he would
be followed, out of curiosity if not by treachery.

By the trough where the horse guards paced he found his
two men playing at fortune dice by a fire. For a long minute he
stood over them as if to watch, but actually to satisfy himself
that they were his messengers—the youngish swordbearer and
the commander of a division who, however, had drawn a captain's mantle over his insignia.

For that moment Piri Pasha felt the bitterness of countless
decisions, the weariness of anxiety lest he make a mistake and
cause more men to die. For a fleeting instant he longed to ride
away in the place of one of the messengers, to rest in his tulip
gardens by the water of the Bosphorus. But he could not do
that.

2

THE SUMMONS

Once it was known beyond doubt that Selim had died, there would be a few days of uncertainty. Until the Sultan's successor was girded with a sword at the tomb of Ayub, risings might take place—probably among the wild clans of Asia, almost certainly among any enemies of Selim. Yet Selim had left few enemies alive and he had only one son living.

That son was Suleiman, far down the Asian coast.

More than anything else, Piri Pasha distrusted the city, where the imperial treasures were stored, where foreigners still dwelt in palaces and a riot might be set going by a chance word or a bribe. He, the Vizir of the Osmanli Empire, had been living when first the Turks reined their horses into the city. After sixty-seven years he still thought of it as alien, and he had made his own home by the blue water out of sight of its walls——

Aware that the two players were watching him quietly, the Vizir stifled his anxiety and said, "The hour is late for such gaming as this." He accented a little the word *sa'at*, the hour. This was the key word, to start them on their mission. The three had already agreed on what must be done.

Obediently—for the Vizir of the empire spoke with the authority of the Sultan himself—the players pouched their wooden dice and rose. "May God be with you, Piri Pasha," responded the older officer courteously.

As they were going Piri Pasha stopped the younger and handed him a slip of paper with an unsigned scrawl upon it. "See that this count of the Kabarda horses is correct," he ordered, as if giving the swordbearer a duty task in mild reprimand. Almost certainly his words would be repeated throughout the encampment.

Waiting only long enough to see that his messengers were not followed before they could be in the saddle, Piri Pasha went to his tent. By the time he reached it, he knew, the others would be racing south through the hills, the divisional commander toward the great city, Constantinople, there to wait to make head against any rising while the swordbearer carried his

3

written message at the speed of hard-ridden horses across the Bosphorus into Asia, to search for Suleiman, the son of Selim.

Piri Pasha had hoped to carry out his pretense that the Sultan was still living for a week. But at the end of five days he could tell that his secret was known outside the imperial tent. It was known, but not yet proved. Weighing the time he had gained against the moods of tens of thousands of armed men, he decided to supply the proof himself. Going out abruptly to the standard where the seven white horsetails hung, he announced that Yavuz Sultan Selim had died in the night.

At once the nearest troops, the janizary brotherhood, felled their tents by slashing the cords, and tore off their headgear in mourning. Shouts of grief echoed through the camp streets.

Experienced as he was in the varying moods of the army, Piri Pasha felt fleeting astonishment that these janizaris, who had suffered from the cruelty of a man tortured himself by spasms of agony, should grieve like children at his death.

The army was safe, Piri Pasha thought. And at once he decided to leave the encampment. Placing his seal on all money chests and on Selim's personal treasure, he gave over the command—but not his seal ring—to another general, advising him how to lead the funeral cortege south by slow stages. That night Piri Pasha rode after his messengers, in disguise, toward the city.

By the ninth day, he calculated, Suleiman should arrive at the city. If something went wrong and the son of Selim did not appear, why then the Bearer of the Burden would have to cope with the situation in some way——

As he galloped without torches to light his road, suddenly he was aware that he missed Selim, whose hard purpose had never faltered before danger or difficulty.

On the fifth day Suleiman rode north along the coast road toward Europe.

4

He rode easily, resting his long, thin body at times by leaning forward on the shortened stirrups. He loved horses and enjoyed most the hours he spent at the upland breeding farms. The hand on the rein was brown and muscular. He gave to the saddle with almost womanly grace, his restless gray eyes, his thin lips and narrow beaked nose sensitive to the touch of the warm wind on his face.

Except for a slight mustache, he was shaven, and the loose cloth wrapped around his lean head gave him the semblance of a young and energetic monk or dervish. The son of Selim was no more than twenty-five years old. As he rode he noticed the stacked hay, the fertile red earth, bare for the spring's plowing. The road twisted around inlets where he counted the masts of fishing ketches moored against the red-roofed villages. This southern coast had been assigned him to manage and he had done his best with it, as he had with the district in the sun-warmed Crimea, knowing all the time that he was being tested and a record kept of his mistakes. But he liked best the great city where he had had his schooling, in the barrack under the plane trees.

For sixteen years Suleiman had served an apprenticeship at caring for human beings and cattle, with experienced officers to advise him and even a miniature court like his father's—but never having the advice or companionship of his grim father, who had been absent in the wars.

In his girdle he carried the brief note from the Vizir, almost a stranger to Suleiman, telling him only that the sword of the House of Osman awaited him at the shrine outside the city—the summons that his own advisers had distrusted, warning him that it might be a trap to bring him headlong to the city with only a small escort. "Ears deceive, eyes reveal," they had warned him.

But the exhausted messenger had sworn that he had the writing from the hand of Piri Pasha. Then the Greek, Ibrahim, argued that if the message were a lure to draw Suleiman north, it would have said that Selim had died, or that Piri Pasha urged Suleiman to come. Instead, it merely mentioned the family sword. And Suleiman himself had noticed how the rider had fallen asleep immediately on a carpet under the olive trees, not even holding to the purse of gold coins that Suleiman had given him. It looked as if the man had actually gone without rest for several nights. Suleiman had decided that he would obey the summons. Then ride, his companions urged, without wasting more time. It did not seem strange to them to start off that moment, without thought of Suleiman's family or their own.

The dervish had angered him, catching at his rein to chant that he was fortunate beyond other men, he who bore the name of that earlier wise Solomon. . . . Suleiman was the tenth of the House of Osman . . . called to rule at the dawn of the tenth century of Islam. *"In every age one is appointed to grasp the age by the horns"* . . . as if it had been a bull.

They had given him orders, hastily prepared, to sign. And they had watched with new interest while he traced the curves of his signature. As if it were in some manner different from the evening before.

In their minds, he knew, he had already become the Sultan, the ruling member of the House of Osman. He was alone. He had no longer any brothers and Selim had left no uncles living. If he lost his life at the hands of unknown conspirators at the ferry to the city, the House of Osman would cease to be.

His ancestors for the last generations had been alone, because of the strict law of their household. There had always been so few of them, and so few of the Turks. They had been given such odd nicknames, Ghazi and Kaisar-i-Rum—Victor and Caesar of a new Rome. So foreigners put it. Yet they had never had a people or an actual empire of their own. Mehmed Fatih—Mehmed II, the Conqueror—had, of course, wrested Constantinople from the Europeans, but that same versatile Sultan had also laid down a rule. Henceforth, Mehmed had declared,

6

a Christian would be the equal of a Moslem—a Greek born, of an Anatolian born.

Once spoken, the Conqueror's word had become law. After him his son, Suleiman's grandfather, had laid down another rule. The people, the Osmanlis, must be educated above the other peoples of the Europe they had invaded. That had been Bayazid's idea. And during the sixty long years of their reigns these two ideas had been carried out. Could such ideas shape and hold together a nation that did not exist except for them? Two men and two ideas, and then the reckless Selim breaking through the mold the older men had made, to conquer new territories——

Abruptly Suleiman realized that the road ahead of him was blocked. A peasant's cart had jammed its wheel on a narrow stone bridge across a stream. The load of wheat sheaves on the cart had toppled into the road. The two outriders who preceded Suleiman to clear the way had dismounted here to struggle stupidly, trying to help the peasant clear the wheel.

Approaching the cart, Suleiman reined in. At once he heard the beat of galloping hoofs behind him. Today his companions, whatever their rank, had remained discreetly a javelin's cast behind their prince. Now at sight of the tangle on the bridge, they were rushing up to protect him.

Impatient at the delay and the needless shouting, Suleiman twisted the reins in his hand. His splendid gray pacer turned down into the gully, splashed through the stream and lunged up the far bank to the road beyond the block. Then the anxious outriders raced past, to take up their posts again. It crossed Suleiman's mind that he might have galloped into an ambush at the stream, but he had thought only how he might get past the cart. And he did not relish being left alone. Over his shoulder he called, "Come up, Ibrahim."

Often when he was troubled he called for Ibrahim, the First Falconer, who had been born a Christian and a Greek at the edge of the sea. Ibrahim was older than he, dark and slender

7

with long outthrust jaw and eyes quick to see the way past any difficulty. Usually Ibrahim played the guitar for him or read aloud from books unfamiliar to other men. Suleiman had a knack of solving practical difficulties without effort, but he liked to hear the quick-witted Ibrahim dissect a problem. "Eh, Ibrahim," he asked, "do you think the army believes that my father poisoned Bayazid, his father?"

For once the Greek had no ready answer. Because the army did believe exactly that. Had not Bayazid, the mild and far-seeing, abdicated the sultanate to Selim, the ruthless? And had not the aged Bayazid died soon after from an unidentified illness while journeying away from the city to live in peace at his birthplace? Certainly he must have died from poisoning. Yet there was no proof. And the Greek did not know what answer would satisfy Suleiman. It would not do to lie to him.

"The army believes it," he agreed carefully, "because the Yavuz Sultan was determined to hold all power, alone. While Bayazid lived, wherever he might be, there were still two sultans."

Suleiman gave no sign of assent. When he withdrew his mind like this, the Greek could not guess his thoughts. At times Suleiman had a way of taking questions before some inner tribunal of his own. The practical side of the prince Ibrahim understood very well, but not this mysticism. Anxiously he probed at the mood of his young master.

"You cannot change what has happened. Before this morning. The morning of your power lies ahead along this road." (Suleiman could be deceived easily enough, yet it was always danger-ous to do so, because he had a quick temper that he hid carefully under his silence, and his whimsey.) "Everything that has hap-pened has been fortunate for you, as that dervish said. Bayazid himself said that you would rule. Perhaps the late Sultan Selim feared that you would be named in his place"—quickly Ibrahim glanced at the sensitive, impassive face beside him. "Don't look back. Look ahead. You *are* fortunate." In his eagerness he

8

dared raise his voice. "No brothers to race you in to the imperial city—no enemies to draw their reins across your path. All power waits for the touch of your hand. Even the Vizir waits to bend his head before the shadow of God on earth. With luck like yours, there's nothing you can't do."

Suleiman smiled. "Except turn back upon this road."

Voices of the City

He did not turn back. For three days he rode fast. Then he left behind him the quiet moist earth and the smoke of charcoal burners in the shielding forest. The hoofs of his horse jarred on the smooth stones of a road that had been made by Romans. It led to a height that was Chamlija, the Place of the Cypresses, where the dead waited and the living passed by. Beyond that height shone the blue of the water of Marmora.

So he left the quiet of the open land, and came within sight of the city he was to rule. Already things were different. Here the folk did not bend over green barley or move gently with the herded sheep; they thronged to the stone road to stare at him and he knew that in some fashion the news that had come to him had reached the city also. In the city rumors ran from caravan lodging to street, they bred in the vapor of the baths and passed with the rowing caiques up and down the water front. As he rode between the throngs of people, voices murmured, "Now may good fortune be with the son of Selim!"

At the shore a ferry waited with a carpet laid over the tiller seat. Across from him the great city waited, displaying no sign of resistance. Like a lovely and disdainful woman it lay between the waters, heedless of all that was commonplace, seeking only the man who would enter as master. Suleiman had governed it during the absence of Selim, and had grown familiar with its moods, as he had come to know its landmarks from the minaret towers of the Aya Sofia rising over the plane trees to

9

the far burned column the Romans had left standing near the gate of his palace.

When he stepped from the ferry barge to the boat landing in the garden, the gardeners hurried to greet him without command. Down the slope raced young soldiers, leaping the flower beds, the neck drops of their gray caps tossing. These janizaris, the Young Troops, guardians of the city, rushed around him, crowding against him, the knives in their girdles brushing his arms. Having sighted him, they were clamoring, "The gift! The payment—make the payment!"

Excitable, and dangerous if they got out of hand, the janizaris were calling for the customary reward, paid of late upon the succession of a new sultan. Their active muscular bodies pressed around the slight, tall prince. Through them pushed the veteran Agha of the Janizaris, puffing after his run, grinning and holding out a red apple in his scarred hand. Staring at Suleiman, the agha struck him lightly over the shoulder—the customary greeting to a new chief of the janizaris. "Can you eat the apple, son of Selim?"

This apple signified to them in some way the legendary antagonist of the janizary brotherhood, the Rome across the water in Italy.

"In time," said Suleiman briefly, taking the apple.

"The gift! Make the gift!"

"In its time." Suleiman pushed on through them. The agha grunted and the others fell back silently. From the fountain under the trees the divisional commander whose mission had been to hold the city quiet drew a long breath of relief and disappointment. Suleiman had said too little. He had shown no fear of the household guards, yet he had not forced their respect. They had hardly found him to be the true son of Selim.

Suleiman ate alone that noon. From the small bowls placed on the clean cloth in front of his knees he took tiny squares of meat broiled in herbs, and portions of squash stuffed with rice, and figs in sour cream, pretending to enjoy them. He touched the gold goblet, and a silent boy stepped forward to pour sherbet into it.

Although he managed to appear coldly content with his food and the service of the watchful pages of the inner palace, Suleiman felt the dry fever of anxiety. The eating compartment was ugly and narrow, and alien. And he had managed himself badly before the tumultuous janizaris. He could never win their devotion, as Selim had done. . . .

Ten years before. Selim, rebelling against Bayazid, defeated in battle by the old Sultan, retreating into the seabound fastness of the Crimea, where Suleiman had been sent with his mother—Selim laughing at the order of his father to send the youthful, studious Suleiman to govern Constantinople—Selim riding off with the wild Tatars, their drums throbbing, going against the city and the Sultan his father. The matchless janizaris marching out under orders to drive back Selim and the Tatars, and then at the first sight of Selim riding against them, the janizaris rushing forward to cry Selim's name, and touch his stirrup, swearing no other man should lead them . . . by that act the janizaris had disowned their Sultan and chosen a new leader. Bayazid had had to yield the sword of Osman and then to yield his life . . . if he had not been given poison at Selim's order, he had lost the will to live . . . the bitter memory of that year lay between Selim and Selim's son, who had been kept at a distance from the army and the companionship of his father . . . Selim's last words to Suleiman had been spoken years ago, half contemptuously, half pleading: *If a Turk dismounts from the saddle to sit on a carpet, he becomes nothing—nothing.*

Sitting alone at his food, washing his hands in the silver basin brought by another page, Suleiman could not help thinking how they would have served another man in just that fashion. Until Piri Pasha came, and the high officers swore obedience to him, Suleiman was nothing. And Piri Pasha, who should have

11

been waiting to greet him at the ferry, had not appeared.

After eating, the household pages expected him to sleep awhile. They unrolled the mattress in his sleeping room. But Suleiman could not bring himself to lie down. Instead he paced by the wall, fingering his old belongings carefully stored in niches—manuscripts copied in the clear hand of Kasim, his tutor—old examination papers he himself had written, on the movements of the stars or decisions of the Law. A small clock case he had made out of gold when he had had to learn a handcraft. Since he liked the feel of smooth gold and fancied the precision of European watches, he had enjoyed making this case.

The school lessons and the clock had no meaning now. They belonged to a boy who did not exist——

He felt a sharp stab of loneliness, for the touch of Flower of Spring, and the sight of his own boy again, for cheerful Ibrahim making music when they sailed in the moonlight after digging shrimps along the shore. A man could not enjoy such things alone.

"Sultan Suleiman Khan!"

Although the voice startled him, Suleiman turned casually to the curtained entrance, as if mildly surprised at being disturbed in his thoughts. Through the curtain strode Piri Pasha wrapped in a funny mantle, looking old and tired. He caught Suleiman's hand to his heart and kissed it. His voice quivered with the emotion of the aged as he explained how he had hurried to the utmost of his poor strength, and how the sight of his young master in health restored his failing spirit. His words had the artificial cadence of the court, but he was sincere. Suleiman could detect truth in a man, as he knew gold by the touch.

Moreover, the veteran Vizir began at once to issue orders in Suleiman's name for a new clock in running order to be brought, and black garments of mourning, and prayers to be said publicly for Selim that sunset. At this an orderly hum of movement filled the palace that had been like a caravan *serai* awaiting guests.

12

Under the new black robes Piri Pasha advised Suleiman—when they were alone for a moment—to wear a tunic of cloth of gold. "Never be without splendor," he explained. "People may love you for yourself but when they look at you they must see you in some manner as a ruler of rulers."

Not satisfied with the glint of gold, he had two red heron's plumes brought to fix upon Suleiman's headcloth with a gleaming ruby clasp. "Why not?" he said gently. "A time of fear has ended, a time of hope has begun—God willing."

"A time of hope?"

Piri Pasha hesitated, brushing his gnarled fingers through his gray beard. "Yes. The reports of your district of Magnisiya came under my eyes. You gave too much of your time to hunting and sailing, as young people do. Yet it was also said that you gave justice to any person who asked it, whether foreign or peasant or Christian *raya*. Because of that, I hope. I am a foolish old man." His beard twitched in a smile. "The ancient Solomon, upon whom be blessings, showed his wisdom in his judgments. He asked only for an understanding heart, and he lived to wear emeralds as well as rubies."

The gray eyes lighted, amused. "No, Piri Pasha, it is you who have given me hope."

The old man bent his head, a courtier again. In the outer corridors he took anxious note how everyone stared covertly at the slender figure in black, the white impassive face under the regal heron's plumes. And he let fall chance remarks about a second Solomon and a time of hope that would come with him.

Outside the gates where janizaris stood motionless on guard, Venetian spies listened to the gossip of servitors as they tried to pick up clues to the nature of the Sultan-to-be. "A time of hope has come," they heard.

From afar the spies watched the burial of the late Sultan, after Suleiman and Piri Pasha had ridden out to meet the funeral cortege, and had dismounted to walk beside the great officers bearing the casket. A few men, walking up a rubble-strewn hill where fires burned to keep away evil spirits. Taking a shrouded body from the casket, and lowering it into a hole in the ground. All this was done as old custom required.

Suleiman repeated the customary phrase, "Let the tomb be built, and a mosque joined to it. Let a hospital for the sick and a hostel for wayfarers be joined to the mosque." Then he added a thought of his own. "And a school."

A startled secretary taking silent note of his spoken words asked, "Where?"

Suleiman glanced around the hill. Close to him the shell of a Byzantine palace stood, tenanted only by some tribal families. The granite stones and marble columns of the palace would yield good building materials for the mosque tomb of Selim, and the families could move elsewhere. "Here," he said.

Then, as custom required, the cavalcade rode back outside the city wall to the gnarled cypress trees around the tomb of a soldier saint, Ayub. Here waited a white-bearded man robed like a wanderer but holding a slender curved sword sheathed in silver that gleamed with precious stones. He was ·the head of the Mevlevi dervishes, the brotherhood that had aided the Osmanlis from their earliest struggles. The sword was the symbolic weapon of the House of Osman, never to be put aside when it had been accepted.

Taking Suleiman by the hand, the head of the dervishes led him to a dais where he could be seen by the crowd as the old man announced loudly that God had willed him to be the Sultan, head of the House of Osman.

Girdling the sword over Suleiman's hip, the Mevlevi cried in warning: "We who believe from of old give to thee the keys of the Unseen. Be thou guided aright, for if not, all things will fail thee."

Few of the listeners could understand the Mevlevi. They saw only that Suleiman had accepted the sword that made him responsible for the nation. How could a leader be guided, except by his own wisdom? What else had guided the Yavuz Sultan who had conquered such vast lands with his sword? From that moment Suleiman was bound to serve his nation.

Riding back into Constantinople behind the new Sultan, Piri Pasha, the minister, felt that he had carried out the full of his obligation to the Yavuz Sultan. Selim's successor had been accepted by the army and greeted by the people. Even if he himself could not retire to his garden on the Bosphorus, his mind was at peace.

He let drop a hint to Suleiman, because he had noticed that the new Sultan would listen carefully to advice. A first act, like the first note of music, was important. Suleiman's first act might be one of mercy, he hinted. Certain Egyptian merchants had been imprisoned for no cause except that they had angered Selim——

Suleiman ordered them released, without payment. It gave him a warm, good feeling to speak the words. Then, observing the sentinels on duty outside his gate, he remembered the gift to the janizaris that he had promised, in time, and he decided to give it quickly. Already observers noticed that he would brood in silence for a long interval, but he had a way of acting swiftly, as if to get a thing out of his mind. The janizaris of his own guard were awarded the amount Selim had given, no more and no less; yet all others shared with them alike, so the sum of the payment was more than before.

From the faces of his household guards Suleiman could not tell whether they were pleased or angered. They stood their posts motionless, athletes swathed in blue cotton, only their eyes moving under their gray dervish caps. They were his personal guards, bound to follow him now where he went, without thought of their own lives. Yet he could not forget how they had turned from Bayazid.

After sunset, at the hour of lamp lighting, Suleiman heard the late prayers said. Alone, he sat on an age-old carpet upon

15

the half balcony above thousands of bowed heads. The tiny flickering of lamps could not light the dimness of the vast mosque built by his grandfather.

Opposite him a strange reader stood on the prayer stand, holding a sword in one hand, a Koran in the other. When this imam raised his voice sharply, a faint echo answered from the dome overhead. The voice and the echo chimed: "The mercy of God, all pitying, all compassionate, be upon the sultan of sultans, the ruler of rulers, the shadow of God and dispenser of crowns upon earth, Lord of the Two Worlds, Lord of the White Sea and of the Black Sea . . . Sultan Suleiman Khan, son of Sultan Selim Khan."

So was his name read into the prayer. He was acknowledged Sultan.

Before the last echo had died, an impulse of fear chilled his motionless body. He was alone, raised above the others. By title, he was head of the janizaris, among whom he had not a single friend; he was head of the nation his ancestors had striven to create out of their own minds, their passions and unceasing courage. Yet what reality had the Turkish nation, except for the fact that for a while hundreds of thousands of men of all sorts scattered over a great portion of the earth would obey his pronounced commands?

More, he was named head of a religion—the shadow of an unseen God—about which he understood less than the majestic man in the stand across from him. The last echo clung to the air. Truly, he, Suleiman, was no more than the son of Selim Khan. . . .

After a few days the Venetians in the palace of the Bailo across the water of the Golden Horn studied the reports of their spies and wrote down their descriptions of the new Sultan and their predictions of what his reign, as they put it, might mean to Europe.

Bartolomeo Contarini wrote: "He is no more than twenty-five years old, tall but wiry—his neck long, his face thin and very pale. He has only the shadow of a mustache and his manner is noticeably pleasant. The talk is that he is a wise Lord, given to much study, and men of all types hope for good from his rule."

Such reports went to the anxious Signory at Venice by the first fast galleys to clear from the Golden Horn.

By autumn of that year of our Lord, 1520, the reports sped to Rome in the pouches of couriers. There the young Pope Leo X—he who had been Giovanni de' Medici—gave thanks that the Turkish terror had been stayed, if not ended, because the Sultan of the Osmanli Turks who had flashed across Asia like a comet had entered Europe only to die there, without further harm. Had he not been the champion of the idolatrous prophet *Mahomet?*

Leo's favorite news commentator, Paolo Giovio, a physician who had taken to digesting tidings from the outer world as a hobby, made note accordingly that "Pope Leo, having made certain of the death of Selim, gave command that prayers be sung throughout Rome, and men should go barefoot to the prayers."

In Paris the young scion of the House of Valois, Francis I, heard the news carelessly as he heard everything. Paris was far from Constantinople, and already the gifted Francis was being called the first gentleman of Europe.

By chance they were all young, these princes of a continent seething with the ferment of renaissance, seizing upon new ideas and exploring for new worlds beyond the oceans. At Aix, the family shrine, Charles Hapsburg had just been crowned as Charles V, Emperor of the Holy Roman Empire—having defeated Francis' attempt to elect himself to that high office. Old Jakob Fugger, of Fuggerau in the Tyrol, had lent Charles enough florins on security of a mortgage on the silver mines at Guadalcanal in the New World to buy his election. Then, too, Charles had gained the approval if not the liking of truculent

Henry of England, who had taken as his first wife Charles's aunt, Catherine of Aragon.

In those particular months Charles V was being bothered by a stubborn monk, Martin Luther, who had written a challenging tract entitled *On the Liberty of a Christian Man*. The new printing presses circulated this pamphlet through the German cities in spite of the fact that it challenged the authority of Leo as the head of the ancient Church, and of Charles as head of the remnant of the Roman Empire. No, all in all, Charles could have given little thought to the appearance of a new Turkish sultan.

When Paolo Giovio had compared the different letters from Constantinople, he summed them up in a prediction. "All men agree that a gentle lamb had succeeded a fierce lion . . . for Suleiman is young, without experience—altogether given to quiet repose."

His prediction proved to be much mistaken.

Seclusion of the Family

Some of the Europeans wrote home that Suleiman was also devoted to his family. Upon that family they never set eyes. But this time what they wrote was true.

Within a matter of days after he had made his ride to Constantinople, Suleiman's household servants had escorted Flower of Spring and her infant son thither, carefully screened from the watching eyes of the world. It was easily done, because the Turks were accustomed to traveling light. Gulbehar—Flower of Spring—and her son arrived with no more than a few garments folded into saddle sacks and small trinket boxes. And at the Serai, the House, the quarters prepared for them were no larger than the niches and nooks of a caravan serai, where travelers slept the night upon the road.

In that Serai, however, a corridor divided the women's apartments from the Sultan's outer chambers. When Suleiman wished to enter the women's part of his household, custom required him to send a message in advance before he walked down the corridor past the women's guards to his sleeping room there.

No other man could enter this secluded part. Only slaves lived behind the doors of the harem. He never failed to sense the irony of it—that the place he knew as home was a labyrinth of slaves. They kept his house for him, such as it was.

A fire of scented wood crackled in the hooded hearth. Light rippled pleasantly along the tiled walls. Trees and flower borders painted on the tiles gave the room the aspect of a garden nook. Once he had entered it, Suleiman threw off his headcloth and flung himself down on the wall couch.

His head was shaved except for one long lock of hair; he shaved his chin after the manner of the army. Without moving he watched the hearth fire until Flower of Spring came in, through the other curtain. And he checked the ceremonious greeting that she tried to repeat, her slight forehead wrinkled. She had been made to memorize it, he knew.

"I may be lord of your life," he assured her, "but I am not all those other things."

With Flower of Spring—the name of Gulbehar had been given her when she had been fetched from the Circassian mountains—he did not feel alone. Her supple body moved lightly, as if wind-blown. Their son had her fair hair.

His pride, always fastidious, was satisfied by her loveliness. Yet he disliked bringing Gulbehar here, to be pent up with scores of other women, all of whom had duties and privileges of their own—having been attached in one way or another to the service of the Osmanlis.

Freed from the necessity of repeating her lesson, the slender girl curled up on the carpet by him and showed him a present she had made, a brocaded bag with drawstrings.

"Open it," she urged, when he admired it.

To his surprise it contained rolls of paper on which he had

19

written verses. He had labored at the verses, in Persian which he disliked. And he knew they were not good. It was typical of Gulbehar that she kept the old poems carefully, and made an absurd bag for them. She could not read them.

"Do you know what these are?" he asked suddenly. "What they really are?"

"Truly." When she moved restlessly, the scent of dried jasmine came from her clean body and hair. Jasmine, he thought, not roses. "They are writings by your hand, splendidly made as —as—"

Truly she had never heard such names as Maulavi, the mystic, or Ghazali either.

"As old Kasim could make," she ventured hopefully.

Suleiman touched her hair and pointed at the signature. "Yet it says here, they are by one who seeks a friend. No more than that."

Again the girl's forehead wrinkled over the kohl-darkened brows. "Am I not a friend?"

"You are more." He smiled, not wishing to tell her she was both more, and less.

It amused Suleiman that when he visited his infant son or slept with Gulbehar, he himself had to conform to the silent ritual of the household. Mute African slaves took post outside the harem bedroom and other women were sent away beyond hearing. When he left the Circassian girl, he was expected to steal back at daybreak to his outer sleeping room. There the boy pages would turn their backs quickly, if they happened to be awake by the night lamp.

Later the wardrobe page would bring him a waistcloth and huge bath towel, and Suleiman would go obediently to his private bath, there to be shaven and scraped, steamed and washed, rubbed and rinsed down, and finally allowed to dry and cool himself at his leisure.

Otherwise, he never saw Flower of Spring. Even when she

20

ventured out to prayer escorted by elder women in closed car-
riages she remained veiled, and hidden behind the marble
tracery of the women's gallery. She could not share his
thoughts. The judges of the Law assured him that such women
could have no souls; like animals, they ceased to be when life
left their bodies.

With this the wise Kasim disagreed. Exceptional animals, said
Suleiman's tutor, lived on in paradise by reason of services they
rendered men—beasts such as the ass of Baalam and the whale
that cast Jonah safe ashore. Could not some women achieve
the same merit as these animals, and so survive?

A discerning foreigner declared that women here were meant
only for service, like horses. "The women are commonly beautiful, straight and well-shaped; they are very fair, for they stir
but little abroad and when they do they are veiled. They add
Art to their natural beauty, for they paint their eyebrows and
eyelids with a blackish color; they also paint their nails with a
reddish brown color called *al hanna*. They are very cleanly and
neat, for seeing they go twice a week to the baths, they have no
hair upon their bodies . . . they are all generally very haughty,
and clad like the men, or in flowered stuffs . . . in the streets
they let the sleeves of their smocks hang down over their hands,
thinking that if so much as a hand is seen they will be looked
on as women of no repute."

Suleiman seldom ventured beyond the guarded corridor. As
Sultan, his home lay in the tents of the camp; the Serai itself, ill
fashioned of secondhand stones and rubble, was intended to be
no more than a brief stopping place. So old custom ordained.
Within it, the girls and elders of the House of Osman had protection; it formed a court of its own ruled to the smallest detail
of the nursery and kitchen by his mother, the Sultan Valideh.

This authority had belonged to the eldest woman in ancestral
times when the Turkish women had journeyed unveiled with
the clan, with men and herds to care for. Their strong tribal

stock had not been weakened by the infusion of girls from the far frontiers—Slavs, Georgians, Circassians, Tatars—of late years. The Sultan Valideh ruled the harem with the authority of an ancient *khatun*, a tribal princess, selecting her own managers, the Keeper of the House, the Keeper of the Storerooms, the Keeper of the Jewels, and the others, allotting money and tasks to every worker in the harem. For without work, the Sultan Valideh believed, a woman's hands would be idle and empty.

The Valideh, Suleiman knew, had once been a Christian; like Gulbehar, she had been bought young in the eastern mountains, to be trained in the imperial household, there to please the eye of its master. She had the lustrous dark hair and gray eyes of the Georgians, lacking Gulbehar's fairness. He had wondered how she endured the moods of the sardonic Selim. After his boyhood he had not been allowed to see them together, nor could she tell him much of Selim. As a girl she had known poverty; now, impatient and kindly, she had a fondness for colored satin vests, and mother-of-pearl with garnet glass worked into flower patterns to set in her hair. When he praised her splendor, the Valideh shook her head, thinking of more than she would say: "Haggard and old, I am not splendid now."

Yet he noticed how newcomers to the household, little more than shy children, took refuge in the kindness of his mother. Of the feuds and the distress of the women he could observe little; they served in their different ways, warring among themselves but presenting gay faces to the master of the house. Gulbehar asked for nothing except trifles, tortoise-shell combs or some bit of Venetian satin, or silk from Baghdad; she felt secure, being more than "in the eye" of the Sultan, aware that she was loved by him, and that her son would follow Suleiman, making her, if she lived, the next Sultan Valideh.

The good fortune of the new ruler seemed to extend to his household of women.

Yet either because he disliked the old Serai or because old custom required it, Suleiman spent most of his time and often slept at the Serai Burnu, the Palace Point. Here at the edge of the city in courtyards surrounded by plane trees and gardens the sultans carried on the task of administration. Here the Conqueror had tried to escape from the city streets, even erecting a kiosk or sitting place in the gardens.

First Suleiman made certain that one companion would be with him at all times. He named Ibrahim, the Greek who had music in his spirit and wit to cope with any problem, to be Captain of the Inner House. (Even now the Osmanlis gave army rank to all officers serving them.) More than that, he asked Ibrahim to share the evening meal with him, after the routine of the day.

For once the volatile Greek looked serious when he knelt across the supper cloth. He asked, "If you share water and bread with a servant, does not that make him a friend?"

Suleiman looked at his companion and nodded. "Yes, it does."

In his dread of loneliness he wished for nothing more than to have a friend. After supper they could talk undisturbed by ceremony; Suleiman could read and question Ibrahim, who answered readily even while fingering the muted strings of his violin. Ibrahim, who seldom needed to study books, was fluent in at least two languages—Persian and Italian as well as his native Greek and acquired Turkish—that his master barely understood. At will the brilliant Greek could tap the riches of classical Persian poetry, or quote from Dante. He could go far ahead of Suleiman's thought.

"*What need to build palaces or cities,*" quoted Ibrahim, "*for they will be ruins anon?*"

"Then what endures?" demanded the Sultan quickly. He had seen Roman ruins enough.

"Wisdom, and this music I am making!"

"And Angora goats!"

"Ay, truly."

Suleiman's amusement was touched by anger. At times he could not be certain Ibrahim was not jesting. For the Greek

23

could be arrogant, in quickening his master's plodding mind. And at times when Ibrahim made fun of things he seemed to be leading his companion into new realization. Music like the hymns of the Christians *might* be more permanent than Constantinople itself.

One book Suleiman brooded over, because he could not understand it very well. The *Sikander nameh*, the story of Alexander, usually accompanied him in his journeying. He wanted very much to learn how the great Alexander had meant to unite the peoples of the east and the west. But Ibrahim much preferred to discuss a certain Hannibal, who he said had known how to defeat the armies of Rome. Suleiman did not care to read about wars, especially when chronicled by Livy.

"It's important," his Captain of the Inner House urged.

"Why is it important?"

Because, the Greek thought, this Hannibal represented one man and one purpose, opposed to an empire. Look at his army: it was made up, like the Turkish *asker*, of motley elements— in his case of Africans, slingers, elephants. Yet because Hannibal had been a single gifted man with one indomitable purpose, he had worn down the strength of the Romans. "In the conflict of wills, Hannibal prevailed."

"What did he win?"

They argued a point like this, the master interested in practical consequences, the brilliant servant seeking to understand the means that gained an end. Ibrahim had spent most of his thirty-three years in schooling under the Turks, relying on his own wit, challenged by minds as keen as his own, searching for weakness in others by which he might profit. Until now he had never had authority of his own, and he understood perfectly that that authority rested entirely upon Suleiman's favor. "My emperor," he said humbly, "in conflict, a leader must subdue others or be subdued himself. His life will be a conflict with others. You cannot escape that."

At this Suleiman fell into one of his silences. He had a way of remembering every least word spoken, when he was pleased or angered.

Men said of them at this time that the Sultan had a woman's beauty and gentleness, while the favored Ibrahim had masculine strength and purpose. Those who were jealous of Ibrahim's new rank whispered that the younger Suleiman kept him to share his bed at night. And it is true that Suleiman often told the Greek to pass the night in his sleeping room, where they could talk freely again after the morning prayer.

On certain nights the Captain of the Inner House was observed going out at a late hour. During such excursions he could not easily be followed beyond the gate because he wore a dark dolman and no insignia of rank on his head. Yet apparently he did not make his way to any one house. Instead he was seen searching through the alleys leading down to the boats moored along the Bosphorus. He turned into wine cellars kept by his former countrymen. There he searched until he found a certain man much the worse for wine. Then the two would go off together.

When Suleiman heard the rumor, as he heard most rumors in time, he had a messenger of the Serai follow Ibrahim with an escort, to discover the meaning of his search.

The messenger made his report only when he was certain. "The captain finds this man sometimes sleeping in the gutters, sometimes still drinking. He tries to get the man on his feet, to take him to a hostel or mosque courtyard to sleep. Once the captain carried clean clothing for the other to put on, telling him that he must not live longer in this way in the dirt. Whenever he gives money, either gold dinars or silver, the other will buy more wine to drink. The man is his father, who was once a Greek seaman."

Suleiman ordered that Ibrahim was not to be followed again.

Every morning the page of the wardrobe put thirty-two pieces of gold into the Sultan's belt wallet for him to give away during the day. For when he ventured beyond the Serai gate, even in parade with spahis going before and swordbearer and messenger and the others following, people would break forward to reach at his stirrup and ask for alms, or for employment, or to thrust up a petition in a cleft stick. Sometimes a gift was tied to the stick. It was the *Ayin*, the old custom, that whoever appeared before the face of the ruler must be heard or rewarded by him.

Sometimes he had to give judgments from the saddle, on unexpected questions, and he had come to regret that the Solomon of ancient times had been so wise in judging. A bathman from Sivas, being hauled away by an inspector for drinking the new dark brew, coffee, appealed to him loudly in the street. Coffee, the bathman claimed, was not illegal. True, some people called it the black enemy of sleep and copulation, but no law forbade it. Did any law laid down by the Prophet of God forbid the drinking of coffee?

As always when appeal was made to him in public, a great crowd gathered in silence to hear his response. For Suleiman's word could imprison or free an offender; it could kill or give life instantly.

It crossed Suleiman's mind that coffee had not been known in the time of the Prophet, ten centuries before. Yet he had to answer the bathman's appeal with a decision. "Do you think, man of Sivas," he demanded, "that the Prophet of God would sit on a street corner drinking coffee?"

The man considered and answered, "No."

"Free him," Suleiman told the inspector, and rode on.

Not only did he have to give judgment continually; he had to take notice of any praiseworthy or offensive action within his sight as he passed. The Ayin required that. Kasim never tired of telling how the soldierlike Murad—the Sultan who had formed the janizaris into an invincible fighting force—had once ordered a saddle put upon a passer-by. Murad had noticed a peasant standing at a food stall munching bread and garlic while the man's horse waited with a heavy load on its pack-saddle. Murad had stopped instantly, and had ordered the peasant to put barley before his horse and then to remove the packsaddle and shoulder it entire himself while he ate. So the forthright Murad had impressed upon the peasant, and upon all who watched, that a man must not take his ease until he had cared for his horse. (And since Murad had established this point so clearly, Suleiman had to take notice if any rider abused his horse.)

It was a saying in the country: *A command once given must be carried out always.* What was old was sanctioned, and what was sanctioned must not be changed.

Sheepskins in the Treasury

The Ayin, the old Turkish custom, followed Suleiman wherever he went. Always he appeared before the eyes of his people mounted in the saddle. Even when he went from the Old Serai gate to the Great Gate of the garden point, where he attended councils, he never walked, or rode in a chair or carriage.

Still, if he happened to meet a porter bent under a heavy load, or a sick man being carried to the hospital, he was expected to keep out of the way. He enjoyed riding past the soaring mass of the Aya Sofia, turning under the plane trees into the Great Gate. There his people swarmed, pressing in and pushing out, like sheep at the fold entrance. (This portal would be called by foreigners the *Sublime Porte.*)

Within this white gate, the hospital grounds lay on his right hand but he always glanced instinctively to the left where behind a giant plane tree stretched the barracks of the janizaris. Some of these warriors of his personal army were always waiting by the brass drum at the door. But the young Sultan glanced that way to discover if huge soup kettles lay there, overturned. As the janizaris cut down their tents as a sign of mourning, they threw out their soup kettles when they had a grievance for the Sultan to notice. Until now they had not overturned their kettles. . . .

Only he, the Sultan, could ride through the second gate upon the clean lawns where the small council chamber with its watchtower faced the kitchens.

Beyond the third gate no one ventured except the officers and guards of the household who had the duty of caring for valuable things—for the Mantle of the Prophet brought by Selim from Mecca, for the library of scientific books that Mehmed the Conqueror had started to collect. These were valuables of the House of Osman. Across from them stood the schools of the young apprentices. Often as he passed by he heard flutes or viols playing where these boys who were studying to rule an empire snatched a moment of pleasure, unaware that the Sultan was listening.

Suleiman, of course, could go where the whim seized him. No door from the Danube to the end of the Nile was closed to him. Tall and withdrawn, seemingly cold and sure of himself, he drew only admiring glances and murmured salutation from observers, "Long life . . . many years to the fortunate son of Selim."

His perfect attire, usually in matched gray and white, or black and gold, his careful manner, hid his shyness and his dread. Inwardly he shrank from the task awaiting him, of finding sustenance and giving laws to the hundreds of thousands who now depended on him.

He went through the daily routine expected of him, grateful that in the stress of these first months no one had leisure to observe his weakness. Ibrahim's words chimed with his thoughts: *One man, and one purpose.* Within his family he felt at ease, and when he could steal off to hunt with a small group. He repeated words of his own, "My family, and my people." Vainly he tried to think that the one might become like the other, someday. But he did not have much hope of that.

28

Even when he was escorted through the treasure house by the Steward of the Treasury he felt terror of the task imposed on him. Among the bundles carefully labeled and sealed, they showed him the heavy sword, almost straight, of Mehmed the Conqueror. He did not want to take it into his hand. They showed him the peacock plumes of Murad, and the gold brocade that had been worn at feasts by his own father. Suleiman turned to clocks encased in mother-of-pearl, gifts of the Europeans, and to stacked dishes of delicate green and deep blue Chinese porcelain. "I would like to have these used, instead of stored here," he explained. And at once the dishes were taken from the shelves by the steward's servants.

In fact the Treasury was like a storehouse. It held pearl-sewn saddles, silver-gilt stirrups, even a jeweled fly swatter. Most of the things had been gifts to the sultans, who in turn made gifts from their stored treasures at the feasts such as New Year's or the Prophet's birthday. It was wrong to hoard wealth. A chest of gold ducats, tribute paid in by Venice, was marked to be sent over to the Arsenal, for shipbuilding . . . in a dark corridor Suleiman observed plain garments of heavy white felt and black lambskin. These, he was told, had belonged to the ancestors of his house, to Osman and to Ertoghrul.

Again the steward had to tell him the legend of the shadowy Ertoghrul. How the Osmanli clan of no more than four hundred and forty-four families under their chieftain Ertoghrul had wandered across the Anatolian plain over two centuries ago, when more powerful peoples were fleeing west from the sweep of the victorious Mongols. It had been a time of starvation, but Ertoghrul had kept his herds together and his people had survived, until the day when they sighted a battle in progress on the plain below them. They watched it, knowing nothing of the battle.

Then Ertoghrul led them down into it, rushing to aid the horsemen that were having the worst of the affair. This unexpected charge of the Turkish clan had aided the mighty Sultan

Kaikhosru, whose horsemen had been the Seljuk Turks, to defeat and drive off a Mongol army. In reward, so the legend said, Kaikhosru had bestowed lands on Ertoghrul's clan——

That small holding of land, Suleiman understood, had been the beginning of the fortune of the Osmanlis, near the Ankara River. The fighters of the clan had served at times with the weakening Seljuks, at times with the Byzantine forces clinging to the last frontiers of Rome. Fighting men, breeding and recruiting others, looting along the limbo of the frontiers, daring to encircle great cities, capturing the cities after years by their stubborn land blockade—how could a walled city survive when all roads to it were cut off?—then capturing cannon and technicians to cast new and larger cannon, then taking tribute from wealthy states as a price of their protection, such had been the first Osmanlis, a flotsam of swordsmen, swirling among the human tides. And then, the Seljuks vanishing, with Kaikobad and Kaikhosru, while the Byzantines sickened and wearied behind the triple walls of Constantinople, leaving the Osmanlis the only strong nucleus of men under discipline, and under leadership so daring that it held back at nothing—crossing the swift Dardanelles when an earthquake crippled the forts on the far side, dragging their ships over a neck of land into the Golden Horn, breaking down the triple walls of impregnable Constantinople. Such had been the incredible rise of the Osmanlis.

They were the first tribal people of mid-Asia to break their way into Europe, there to stay and to rule.

It had been accomplished, Suleiman believed, by no miracle or God-given fortune but by the ability of the Osmanlis themselves—by the exertions of nine extraordinary men. Osman had worn this coat of rough animal hair. Selim had worn the banquet robe of spun gold. If one of the nine had been a weakling during the two and a half centuries of their rise, the chain of success would have been broken and the Osmanli Turks would have been no more than another warlike nomad nucleus, like the dour White Sheep Turkomans. Some of the nine had shown weakness. Murad had been reckless, and Selim callous in his cruelty. Perhaps in memory their great qualities had been told and their faults forgotten. Yet the careless Murad had organized an invincible army, the Turkish *asker*. And Selim, a visionary, had led that army in a triumph like the storied Alexander's across Asia from the Nile to the snow mountains of Kurdistan. No, if one link in the chain had actually failed, the chain would have broken.

Now he, Suleiman, stood in the odd Treasury of his family, the tenth of the line. Already the Europeans, and Ibrahim, spoke of him as emperor. In what direction was he to lead, and what destiny could he grasp for his people? Did not the great task become increasingly difficult with each generation's rise? Or had the Osmanlis, by overcoming incredible difficulties, earned for their people a still undreamed-of destiny?

Not even Piri Pasha could answer that question for him. Ibrahim might, in time. Suleiman, impartial and keenly intelligent, understood his own failings too well. Sensitive, he took refuge in gentleness; fastidious, he wanted only fine things close to him, like the lovely Chinese porcelain. Without clear purpose of his own as yet, he depended on others; he felt that wiser men must guide him. Without any desire to lead an army —his father had kept him at posts far from any military command—he realized that he must either allow the Osmanli army to go its own way, or he must alter the nature of Osmanli rule in some way to dispense with the all-powerful army. Neither of these alternatives seemed at all possible.

Certainly the Ayin warned him not to tamper with the army. In his nursery Suleiman had learned the old song about the four vital things:

> *To hold a land you need armed men,*
> *To keep armed men you share out property,*
> *To have property you need a rich folk,*

31

SULEIMAN THE MAGNIFICENT

Only by laws can you make folk rich—
If one of these lacks, all four will lack,
Where all four lack, the land is lost.

About this time, without confiding in anyone Suleiman decided to set himself against the ancient Ayin. In doing so he would change the army. He would make law the first of the four vital things. By new laws he would rule the land, and it would not be lost.

In one corner of the Treasury stood the first standard of the Osmanlis, a small pole with a battered brass crescent under which hung two dried-out white horsetails. The ancient wood was carefully oiled, the long hairs combed smooth. Smiling, the attendants told Suleiman that a chieftain long before Osman had lost his standard in a battle, and had slashed the tail from a horse to make this new one, on the instant.

To these men who crowded around him respectfully, he, Suleiman, was no more than the youth who must carry out the task of ruling; they wanted him to feel the importance of a wooden pole and a horsetail.

(He could not know, because the memories of those around him held no vestige of it, how the people still depended on one chieftain. In the past they followed that chieftain or they deserted him, as they desired. Theirs had been a voluntary association. They still kept the order and the discipline of the nomad group that had been obliged to transport itself as a unit over pasturelands, with each member sharing in the labor. They still hoarded old garments and chests because in their arduous passage over the plains such articles had been rare, and hard to make. They still waited for the chieftain to point out the line of march, which they might or might not consent to follow.

(It was the peculiarity of the Osmanli Turks that they migrated through many changes but changed little themselves. To these Turks the ancient horsetails, like the fires on their hearths, represented their own past, their continuing existence.)

Unmistakably Suleiman realized the first need of his people. Fertile land to produce ample food and the good grass on which herds thrived, whether horses or Angora goats. From the day of Osman and the earliest owned land, everything had been based on peasant farming. This base of the peasant with his ox and wooden plow could not be altered or disturbed. The army, for instance, might bring in loot from far afield—as the nomad riders of the clan had carried back spoil—to add to the stored-up treasure; but primarily the army must acquire new lands along watered valleys or rich riversheds, to feed the increasing numbers of mouths.

In consequence, the first duty of the new ruler was to nourish the hundreds of thousands who adhered to him. Whenever Suleiman came out of the Treasury, he thought how little a thing it was compared to the vast raw earth seeded for harvest. In very truth he himself was the servant of that earth.

The Rose Garden between Two Worlds

His first laws had to do with care of fallow land, and summer and winter pasturage, and tithes to be paid by keepers of beehives. In such matters his spoken word, *urf*, became *kanun*, a law to be obeyed.

Only by custom and courtesy was his minister, Piri Pasha, acknowledged to be the Bearer of the Burden. In reality the burden of responsibility lay upon the Sultan, and now, entering his twenty-sixth year, he accepted it to the full—"to feed and to lead." It is quite clear that he decided at once to lead his people toward Europe.

Probably he decided it in the fourth courtyard of the Serai Burnu. This space, lying behind the other three busy courts, was really a miniature forest of old pines and twisted cypresses on the very point of the Serai where the three-mile encircling wall came down close to the water. Successive sultans had made it their private garden, and the gardeners had made a toy lake, a nest of rose beds and a secluded meadow where they could pray by the fountains. Only the back windows of the Treasury of the Holy Mantle overlooked it.

But the garden point overlooked the outer life of the city. Down one slope beyond it stretched the training fields where young apprentices raced their horses, sporting with a wooden ball or hard-thrown javelins. They stabled their horses in the empty shells of Byzantine monasteries.

When Suleiman climbed the Path That Made the Camel Scream—so christened by the young gardeners who were also apprentices, learning to aid him in government—the winds of outer space buffeted him. Here he stood, actually, between his two worlds of the east and west. Across from him in Asia the cypresses of Chamlija rose against the sky. To his right dim islands lay along the White (Marmora) Sea that led to the vaster Mediterranean in the west. To his left the wind ruffled and whitened the water lane of the Bosphorus that led to the Black Sea and the caravan tracks of the east.

Nowhere else on earth could a monarch walk in his garden and behold the vistas of his power stretching away from him to the coasts of two continents, the waters of two seas. Behind him the sunsets glowed on the twisted harbor fringed by masts of moored fishing craft and galleys, the teeming shining inlet that resembled a ram's horn in shape and so was called the Golden Horn. Beyond the forest of masts lay the sheds of his Arsenal, the dark warehouses and palaces of the Venetians, the Genoese, the Greeks and Ragusans who carried on their trade by his sufferance.

On such walks the gentle Piri Pasha accompanied him, because Suleiman could take no rest from thought until he slept after the last prayer. Piri Pasha urged him to think as a judge and to be in no haste to act. "Haste is from the Devil and patience is from God."

And patiently Piri Pasha drew the mind of his young master toward Asia. There lay the security of old familiar things. What matter if the dhows drifted slowly down the Nile, if the Nile at flood brought rich black earth down to its desert banks? What if the donkey trains of Jews plodded slowly past Aleppo, to seek the road to Samarkand? They brought back, in time, their loads of white paper and blue turquoise, of spice and Chinaware. Why should pilgrims rush along the other roads to the Dome of the Rock, at the Holy City (Jerusalem), or the desert path to the shrine within the Ka'aba of Mecca? They brought back with them a foretaste of salvation. Against that, what mattered the sacks of gold ore that Berber camels fetched out from the hidden mines of Africa to the trace of the Roman road that wound along the African coast from the fallen domes of Alexandria to the bustling port of Algiers—the Island—in the far west. No, let trade take its course to the west, and westerners weigh their silver and count their piled-up coins. Their profit availed nothing after death. Then the slow-striding pilgrim would overtake them, on the way to God's mercy.

"Eleven armed men cannot rob me," quoth Piri Pasha, "if I have nothing in my wallet!"

As for wealth, let Suleiman the son of Selim count if he could the incalculable treasures of Asia. Up in the farther mountains streams flowed without ceasing from the snows of Argh' Dagh, the Mountain of Noah's Ark; more than sapphires was the blue of the great Lake Van; more than emeralds the green of the Syrian prairies fed by the headwaters of Euphrates; more than gold the ripple of ripe wheat where the streams of Tigris flowed from the hills. Even from their depths the mountains yielded salt without stint. On the bare breast of the Anatolian plain the finest horse herds fattened and increased. Such wealth as this did not vanish overnight; it came from the hand of God.

Piri Pasha would point across the water to the opposite height. "V'allah! Before the memory of living men Europeans came there, to build their City of Gold. Perhaps they were Greeks. Where is it now, their city? Only the green grove of Chamlija remains."

"And only the dead stay there," Suleiman reminded the old man. "The living come from here."

"What is dead! In that early time the Greek Pythagoras taught that all substance endures, to immortality. All relates to all, and never does anything new enter our visible world. Although he was a Greek, he spoke the truth."

Unmistakably Piri Pasha disliked the ways of Europeans, and especially of Ibrahim, the Captain of the Inner Household. In Europe, he insisted, they did not breed proper horses, they built dwellings not to be serviceable as tents but to tower in the streets shutting out the sunlight; they hugged their fires in winter, and bathed their bodies internally with wine, to get food in their cities they struggled, shouting as if drunk, in the market place. They wrote down their affairs and *sciences* in books, but did not honor a spoken word. As for religion, did they not burn the head of one of their dervish orders, a certain Savonarola, at the stake; did they not try to buy salvation with money at their churches? In very truth, they strove murderously for temporary gain, passing by what was permanent.

Still Suleiman in the energy of his youth resolved to turn his back on the Black Sea and seek the Mediterranean, and to lead his Turks among the Europeans to learn their way of life. Was he not, as they were, of a white race? Were not his eyes as light as theirs, his skin as clear? If he changed garments with one of them, he could appear to be one of them.

When the snows melted away that first spring of 1521 the army mobilized. When the freshets had dwindled and the new grass afforded grazing to the horse herds, the scattered divisions of the army began to move north to carry out the task that

36

Selim had set for it, which had been delayed by his death. That task was to break into eastern Europe.

Suleiman had almost nothing to do with it. Piri Pasha and the other veteran generals saw to it that he had no responsibility to shoulder. They knew his lack of experience in warfare. They even made much of a grievance that caused the Turks to march again. A certain messenger sent, they said, to the Hungarian court to announce Suleiman's accession last autumn had been mistreated—his ears and his nose had been sliced off. So the army was moving against the Hungarians in retribution.

That, if true, was no more than a pretext. The army in reality was carrying out the wish of the Yavuz Sultan, to push the invasion of Europe. To be exact—and Piri Pasha showed Suleiman how it appeared on the map—the army would accomplish this summer what both Selim and Mehmed the Conqueror had failed to do, shatter the European defense line of the river Danube. It would capture the White City, Belgrade. This White City, strong on its height on their side, south, of the mighty Danube served as a bridgehead for the Europeans. It reared insolently in the gap where the Danube left one mass of mountains and entered another. By capturing it the army of Suleiman would open a road between the mountains to Buda and Prague and Vienna.

Suleiman grasped the significance of the map. There was no alternative for him, except to decline to lead the army to open that road of invasion. Without him the janizaris, for example, would refuse to march.

"Yes," he agreed, "we will go to the White City."

Then, they told him, he must give an order for the sounding of the great bronze drum that was the drum of conquest. With a word he gave the order, and almost at once he heard the metallic *bong* of the drum by the Great Gate. It was a strange sound, the reverberation of the drum in the winding streets of the city, as if a brazen voice called to the throngs, *Take the road that waits—march out to the far lands.*

Piri Pasha said it was the voice of the Young Troops, the
Yenicheri that Europeans called the janizaris.

Long before in the steppes of Asia, said Piri Pasha and the
distinguished old men, the Osmanlis who had never numbered
more than a few thousands had trained captured boys to ride
to war with them. The Osmanlis made use of strange peoples
as the early steppe dwellers made use of animal herds. Out of
recruited boys they organized new conquests, thus obtaining
new land and the service of still other peoples.

Here in Europe they continued to add Christian captives to
the number of the Turkish boys; but they also drafted boys
every three or four years from the Christian families of the
"inner nations." From each family they took a son of seven or
eight years, young enough not to be bound by the ties of his
home. These boys were examined at receiving centers from
Adrianople, the old Turkish capital, to Brusa where stood the
tombs of the earlier sultans. Then the recruits were given new
names and sent to field work where they would be strengthened
and learn to speak Turkish.

These selected youths were nourished and clothed and
watched carefully, the brightest minds being sent to the schools.
The greater part became *ajem-oghlans*, "foreign boys" working
in the gardens, on the ships at Gallipoli, or serving at the messes
of the graduated janizaris, as they chose. These last had constant training in the weapons of war, particularly with the light
swords, slender steel javelins, or the short powerful Turkish
bow. Usually they disliked the new clumsy firelocks. Some
chose to train with horses, thus becoming spahis, or riders.

At twenty years of age the ajem-oghlans had become athletes,
expert with weapons, disciplined and bound by the ties of their
brotherhood. Barracks had become their homes. After that
they graduated into the ranks of the janizaris, qualified to wear
the long dervish cap, or they entered the troops of spahis as
vacancies occurred.

It did not matter whether they had come originally from

privileged or poverty-ridden families. (Many foreign parents tried to have their sons entered among the Sultan's apprentices who might rise to posts of high responsibility; many of the boys remained Christian at heart.) In this severe training with almost no pay the Young Troops had nothing but their ability to aid them, and their loyalty was given only to the Sultan.

They had the unruly spirit of the young, long confinement in the city irked them; they had been trained to march, to give battle, and to police captured territories. They longed to be moving on the roads at their swift pace that was half a run toward fresh lands and opportunity.

"It is not good for them in the city," said Piri Pasha, "where they chew the bitter root of drill and eat in house kitchens. But you must lead them."

When the drum of the janizaris began to sound outside their barracks, Suleiman upset tradition unexpectedly by appearing among them on foot. At the moment they were lined up to draw their pay, before marching. For generations the sultans had been their honorary commanders, and they were very jealous of that distinction. Now this young and handsome Sultan came among them, actually, to draw his pay as an officer.

In expectant silence the disciplined figures in their baggy trousers and soft leather boots made way for Suleiman. The stalwart Agha of the Janizaris pulled at his long mustache as Suleiman took a heavy handful of silver *aspers* from the paymaster. That would be something, the agha promised himself, to tell the cavalry. Nothing could have touched these lifetime soldiers more than to witness the Sultan himself pouching his pay. This youngling, they boasted in barracks afterward, was no longer wet behind the ears; no, he was a true foot slogger, a Young Trooper at heart, and the spahis, the Riders, could move to the rear now where they belonged. The son of Selim wanted no pay as a spahi.

It had been a gesture on Suleiman's part, but a most timely one. He had joined the wild brotherhood that he feared most.

Nor did he try to seclude himself on the march north as he had in the city. He went among the troops constantly, questioning the oldest of them, and making decisions only as the more experienced commanders advised him.

Although he appeared to be leading it, Suleiman actually merely followed the fighting front. So the thing he had dreaded became a pleasant journey, up into the northern valleys where European castles stood like landmarks of earlier advances. Daily he heard discussion of great victories of the past. At Nicopolis the last Christian crusade had been annihilated; at Kossovo—the Field of the Crows—the proud Serbs had submitted to the power that never since the day of Mehmed had known defeat.

The White City

Except that he journeyed forward each day and slept in a luxurious tent guarded by a select band of archers, his routine remained much like that of the Serai. The Organization, his government, traveled with him, from Piri Pasha to the lower secretary-treasurers. The standing army of janizaris and spahis stayed close to him as before. Only their musicians played for him each evening, and workmanlike engineers prepared the road for the passage of the massive siege guns escorted by the cannoneers.

Wherever he moved, a human barrier formed around him— a detachment of *solaks*, who were the hundred and fifty veteran janizaris with the sole duty of guarding the Sultan's life. They carried their bows ready strung, and took their posts outside the ropes of his pavilion at night. On the march another detachment ran beside him, like dogs around the horse of their master. They were the *peiks* or trained runners who carried his messages or fetched him what he desired.

He saw nothing of the foragers and light horsemen flung far

ahead, to pillage supplies from the "Lands of War." Only on the map could he trace the movements of the Army of Europe, and the other Army of Asia. These great masses of horsemen were the feudal levies made up of Turkish landowners, with armed followers. Mobilized each season, drawing no pay, they foraged for themselves, coming in as the grass ripened from the warm south to the cold north. Long camel trains followed the Army of Asia.

These two strong wings of the fighting forces could act independently or fall back upon the support of the Sultan's regular army, the core of the janizaris and the heavy artillery that had never given ground to an enemy.

As Suleiman rode north, these distant wings were enveloping and taking the smaller castles along the Danube. Piri Pasha had laid siege to Belgrade itself. Meanwhile up the water route of the Danube war vessels and supply barges were pushing their way against the current. There was little for Suleiman to do except observe, and sit in council when the occasion called for it.

Suleiman kept a daily journal. It has survived the centuries.

So little he wrote each day, it seems as if he meant one word to suffice for one day. At such and such a place they halted, he noted. Or, simply, "Rest." But beyond the terseness and the cold accuracy, the journal reveals a curious interest in the different people who came before the Sultan's eyes. A certain rider was beaten with staffs because he trampled growing crops in a field; an infantryman was beheaded for stealing turnips from a garden. (They were still in the "land of peace" under Turkish responsibility, and rigid orders forbade the troops to damage the countryside. Once they crossed into the enemy Lands of War the situation was to be different.)

July 7. "Word comes in of the taking of Sabaks. One hundred heads of soldiers of the garrison who did not escape with the others, arrive in camp. . . ." July 8. "These heads are placed along the line of march." . . .

41

At the river Save a bridge must be built over the flood. July 9. "Halt. . . . Suleiman [so he speaks of himself] quarters himself in a hut to speed up the bridge building by his presence. . . . The Sultan shows himself constantly near the bridge."

July 18. "The bridge is finished. The Save rises to its floor."

July 19. "The water flows over it, making passage impossible. Order to make the crossing in flatboats."

The heavy supplies are detoured another way. This task of crossing the flooded Save becomes important to Suleiman; being present, he is responsible.

After his arrival at besieged Belgrade, the journal gives the same laconic, clear details. Yet, piecing them together, we see a picture of the unconquered sentinel city falling. Its flanking cities have gone; Turkish ships have closed the river behind it; detachments of janizaris hold the islands. Heavy siege guns on both sides of the river batter down sections of the outer wall of Belgrade.

August 3. "The Agha of the Janizaris, Bali Agha, is wounded."

August 8. "The enemy give up the defense of the city, and set it afire, retiring into the citadel."

August 9. "Order to mine under the towers of the citadel."

August 10. "The cannon placed in new batteries."

After a week the garrison, cut off without prospect of relief, offers to surrender. The commandant comes out to kiss Suleiman's hand and be given a kaftan. "The believers are called to prayer, and the army musicians play three times within Belgrade. Suleiman crosses the bridge and enters Belgrade, where he goes to Friday prayer in a church of the outer city, changed over into a mosque."

The next day Bali Agha is presented with three thousand aspers. Hungarian captives are allowed to cross the river and depart. The Serbs among them are sent south to Constantinople (where they settled in a suburb that they named Belgrade). Suleiman rides through all the captured city to inspect it, and

then goes hunting. For the new governor of Belgrade he selects
Bali Agha.

A note of pride appeared in the journal's entries after that.
Suleiman had played his part well. His army had taken over
the line of the middle Danube—with Sabaks, Semlin, and
Semendria as well as Belgrade—turning the captured batteries
north across the river, cutting down the forest that screened
the shore. Beyond that front a corridor had been opened toward middle Europe. Suleiman could well afford to ride off
to hunt.

What he had most feared had not happened. Incredibly, no
European army of relief had appeared at the river. It seemed
as if the European leaders had been taken by surprise, or they
had been too occupied elsewhere with the new Emperor,
Charles, to give aid to the doomed Danube. For the first time
Suleiman observed how his enemies were weakened by their
divided counsels. He remembered Ibrahim's saying, the strength
of "One man, and one purpose."

But he was not at all sure that he wanted those same European brother monarchs to be enemies. As to that, he kept his
own counsel, even from Ibrahim.

As if at a signal, at the first frosts of September the Turkish
field army turned homeward, laden with its spoil—which went
to pay for the mobilization. On the way, the armies scattered,
to regain their own countries in time to get in the last harvests.
The horses had to be home before the last grass failed; the
camels could not survive autumn cold in the north. The well-
being of the animals and the crops had to come before military
niceties at the end of a campaign.

Suleiman had been fortunate, and he displayed a new pride
in success when he sent official announcement of the capture of
Belgrade to the two European courts on friendly terms with
him—Venice and Ragusa. The startled Venetians rewarded the
Turkish ambassador with five hundred gold ducats.

"The Turks go to a war as if to a wedding," they complained afterward.

In Rome the energetic Paolo Giovio wrote in his Commentary—saying nothing more about his prophecy that Suleiman would be as a lamb and not a lion—"Their discipline under arms is due to their justice and severity, which surpasses that of the ancient Romans. They surpass our soldiers for three reasons: they obey their commanders without question; they seem to care nothing at all for their lives, in battle; they go for a long time without bread or wine, being content with barley and water."

In England Henry VIII made his own comment. "The news is lamentable and of importance to all Christianity."

When Suleiman returned to his city, people came out beyond the cypresses on the hill of Ayub to greet him joyfully. They lined the streets when he rode to the mosque to pray. Those who had made the hard march he rewarded with gifts; for the city dwellers he prepared a feast under lighted lamps. The Venetians who attended this festival after Belgrade had definite misgivings that in him they were confronted again by one of the great Turks.

II

Lands of War

The Bastard of the Magnifica Comunita

AS THE second year of Suleiman's reign came to its end, Messer Marco Memmo, ambassador of the Illustrious Signory of Venice, celebrated the theoretical feast day of his namesake St. Mark with mingled satisfaction and apprehension. His satisfaction was due to the fact that he had just signed, as token of his own astuteness, the first bilateral foreign treaty of the young Sultan, on behalf of his native Venice, thereby stirring the jealousy of his rivals the podesta of Genoa, the envoy of Ragusa and the agent of the King of Poland. These were the only representatives of European powers dwelling among the infidel Turks, and of this small diplomatic corps Messer Marco rightly deemed himself to be the most important.

His apprehension was caused by observing from the roof gallery of his palace adjoining the Baillio in Galata an increasing activity in the Turkish Arsenal below him. From the shipways of the Arsenal galleys were being launched that strangely resembled the finest Venetian warcraft. Memmo suspected that they had been built from Venetian plans, although he could not discover who had sold the plans to the Turks. Nor could he learn definitely how the unpredictable Osmanlis intended to make use of their new vessels.

It annoyed Messer Marco that he himself should have so

45

much appearance of power with so little reality. In his *Magnifica Comunita*—his city within a city—halberdiers took their posts around the walls with beat of drum and parade of flags. From the summit of his massive Galata tower he looked across the entrance of the Golden Horn to the woodland point where the great Sultan dwelt in gardens that had nothing martial about them, except perhaps the slender watchtower projecting from the treetops. Yet at a word from Suleiman he and the foreign colony would be obliged to evacuate their Magnificent Quarter. They remained there because Mehmed the Conqueror, who had captured Constantinople, had said that they could do so. By his permission they could enjoy all their old privileges of bartering for Turkish grain, slaves, horses, silk or spice. He had merely asked that the keys of the Galata gates be sent over to him in token surrender, and that the Christians take down their church bells which disturbed the Moslems at the hours of prayer. So Messer Marco remained as the guest of the Osmanlis, never quite certain what the morrow might bring. Being a nobleman of intelligence, he understood but would not admit that the sea power of the Illustrious Signory was on the wane, while the makeshift fleets of the Turks were venturing farther and farther out into the sea lanes. "They say," Luigi Gritti assured him, "that we are old, and remarkable for our wealth and treachery."

At Marco's feast in the gilded hall of the Baillio, at his table loaded with venison flavored by Chian wine, with stuffed pheasants, rare swordfish from the White Sea, lobster from the Bosphorus, dainty truffles and sweetmeats to go with the Oporto, this same Luigi Gritti sat like a skeleton at the feast of gourmets, a mocking mask, an unbridled tongue. Luigi Gritti, the bastard of the respected Andrea Gritti, out of a Greek woman of the islands, was accounted half a renegade, for he bolstered his cynical pride by going among the Turks who made no difference between a bastard and a lawful son. He spoke their barbarous language. Messer Marco invited this voluntary exile from the Serene Republic to his board for the reason that Gritti was apt to have ferreted out the secrets of the Turks.

When Memmo, warmed by wine and success, confessed that he had gained by his new treaty a yearly carrying trade for Venice worth tens of thousands of gold ducats, the Gritti bastard dared ask him if he had gained so much, what had he lost?

Nothing, said Memmo, or next to nothing. A detail only. Under the new treaty Venetian vessels would heave to off Gallipoli light, to report themselves and request formal permission to enter Turkish ports.

A detail only, the lean and ranting Gritti conceded. Yet without that slight punctilio, no ship of the Signory might land a cargo. Was it for that the Magnificence, the ambassador, agreed to pay tribute?

Touched in his pride, Memmo pointed out that he had agreed to pay little for a valuable concession, to wit: ten thousand ducats a year as rental for the island of Cyprus and five hundred for tiny Zante. "We have never paid tribute."

"Until now," corrected Gritti.

It irritated Memmo that this should be true. Since Cyprus and Zante still belonged to Venice, the money paid ostensibly for their hire and usance was actually tribute.

"Mark you," Gritti pressed, "how gently it is done, with what solicitude for our self-esteem? I see Suleiman's hand in this, not Piri Pasha's."

Not a word of Memmo's astuteness! Angry now, the ambassador stormed at the knowing bastard. This same Suleiman, this *gentil-homme par excellence*, had offered him a gift after the ceremony of signing the treaty. A truly courteous gift. Wrapped in a silk kerchief, a human head. An evil-smelling head cut off from the body of a rebel, they said, a Ghazi Something——

"Ghazali's. Ferhad Pasha, the Third Vizir, brought it from Syria."

"And your mild-mannered Suleiman offered it to me." With a grimace the ambassador wiped his hands on his ample skirts.

47

"I was obliged to thank him—I had much ado to refuse it without offending old Piri Pasha. By the three Archangels, why did they offer it? What do you make of it, Luigi?"

After considering a moment, Gritti held out four fingers. "Four items I make of it, Magnificence. Item one: these Turks have a saying, in making a promise, 'On my head.' Item two: they also have a saying that our Signory is sagacious and full of treachery. Item three: Your Magnificence, a righteous man but still an ambassador, had just signed a pledge of faith. Item four: the head of another wight who did not keep faith is dumped in your lap for a going-away gift. *Ecco*—add together these four items and what answer do you arrive at?"

Ruefully Memmo caressed the back of his stout neck. These Turks had a barbarous habit of holding diplomats personally responsible for a treaty. They did not, or would not, understand diplomatic immunity. "I might have expected it of Selim," he murmured, "but not of Suleiman."

Gritti thought, They have been looking at heron's plumes and a gentle smile. What if gentleness can mask a fiendish strength?

"I say we have been blind when we reported him young and careless and gay, utterly unlike Selim. Selim, I grant you, was fearsome. But his son who rides so merrily to hunt may be terrible."

Not long after that, Luigi Gritti began to cultivate the friendship of those in the palace across the water. Since it was impossible now to gain admission to Suleiman, he sought for one whom the Sultan favored, and found him in Ibrahim. The bastard and the Captain of the Inner Palace had certain things in common; both had Greek mothers, and a sense of hard reality.

School of the Tribute Children

Like almost all the others who held command under the Turkish Organization, Ibrahim had graduated from the School.

More, as Gritti soon found out, the favored Greek had graduated with the highest honors.

As to the School itself, the foreign observers disagreed heartily. Some believed it to be stricter than the monasteries of Europe proper. At least one said, "If this is a monastery, I vow that all the devils must be cloistered there."

Not that the School had been made a mystery. It was simply the *Enderun* or Enclosed School. Situated in the third court of the palace grounds, actually housed within the broad wall itself, the School was truly enclosed, and few foreigners ever laid eyes on it.

Suleiman sometimes visited the halls of the School in the small hours of the night. Old custom required the Sultan to do this, as if he were a watchman. With a gray felt mantle drawn over him and candles carried behind him by the night watchmen, he passed silently through the dormitories. In those dormitories slept some six hundred boys, aged from eight to eighteen.

Whenever Suleiman passed through the schoolrooms, he felt the impress of the mind of his great-grandfather, the Conqueror. The huge wall map of the known world hanging in the eating hall had been made at the Conqueror's demand. In fact Mehmed had started the garden outside the hall with his own hands. He had sought avidly for Byzantine philosophers, to translate geographies and the sciences—even demanding manuscripts instead of money as tribute from the enlightened city of Ragusa.

So intent had the Conqueror been on the wisdom of the Byzantines that it was said his School had become like Plato's Republic, creating fine minds in hardened bodies. (Before his time the School had served only to train youths physically for the janizaris and other war corps.)

Now in the opinion of foreigners like Gritti, the School was the secret of the amazing rise to power of the Turks.

For the boys of the School were not Turks at birth. They were the children of outlanders, Albanians, Serbs, Slavs of the north, Georgians and Circassians from the eastern mountains, Greeks from the seacoast, and even Croats and Germans. Most of them came, like Ibrahim, from Christian families.

Often they had been the "tribute children"—three thousand being required from the outlying peoples every third year—or slave children purchased from the markets at Lemnos or Kaffa, or sons brought in by their parents, to be registered in the School. (The Palace School of Suleiman had only the pick of the children, carefully selected from reception centers throughout the lands; they were the chosen few, the candidates for the rule of the Organization which in turn, under the eye of the Sultan, ruled the empire.)

Parents frequently wanted one of their children to become a student or apprentice of the Sultan, because the boy might excel over others and be appointed regimental commander in the spahis, a Judge of the Army, a treasurer, or even minister, like aged Piri Pasha. By recruiting youths trained to arms in this fashion, the farming peasantry of the Osmanlis was not drained away from the soil.

When a boy registered in the School, he left his old ties behind. He was separated from his family and given a new name. Once he passed through the Great Gate as an apprentice student, he was not allowed to leave, except to go with those of his own hall to the archery fields on the heights by the cemeteries, or to accompany the Sultan, rarely, on a special mission.

The thirty boys of finest appearance, who passed the tests with the best marks, were taken into the personal service of the Sultan as pages. To this Sultan the boy's loyalty was given; for years he learned obedience, standing motionless with crossed hands and lowered eyes if he happened to be sent into the presence of his Sultan; at the end of the years, he was released from the Great Gate to full responsibility far afield. Yet he knew that the training of the Sultan himself had been no less rigorous.

Once graduated, he was not allowed to set foot in the School again, unless by chance he became the Vizir, or the Mufti.

"His ministers," Machiavelli called them. ". . . his ministers being all slaves and bondmen, can only be corrupted with great difficulty, and little advantage can be expected by doing so . . . hence he who attacks the Turk must bear in mind that he will find him united . . . but if once the Turk has been routed in the field in such a way that he cannot replace his armies, there is nothing to fear but the family of the prince."

The boys were not slaves. Suleiman himself was the son of a woman who had been a slave, but was now empress-mother. They were being trained as warrior-statesmen. He had been trained to lead them. The tie between the boys and the Sultan was one of loyalty, in both. . . .

They wakened when the night watchmen came through the dormitories to light all the candles. Then they had a half hour to wash themselves at the copper taps over the marble basins—the Enclosed School had the same fittings as the palace—to put on skullcaps, tight tunics and baggy trousers, with their soft slipper-boots ready to their hands. At the end of the half hour their bedding must be rolled snug and hung against the wall behind them. Their personal belongings must be packed away in the large wooden chests. Behind each chest a boy knelt, with his notes and books arranged on the chest top between two lighted candles.

As the half hour ended, before the first streak of dawn, music sounded. Over in the second court the band of the janizaris played reveille for the Sultan's rising. The chime of bell-staffs, the shrilling of flutes and the diapason of deep voices singing had a merry sound.

While they waited one of them who had a musical voice read aloud from the Book-to-Be-Read. "*Say: I betake me for refuge to the Lord of Men, the King of men, and to the God of men—against the evil of the stealthy whisperer, who whispers in man's breast, against him—*"

As the last stars faded, a command was spoken and the boys

51

filed out silently, slipping on their boots and swinging through the darkness with arms folded across their chests, to the School mosque, for the dawn prayer.

Then began the work of the day. At the third hour after sunrise they had their first meal of soup, broiled lamb and a slice of bread. It was always the same, and sufficient to keep up their strength.

They had their jokes in the halls. A sleeping place once occupied by Egyptians, they named the Stall of Fleas. Asked how they passed the hours of the day, they would answer gravely: "We rest from study by learning to wrestle and ride in the playing fields; we rest from such manual exercise by learning to play flutes, viols and bagpipes indoors; when we eat, we are entertained by prayers, and when we sleep, the watchman wakes us up."

After full dark, their evening study began in the dormitories. A boy could choose a subject of his own to follow out—apart from the required religion, philosophy, mathematics, athletics and military exercises and music—provided he did well at it. At that hour, too, the instructor who lived in the hall—"He Who Trains"—read out the totals of commendation and punishment earned by each student during the day. Punishments ranged from a public scolding to beating with wooden staffs. Such punishments had to be administered carefully, however. If the instructor was too hard on a boy he himself had to take the public beating he had administered, or he might have his right hand cut off.

Suleiman asked to see a boy who had refused a robe of honor, bestowed for fine work. This eighteen-year-old Mehmed Sokolli requested instead of the robe permission to visit his parents. That was not allowed. Besides, Sokolli had earned a large total of beatings in his earlier years.

The case interested Suleiman because Ibrahim alone had been granted such permission, to leave the Great Gate to visit his father, when he had been in the Enclosed School.

When questioned, Sokolli, whose record showed him to be a captive taken at eleven years from the Croats, explained that his family had journeyed to the city to see him and had waited there for years.

"There is no record," Suleiman pointed out, "of the special study you have chosen. What is it? You may speak."

"My masters," replied the boy impassively.

It could not have been impertinence because he was speaking before the face of his Sultan. It might then be the simple truth.

"Why?" Suleiman asked curiously.

The boy's gray eyes lifted, restlessly. "Because I do not understand them."

For that answer he might have been sent from the School to serve as a gardener or a barge rower. Suleiman wondered if this outspoken boy from the northern mountains did not find it necessary to grasp the purpose of his tutors before he would serve them. He dismissed Sokolli, and told Piri Pasha to have the School offer no more rewards to the student but to allow him to do as he wished, including visiting his family.

Later, after Sokolli had graduated, he asked what post had been given him in the Organization. He learned that the Croat had been appointed assistant to the Judge of the Army of Europe—a post high in the scale, with a good salary.

Years afterward, when Suleiman's personal influence had wrought change in the Organization, Ogier Busbecq, an acute observer from Europe, made this comment: "The Turks rejoice greatly when they find an exceptional man. It is as if they had gained a precious object, and they spare no labor in cultivating him—especially if they notice that he is fitted for war. Our way of doing is very different; for if we find a good dog, hawk or horse, we are greatly delighted and we spare no effort to make it the best of its kind. But if a man happens to possess an extraordinary disposition, we do not take such pains [with him]. Nor do we think that his education is especially our affair. We get much pleasure and service from the well-trained horse, dog, and hawk—but the Turks much more from a well-educated man."

Naturally other residents of the Magnifica Comunita were sorely puzzled by the anomaly of the School. They could not understand why the all-powerful Turks allowed themselves to be governed by foreign boys. When they asked the question of Turkish-born acquaintances, they were answered: "Because the Sultan's *kullar* are better able to do it than we are." When they asked if such boys, captive and Christian for the most part, could be trusted, they were assured—"Have you ever heard of one of them who betrayed us?"

Only a very few of these foreign residents across the Golden Horn—who had come thither to bargain for concessions in the rich oriental trade—realized the truth. The graduates of the School were the best-educated group in the Osmanli dominion. They were better trained than western students in the universities of Paris or Bologna, at that time. And in Suleiman they had a leader capable of using their minds to greater effect than the steel tempered into swords at the Arsenal.

When the snow melted and jasmine bloom touched the gardens with white in the spring, in the year 1522, Luigi Gritti called Marco Memmo's attention to the youths riding out upon the fields of sport across the water. Over there, he said, was nurtured the greatest peril to the Christian Commonwealth. "Nimble and gay," he nodded, "yet they pray; they read their prayers, yet they study the books of the new learning. With what weapon are you going to stop the career of such young-lings?"

Messer Marco felt convinced that the bastard was becoming a renegade. His distrust of the gibing Gritti was heightened by realization that he himself served as little more than a spy here in Galata, while Gritti had a way of proving himself right in his prognostications about the infidel Turks. "By the lion of San

Marco," he retorted, "I see nothing fearsome in these mammets and their mummeries! Nor do I hold in regard any such learning, which smells of the arts of Paracelsian physicians! If you had the eyes of a true Venetian you would take heed of what is being launched upon the water beneath us. There lies the danger we must reckon with."

Along the docks of the Arsenal storeships and transport galleons were moored with the new galleys. Shipping of all sorts crowded the Golden Horn. Memmo, experienced in such matters, pointed out barges decked with planking heavy enough to hold cannon that fired huge balls, ten hands' lengths around. Whither was this new armada bound?

Reports from Venice and Vienna both had it that the Turkish army of invasion would move north again, through the Danube gateway that had been opened the year before. But Memmo could not believe that such heavy sailing galleons as these were bound for the river run up the Danube. No, they must be bound for the open sea. Yet not for forty years had the Turks ventured thither——

The riddle nagged at him, because Venice itself lay within easy sail up the Adriatic that had been until now a Venetian lake.

"Has Your Excellency forgotten," Gritti asked provokingly, "the treaty of accord and friendship Suleiman signed with you last autumn?" It amused him that Memmo bewildered his brain about the armament of a fleet instead of the purpose of Suleiman, who would direct it.

Memmo spat in voiceless anger. He ejaculated that such a treaty often served as a screen for an invasion.

"But not by the Turks. Not by Suleiman, I think." Carefully Gritti pondered. "I heard—there is a certain secretary of the Divan who owes money to an Armenian goldsmith who has a woman, a spice seller in the Covered Market. She whispered to me that the Sultan could not agree with the Vizir and the commanders of the army as to what they would do next."

"Bazaar talk! Dust in our eyes! They have agreed well enough, the Sultan and his Divan." In his turn Memmo meditated. "My eyes tell me they will take their armed host some-whither by sea. The moment favors it. The Holy Roman Emperor and his warcraft of Spain are engaged in conflict"—bitterness crept into his voice—"with the Most Christian King of France. Only the fleet of our republic stands in the way of the Turks."

"Only"—suddenly Gritti laughed. "But does it? To enjoy your trade with the Turks, you must keep the peace. Your Excellency's hand signed the new treaty. Will you hold to it?"

Thoughtfully, Memmo nodded. "By all the Archangels!"

"*Ecco,*" said Gritti, "they have opened the way to Rhodes."

Rhodes

Everything about the island of Rhodes was strange. It lay, for instance, within easy sight of the Turkish mainland. A little south of the coast where Suleiman had lived two years before, this large island rose from the tranquil sea like a citadel within its ring of smaller hilly islands. It had a strange aspect—a hard gray northern citadel in a semitropical sea.

The Knights of Rhodes held it. And they were themselves a remarkable anachronism. They were the belligerent ghosts of all but forgotten crusaders. As the Order of the Brotherhood of the Hospital of St. John the Baptist in Jerusalem they had once played their part in the Holy Land, which was now within Suleiman's dominion. Retreating thence to the nearest island, Cyprus, they had retreated again, northerly, to Rhodes. Within their heavily fortified city they still had a hospital but they were no longer called Hospitalers. The Turks, who respected them for their hardihood, called them, collectively, the Religion, and their citadel the Stronghold of the Hellhounds.

Being at such a great distance from their native Europe, the

Knights perforce raided and traded for supplies along the adjacent Turkish mainland, their fast galleys went out against the grain ships coming from Egypt. Then, too, being by now a political entity—with their commanderies scattered through Europe—the Knights had made war or treaties with their late rivals the Templars, and with Genoa. Altogether these survivors of the crusades had displayed more hatred than good will toward each other.

In Rhodes itself a remarkable state of affairs prevailed. On the broad Street of the Knights separate chapter halls housed the Knights, with different shields of arms over the massive doorways, shields of now vanished Aragon and Provence as well as new nationalities such as France and England. Within these very comfortable hostels the Knights and men-at-arms spoke the "Tongues" of ancient days. The Portuguese, being newcomers, had been shoved in the house of an older Tongue.

Their leader was a figure two centuries behind his time—a white-bearded Frenchman whose portraits show him in full plate armor, a banner in one gauntleted hand—the Grand Master, Philippe Villiers de L'Isle Adam. Between the old De L'Isle Adam and the youthful Suleiman there lay the cleavage of time, and of religion. Each stood for an idea and a way of life. But the obdurate Frenchman was also a skilled soldier: Suleiman was hardly that.

Suleiman in his summons to the master of the Knights offered more than terms of surrender. If the Grand Master yielded the rule of the island to Suleiman, he and his people could remain as they were, with freedom to practice their religion, or they could evacuate with their arms and possessions, being ferried where they chose to go in Turkish ships. The reply of De L'Isle Adam, of course, was only routine. He would not surrender.

It was odd that the young Sultan of the Osmanlis should have set his mind on this island of the sea, troublesome though it might be. The dominion of the Turks had expanded over the land. Still, he had spent most of his life along the coasts, whether on the Crimea or Magnisiya. And Constantinople itself lay between the waterways of two continents. Whether he had pondered the strategic possibilities of the sea or not, he had a fondness for it. Moreover, there was an old score to settle with the Knights. In his last years, Suleiman's great-grandfather, the Conqueror, had attempted to wrest this island from them and had failed.

Suleiman's Vizir, Piri Pasha, argued against the expedition. It would be dangerous to move the field army and the Sultan to an island where both could be cut off. The strength of the army lay in its horsemen, who would be at a great disadvantage against walls on an island. Whereas they could break through the Danube gateway with little risk and a secure retreat behind them. Moreover, Piri Pasha distrusted (and, as the event proved, rightly) the information of the Jewish physician arrived from Rhodes—that the city of the Knights lacked adequate supplies and was commanded by an old man newly out from France.

Piri Pasha did not mention what he most feared, Suleiman's lack of experience.

Unmistakably at this point Suleiman took active command of the armed forces, overruling Piri Pasha and ordering the expedition to set out by sea and land. He went himself with the Asiatic mobilization, down the coast to a harbor opposite Rhodes, where transports waited. Somewhere along the line there had been delays. And Suleiman gave evidence of the temper that he held in restraint. In his diary he noted that they made four of the last stages in two days; the day after the leading column reached the shore it began to embark, which was quite a feat in itself. Still, Suleiman's portion of the army did not land on Rhodes until July 28—late in the summer. The other commanders had occupied the island, protected by the battle fleet of galleys, landing stores and heavy artillery and 10,000 troops, the month before.

When Suleiman reached the quarters prepared for him on a height opposite the walls, that same twenty-eighth of July, the guns opened up. Evidently he had assumed full responsibility.

And at once the results proved to be discouraging. Suleiman's laconic diary reveals how the return fire of the city fortress flattened down the advanced trenches; counterattacks swept over Piri Pasha's batteries, putting them out of action for weeks.

"The Sultan changes the position of his camp," the diary records, "to be nearer. Heavy bombardment silences the guns of the city."

(The defenders have taken to bombproof shelters.)

"A shelter of tree branches is put up for the Sultan, so that he can direct the movements of his forces better."

(Something unexpected is happening. The diary lists too many high officers as casualties.)

"The commander of the cannon is killed . . . the chiefs of the firelock men and of the cannoneers, wounded."

Weeks pass, and the walls of Rhodes appear as impregnable as before. The Tongues of the knighthood of Europe are speaking with unmistakable meaning.

The fortifications of Rhodes had been designed in a new manner, and were probably the strongest in Europe at the time. Instead of the plain curtain wall with corner towers of the early days of gunpowder, the Knights had constructed low-lying but deep works of massive cemented stone. These had projecting bastions thrust forward into the plain. Fire from the bastions swept the front of the main ramparts.

Inside this vast structure of masonry, corridors and shelters permitted the defenders to move safely from point to point. Half of the Stronghold of the Hellhounds fronted the sea. Out from it two moles, ending in towers, formed the breakwaters of the small harbor. On the side toward the sea, Rhodes could not be attacked. And aid from the sea might reach the city by way of the protected harbor. So narrow was the water entrance that a chain could be drawn across it.

Within the walls Rhodes had been built by the Knights to be a true citadel of massive stonework, from the house of the Grand Master to the cathedral of St. John, and the hospital. There were no ramshackle rows of wooden dwellings to burn, or flimsy roofs to give way under the dropping fire of mortars.

In their siege trenches, pushed at great cost close to the walls, the Turks had such mortars; they had long iron cannon capable of smashing down the older type of high encircling walls, they had brass siege pieces sunk into the ground, firing huge balls and newly designed explosive shells at a high angle, to fall inside the city; they had light sakers that could be carried forward in the rush of an attack, and set up on temporary positions.

Even such siege batteries as these could not breach the new defenses of the Knights. In the long duel between firepower and fortification, now just beginning, the ramparts of Rhodes had a decisive advantage. In proof, they are still standing, repaired but unchanged, as the Knights designed them, to make their island invulnerable.

Among the men of the Tongues, moreover, there was an Italian engineer, Gabriel Martinengo, who handled guns with loving skill. Martinengo had spotted the ranges for his cannon to all points outside the walls.

Defeated in their efforts aboveground, the Turkish engineers went underground, pushing mines laboriously through the stony earth, to blow up the walls. Martinengo devised mine detectors out of the upper halves of drums set a little into the earth so that the vibration of digging beneath sounded in the drumhead. Other devices met the attackers in their tunnels and in their rush aboveground after the explosion of a mine.

"The miners meet with the enemy," Suleiman's diary relates, "who use a great quantity of [flaming] naphtha, without success. . . .

"The troops penetrate inside the fortress, but are driven out with heavy loss by the use the infidels make of a new kind of catapult. . . .

"Some Circassians break in, carrying off four or five banners and a great plank that the enemy had filled with metal hooks to tear the feet of the besiegers. . . ."

No real break can be made in the defenses, the human tides sent against the openings are driven back and down; all the batteries open at once against the fronts of the Tongues of Auvergne, of Spain and England and Provence, against the bastion of St. George, the Tower of Spain, the gates of St. Mary and St. John. The guns cannot reach the human defenders, nor break down the stubbornness of old De L'Isle Adam, or the genius of Martinengo.

August has passed and September is ending. Suleiman ventures to order a desperate measure, an attack at all points. The evening before this, messengers go through the encampment, calling out, "The earth and the stonework above the ground only will be the Sultan's; the blood of the people inside and the plunder will be yours."

The general attack fails.

Suleiman cannot understand this failure of his armed forces to penetrate a rubble of stonework held by no more than a tenth of his strength, in numbers. His temper flares in the council of the army leaders.

September 26. "Council. The Sultan in his anger puts Ayas Pasha under arrest."

(Ayas Pasha, a single-minded Albanian, had pressed his attack all day against the fronts of Auvergne and the Germans, and had suffered the greatest losses.)

September 27. "Council. Ayas Pasha is restored to duty."

(Not only that, the steadfast Albanian soldier is given reinforcements from Piri Pasha's lines. Piri Pasha, ill with gout and wearied, has no mind to continue the battle.)

Unmistakably Suleiman himself is suffering. He has given

orders that cannot be carried out. Wherever he rides now through the lines the men watch expectantly, waiting for him to order the withdrawal from Rhodes to the mainland.

Most of all the unarmed peasants suffer, who have dug the siegeworks under the diabolical blasting of guns above their heads. They have gone with little food, and lie sick and shivering under the lash of the autumn rains. For one man who dies in the trenches another dies in the lines from sickness. It is time for these peasants to be marched homeward, to get in the last of the crops . . . the useless horses of the army are dying off from lack of grazing.

Moreover, by now the survivors are endangered. Too much time has gone by. Scout vessels bring in tidings of a Venetian fleet gathering off Crete. Relief from Europe can be expected any day. And Suleiman might be cut off on the island where he could not feed his army.

True, commanders like Ayas Pasha and the Slav, Ferhad Pasha, think only of new attacks, of the hideous throwing of human beings against broken stones and exploding guns. But Suleiman realizes his own mistakes too clearly. Grim Sultan Selim would never have been caught sitting helplessly in a tent of tree branches in the rain, on an island. Selim understood the insatiability of war; how you must trick war by marching swiftly, striking with terror, and passing on—never staying, never letting yourself be caught and held to face merciless war itself. . . .

The diary tells that Suleiman rode off in intervals of quiet to visit garden spots, bare in the autumn storms. He went off to the ruins of ancient Rhodes where the sea kings of long ago had their dwellings. These ruins he ordered restored, to make winter quarters for the army. At such times, watching the work in the gardens and the ruins, he could escape for a little from the thudding of the guns and the haggard faces of his men.

He ordered fresh supplies to be ferried from Egypt, and the garrisons of janizaris posted in Anatolia to be brought out to the island. To show his men that he meant to stay, he moved from his makeshift tent into a stone house.

Word went through the huts of the army: "The Sultan will not retreat."

Of all the alternatives he might pursue, retreat was the worst. That would mean the slaughter of thousands of his followers had been useless—a foolish mistake made by a Suleiman who did not know how to lead in warfare.

October passed. Suleiman allowed no more general attacks. When even the janizaris began to gather in groups and complain, he ordered the supporting fleet to leave the island anchorages and take shelter in the mainland, thus ending the possibility of retreat.

The Surrender

November went by. Suleiman chose to outlast the enemy, relying on the weariness bred by time itself, protecting his forces as best he could contrive, relying on intermittent gunfire and mining, pressing forward at night for gains of a few yards into the labyrinth of stonework.

The first day of December he made use of a new weapon. An unarmed man, making his way into the Stronghold, told the Christians that the Sultan would end the siege by granting the terms he had offered beforehand: the Religion and the townspeople could leave or stay, with their liberty, their arms and wealth untouched. This was no official offer, only a report passed in, but it spread through all the households of Rhodes.

It had an unexpected impact, psychologically, upon the badly exhausted defenders.

"This device served the enemy to greater purpose than anything he had done before," Richard Knolles, a chronicler of the later Elizabethan age, relates. "The enemy . . . little by little creeping on further, drove the defenders to such extremity that they were glad to pull down many of their houses, therewith to make new fortifications, and to make their city less by casting up of new trenches, so that in a short time . . . they could not well tell which place to fortify first, the enemy was now so far crept within them. For the ground which the enemy had now gained within the city was almost 200 paces in breadth, and 150 paces in length.

"*Solyman* . . . persuaded that nothing was better than clemency, commanded Piri, the old Pasha, to prove if the Rhodians might by parley be drawn to yield their city upon reasonable conditions. . . . Many, who in time of the assault feared not any danger but were altogether become desperate and careless of themselves, after they had understood that the enemy offered parley, they began to conceive some hope of life. Resorting unto the Grand Master, they requested him that he would provide for the safety of his people, whose warlike forces were weakened, and the city beaten down about their ears."

Not only that: the long ordeal and the hand-to-hand struggle for street corners and parapet crests had embittered men chilled by winter frosts. De L'Isle Adam and his surviving officers— only 180 Knights remained on their feet, to lead 1500 men-at-arms and Greeks of the town—could expect merciless killing when the crippled Turkish forces broke through the last barriers. They had hoped for relief from Europe. They had sent out messengers in the first days to urge that, with fresh troops and powder, the walls of Rhodes could be held.

"The Grand Master," Richard Knolles sums up, "sent one of the knights of the Order into Spain, to Charles the Emperor, and another of the Order also to Rome to the Cardinals and Italian Knights, and from thence into France unto the French king with letters: craving the aid of the Christian princes for relief of the city by land and sea besieged. But all in vain, for they, carried away by the endless grudge of one against another, or respecting only their own states, returned the ambassadors with good words but no relief."

De L'Isle Adam had a bitter choice to make. By his own code there was no surrender. No one around him had confidence that the Sultan would keep his promised terms. On the other hand, resistance would sacrifice thousands of the townspeople, Greek Christians, who were breaking down under the ordeal.

He asked for a three days' truce and got it. Then happened one of those mischances that act as a match to powder in hours of tension. A ship came in by night, showing no lights. It was the first from Crete, and proved to be a wine ship carrying no more than a hundred volunteers who had sailed against the orders of the Venetian Signory. Turkish observers naturally thought that the relief ship carried more than it did, breaking the truce by its arrival.

Then a die-hard Frenchman discharged two cannon into a crowd of janizaris who had come up during the truce to stare at the walls. The result was a wild attack by the Turks on that section of the walls.

At the end of it, Rhodes still stood. The Grand Master took the testimony of Gabriel Martinengo, who had headed the defense. Martinengo summed up the situation: they had twelve hours' supply of powder, and the powder mill at the harbor could no longer keep up that much reserve; they had combatants enough to hold only portions of the walls; a general attack for more than twelve hours would be the end of the defense.

De L'Isle Adam heard his engineer's testimony and took the vote of his officers and the burghers of the town. It was for surrender, and he agreed. He sent out an envoy and the siege was over.

Then happened something unexpected. Suleiman reaffirmed his old terms, explaining carefully that the churches of the townspeople would not be commandeered as mosques; the people themselves would not be pressed to turn Moslem; their children would not be taken. Those who decided to leave might carry the cannon with them, and all their property if they wished; Turkish ships would transport them to Crete.

This the Knights could hardly believe. When unarmed janizaris rioted inside a gate—these were the reinforcements from
the mainland, angered by the command against plundering—
De L'Isle Adam went out with one companion through the rain
to the Sultan's house. The two leaders met—the soldier of the
west, and the new emperor of the east. Suleiman gave the
Grand Master a robe of honor, remarking to Ibrahim, who was
with him, "It is a pity that this fine old man should be made to
leave his home."

He sent janizaris of his guard to stop the rioting. More than
that, he made an effort to retrieve something from the devastation of the last five months. As if calling on a friend, he returned the visit of his enemy.

It broke all precedent, for a reigning monarch of the Orient
to venture into the armed lines of the Christians. In doing so
he had only the Grand Master's word to protect him. When
Suleiman rode through a demolished gate without a following
except for one of the pashas and Ibrahim to interpret, he took
a step toward a better understanding with his hereditary foes.

Dismounting in the courtyard of De L'Isle Adam, he approached the amazed Knights on foot, explaining that he had
come to ask after the health of their venerable master. Against
the hard gray of the massive doorway the slender youth in white
and gold appeared friendly and gay. For the first time the anxious Christians understood that he meant to keep his word as to
the terms of surrender.

Later when a guard of janizaris marched in, the Knights had
another moment of surprise. One said, "They came silent, moving as one man without a word spoken."

It softened the tight bitterness of the soldierly Grand Master, who is reported to have said, "You are worthy of praise because you vanquished Rhodes, and showed mercy."

The evacuation was carried out as agreed. When the surviving Knights were landed safely at Crete, they found the Venetian battle fleet immobilized there, with orders to take no action

unless the Turks should threaten Cyprus. Two thousand recruits had been gathered at Rome, to relieve Rhodes, but no shipping had been available to them.

The Emperor, Charles, dismissed the loss of the island with casual irony. "Nothing in the world," he said, "has been so well lost as Rhodes."

He was wrong. Until then there had been at least the pretense that Europeans could unite in a crusade, at need. There had been the sense that, in spite of its internal conflicts, Christian Europe made a whole of some sort. After Rhodes had been left to surrender, and the wounded Knights to be shipped back carefully by the Sultan, that semblance of unity became a wraith of the past with the memory of the Caesars of Rome and Charlemagne.

For years the surviving Knights wandered haphazard around the Mediterranean shores, visiting courts that listened indifferently to their demand for a new stronghold. These veterans of a remote battle were really something of a nuisance. Monarchs who entertained them perforce wearied of hearing how Rhodes had been held for five months against fourteen attacks. These wounded men brought the bastion of St. George with them everywhere.

After seven years Charles granted them the rocky inhospitable island of Malta lying far to the west in the narrow gut of the sea between his own Sicily and the African coast.

Meanwhile at Rhodes, the Turks had gained their first base upon the sea.

The Cost of the Capture of Rhodes

The Sultan had departed from Rhodes as soon as the Knights had been shipped off and the necessary orders given. He had not questioned the efficient Martinengo, or made an examination of the formidable defenses. He was anxious only to leave the place, and he never returned within sight of it again. Characteristically, he made time to reward some Greek women, expert swimmers, who had given aid by carrying messages to and from the city.

Strangely enough—in European opinion—most of the Greek citizens elected to remain in their homes under Turkish rule. They had not found service to the feudal-minded Knights to be an easy one. Under the Turks they had freedom from taxation for five years, and after that only the yearly house tax of ten pieces of silver to pay. No demands were made on them for cattle or wine, and their daughters were not molested.

At Constantinople Memmo waited upon the Sultan, to congratulate him. For Memmo, mouthing praise of the Turkish victory, Suleiman felt only contempt. Memmo was lying, fluently and obsequiously. It amused Suleiman to hear the lies so deftly phrased—as Ibrahim translated them impassively—and it flattered his inward pride to have the envoy of a once powerful European state render lip service to his achievement. But he had a faint physical dislike of Memmo, who gorged his body with meat and soaked up wine.

For his antagonist, the Grand Master, Suleiman had felt real pity and involuntary respect. The white-bearded man had been loyal to a religion and a code. The religion, of course, had been that of the Evangel, not the Koran. But the important thing was that the old man believed in his religion.

Long ago Kasim had taught Suleiman that there were only three true believers, the three Peoples of the Book—the eldest in time being the Jews, who held to the ancient Torah, the next being the Christians, who held to the Evangel, and the latest being the *Muslimin* (Moslems) of the Koran. All had Prophets of their faith, whether Moses or Abraham, Jesus or Muhammad. Suleiman was terribly earnest about inward conviction. He could not be sure—in spite of the arguments of the imams—that a Moslem who gave only lip service to his religion was equal in

68

the scales of judgment to a Christian who lived by the word of his religion.

So in this moment of apparent triumph we find Suleiman to be a man rigid in keeping his word, sensitive in his judgments, susceptible only to flattery that touched his pride, and groping confusedly toward a concept of brotherhood among peoples.

The notion of a brotherhood was not his own. He had grown up solitary, as the son of Selim, yet in touch with two very active brotherhoods. Both the Mevlevi and the Bektashi dervishes wandered by him, some merry with their token begging bowls, some withdrawn from ordinary life, the hermits of the mountains. They had active minds; they laughed and mocked and again they wept over the ills they beheld along the roads. "We cannot be counted by numbering," they said. "We cannot be ended by defeat."

Even the *yuldashlar* of the janizaris in their barracks had formed a rude brotherhood. You could not harm one janizary without having to deal with his comrades. If you aided one of those Young Troopers, you had the gratitude of the others. So, in a sense perfectly comprehended by Suleiman, the Grand Master had been the head of a brotherhood.

Often Suleiman wondered about the Pope in Rome. As the head of a Christian brotherhood the Pope was understandable, as was the Sheyk of Islam (the Mufti). In fact most Turks felt awe of the solitary man who served a great religion. But as the head of a political power, pent up in the enclosure of the Vatican, the Pope was not so easily understood.

Suleiman had known intimately the ties of loyalty, the bonds of belief, the needs of common folk, and their vagrant impulses toward something better. He had no acquaintance with nationality as such, or with the European courts that dominated the nations there, or with the class of nobility—except for the Venetian ambassadors—that in turn dominated the courts.

At that time he was groping his way toward a new understanding between rulers. If rulers served their different peoples, and if there could be friendship between rulers, why then the ordeal of ordinary living might go better among the peoples than it had gone, for instance, under the Yavuz Sultan.

If there could be a new bond, simply of friendship . . .

Diffidently he confided this thought to Ibrahim. He never could find the eloquent words to express a thought; nor could he make a speech. And after Rhodes he had a definite plan for Ibrahim. Partly because of that and partly—being oriental in his thinking—because he wished to test the self-sure Greek on this point, he put his thought into a question. Could there be actual friendship among rulers, as between ordinary men?

He got his answer immediately. Ibrahim was amused. "Certainly the Lord of the Two Worlds can have friendship for the asking. At a fine feast, all the guests will be fast friends indeed of the host. But a beggar is another matter."

Carefully Suleiman pondered this, disregarding Ibrahim's habitual mockery, detecting a certain defiance in his friend. The gifted Ibrahim could never forget that he was passing his life in service to a more stupid Turk. This instinctive resentment he concealed carefully.

"Actually," he added quickly, "you can accomplish much by that—more perhaps than the Conqueror ever did. For one thing, you might manage to disarm your enemies while increasing the loyalty of those who believe as you do. It would be something new in the world to use peace as a weapon. Only a very strong ruler could do that. Imagine how you would confuse Memmo if you held out the hand of friendship to him." He smiled, pleased. "I would like to be there to see his face. Why, diplomats would soon have to take to begging bowls, and dervishes would sit in council!"

Suleiman pictured that in his mind and smiled. "I would like to be there to see that."

Immediately Ibrahim foresaw real benefits to be gleaned from his master's visionary idea. The Venetians would gain favor as being the first friends of the Turks; and the Venetian fleet was worth having. The Greek minority would have more privileges—and Ibrahim was a Greek. Beyond that, a new entente could be set up in southeastern Europe, around the House of Osman, a group of peoples declaring for peace. How much he, Ibrahim, would enjoy balancing such a league of peaceful warriors against the dominion of the Emperor of the House of Hapsburg, who ruled warlike civilians.

Even beyond that—Ibrahim's clairvoyant mind caught at remote possibilities—Suleiman's new idea might appeal to some of the oppressed European *rayat*, the common folk, the peasantry. And if the Turks could be persuaded to put aside weapons for a generation or two, they might be seriously weakened. They had a saying: *Take arms from a people, and strength will leave them.*

Then bitterness returned. Only a Suleiman, with an invincible army at call, could pose as a humanist in this time of strife.

Yet Suleiman was earnest in his groping. The siege of Rhodes had left its indelible impression on him.

The exultant acclamation of his city had surprised Suleiman at his return. When he rode for the first time out the Great Gate, to go to the mosque on Friday, masses of people lined the way that had been swept and sanded before him. The four pashas rode before him, in their fur-edged kaftans. Behind him trotted Ibrahim and the weapon-bearers, stiff in white satin and gold. Beside him ran the archers of his guard, like watchful hounds.

The people of the streets strained to catch sight of him as he sped by. They threw precious flowers, they knelt to pick up the sand the hoofs of his white pacer had trod. And always they murmured his name, and the word "Fortunate."

Fortune had followed him like the benevolent unseen angel upon his right hand. The fall of Rhodes. A boy child born to Gulbehar. Islands of the sea and fortresses of far lands submitting, after Rhodes. Messages of congratulation, not only from

Venice but from the Sherif of Mecca, the Tatar Khan of the Crimea, and, beyond expectation, the first envoys from his most bitter enemy Ismail the Shah-in-shah of Persia, and from an almost unknown city, Moscow. . . .

Yet when the ride ended and he knelt on his half balcony in the obscurity of the mosque, he smelled the mud of the earthworks, and the stench of sick men lying on the wet ground of Rhodes. He felt the sweat chill upon his own body as he turned and twisted under brocade and fur coverlets through the hours of darkness, hearing the drip of water from the branches of his hut to which he had clung stubbornly, torturing himself, alone, for his mistakes and his helplessness before Rhodes.

He had not spoken about that. For one thing, the Osmanli Sultan could not well explain his misgivings or his hopes; for another, Suleiman found it hard to explain anything. In his laconic diary he wrote a customary phrase—God gave the victory to the Padishah (the Emperor). Yet in his diary after Rhodes he made constant note of rain, of storms, of animals and men caught in the mud, sickening—of rivers flooding, and of rain, rain, and rain. It became almost an obsession.

His revulsion against waging war after that showed in his acts. Next spring the drum of conquest did not beat; there was no campaign for three years. This was the first respite in the fourteen years since Selim had taken the Osmanli sword.

The Osmanli sultans had the duty of using that sword. Beyond their dominion of peace lay the Lands of War—the pagan lands against which the Moslem arms must be led. From the time of Ertoghrul this duty had been carried out, except during brief years of the rule of his grandfather, Bayazid, the recluse and dreamer. In putting a stop to the outward march of conquest, Suleiman was violating old custom. He had no way of knowing what the consequences would be.

At the same time he acted even more radically in changing his helpers. He rid himself of what might be called the old army type. In Suleiman's case this meant more than if a European

monarch, Henry VIII for example, had dismissed his ministers.
For under the Osmanlis, the different heads of the Organization
had direct responsibility for what went on beneath them. The
ailing Piri Pasha held the imperial seal and was in very truth the
bearer of the burden of administration.

When Suleiman informed Piri Pasha that he would be relieved of duty and could retire, the lined face of the old man
sagged in weariness. He did not seem to understand that he
had committed no fault. Instead he muttered as if to justify
himself that he was raising a new blood-hued variety of tulip.

Suleiman had heard of horses so accustomed to the traces
that they pushed against the pasture fence when a wagon train
creaked by. "You can raise the new species now, Piri Pasha,"
he said. "On my head, your hours are your own."

When he mentioned the enormous pension of two hundred
thousand aspers to be paid the retired Vizir, Piri Pasha only ex-
pressed gratitude for the kindness shown by his Sultan. The
money had little meaning, else, to him now.

Although they had expected it, the leaders of the Organization felt bewilderment when Suleiman named Ibrahim First
Vizir of the empire. The Greek had been advanced over the
heads of experienced officers his seniors. Besides that, Ibrahim
was to have the military rank of Beylerbey of Roumelia—Commander of the Army of Europe. This gave him responsibility as
great as his authority. (The two other pashas were veteran
Albanians, inarticulate, fond of sleeping between campaigns
in the field.)

Before then, they had talked it over together. At first Ibrahim
had been reluctant to accept the exalted rank. His quick mind
seized on the innumerable dangers to him, of misunderstanding,
of whispering campaigns by those who envied him. Remembering Selim, he was afraid of the repressed moodiness of Suleiman. But Suleiman had thought it through carefully and he was
obdurate. He wanted the Greek to act not as a servant but as
the man he was, brilliantly able to disentangle the complexities

of ruling; he wanted genius, not a routine mind. It was without precedent, for both Sultan and Vizir to be so young, but was that in any way a bad thing?

Still distrustful, Ibrahim exacted a promise from his master, and Suleiman gave it. "I will never dismiss you, in disgrace, from office."

To that promise the new Bearer of the Burden could hold confidently. Suleiman was incapable of breaking his word.

On his part, it is clear that the Sultan meant what he said. His *alter ego* could carry on the outward task of government, counseled, restrained and urged on by Suleiman, who craved seclusion. It was a daring experiment, to single out an obscure foreign-born graduate of the School, the best mind in his dominion. But Suleiman was an astute judge of character.

Having named Ibrahim, he went to great pains to publicize his choice. Ibrahim was to have twelve rowers in his service barge, five horsetails on the standard carried before him. He was to marry a sister of the Sultan.

Probably it occurred to neither of them to wonder if other Osmanlis after them would raise a personal favorite to the highest authority. Suleiman had been the first to do so.

Very soon, in selecting his own officers, Ibrahim appointed the useful Luigi Gritti to be Dragoman of the Gate—that is, liaison officer for foreign affairs. Gritti, of course, was still a Venetian and a Christian. And Ibrahim was to depend on the quick-witted Gritti, as Suleiman depended on him.

So, in the years of change-over, 1523–25, Suleiman turned away from the elder Turkish minds toward the minds of the west. It was noticed that he began to talk with men of the European dominion, with Serbs and Croats, in their own language. As in the case of the graduate, Sokolli, who became assistant to Iskander Chelebi, the Treasurer.

When the Mufti died—and not even Suleiman could have dismissed the head of Islam—Kemal, a philosopher and a great legalist, was named in his place. Then, too, Kasim, the former tutor of Suleiman, gained office with the title of pasha. These two men were notable for their intellectual integrity, resting upon fine scholarship.

Mainstays of the Organization

Upon personal integrity rested also the whole ruling Organization of the Osmanlis. It differed from other governments in that it remained sharply separated from the rest of the nation, probably because it was composed of a special class, graduated from the schools of the tribute children.

Somewhere along the line of their migration, from the Persians or the Byzantines, the Turks had picked up the idea that the household of the ruler must be apart from the government of the land, and so it was. Suleiman's following, from chief swordbearer to keeper of his private stable, had no other duty than to attend him.

That left the management of affairs squarely upon the shoulders of the three vizirs, or ministers. They, in turn, headed the Divan or council. This sat in the Hall of Audience and heard all who came thither with business for the government. Such hearings went with speed and few words, as in the old days when they were held on horseback by the tent of the khan.

Fiscal responsibility lay upon the chief Treasurer, but all accounts passed through the *Kalemi* or central clearing bureau. Secretaries kept the books with rigorous exactitude.

Here another peculiarity of the Osmanlis played its part. They held to their old idea that the nation must be organized for war. In consequence, all officers of the Organization also held rank in the army—except for a residue of secretaries who remained at home to keep the books. And active officers of the army, like the Agha of Spahis, had beneath them their own team of treasurer and accountants.

Beyond this central administration of Constantinople, the

eight beylerbeys in charge of the divisions of the dominion each had his own similar administrative personnel, with treasurer and Kalemi. Farther out in the smaller districts and all through the provinces, the sanjakbeys had their miniature staffs. Naturally, they, too, were part of the national mobilization in time of war. The Beylerbey of Anatolia headed the levies of Asia.

So it befell that responsibilities were fixed, yet dependent upon personal integrity in their carrying out. The Beylerbey of Anatolia, receiving a fixed amount of revenue each year, must produce a certain number of troops fully equipped at demand. Such officers paid no taxes; they received their support from the central Treasury, and were not expected to indulge in any money-making enterprises of their own.

Separated from this dynamic force of the school-bred Organization, the judges of the Law, the graduates of religious schools, held the balance of juridical power, in accordance with the Koran. A Venetian bailo, Marcantonio Barbaro, put it rather quaintly: "As the arms and forces repose altogether in the hands of those who are all Christian-born, so the carrying out of the law is altogether in the hands of those who are born Turks."

Within the fabric of this Organization, and subject to the final judgment of the Law, the inner nationalities, the *millets*—the Greeks, Armenians, Jews, Bulgars, Circassians and others—held to their own customs, and laws. Non-Moslems paid the *kharaj*, or head tax, and attended their own churches.

So long as the officers of the ruling Organization were men of integrity, this system of interrelated responsibility worked well. It also presented a rigid framework difficult to change. And the Turks to a man disliked to forsake their own way of doing things. In his attempt to alter it, Suleiman could only rely on changing the basic laws, a slow process, or on appointing finer minds to administrative posts, a quicker procedure.

He made his most drastic change almost at once when he increased the power of the First Vizir, who had been little more than head of the Divan before. Now Ibrahim fairly held the reins of government as a sort of prime minister-on-trial. Suleiman anticipated rightly that Ibrahim on his own account would bring about great innovations. But he could not have anticipated the nature of those innovations.

Meanwhile the sole responsibility, from deciding upon the pension of a keeper of garrison stables in Mosul to the making of war and peace, rested upon the Sultan himself. While he was not expected to interfere with routine, he was obliged to take notice of any dispute, and to act himself immediately in a crisis.

Very naturally most European observers beheld in him a supreme oriental despot, an *Ottoman emperor.* Few of them realized that he was also the head of the most democratic government of their time. Or that his authority was limited by the *She'ri,* the sacred Law. Suleiman conceded this limitation by allowing the Mufti unchallenged authority in religion, as he made over to the Vizir the entire economy of the nation.

Foreign policy—which centered in the case of the Osmanli sultans upon the perennial question of war or peace with the powers beyond their dominion—was to be decided only theoretically by the old-fashioned Divan. Actually under Suleiman it was decided by himself, Ibrahim, and the Mufti.

For himself in these first years of his reign Suleiman reserved an extraordinary authority. He wished to make himself the sole arbiter of the moral law. What was right and what was wrong he alone would decide—whether a peasant might claim a passing swarm of bees, or an imam might call for prayers at a roadside shrine.

This concept of himself as a monarch without portfolio, a despot going about with a lantern of Diogenes, was incomprehensible to Europeans. Yet it was to have great effect upon the affairs of Europe for forty years. And in the end it was to compel Suleiman to act as a judge within his own family.

When Suleiman judged the case of Ferhad Pasha, he fairly startled the foreigners across the Golden Horn. Ferhad Pasha, a Slav from the Dalmatian coast, had become the most dashing soldier of the army. As Third Vizir he had crushed that early revolt in Syria, sending the head of the leader of the revolt, Ghazali, to the Sultan; he had done much at Belgrade and had fought savagely at Rhodes. He had been given a sister of Suleiman in marriage. Yet savagery had been a part of his nature; he had arrogated power to himself in distant posts and had executed personal enemies, against the Law, as enemies of the Osmanli state. Suleiman would have none of a man who used threats to advance his interests, and Ferhad was dismissed from his *pashalik* and recalled.

He had friends who admired him, and one woman who loved him. Suleiman found that his mother, the Valideh, and his sister argued Ferhad's case in the harem beyond the corridor. The influence of the harem, in ways known to women, was exerted for the accused commander. Suleiman put Ferhad on probation, sending him to govern a frontier district on the Danube, only to hear that the soldier abused his power as before. Called again before Suleiman, he was sentenced within a few moments and put to death at once by the executioners, who strangled him with a bowstring.

This death his sister could not forgive Suleiman. Clad in dark mourning, she confronted him in the harem. "I hope it will not be long," she dared to say, "before I wear mourning again, for my brother."

It was in the Law of the Osmanlis, laid down by the Conqueror, that a man should be slain if by living he endangered the lives of many others. That was applied even in the case of the brothers of a prince who became Sultan. To prevent any civil war in the Osmanli lands, such brothers were sought out and killed. Mehmed had decreed that it was better for two or a half dozen, even in the family, to be executed than for civil war to break out. Suleiman had been fortunate in having no brothers.

Appearance of the Laughing One

By then Suleiman had chosen the Laughing One from among the younger girls of the harem.

She had come from the north, bought from a Tatar dealer. A slight thing with fair hair, unmistakably a Slav, she had been given the name of Khurrem, the Laughing One. The Keeper of the Linen named her that because she had a merry way of singing. She would take a guitar and pick at it and sing, with her high heels tapping the carpet.

Because Khurrem embroidered swiftly, making odd designs of crowns and castles, the Keeper of the Linen took her in charge, paying her slipper money. The Russian girl had her own way of doing things. From the flame of a lamp with her hands she could make shadows dance like demons on a screen. After watching the other novice working girls playing at tossing a ball, with their legs showing against the sheer white silk of their trousers, Khurrem joined them, binding her loose hair with a satin cord since she had no rope of pearls. Her skullcap was blue velvet, because she had no cloth of gold like the others. When she sewed the buttons on a tunic of the Valideh, she stared and laughed on learning they were diamonds, and precious. Such precious stones, she said, made clumsy buttons. Often when she laughed like that she was punished by a beating across the back. But she did not weep like the others. Wiping her eyes, she did exactly as before, and she never forgave those who punished her.

To Hafiza, the Sultan's mother, who asked about her, the Keeper of the Linen declared that the Slav girl was clever and quick and hard as the diamonds she mocked. Hafiza said she could well believe that, because a foreign girl who had been a captive and then a slave and then a servant would have a hard will and a stubborn way. Although Suleiman had been given

79

some of the kerchiefs Khurrem embroidered, he had hardly seen the girl's face until the time he heard her singing where the elder women could not hush her. Since he had learned some of the dialects of the north, he listened to the words of her song and asked her name.

Then he sometimes stopped to talk with her in outlandish speech. She laughed merrily when he said the wrong words, but he showed no anger at that. Not even the Keeper of the Linen could punish her, now that she was in his eye.

By the law of the harem a young girl in the Sultan's eye was given a separate sleeping cubicle, with sheer garments, body servants of her own, and an allowance for pearl and gold ornaments. She could call for bath masseuses and hairdressers to come when she wished.

The Laughing One did all that, and set the heel of her slipper on the foot of the Keeper of the Linen, who no longer had the right to punish her. The Valideh Hafiza summoned her and talked to her sternly. The Laughing One stood respectfully with clasped hands before the Sultan's mother.

Of late the Sultan had not looked closely at any woman of his household other than Gulbehar, the *kadin* or favored girl. It seemed as if Khurrem amused him with her tricks and outlandish speech. Without warning, in passing her after the sunset prayer one evening he drew his kerchief over her shoulder and left it there. Khurrem smiled when she observed that the kerchief was one she had embroidered. Now it was a sign that he would sleep with her.

By the law of the harem Gulbehar should have prepared the Slav girl for her first night with her master. But Gulbehar did not like the Slav, and would not concern herself with the girl who had been a Christian.

It had to be done by others, hurriedly—the Keeper of the Baths taking her off, adding perfume to the bath water as it flowed, summoning slave women for the massage, the nail trimming, and anointing. These women whispered that the Russian had not the softness of the skin of Gulbehar, or the soft fair hair. Certainly Khurrem did not wear sheer silk as well. But, cleverly, she put on few ornaments.

An old Moorish woman of the nursery instructed Khurrem in the details of approaching her master, how to go past the guards at the Sultan's inner sleeping room, and to make a half prostration toward the bed, then to go to the foot and touch the coverlet to her forehead, to remove all ornaments with her garments and to slip beneath the foot of the coverlet, to draw herself up beside her master. Then before dawn the woman of Africa would come with a lamp to summon the girl back to her own sleeping niche and to testify that she had lain with the Sultan.

It was not the only time Suleiman called for her. Whether she pleased him with her laughing ways, or simply because she differed so from Gulbehar, the harem slaves did not know. Often he would summon Khurrem to a meal, and talk with her of the north and the lands beyond the Danube. In doing so he seemed to value her as a companion and not simply as a woman to take pleasure from.

As a recognized kadin, the Slav had an increased allowance; she could send her attendants for garments or caskets that she wanted. Not that she cared much for bracelets or jeweled anklets; when the whim seized her she bought a great many, and gave them away as quickly.

The Valideh talked with her again, and decided that the girl pleased the Sultan with the strange guitar music she made. Before then no one had fancied that he liked the playing of music, except for the songs of the students in the courtyard of the School. Although he had stopped his horse often to listen to the bell-staves, flutes and drums of the janizaris.

As a favored kadin, she now had authority. When she told the Valideh that she was pregnant, that authority increased. Slaves in trouble sought her protection, and served her in recompense.

Only the Valideh came before her, with Gulbehar, who had borne the Sultan a son. She was called Second Kadin.

Yet the eyes in the harem noticed—for they kept careful count—that the Sultan spoke more and more often with this Slav who had been a captive and then a slave. Gulbehar was First Kadin in name, and in right. But was she first in reality?

From the chambers of the harem, the gossip ran from the black eunuchs to the white outer guards, to the buyers of spice and sugar, to the Covered Market.

For the first time foreign diplomats began to take notice of the gossip about a woman of the Sultan. Gulbehar's name they had hardly known, but this was a stranger, this was a new favorite. When they discovered that she was Russian-born, they called her Russelanie, or Roxelana.

The First Show at the Hippodrome

His new policy of not going to war made it necessary to stay at home in the city. Being incapable of halfway measures, Suleiman tried to make the city his home, almost as if in escaping from Rhodes he sought for shelter in Constantinople.

He had always been drawn toward the city, which he understood much better than the aged Piri Pasha, who had desired to avoid it, or Ibrahim, who wanted to use it as a lever to uplift the outer dominion.

Yet in the city he lived with ghosts. They were very real ghosts, forever intruding on him, with memories of Byzantium. The clear water that splashed into his marble bath flowed from Byzantine cisterns; the very stones of his Serai were the stones of Byzantine palaces. When he prayed in the vast Aya Sophia he felt awed by the immensity of the gray, green and purple marble edifice built by an Augustus Caesar, Justinian. True, the altar of the Christians had been taken away, and a rather shoddy *mihrab* had been set up, cattycorners, to show the direction of Mecca; the brilliant mosaic murals of emperors and empresses had been whitewashed over. Yet it was impossible to enter the magnificent edifice without sensing that it was still the basilica of Justinian.

Besides, Turkish architects had copied the Aya Sophia when they designed the great mosques of the Conqueror, of Bayazid, and of Selim.

The Turks had captured Constantinople three generations before but in turn they had yielded to the influence of the queen city. It was very much like taking a woman captive.

Even when he walked in the seclusion of his private garden under the tree mesh, Suleiman encountered vine-grown marble columns that had marked the triumphs of Byzantine emperors. The sunburned dervishes who chattered to him cheerily about the Wine of Life might have been the pallid monks who eased the soul torment of Byzantine autocrats.

When his private barge sped up the cool vista of the Bosphorus, Suleiman reclined under the awning of the stern dais as great ladies of the Byzantine families, the Comneni, the Ducases, the Porphyrygeniti—those "born to the purple"—had lain in the smoke of incense on their gilt speedboats. He had more than a trace of their blood in him, for Byzantine women had been given to his ancestors.

And his ancestors had imitated the seclusion of the Byzantine noblewomen in penning their own households within harems; they had begun to use castrated black slaves to serve and guard the inmates of the harem, as the Byzantines had done. The Conqueror especially had found it useful to do as the Byzantines had done in more ways than one. His School had been modeled on the palace school of elder Constantinople. His Grand Vizir had been given the powers of the Grand Domestic of the vanished emperors.

Yet the need of the Turks in Constantinople was utterly different from the need of the last Byzantine rulers. *They* had sought security behind vast walls, creating here the last refuge

83

of a cultured, inbred society, headed often by brilliant women like Irene—whose church stood by the barracks of the janizaris—and Theodora. Under them the regal city had become half depopulated, poverty-ridden in the midst of its splendors, draining sustenance from the Anatolian countryside, borrowing money from its churches to hire barbarian soldiery to defend it. The Byzantine city lived on because it contrived not to die.

The Turks needed no protection here; they turned the city into an administrative center of their dominion, a heart from which the blood could pulse outward through the arteries.

The result was a cosmopolitan city. Almost next door to the Great Gate (and to Suleiman's stables) the Patriarch of the Orthodox Church ministered to the Christian Greeks. Across from Suleiman's Serai, the Magnifica Comunita dealt submissively in foreign trade.

When Suleiman rode up toward the new Covered Market he passed through streets rebuilt—although with wood and clay—by another community, refugee Jews from Spain. They worked unceasingly at handcraft and shopkeeping, with the Armenians who came from everywhere to their quarter, and with the Moors who had also been driven out of Spain. Beyond the Market the Serbs from Belgrade had built a new community, called Belgrade. Down along the tideless harbor Berbers from Africa and the Arabs from the far Red Sea quartered themselves in warehouses that sheltered their imports of spice, ivory, silk, glass lamps and even pearls from the east—the new luxuries of the Turks.

So the city was filling up with outland peoples, seeking the trade of the great Covered Market and the splendor of the Serai. These newcomers sought to shelter themselves within the Turkish power—the new power rising between the older peoples of the east and the nations of Europe.

All these foreign communities governed themselves, and thronged to churches of their own. They paid a yearly tax of a tenth to the Turkish secretary-treasurers—a tax in almost every case less than they had paid in their old homes, whether in the east or the west. They tried their own criminals, except when a Turk was involved in a case, and even before a Turkish judge the foreigners could expect a fair and quick decision. Moreover, like the Venetians, most of them had privileges. The Jews and Armenians were exempted from the draft of tribute children, and military service—as were the Arabs and Berbers. On the other hand, no inner nation could possess arms or mount cannon on their ships.

The result was that Suleiman held only ultimate authority over a dozen different peoples with as many variations of religious belief, who kept their languages and customs intact. The Osmanlis had never forced those peoples—the separate millets—into a Turkish nation, with a single language and religion. The consequences of this variegation were slow in making themselves apparent, but they were sure.

So Suleiman passed through his city with the wraith of a Byzantine autocrat accompanying him, unseen. The horsetails of the standard carried before him had come from the hinterland of *Tsin* (China) but the gold crescent now displayed above them had been copied from the Byzantine symbol of the crescent moon. Suleiman never beheld it without misgivings. His Turks had no institutions as yet, like those of China or Byzantine; they had no more than the skeleton of their Organization and the driving wills of their sultans. The sultans before him had been able to conquer territories and peoples, but what had they created from their conquest?

Suleiman was the first to take the sword of Osman as an educated man. After Rhodes it became clear to him that the Turks must abandon the path of war and go forward in a new direction. If they were to follow a new path he himself must lead them.

His first efforts to do so in the years of decision, 1522–25, were a bit pathetic. The Mufti counseled him to take money from the Treasury to construct roads and wells, hostels and mosques for the poorer folk. Was it not written in the Koran that wealth brought no good unless it was so used?

Summoning young architects, Suleiman tried to explain that he desired a garden haven for his city, with clear water in it. The architects brought back to him sketches of gardens copied from the Serai. He did not want another Serai. So he set them to work on a new aqueduct to bring fresh water to the city. They could do that because they could use the old Byzantine aqueduct as a model. For himself he had a summerhouse built by the Sweet Waters of Asia.

Ibrahim counseled him to go about the streets disguised, to hear the unguarded talk of the workers on the docks and the veiled women who thronged to the cemeteries on Fridays to gossip.

That Suleiman would not do. But after he thought it over he decided to play host to his people. In the spring month of 1524 he held a public festival for nine days in the half-ruined Hippo-drome where the Byzantines had raced their chariots. The stone obelisk from Egypt still stood there. On the first day he tried to make a speech when Ayas Pasha and the Agha of the Janizaris informed him that the festival awaited his word to begin. He managed to utter some praise of the new Vizir, Ibrahim, then took refuge in handing out gifts.

Each day he sat patiently on a gold settee beneath the wind-whipped pavilion, and each day the merrymaking was for a different group of his people, from the beylerbeys and sanjak-beys down to the scouts and men of the pen. In the arena beneath him the sports varied accordingly—archery and wrestling giving way to juggling and racing and reading of poems. As host Suleiman ordered sherbet and julep to be given by pages of his household to all the watchers. He made gifts of horses and silver-worked saddles from his private stables. Thousands of his people lined the rim of the arena and climbed the trees around it to enjoy the sight of their Sultan in silence. But to

Suleiman it seemed that this festival in the Hippodrome lacked gaiety because he had been an unaccustomed host.

At the end of the last day there was merriment enough. Breaking all precedent, Suleiman went as a simple guest to the wedding feast of Ibrahim—who was taking the Sultan's sister as bride—in the new fine house of the Vizir at the corner of the Hippodrome. There he was surprised to find the entrance sheathed on one side in cloth of gold, and silk brocade on the other. Gold dishes shone on the supper cloth.

And Ibrahim, drawing them all toward him by the magnetism of his presence, offered his distinguised guest a sip of julep from a cup cut from a single turquoise. Ibrahim's dark eyes shone with joy. When he seated Suleiman he laughed and said, "Your feast cannot be compared to mine!"

Surprised, the Sultan looked up at his favorite.

"Because I alone among living men," explained Ibrahim, "have the Lord of the Two Worlds as my guest."

It was a deft compliment that Suleiman returned very soon by allowing the Greek to go upon a mission that he himself should have undertaken, by tradition. In Egypt, always restless under the Mamelukes—whom Yavuz Sultan Selim had allowed to retain the nominal rule of the land, after he had conquered it —a bad situation had arisen under the government of Ahmed Pasha, whom Suleiman had dismissed in disgrace from the siege of Rhodes. Ahmed Pasha, an older man, was also jealous of the rapid rise of Ibrahim to favor. The fellaheen, accustomed though they were to oppression, had complained furtively of exploitation by Ahmed and the Mamelukes. Since the fellaheen had become Turkish subjects, their grievance must be remedied. Because the difficult Ahmed might join in rebellion with the Mamelukes, the situation had to be handled with care and restraint. By giving Ibrahim an honorary guard of five hundred janizaris, Suleiman made it evident that his new Vizir carried with him the full authority of the Sultan.

He himself remained in the city for that third summer without a summons to war. It was a happy summer, because during the festival of Ibrahim's marriage, a son had been born in his own household to Roxelana (Khurrem). The Russian girl seemed to have been born herself under fortunate stars because her first child was a boy. Suleiman gave to the child the name of Selim, his father.

By becoming a mother, Roxelana gained prestige in the harem. The Sultan had only one son older than Selim—Gulbehar's boy, Mustafa. There was always the possibility that Mustafa might die. By that same token Roxelana might become the Sultan Valideh after Hafiza died. She was still Second Kadin; Hafiza ruled the women's quarters, and Gulbehar remained the mother of the first-born. But Roxelana had now become a member of the household.

Moreover, with Ibrahim away, Suleiman sought her companionship. The servants noticed that he seldom brought gifts to the favorite. Often he sat with her, talking of weighty matters as if she had been a man. Since the Russian had come from the Lands of War, she knew the miseries and the hopes of the outlanders of the north.

The servants whispered that she must have laid a spell upon their master. In the very hearth of his home the Sultan had turned to a Christian-born woman with tawny hair. There seemed to be no way of breaking his attachment. If it was fated to be, why then it must be.

The quiet of the city did not last through the winter. Like a blast of the north wind, the Young Troops broke out in revolt.

Janizaris Overturn Their Kettles

Benedetto Ramberti wrote of them: "The janizaris number about twelve thousand, and each of them is paid three to eight aspers a day. Once a year they are given poor blue cloth for garments by the Signor. They live in two barracks within Constantinople. When they take the field every hundred of them bear along a tent; every three lead a horse with their belongings. And when they grow too old or displease the Signor, their names are struck from the book of the janizaris and they are sent off to be castle guards. In this way none of them suffers hardship, while those who do great things in war are made governors.

"They come in boyhood to this soldiery. Those chosen are the healthy ones, strong, and quick above all, and more cruel than compassionate. They are taught by the older, experienced ones. In them rests the force and the firmness of the army of the Turk. Because they all exercise and live together, they become as it were a single body, and in truth they are terrible."

In this description of the Italian the germs of revolt by the Young Troops are evident. Their one garment a year, which they had to wash themselves; the few cents pay in a day, to buy their soup and bread; the harsh discipline which kept them training while pent up in the city—these could be balanced only by the spoil they could snatch in a campaign, or the recognition they might win in battle.

For the last three years they had not been led out to war by the Sultan.

More than that, the veterans among them remembered how they had been denied the looting of the Stronghold of the Hellhounds at Rhodes. They all resented the promotion of the Greek, Ibrahim, from the Enclosed School, over the heads of veteran pashas. Having too much time to brood in their barracks, they imagined how many girls or dinners could be bought with the twenty-four thousand gold Venetian ducats Ibrahim got as salary. Beyond the courtyard of the Aya Sofia they could see Ibrahim's new residence, filled with luxuries, above the empty Hippodrome.

So long as Suleiman remained in the city they nursed their grievances. When he went off during the winter—breaking tradition in leaving them—merely to hunt at Adrianople, taking the Divan and higher officers with him, they felt their injuries anew. Ibrahim was off elsewhere at the fleshpots of Egypt.

Weary of cold and inaction, the janizaris at the Serai gate threw out their soup kettles and took to the streets. Armed with some firelocks, their slender iron javelins and powerful bows and sabers, they fired houses for warmth, plundering the workshops of Jews near the Covered Market, and breaking into the new palace of Ibrahim Pasha.

At once Suleiman rode south. Instead of venturing through the rioting to the Serai, he went to the kiosk up the Bosphorus at the Sweet Waters of Asia.

From the water he made his way with a small escort to the deserted Hall of Audience near the barracks of the janizaris. Then he summoned their regimental officers to appear before him. A mass of troops pressed in with the first officers. Some swords were drawn, amid a confusion of voices. There was a moment of great danger, when the janizaris might have thrown themselves against the Sultan's escort.

Suleiman drew his sword. He killed the soldier nearest him and wounded another. There was only the fleeting clashing of steel, and then quiet. Seeing the blood on the carpet beneath them, the rioters put down their arms.

Punishment was just and cruel. The Agha of the Janizaris and the leaders of the outbreak went to execution; the mass of men returned to their barracks and their duties.

With the end of the winter's snow and the coming of the first grass, Suleiman ordered the drum of conquest sounded. He had no alternative but to lead the army out again.

From his palace across the Golden Horn, Marco Memmo observed the familiar signs of preparation for war. When Ibrahim returned in haste by sea from Egypt, His Excellency concluded that the expedition would be full-scale and immediate. His spies confirmed that, adding the fact that supply convoys were leaving for the northern mountains, so the Turks must be moving upon the gateway of the Danube. Messer Marco on his own account reflected that their Divan had just signed a treaty of accord with Poland. Such a treaty already existed with his republic of Venice. Therefore neither the Poles nor the Venetians were expected to interfere with them. And—he applied Luigi Gritti's test to this fact—what Lands of War lay closest to Venice and Poland? Austria of course, with Bohemia and Hungary.

Still His Excellency could not rid himself of doubts of such apparent certainty. Since there was only one person who could resolve his doubts, he ordered his carriage to go up the Bosphorus, where Gritti now owned a small palace with a terrace opening pleasantly on the water. Gritti might be Dragoman of the Gate, in the Vizir's pay, but Memmo suspected that he would not try to delude his visitor if Venice were threatened. It irked the ambassador that he should need to seek out the adventurer to assure himself of the destination of the Turks.

On his terrace Gritti greeted his friend with no surprise whatever. "Is there a report to go to the ducal palace?"

Memmo noticed that a bracelet gleamed on his wrist, set with an emerald of great size. Deciding not to take offense, he nodded affably. "You have seen the sailing galliot moored by our barge?"

"No, Excellency—but I knew it must be there because you are here in my poor abode. And your report? It will be that the Sultan and his Turkish *asker* march to the Danube?"

This the ambassador did not care to admit. It would not do to trust Gritti too readily. "Signor, I have only fragments of information—that three years of truce have emboldened the Hungarians beyond Belgrade, so that their worthy archbishop, Paul Tomori, and, yes, the venturesome Count Frangipani have been assailing the Turks with their Hungarians. It seems a slight matter." He paused, to say forcibly, "Venice lies not far from the Danube."

Something hard came into Gritti's voice. "It will not be Venice this time."

91

Straining his ears to catch the low intonation, Memmo nodded. If the objective of the Turks were not Venice, it must be the Hungarians. If the bastard could be believed. Abruptly he probed at the other's thought. "Do you speak as the son of the Illustrious, the Doge Andrea Gritti, or as the Dragoman of Ibrahim?"

Once more the dark eyes mocked him. "Am I not both?"

"By the lion of San Marco—why do you serve the Turk?"

Gritti's hand swept across the terrace, and the emerald flashed on his wrist. "I take joy in my new home. And—have you forgotten my interest in Suleiman?"

"I have failed to understand it."

"I did not expect Your Excellency to do so." For a moment Gritti stared at his wrist. "Perhaps only he can bring peace to the world."

The Warning of Mohács

When had there been peace in Europe? There was fear in Europe, greater than the fear of the incoming of the Turks. This greater fear resounded in voices crying from the street corners and at night where men marched on the highroads. It spoke a word that was new and secret, *Bundschuh, Bundschuh*—

What was so dignified and so manifestly a figure of power as the Holy Roman Emperor seated in the Diet or conclave of the Germanic princes and prelates in the flourishing city of Worms in the very heart of Europe, in the center of the Commonwealth of Christians?

In the early month of spring five years before, Charles V, the Emperor, had sat there, listening to speeches in Latin that he barely understood. Threefold fears assailed his mind, drawing his thoughts from the solemn Latin words. One—in his kingdom of Spain the heretical Moriscos were gathering and resisting his efforts to convert or expel them after the policy of Cardinal

Ximenes. In Aragon, in Granada where this Moorish folk still hung around the castles from which they had been driven . . . Two—the obdurate Francis was mustering his armed forces to assail the lands of Charles's Empire. . . . Three—there in the Diet before Charles a thickset mumbling monk, Martin Luther, was refusing to disavow his writings, saying that they had been taken from the word of God, and he could do no otherwise——

A strange speaker, one Hieronymus Balbus, was making an appeal, driven by a fear of his own. A Hungarian, a Magyar from the east, from the far limit of the Empire, he was shouting, "Who stayed the Turks from raging onward in their madness? The Hungarians. Who checked their overwhelming fury? The Hungarians. Who chose to turn against themselves the full power and onslaught of these barbarians, rather than allow them to open a way into the lands of others? The Hungarians!"

The man Balbus was saying that the Christian Common-wealth would have been invaded, and the vitals of German and Italian kingdoms pierced, if the Hungarians had not set up a wall against the pagan invaders.

"But now the Hungarian kingdom is so stripped of strength and its people have been so struck down that unless it can have aid from the west it cannot long resist the Turks."

Balbus spoke at Worms. And then Luther spoke his few words. It smacked of heresy that a monk, alone, could claim to be inspired by the word of God. An edict was laid against him at Worms. When Luther hurried from the hall people closed around him, German knights and burghers. They raised their clenched fists in the gesture that was a salute of the *Landsknechts*. They hurried Luther out and they hid him.

Then was heard along the roads leading from Worms the watchword of gathering and revolt, *Bundschuh, Bundschuh, Bundschuh*. It passed from the protestant knights to the burgh-ers of the towns and the peasants waiting in the fields. . . .

What could be done to give armed aid to Hungary at such a time? The Holy Roman Emperor almost absently gave the man

Balbus a written answer, allowing the Hungarians to fend for themselves and even to make a truce with the Turks, "provided always . . . that it should not dishonor or injure the Catholic faith, or the Commonwealth of Christendom."

No aid was given to Hungary in that earlier year, and Belgrade fell to the Turks.

Five years later, on August 28, 1526, the rains had ceased along the Danube. But the river was in flood from its upper reaches that flowed around the capital city of Vienna, and past the smaller Hungarian capital of Buda. From Buda the river ran due south across the immense lowlands of Hungary, until it joined with the Drave. There it changed its course again, flowing east through hills past Belgrade. It was this lower easterly course of the great river that the Turks had captured five years before.

The heavy rains had turned hollows into marshes along the banks of the river. Streams had turned into mudspates churning through the gullies.

Where the village of Mohács rose, red-roofed, against the riverbank the army of the Hungarians and some volunteer forces was encamped. Before that encampment, to the south, a waterlogged prairie stretched for some six miles, as far as a line of hillocks overgrown with trees. This prairie was called the field of Mohács. So on August 28 the army was quartered along the upper end of the vast field.

The Hungarian army had gathered there to defend Europe. But behind it lay the tensions and antagonisms of a continent. At the edge of the Atlantic Henry VIII had promised to contribute some money for defense. The King of France, having been captured at Pavia and imprisoned in Madrid by the Emperor Charles, had no least wish to aid the Empire. Charles himself was involved in the struggle now begun between the Romanists and the armed Lutherans, and the uprising of the peasantry throughout the German lands—the peasantry that had believed mistakenly in the Gospel as proclaimed by Luther as a summons to fight for their freedom.

Luther had said about the Turks, "To fight against the Turks is to resist the Lord, who visits our sins with such [chastising] rods." Dimly the common folk, who had the text of the Bible in their hands for the first time, regarded the appearance of the Turks as something out of the Book of Revelation.

Pope Clement VII had stormed at Luther, yet Clement desired to see a breakdown rather than an increase of the power of the Hapsburgs, headed by Charles. Ferdinand, the younger brother of Charles, was occupied at Vienna, and had no wish to ally himself with the troublesome Hungarians. Belatedly the Hapsburgs called a Diet together. By August 28 the Diet at Spires went on record as favoring general measures against the Turkish attack. That was the day before the battle of Mohács.

Nearer at hand, close to Mohács, the same jealousies and antagonisms were repeated on a smaller scale. Not that the peers and prelates concerned were particularly unscrupulous, or—in the new fashion—Machiavellian. It was simply that, faced by an emergency, they sought to safeguard their own well-being and to let the losses fall on their political antagonists.

The man most responsible for the defense of Hungary was its King, an amiable youth named Louis, very fond of tournaments and hunting. Louis had no influence with his people, because he was of Polish descent and ruled Bohemia also—much preferring the festivities of Prague to those of primitive Buda. Besides, Louis had been married off to Mary, the sister of the Hapsburgs, Charles and Ferdinand. And the people, the Bohemians especially, detested the "Germans" of the House of Hapsburg. Mary herself, devoted to court entertainments, was annoyed because the mobilizations interfered with the parties she had planned.

Then, too, between the Catholic Hungarian nobility and the sturdy Bohemian middle classes there lay the cleavage of religious doctrine. The radical teaching of John Huss still influenced the land of Prague, where many good burghers were turning to the doctrine of Luther.

Wider than the religious cleavage, however, was the bitterness in Hungary between peasants and nobles. The half-starved peasantry had turned on the upper classes only a few years before, and the ensuing jacquerie darkened the memories of all of them.

In consequence, the army mustered by King Louis at Mohács consisted almost entirely of the nobles and their horsemen—the Royal Party—while the Hungarian commoners rallied to a certain John Zapolya, a Transylvanian magnate who headed what might be called the Nationalist Party.

John Zapolya's army was coming in from the eastward, but slowly and with great reluctance. The main army of the Bohemians was also advancing farther to the west, delayed because it was composed mostly of foot soldiery who had no desire to join the mounted nobles.

Meanwhile, although it had needed to bridge flooded rivers and capture fortified towns on the way, the Turkish army led by one man, Suleiman, had arrived on the scene. It had been sighted that morning from the line of wooded hills at the lower end of the plain of Mohács. . . .

In the Hungarian camp there had been as many different plans for action as there were leaders. The youthful Louis said frankly that he knew nothing about a battle, but he would try to bear himself bravely. Only one man, who was afraid, suggested retreating to the shelter of Buda and waiting for John Zapolya and the Bohemians to arrive. He was a bishop from Varaždin, unacquainted with war. The others refused to retreat or to abandon the fertile Hungarian plain to the ravaging of the Turks.

A professional soldier, Hannibal by name, in command of the German mercenaries—4000 of them hired with the funds donated by Henry VIII and Clement VII—proposed making a stand behind a palisade with the cannon. (His division, being pikemen, were accustomed to that.) Another experienced leader, Gnomski, a Polish volunteer, advised making a defense line of wagons. (His 1500 infantrymen had made good use of wagons before)

The Hungarian nobles would not do that. Their knights and lightly armed hussars were accustomed to charge the enemy. It would be both cowardly and mistaken to their thinking to stand still like peasants to await the attack of the enemy.

Worthy Archbishop Tomori, who had had years of experience in partisan action against the Turks along the lower Danube, agreed that if they were to give battle they should attack. The greater part of the Turks, he explained, were lightly armed horsemen who might be broken by the onset of the heavily armed and armored Christians, especially on the morrow, which was the day of St. John.

In the end, that evening the leaders at Mohács selected Archbishop Tomori for one of their commanders on the morrow. In vain the courageous archbishop protested that he had had no experience in handling an army. A certain Palatine was to be the other commander.

As to the army itself, the new commanders decided that the German mercenaries and cannon should stay entrenched by the camp as Gnomski had advised; King Louis and his immediate following should wait there also, in reserve. Meanwhile the first battle line should make the charge. Thus everyone except the Pole was allowed to do what he wished to do.

Hearing that, the Bishop of Varaždin whispered to Louis, "And in Rome His Holiness had better arrange for the canonization of twenty thousand Hungarian martyrs."

The death toll of the next day's disaster came almost to twenty thousand, including the bishop himself. Almost the entire army was lost.[1] It had been doomed not so much by its

[1]The Christians at Mohács numbered perhaps 25,000. No exact estimate of their force is available. On the other hand, the Turkish strength has been vastly exaggerated by the European chroniclers, who give it, in

own inexperience as by the dissensions of the courts of Europe.

For the Hungarian horsemen were brave and formidable fighters. Descendants of the Magyars from the steppes of Asia, they were the best riders in Europe.

The charge of their first division on that day of St. John met the advancing Turks and broke through the Army of Europe. It swept on, into the center of the Army of Asia, and cut its way through by sheer physical power.

At that point the Palatine galloped back over the wooded rise, to the line of reserves waiting at the camp. Reaching the standard of King Louis, he shouted that the battle was all but won. At once the young King gave the order to advance and took the reserves forward, away from the German pikemen and the cannon. They galloped over the rise and down the slope, over the ground of the earlier action.

No one except Archbishop Tomori seems to have noticed the Turkish force far out on the flank away from the river, closing in behind them. They had no conception that the disciplined antagonists of the first two battle lines were parting to let them through.

The third Turkish army did not divide in front of them. It consisted of the heavy guns chained together, of the massed janizaris, and Suleiman with his guards, supported by the spahis. Against this formation the first Hungarians piled up, crowded into the cannon smoke that choked them and made their horses unmanageable. Into this confusion the youthful Louis galloped headlong with his reserves.

Wearied, they tried to draw out into some kind of order. They

---

round numbers, as 100,000 to 300,000. At Mohács, Archbishop Tomori estimated it at 70,000. More probably its fighting force consisted of some 9000 janizaris, 7000 mounted spahis, and 30,000 for the combined levies of Europe and Asia—perhaps 46,000. There may have been as many more of the *akinjis* or foraging partisans, engineers and other service detachments. At Mohács the Turkish army had marched six hundred miles from Constantinople, and must have left detachments along the route in garrison and supply service.

were struck by horsemen on both sides. They crowded together, their heavily armored chargers sinking and slipping in the marshy ground. They tried to find their way out of the smoke, and then, desperately, they fled on exhausted horses.

Only detachments of the light hussars escaped from the plain. Two archbishops, six bishops, the officers of the crown of Hungary, and five hundred nobles died there, with their main array of "gentle and simple men." A month later the body of Louis was found buried deep in the mud of a gully.

Between three o'clock that afternoon and sunset, when Suleiman ordered trumpets to sound recall, the leaders and the nobility of the Hungarian nation were lost.

Suleiman's diary reads:

August 29. "We make camp on the field of the battle."

August 30. "The Sultan rides out. Order to the troops to bring in all prisoners to the council tent."

August 31. "The Sultan seated on a throne of gold receives the salutations of the vizirs and officers; massacre of two thousand prisoners. Rain falls in torrents."

September 1. "The Secretary of Europe receives order to bury the bodies."

September 2. "Rest, at Mohács. Twenty thousand foot soldiers and 4000 mailed riders of the Hungarian army are buried."

Opening of the Corridor

It seemed to the army as if Suleiman's good fortune had gained them a new land. Surely never before had fortune in two hours' time won for the faithful such a victory, and such reward! In fact Suleiman's announcement of the victory, written to the far provinces, to Cairo on the Nile, to the Tatar Khan and to the guardian Sherif of Mecca, confirmed their belief, for it said, "God's grace has given to my splendid armies a triumph without equal."

Unmistakably Suleiman was excited, perhaps startled by the climactic issue of the field of Mohács. Particularly it pleased him that Ibrahim's first test as Vizir should have turned out incredibly well. The inventive Greek had proved himself a brilliant organizer. Ibrahim's white turban, trimmed with gold, had been a rallying signal, even when the Hungarian horsemen had hacked their way within a few yards of the Sultan . . . But inwardly Suleiman did not believe that Mohács had been won by any turn of destiny. Better than the overexcited Ibrahim he understood that success had come to him from the blundering of the Christians.

Reflectively Suleiman studied the broad, muscular head of one of them, the Archbishop Tomori, which had been thrown at his feet by an eager swordsman.

An Italian observer describes him at this time as "deadly pale . . . of no great strength, seemingly, but his hand is very strong as I noticed when I kissed it. They say he has strength to bend a stiff bow better than others. He is melancholy by nature, much given to women, free-thinking, proud, hasty, and sometimes very gentle."

In those days of rain while the burial went on at Mohács, he was faced with the problem of what to do with Hungary. The problem required quick solution, because autumn frosts chilled the nights, and the grass on which his horse herds subsisted was dying off. Once Suleiman stopped a passing warrior from Asia, and asked familiarly, "Well, my old one—what shall we do next?"

The question did not surprise the trooper. If he himself had had a grievance, he might have gone over to the council tent to complain to this young man girded with the Osmanli sword. "Take care," he answered thoughtfully, "that the sow does not punish its own litter."

In saying that he merely repeated the talk of the campfires. Suleiman had been unusually severe in ordering all divisions of the army to hold their posts after the battle. Whereas the

army, except for Suleiman's personal guard, had only one desire
—to be loosed over the Hungarian countryside after disposing
of the infidel fighting force.

It was more than a craving for plunder; it was an economic
need, sanctioned by old custom, for the Turkish feudal levies
to glean some wealth from a Land of War once the opportunity
arose. If Suleiman prevented that customary gleaning of reward
he would be punishing his own litter. Or so the timariot—the
feudal cavalryman—thought.

This particular timariot was probably a farmer. Perhaps he
had his land holding in the red plain near Aleppo, with grapevines and a field of corn, a few horses at graze. Early that spring
he had outfitted himself and several riders, his followers. After
reporting to the agha of his command, he had made the march
of more than six hundred miles to Europe, and as much again to
the battle of Mohács. On that journey the timariot had had to
provide for his followers and the feeding of the horses. (The
Sultan's regular army and the higher officers of the levies received some pay and provisions, but usually the small trooper
was obliged to feed and pay himself off the country.)

It would be early winter, and the grapes and corn harvested
by his women and servants, God willing, before the trooper
could dismount again at his farm. If, then, he did not bring back
a handful of silver with a few garments of satin and brocade
for the women, the winter would be a lean one. If, on the other
hand, he could dismount at his door and scatter gold coins and
silver candlesticks—with even a jewel to be traded in the Aleppo
bazaar—his family would boast to their neighbors. No, the
Sultan must not punish his own brood, for the sake of the infidels!

If that was the need of the sturdy timariots, the necessity
of the foraging akinjis was greater. Truthfully, Christian chroniclers called them the ravening wolf packs of the Turkish army.

Beyond coherent need, fierce fanaticism drove on these men.
The dervishes who rode with them and chanted prayers through

the hours of the night sang and danced with joy after the victory. The dervishes sang the promises of the Prophet of God: *"The truth is from your Lord . . . those who have believed and have done the things that are right . . . for them the gardens of Eden under whose shades shall rivers flow; decked shall they be therein with bracelets of gold, and green robes of silk and rich brocades shall they wear . . . blessed the reward!"*

Although the dervishes were singing the great rewards after death, the Turkish riders—coming often from homes in the desert lands—took the promises to apply to the miraculous rushing rivers of the infidel Hungarian land, and to the brocades in the chests of the townspeople.

Above all, the Turks of the feudal levies expected the earth itself to be made over to some of them in fiefs. It was good earth. Old custom required that such a land, a Land of War, be divided up. The Sultan should take his share, the keepers of the Law their portion, and the bulk of the new conquest should be apportioned among the troopers who would henceforth guard this new frontier. Sultan Suleiman, however, did not seem willing to carry out the ancient custom.

Instead he issued orders against burning villages or destroying towns. He made no effort to enforce them, when they were disregarded. The only order the army respected in those days of looting was to preserve the lives of women and children. The youngest and most likely of those were taken along as slaves, to be kept or sold.

So terror swept through Hungary from the Carpathians to the Bosnian heights.

In the week that followed, Suleiman ascended the Danube to Buda. And as he went the army dwindled strangely. Aghas obtained permission to storm the small gray castles that seemed to rear above every village in this infidel land. When they had the castles, they stripped the villages. The cavalry regiments found it necessary to forage into fresh territory, and when they returned they escorted wagon trains of plunder as well as loads of barley and hay. A janizary regiment heard of an untouched walled town and marched thither at speed, only to find that the akinjis had been there before them, leaving gaping smoking walls stripped of everything that could be carried off. Some bands of akinjis raided into Austria, within sight of Vienna.

Cannon disappeared from the artillery train. The guns were taken off by regiments that had penned a mass of peasantry within an improvised fort of wagons chained together. Turning the guns on the wagons, the Turks massacred the defenders. People gathered in massive stone churches to defend themselves, and the churches were burned over them.

No one remained to lead the defense of the helpless country, after Mohács. Mary, the widow of Louis, fled to the protection of Vienna; the Bohemian army withdrew at pace to its own border; John Zapolya led his Nationalist army of commoners back to the eastern hills, there to watch events warily.

When Suleiman reached the small capital of Buda on the river's edge, only simple folk remained there. They came out to offer him the keys of the city, and he ordered that it should not be damaged or plundered. In spite of that, fire started mysteriously in the streets as the army entered.

The diary relates, for September 14: "Fire breaks out in Buda, in spite of the measures taken by the Sultan. The Grand Vizir hastens in to check it; his efforts are useless." Buda burned, except for the castles and its park, where Suleiman was quartered.

There he explored the grounds, hunting with falcons of the late occupants, while he celebrated a Moslem lental feast and pondered the problem of Hungary. When he left, a pair of siege guns captured long before by the Hungarians from the Conqueror were embarked on barges to be shipped back to Constantinople. On his own account Suleiman had the splendid library of the humanist who had been the greatest of the Hungarian kings, Matthias Corvinus, packed and shipped down the Danube. Ibrahim insisted on taking three ancient Greek statues, of Hercules, Apollo and Diana—statues that were anathema to devout Moslems who would have no human images around them.

The homeless Jews of Buda were shipped to Constantinople. On leaving the palace of the Hungarian kings, Suleiman gave orders that it was not to be damaged and this time he meant it.

Already his plan for Hungary is rumored through the army, causing general discontent. The Sultan, having conquered the greater part of it, will not keep it, even as he kept Rhodes—making the land itself the property of the Osmanli Empire, the inhabitants one of the inner nationalities. Instead, he prepares to evacuate it. The army cannot understand why.

Certainly the Sultan is attracted to the country itself. His diary mentions its "lakes and magnificent prairies." This immense, fertile Hungarian plain is watered by rivers flowing down from cloud-reaching mountains that ring it round—it has been the rendezvous of nomads from the east, from Attila's Huns to the Mongols of the Golden Horde. The Magyars have made it their home. But he is leaving it.

Guardedly, the historian of the expedition, Kemal Pasha Zade, sets forth a reason in his record, embellished with official flowery phrases: "The time of joining this province to the possessions of Islam had not yet arrived, nor had the day come when the heroes of the Holy War should honor the rebel plain by abiding in it. So heed was given to the wise saying, *when thou wouldst enter, think first how thou wilt find a way out again.*"

The heroes of the holy war are well aware how far they have penetrated Europe. (Buda, seven hundred miles from Constantinople as the crow flies, lies only a hundred and forty miles from Vienna.) They were perfectly willing to make this paradise of grass a battleground, to keep it. Seemingly Suleiman is not so inclined.

Despite the grumbling of the army, the people of Constantinople greet the return of their Sultan with transports of joy.

After Mohács, they receive him as conqueror of the Lands of War, and some speak of him as Sultan of the world. The diligent Kemal looses all the organ stops of thanksgiving in his period to the expedition: "May the friends of his rule find unending happiness, and the foes of his empire defeat! May his banners fly victorious until the day of the Resurrection, and his armies go on to triumph until the sounding of the trumpets of Judgment! May God always protect the edifice of his greatness!"

Ibrahim's reception is less wholehearted. The young Vizir, pleased with his Greek statues, has Hercules and Diana and Apollo set up on pedestals outside his palace, overlooking the Hippodrome. There they startle the crowds in the streets. And soon the streets are laughing at a rimester's ready verse:

> "The first Abraham scourged his people
> For bowing down to images.
> This second Abraham sets 'em up again."

Yet here in Constantinople lies the answer to Suleiman's brooding over Hungary. It rests in the wording of a letter written by an anxious mother on behalf of her son. These few words will shape the future policy of the son of Selim the Grim.

Appeal of the Queen Mother of France

The letter came unexpectedly months before he started for Mohács. The first bearers of the message were killed on the way by agents of the Hapsburgs. Another envoy, a member of the Frangipani family, got through to Constantinople with letters from the Queen Mother of France, and Francis I, who had sent a ring with a ruby signet.

At that time the volatile young monarch of France had suffered defeat and capture at the hands of the Emperor Charles, in their struggle for possession of northern Italy. He had written as a prisoner without hope, in Madrid. His mother had appealed emotionally to Suleiman as "Emperor of the Turks" to restore freedom to her son. "We invoke thee, great Emperor, to show thy generosity and bring back my son."

Frangipani was more specific. He asked Suleiman to attack the Hapsburg empire, and force the liberation of Francis. Otherwise, he hinted, the unfortunate French monarch would be made to sign away lands and rights to the Hapsburg, who would then become unquestioned master of Europe. Nothing could have better suited Suleiman, who was planning at the time to march on Buda.

It seemed almost providential. For centuries the Turks had been led to think of the King of France as the foremost monarch of Europe. Had not Charlemagne (who sent gifts to Harun ar Rashid in Baghdad) been King of the *Franks?* De L'Isle Adam, the defender of Rhodes, had come out from France

Moreover, Suleiman had heard that the youthful Francis resembled himself in many respects, being called the first gentleman of Europe. It was as if the chivalrous Francis—who lost nothing in Frangipani's description of him—had buried the enmity of the past, and had reached out the hand of friendship to a Turk. The appeal to his generosity was the strongest possible appeal to Suleiman.

Suleiman was both credulous and hopeful. The letter of the Most Christian King of France opened up an entirely new vista to him. It was the first break in the Lands of War lying to the west of him.

Although Frangipani brought no gifts, he was received at the Serai with the utmost hospitality (and Francis' ring turned up later in Ibrahim's hands).

He carried back with him Suleiman's eager acknowledgment of the new friendship: "I, Sultan Suleiman Khan, son of Sultan Selim Khan, to thee Francis, King of the land of France: You have sent to the sanctuary of my Gate a letter by the hand of your faithful servant Frangipani. He has made known to me how the enemy overran your country, so you are now a cap-

106

tive. You have asked aid, for your deliverance. All this your saying having been set forth at the foot of my throne, the refuge of the world, has gained my imperial understanding in every detail, and I have considered all of it.

"There is nothing wonderful in emperors being defeated and made captive. Do you, then, take courage and be not downcast. Our glorious predecessors and illustrious ancestors—may God keep alight their tombs—never ceased from making war to drive back their foe and conquer his lands. We ourselves have followed their path; we have at every time conquered provinces and citadels both great in strength and in difficulty of approach. By night as well as by day our horse is saddled and our saber girded on.

"May God the Most High advance righteousness! May His will, whatsoever it portends, be accomplished. For the rest, ask it of your envoy and be informed. Know that it will be as said.

"Written . . . from the residence of the Empire, from Constantinople, the well guarded."

Under the ceremonious phrasing—and Suleiman was careful not to put in writing exactly what he agreed to do—this letter shows a desire to gain Francis' friendship, and to co-operate with him against the Germans. Francis is greeted as an equal, and mentioned as being emperor (in the estimation of the Turks there was only one emperor in Europe and he was Suleiman). Reading between the lines, we feel that the Turk is happily convinced of two things: he can follow the way of the Osmanlis, his ancestors, by going farther into Europe on Francis' behalf; at the same time he is hopeful of making his city, Constantinople, a sanctuary for the oppressed.

Probably not even Frangipani, a shrewd negotiator, understood how fully Suleiman meant what he said. "Know that it will be as said."

For the first time the Osmanli Turks entered European affairs as more than barbarians who had pitched their camp in the

Balkan mountains. During the next years the European courts would look toward the east in a crisis.

The first consequence of the Queen Mother's letter was that in January 1526 Charles released the ailing Francis. To win his freedom the French King had to sign the famous treaty of Madrid, by which the House of Hapsburg exacted much from the House of Valois. As soon as he crossed the frontier Francis disavowed the treaty, claiming that it had been signed under duress. Just as lightly he disavowed Suleiman. As the "Most Christian King" who had announced that he would lead a crusade against the Turks when he had been a candidate in the election that Charles had won from the electors six years before, he would not admit that he had an understanding with the Sultan.

Charles, however, had learned the facts of Frangipani's mission from informants. He was quick to announce that he seemed to have two enemies, in the west and the east, the Most Christian King of France and the Commander of the Faithful. Ironically, his ministers commented upon "the sacrilegious union of the Lily and the Crescent."

But Suleiman was very earnest in seeking the friendship of France.

As he had suspended conquest after Rhodes to set his own Osmanli house in order, Suleiman held back after Mohács from further invasion of Europe for two years. In those two years, 1527–29, he studied the eastern face of Europe proper with great care. On one pretext or another he remained at the Serai to do so.

It is often said, too carelessly, that those years marked the height of his military glory. In reality they marked his change from warrior to diplomat. A door had been opened for him, as it were, into western and Christian diplomatic society. Into that door he resolved to enter, to take his place beside his only equals, Francis I and Charles V.

Remember that he had not been the one to seek alliance with France or enmity with the Empire. He must have reflected with amusement when he passed the Roman column of his inner garden that this same Charles Hapsburg still called himself Roman Emperor. This city which had been the seat of the eastern Roman emperors for a thousand years was now Suleiman's city!

Then, too, whenever he passed the small marble Treasury of the Prophet's Mantle, he was reminded how he was titular head of Islam. As such he was bound to be the antagonist of the Pope, the spiritual head of Christendom. When he visited the Divan, his own officers voiced the urgency of the holy war against Europe which lay so temptingly close to his new frontier of Buda and Pesth. Suleiman, in their minds, had become invincible. The next march forth would penetrate further into the vitals of weakening Europe. What mattered it who wore the crowns there?

"It is not the metal of crowns," Mustafa, oldest of the pashas, told him, "it is not gold but the iron of the sword that will rule a country."

Europe's Kaleidoscope Changes

While he watched the continent in which he meant to become a resident, Suleiman was forced to imagine what it might be like beyond the mountain ranges of Hungary. True, he had studied Aristotle, and, like the pages of the School who waited on him, the philosophy of Maimonides, but he had never beheld the European life of his time. He had only one ambassador there, at the halfway point of Venice.

Not being merchants, the Turks had no trading posts there; Turkish ships kept as yet to the Asiatic shores, along the Black Sea, or perhaps across to Egypt. As for the shipmasters from the west who flocked into the Golden Horn, they came searching for profit in trade from such things as silk or ivory or spice.

Fragments of their gossip along the water front drifted up to Suleiman. What could he believe of it? Occasionally an envoy like Frangipani on special mission sat in talk with him—to gain something from him. An envoy like Memmo could be counted on to trick him.

So Suleiman, pondering in seclusion the problem of Europe, began to press Ibrahim to draw information from foreigners. In his turn the Vizir depended upon Luigi Gritti, and suggested that the Sultan go with him to Gritti. Suleiman broke the tradition of the Osmanlis by doing so. On the terrace of the exile's palace they could talk without being overheard. Of course they were seen, and devout Moslems felt aggrieved because the Lord of the Two Worlds had gone like a common man into the home of a Christian who took bribes and drank wine.

Of the three who sat together on the terrace by the Bosphorus, two were reaping fortunes. Ibrahim concealed from Suleiman how greatly he was making use of Gritti. Both urged on the Sultan the importance of close alliance with Venice. (Gritti was working for that for personal reasons, while Ibrahim, who exploited the foreign trade, planned to channel traffic from Asia through Constantinople into the hands of foreign merchants, and in so doing had need of Venetian merchants and their fleets.) Venice, they said truthfully, was now the natural enemy of the Hapsburgs, fearing their rising power. The French, too, should be given trade concessions in Egypt as a token of Suleiman's good will.

Suleiman could not understand the conflicts around his antagonist Charles. As King of Spain, Charles was opposed by the Portuguese in the New World, whence he drew fleetloads of silver.

The Portuguese, Gritti pointed out, were sailing eastward as well, circling around the Turks, to glean new riches direct from the ports of far Asia.

But why was a great monarch like Charles in debt to a family of bankers like the Fuggers?

Because he lacked ready money to pay his numerous armies.

If Charles was indeed the friend of the great Pope, why had his armies just now ravaged the city of Rome, making the Pope himself a prisoner in his castle of St. Angelo?

Because his armies had looted the Pope's city, to get money. Most of them were mercenary Swiss pikemen and German Landsknechts. After Suleiman had turned back from Buda, they were free to go down to loot through Italy—with the Germans paid by Ferdinand, the brother of Charles.

Then, if the Pope were indeed the supreme head of the Christians, why did he not prevent this intrusion by the unruly armed bands of Charles?

Because he had no armies of his own.

After considering this kaleidoscope of ambition and violence, Suleiman agreed to encourage the Venetian merchants and to grant some of the Egyptian carrying trade to the French. He would have two friends upon the sea. As to the land, the picture was not clear to him. He would wait and see what happened in Hungary after he had vacated it. Silently he decided that Charles was a very capable ruler.

So intent was he on the European scene that when an outbreak came that summer in Anatolia, where dervishes had stirred Turkoman tribes to take the field, he sent Ibrahim there instead of going himself to restore quiet.

His patience was rewarded. While he had found it hard to understand why a Christian army had sacked Rome, he had no difficulty in observing what happened to the great Hungarian plain that had been left without a master.

The Hapsburg brothers moved into the defenseless corridor. Suleiman had hardly left the Danube behind him when, with Charles's approval, the younger brother Ferdinand was proclaimed King of the harassed land by one of the few surviving bishops. (Through his wife Anne, the sister of the dead Louis, the stubborn and narrow-minded Ferdinand had a claim to the throne.)

So the shape began to appear of a middle Europe to be ruled by the Emperor—a "fortress Europe" built around Vienna, with the bastions of the German lands to the west, and the bastion of Bohemia with the Hungarian plain to the east.

But one portion of Hungary would have none of the Haps-burgs. In the southeastern mountains John Zapolya, Voevode of Transylvania, still had his army of commoners. (Moreover, Suleiman's army had not devastated Transylvania.) John Za-polya, in his turn, had himself crowned with the iron crown of the Hungarian kings.

Very slowly Suleiman began to move against the European fortress of the Hapsburgs, in a fashion of his own. He did it so quietly that the movement was not perceived at first. A clue to it lies in the evidence of another Italian: "There are in the city besides the Turks countless Jews, or *Marrani* [Moors] ex-pelled from Spain; they have taught and are teaching every useful art to the Turks, and most of the shops are kept by these *Marrani*. In the *Bezestan* [Market] they sell and buy all sorts of cloth and Turkish wares—silks, linen, silver, wrought gold, bows, slaves and horses. In short, all the things to be found in Constantinople are brought here to market."

So in Rhodes the islanders had been encouraged to carry on their work; in the Morea, the southern portion of Greece, the farmers were thriving more under Turkish rule than under the exactions of the Venetian *signori*. Another inner nation, the Armenians, handled the bulk of the carrying trade.

From the sea, also, foreigners were seeking privileges in Turkish markets; Greek shipmasters profited from the coastal trade. Frangipani, returned to the city, asked further privileges for French merchants.

Evidently Sultan Suleiman was offering refuge to the human flotsam and jetsam of wars elsewhere. And by degrees the sta-bility of his rule began to be recognized in the west. Instead of the "Turkish terror" chroniclers spoke more in the last year of the *pax Turcica*, the Turkish peace that offered so great a contrast to the now endemic conflicts of middle Europe. (Paolo Giovio had said of the year of the sack of Rome—in which most of his own papers had been lost—"the events were too grievous to relate.") By cautious steps the barbarian Turk was entering the diplomatic society of Europe.

No one as yet realized the Sultan's determination to do so.

In Hungary, now the no man's land between the House of Osman and the House of Hapsburg, he did not appear with his army for three years. Instead he advanced his missionaries into the mountains along the Danube on either flank of his gateway of Belgrade.

Eastward into the Transylvanian Alps held by John Zapolya's bands went wandering dervishes; westward into the ranges held by the sturdy independent chieftains of the Bosnians and Croats (*Khrats*) went armed columns of Turkish frontier forces under the sanjakbeys, who occupied the valley routes without molesting the mountain villages. Suleiman took pains to cultivate them, aided by the Frangipani from the French court, who had been born a Croat.

In so doing he was adding to his nucleus of Danubian peoples, who had been converted more than conquered, the Wallachians (*Vlakhs*), Bulgars and Serbs. Understanding this, Luigi Gritti had made with much reason his startling remark, "Perhaps only he can bring peace to the world."

In years to come Suleiman would turn to the highly intelligent Croats who were graduates of his School, to rule his dominion under him.

Within that dominion, while he waited on events in Hungary, he was making some changes very patiently because he could not by sudden action shake his Turks loose from their old customs.

Laws and Human Needs

Rather surprisingly Suleiman withdrew from his Divan.

The Divan gathered after daybreak in the small chamber under the watchtower of the second court. The Vizir presided, sitting in the center of the cushioned dais opposite the door, through which the chief of messengers escorted folk with petitions, or cases to be tried, lawyers to make appeal, or foreign envoys to negotiate affairs of their own. Beside him sat the two judges of the army, the other pashas, and the first Secretary-Treasurer.

Outside under the grilled portico crowded those who sought to be heard, as tribesmen had waited outside a tent. Through this small space of the Divan, publicly heard by all who could listen, passed the affairs of the Osmanlis. The council sat four days in the week.

At midday the room was cleared for a brief rest while the members ate the food brought in on small tables set before them. The Vizir had a bowl of sherbet, or julep, the others water from the fountains. .

Since the time of the Conqueror, the sultans had sat apart at the side behind a lattice screen, where they could observe and intervene without being watched. (The story goes that the Conqueror sat with the others against the wall until a peasant wandered in to make a complaint and asked, after staring at all of them, "Which one of you might be the Sultan?")

In the afternoon when the public hearings ended, the Sultan retreated into his private reception room, where the Divan members came to make their individual reports, and others like the aghas of janizaris or spahis brought affairs to his notice. Often the last of them did not leave until sunset.

Suleiman changed that, after Ibrahim became Vizir. In the rear wall over the council seat he had a window cut, with heavy

114

grillwork projecting from it. Here, concealed from observation, he could sit, listening to what was discussed below. The members of the Divan could not know if he were listening or not. This withdrawal seemed to be a slight change, and it had no effect at first, except to make Ibrahim more visibly the head of authority.

There was a reason for Suleiman's withdrawal, beyond his dislike of a crowded room and argument. Probably Mehmed Fatih, the Conqueror, had decided to sit apart because no human being—even such a tireless driving personality as the Conqueror's—could sit listening to all the minute cases heard by the council for six hours or more a day, and still retain any clear grasp of the affairs of the dominion as a whole. Both Bayazid and Selim had worked nights as well as days.

Selim's conquests in Asia had almost doubled the area of the dominion. Besides, Selim had brought back with him the Mantle of the Prophet from Mecca. In consequence, the Osmanli sultans had become the visible successors to the kalifs of earlier days; they now had the duty of protecting the holy places, and this entailed responsibility for the annual pilgrimages to Mecca. Suleiman had to listen to arguments about the possession of the holy places in Jerusalem—in *Al Kuds*, the Sacred City— where churches of the different Christian sects mingled with Jewish shrines. These other Peoples of the Book had pilgrims of their own journeying to Jerusalem. They had ancient privileges, especially upon the Mount of Olives and Mount Sinai, to which they clung stubbornly and because of which they fell frequently into strife among themselves. Suleiman had to judge strange disputes about the right to rocks and olive groves where David had dwelt and Christian Apostles had gathered.

It sometimes seemed as if the possession of a yard of earth, or the right to keep a door open in their holy places within Jerusalem, meant more than any other matters to the Christians. This Suleiman could understand. Religious faith superseded ordinary laws. And, on their part, written laws must serve human beings. You should not sacrifice a living person to a written word. Suleiman had ideas of his own about the kanun, the law code.

As to Jerusalem, he was soon to give his judgment: "The Christians shall live peaceably under the wing of our protection; they shall be allowed to repair their doors and windows, and to preserve in all safety their places of prayer and of living which they actually occupy. No one shall prevent or terrorize them in doing so."

From unsuspected corners of Asia envoys came to stand before him and make their requests. From beyond the steppes ruled by the Tatar khans of the Crimea, a strange individual came with gifts of sable skins—an Ivan Morosov of the obscure city of Moscow, to ask for a mutual defense pact between Suleiman and his master, whom he called Great Prince of Moscow. Suleiman refused the mutual agreement, well aware that the Krim Khan, who gave allegiance to him, was in the habit of raiding the lands of Moscow, which paid yearly tribute to the Khan. The Osmanli Sultan would not bind himself to the Muscovite, who was a source of yearly profit to the Tatar Khan. Instead, he offered to encourage trading for furs with the Muscovites.

This matter of the care of individuals had grown very complex since the day of the Conqueror. The peculiarity of the Osmanli Organization lay in its responsibility for the individual person, whether peasant, shopkeeper, tribesman, seaman or literate lawyer or physician. At death the property of an officer of the Organization returned to the Treasury. No family estates could be created; those who served Suleiman were their own heirs; they had no others. In consequence there existed no class of wealthy men, or of dominant nobles.

When Piri Pasha was retired he became simply an aged man living apart; at his death his property was gathered in by the secretary-treasurers.

Yet constantly cases of need came before Suleiman. The

116

personality of his servants could not be obliterated in spite of the rigid Osmanli law. Widows needed allowances for living; children had a moral right to some of their father's personal property. Suleiman granted such children the greater part of a personal estate.

Those alive in the Organization won their places by ability. In contrast to the system of the Europeans, family and influence did not advance them. This unceasing qualification, meant to winnow out the most able to rule, extended even to the janizaris. By law, no son of a Young Trooper might become a janizary. They were not supposed to have families, but many of them did, in one way or another. Suleiman tried to ease the rigidity of the janizary law by permitting a class of married men. Yet after that it became more difficult to bar out their sons.

As families tended to hold on to some property, the members of a family tended to aid each other. By law an officer, like the able *Defterdar*—the Secretary-Treasurer Mehmed Chelebi—could not appoint relations of his own to posts under his control. Chelebi could appoint Sokolli, the Croat graduate of the Enclosed School, to aid him, but not his own son. This did away with nepotism among the Turks. The Sultan himself could not name a blood relation for office. On the female side his sisters and daughters were given to distinguished men, who could have no other wives than the one of imperial blood. Male children of such marriages might serve in the Organization or as simple army officers, but Turkish custom required them to make no claim to imperial rank, so that no quarrel might arise as to the succession. This unwritten law was obeyed. No child of Ibrahim, for example, appears close to the throne. (There is no truth in the oft-repeated tale that a sultan's womenkind were given to eunuchs to prevent the birth of children; this belongs among the noxious legends that grew from foreign gossip about the harems of the sultans.)

So at his death a sultan would leave no dynasty behind him except in the person of one surviving son, the others being executed at that time in obedience to the ruthless law of the Conqueror.

Against that law Suleiman had set his mind. He would not condemn to death all but one of the male children of Gulbehar and Roxelana, with their offspring. Yet the inexorable law would survive him unless he could in some way do away with it before his own death.

Meanwhile Roxelana was gaining ascendancy within his household.

Each year the solitary Russian was making greater claim upon his emotions. She had given him two sons, whom he named after his own father and grandfather, Selim and Bayazid. Often now he went beyond the corridor into his harem because he needed the companionship of the quick-witted Russian, even more than the relaxation of her body's embrace.

Somehow Roxelana, as the Europeans called her, managed to appear different at each visit. She would wear a small cap of cloth of gold, or she would thread her loose light hair with strings of pearls; she would resemble a slim boy in a military dolman, or a dancing girl in gossamer that revealed the movement of thighs and breasts. In contrast Gulbehar, his first love, appeared always the same, no matter how she darkened her fine eyes with kohl or set flowers of garnet glass into her long tresses.

In similar wise the Russian managed to seem alone in the labyrinth of the harem (although she had her own staff of slaves now to minister to her, and black eunuchs to bring her direct news from outside). Because she never interfered with the management of the harem, the Sultan Valideh tolerated her. Besides, the Slav was always merry.

Then, too, Suleiman gave to his mother the deep respect traditional with Turkish sons. Roxelana made no attempt to alter the delicate balance of feeling between the unworldly mother and the brilliant son. By separating herself, as it were, from the rule of the Valideh over the harem she simply appealed to Suleiman's generosity, even for slipper money. The domestics called her the Khasseki Khurrem, the Favored Laughing One.

So until now in the strict hierarchy of the Turkish harem, the mother had been supreme as Sultan Valideh, Gulbehar second, as First Kadin—being mother of Mustafa, the first-born son, and heir—and Roxelana third, as Second Kadin.

Inevitably, the Circassian girl and the Russian fought a merciless and silent battle. At least once they tore at each other with hands and teeth. Roxelana, the slighter, suffered most from the hair wrenching and face tearing. For days after that she refused to let Suleiman see her, explaining that she was too disfigured. She made no other complaint, and so she gained his sympathy.

Moreover, she professed to be afraid for her two sons, who were helpless infants, playing in the Sultan Valideh's courtyard, at the fountain. Gulbehar's son was past puberty and of an age to be sent to training out of the harem.

So it happened that when Mustafa did go to a province, to the care of army tutors, Gulbehar consented to leave the palace to accompany him. She realized that Suleiman had separated himself from her; in Mustafa, who was destined to rule after him, she had her only tie to him.

That year Bragadino, Venetian Bailo, wrote concerning Gulbehar that "her lord takes thought of her no longer."

Challenge of the First Embassies

And now the first fruit of his waiting appeared. The Hungarians themselves sent envoys to ask his aid in December 1527.

In Hungary, inevitably, the two rival kings had come to conflict. The Hapsburg, Ferdinand, being better equipped and aided by the dour Bohemians, had made short work of occupying Buda and overrunning the middle plain, driving the people's army of Zapolya before him.

And, defeated in the field, Zapolya had appealed to Suleiman. The appeal pleased the Sultan, but not the manner of it. Ibrahim castigated his envoy sharply. "You come too late. You should have come before the crowning of your King. How dared your lord think of himself as lord of Buda? Do you not know that my master was there? Where the horse of the Sultan has trod, that ground is forever his. . . . Brother, you come here as if from a servant. If you have come with tribute, give it; otherwise there is no use talking."

But when envoys appeared from the Hapsburgs, their reception was very different. The versatile Ibrahim played another part—that of a courteous host, interested in all his guests had to say. (He was curious to learn the intentions and the power of the Hapsburgs.)

The two Germans, Hobordanacz and Weixelberger, had the full benefit of ceremony, with the janizaris paraded at their entrance, and all the pashas sitting robed in the Divan. On their part the Germans had a train of four hundred knights, in full panoply There was an imperial air to the meeting, and Ibrahim enjoyed himself vastly, asking if the envoys of the King of Bohemia and Germany—he did not say Hungary—had had a pleasant journey, and if they were comfortable in their quarters, and what had they to tell of their lord?

Hobordanacz said he was happy in the destiny that made him, the King of Hungary, such a near neighbor of the great Turkish emperor.

Ibrahim: "Did you not know that the Sultan has been to Buda?"

Hobordanacz (roughly): "He left signs enough behind him, for us to know he visited it."

Ibrahim: "But the castle; how was that left?"

Hobordanacz: "Whole and undamaged."

Ibrahim: "Do you know why?"

"Because it was the royal castle, apart from the town."

"No, because the Sultan desired to preserve the castle for his own use. God willing, he will keep it."

Hobordanacz: "We know that is the Sultan's idea. Yet even Alexander the Great was unable to carry out such ideas."

Ibrahim could not pass this answer over (knowing that Suleiman was listening, who had debated with him so often the ideas of Alexander). He challenged the envoy sharply. "Then you say that Buda does not belong to Suleiman?"

"I cannot say otherwise than that my King holds Buda."

Ibrahim seized the chance to cross-question him about Ferdinand's real nature and power. "Why do you call him wise . . . what do you understand by wisdom . . . what boldness and courage do you find in him . . . what have you to say about the power of your master?"

Hobordanacz did not fare very well in trying to draw Ferdinand's portrait as an ideal monarch. By pretending naive curiosity and appearing skeptical, Ibrahim managed to get some useful information from the envoy. Only at the end did the Vizir drop his mask of guilelessness. The envoy had explained that Ferdinand was supported by the friendship of his strong neighbors.

Ibrahim: "We know that these so-called friendly neighbors are in reality his enemies." And, as if absently, he asked, "Do you come as at war or in peace?"

"Ferdinand desires the friendship of all his neighbors, the enmity of none."

Having sounded out the envoys, Ibrahim had them conducted into the presence of Suleiman with all splendor. Gifts were offered by the knights attendant on the envoys, and taken by janizaris of the guard, who displayed them to the onlookers. Meanwhile the envoys were kept at the door with their interpreter, until Suleiman asked them to state their master's business. Then each was led forward in turn between Ibrahim and Kasim, who held their arms, in ancient tribal fashion.

121

Hobordanacz said he had come to request a truce, if not a peace. Giving no answer, Suleiman spoke aside to his Vizir, who demanded, "How do you dare speak of the power of your master here in the presence of the Sultan, to whose protection other princes of Europe have been willing to commend themselves?"

Unguardedly Hobordanacz asked who those princes might be.

"The King of France," he was told, "the King of Poland, the Voevode of Transylvania, the Pope, and the Doge of Venice."

That silenced the blunt Austrian, who realized the essential truth of it. Ibrahim added ironically that all but one of these princes were supreme heads of Europe. After a moment's thought Hobordanacz changed his tone, but it did him no good. His mission was an impossible one. During later conferences with Ibrahim he had to admit that Ferdinand expected his sovereignty to be acknowledged over all fortified places in Hungary, in return for an agreed peace.

"I am surprised," Ibrahim commented, "that he does not ask for Constantinople as well."

The Germans made matters worse by suggesting that compensation would be paid Suleiman. Ibrahim, really angry, went to a window and pointed out the ancient city wall. "Do you see that wall? At the end of it there are the Seven Towers, all of them filled with gold and treasure." As for offers, he added, both Charles and Ferdinand seemed incapable of keeping faith.

Not until their dismissal did they go before Suleiman again. And their dismissal was most ominous.

"Your master has not yet felt our neighborly friendliness," Suleiman informed them, "but he shall soon feel it. Tell him plainly that I am coming in person with all my power to give back to Hungary the fortified places that he demanded of me. Tell him to make ready to receive me well."

Nor were the unfortunate Germans allowed to depart with

their message. For a year they were kept confined, to meditate upon their message, while the Turks prepared for war.

Suleiman had decided to remove Hungary entire from the nascent middle Europe dominion of the Hapsburgs. The country of the inviting prairies and lakes would become *Magyaristan*, the land of the Magyars, self-ruled under Suleiman's protection and authority. He had waited long to make this decision. A suitable ruler for the Hungarian state was at hand in John Zapolya, who held the allegiance of the common folk.

Zapolya was acknowledged King of Hungary, freed from paying any tribute—in return for his armed support—and given Gritti as a permanent envoy in Constantinople. "Tell your master," Suleiman informed him, "that now he can sleep with both ears shut."

Road to Vienna

In the rain-drenched May of next spring, 1529, Suleiman marched north to his first defeat.

The great moving encampment of the Turks threaded the familiar roads, past the Roman ruins of Adrianople, up into the mountain gorges, bridging its way, sometimes crossing floods on walks laid over tree branches, swinging through the bare Serbian valleys, sighting again its old frontier at the broad gray sweep of the Danube. As before, the Army of Asia, the horsemen of Anatolia, Syria and the Caucasus, caught up with it and fell in behind.

This time, however, there was a change. A division of Croats came in from the western ranges, and was given a place in the camp beside the contingents of Bulgars and Serbs. On the familiar grassy plain of Mohács, Zapolya appeared with 6000 Hungarians, and Ibrahim rode out to escort him in, to be greeted as King and as ally of Suleiman. Another lord, Peter Pereny, brought in the iron crown of Hungary. Beside these

Hungarians Luigi Gritti pitched his tent. Few as they were these men represented the nucleus of the nations that acknowl edged Suleiman's rule from the Black Sea to Venice. Later Pau Verday appeared from Gran, with the keys of that strong city yielded by its archbishop.

Something rather surprising was taking place. Towns like Szegedin and Stuhlweissenburg which the Hapsburgs had expected to resist the Turks opened their gates to Suleiman's advance detachments. And the Turkish *asker* marched under rigid discipline, without looting, or damaging crops. Suleiman's diary had a laconic entry one day: "A Spahi executed for grazing his horse on growing crops."

Hungary was being protected as a land at peace. The great army forged across the central plain without encountering resistance. There was no sign of Ferdinand or his court. The army marched to Buda as quietly as if to Adrianople. Then Suleiman made a proclamation to it. There would be a new *Serasker* or Marshal of the Army, and he would be Ibrahim, the First Vizir, the victor at Mohács, already commander of the Army of Europe.

More than that, the new Serasker might carry before him a standard of five horsetails. His commands would be as the commands of the Sultan. ". . . all my people, vizirs and peasants, shall hold all he says, or believes fit, as an order from my mouth."

No Osmanli sultan had made such a gift of power to a minister before. Did Suleiman hope to efface himself still more, or to share his popularity with his friend during a spectacular and successful campaign? More probably, since Osmanli custom required the Sultan to march at the head of his forces, he sought to authorize Ibrahim as a commander at need.

Coming into Buda, he met resistance for the first time. A German garrison had been left there, and they made an attempt to defend the citadel, but surrendered in four days. For the next day the diary has the entry: "Sale of slaves."

124

At Buda news from the west reached Suleiman. Ferdinand was far away at a German Diet endeavoring to raise troops for the defense of Vienna. And in Italy the unpredictable French King had signed a treaty of peace with his supposed foe, the German Emperor. This peace of Cambrai had been agreed on only a month before, after Charles had heard that Suleiman had started north to the Danube. Charles, aware of the danger in the east, had granted the unfortunate Francis speedy and easy terms. On his part Francis had agreed to furnish aid in resisting the Turks!

What Suleiman thought of this about-face of his pledged ally is not on record. He went hunting for two days, while Zapolya was installed in his new palace. Then he started with the Turkish army up the highroad along the Danube toward Vienna.

He went fast. Leaving the heavy artillery at Buda, his army pressed on, ignoring harassing attacks in the Austrian hills and bombardment from the guns of Pressburg, covering a hundred and seventy miles by road and river to the wooded suburbs of Vienna in a week.

The Kärtnertor

The siege of Vienna by Suleiman in the autumn of 1529 has become a landmark of history. It has been said so often that the invasion of the Osmanli Turks reached as far as Vienna in that year and was stopped there by the siege.

The most remarkable thing about this "siege of Vienna" is that it never took place. What did occur there on the Danube in that late September was an odd battle which did not at all stop the Turkish expansion. To realize that, consider what happened day by day.

Suleiman, remember, was making forced marches out of Hungary into Austria (a Land of War) with an army mounted for the most part on horses. The horses could no longer graze on frost-blighted pastures; forage had to be provided. Both men and horses were on short rations by then.

Turn to the diary.

September 21. "Citadel of Istergrad [Pressburg—they were passing it under fire]. Difficult stage. Infidels harass the army with continued fire [Austrian detachments firing from the hills along the road]."

September 22. "The army passes three rivers and crosses numerous swamps. At Altenburg we reach the Hungarian frontier. The army enters enemy territory where it finds supplies in abundance."

Once on Austrian soil, the light horsemen are loosed to gather in the all-important forage, supplies, and to ravage the valley hamlets. Some of them penetrate to the forests around Vienna and engage the Christian cavalry.

Suleiman learns that Ferdinand may or may not be in Vienna, but a sizable army is certainly there. He presses on.

In 1529 Vienna was a small city. The castles of the Margraves had not grown into the great Hofburg of later days. It was really pretty much a city of churches and monasteries, grouped around the beloved spire of St. Stefan's, occupying the ground now enclosed by the inner "Ring" and backed against the broad Danube. The wall, except for some of the gates, remained the high narrow city wall of medieval times—unlike the bastioned fortifications of Rhodes.

The large southern gate, on the side away from the river (and the modern Prater park)—the Kärtnertor, with the nunnery of Santa Clara just inside it—led toward Schönbrunn village, and had been fortified.

Vienna was then the capital city of its Archduke, Ferdinand, who had retired prudently to Spires. His brother the Emperor also remained far away in Italy, sending only 700 veteran Spanish cavalry to Vienna. The Diet at Spires named a certain Elector Palatine to be commander at Vienna, who was hardly heard from during the action.

The officers who actually led the defense of Vienna were the experienced Marshal of Austria, William von Rogendorf, and a captain, Nicholas Count of Salm, a veteran of Pavia. They had mobilized a serviceable force of 16,000, mostly professional soldiery, and had also the Spaniards and detachments of volunteer knights, with the Burgher guard of the city to put out fires and repair battle damages. An earth rampart had been raised inside the brittle outer wall. All boats along the river had been sunk and the bridges readied for demolition.

At Vienna, for the first time, Suleiman was faced by well-armed Christian forces, German-led and -disciplined. His approach was very rapid On the twenty-third, Turkish cavalry began to drive in the Christian outposts. By the twenty-sixth, the main Turkish army was quartered opposite the southern wall, with the cavalry withdrawn along the Wiener Wald (across the small Wiener stream). Suleiman's own camp was close behind the Serasker's, opposite the Kärtnertor.

On the twenty-seventh the first of the Turkish flotilla arrived up the Danube, after passing through the barrage at Pressburg. It was used to cut communication between the city and the north bank of the river. Farther to the north Austrian reinforcements were coming in, but they kept their distance. Meanwhile the Turkish light horsemen were fanning out at speed through lower Austria.

By then Salm and Rogendorf had withdrawn all their forces into the city wall, but they had no intention of staying there. By then, or very soon, Suleiman had obtained information from a prisoner that Ferdinand was not with his army in Vienna. But he was not yet certain of that.

His Turks sent a message of greeting to the Austrians: "On the third day we will eat breakfast within your walls."

As soon as they came up, Turkish engineers started to push trenches toward the Kärtnertor wall, and to move guns up through the trenches. The defending captains, surprised that the city was not invested as a whole, puzzled by the fact that the Turkish encampment was only visible in the south, decided to sally out, to sweep away the Turkish engineers and their works.

What happened in the next twelve days is clear in the Sultan's diary and the accounts of the Viennese.

September 29. "The unbelievers make an attack but are driven back as soon as the cavalry mounts to the saddle."

(They sallied out on the east side, by the Stuben gateway, across the Weiner Bach, 2500 of them, and circled around to the Kärtnertor, demolishing trenches on the way, and almost capturing Ibrahim, escaping the counterattack of the Turkish horse from the Wiener Wald.)

By October 1 some of the Turkish guns—which, being only light pieces, have to be advanced close to the wall—are firing.

October 2. "The Bey of Semendria drives back a sortie, killing thirty men and taking ten prisoners."

(The Turkish infantry begins a covering fire from arquebuses, while the real work is undertaken, the shafts of two mines being started toward the Kartnertor wall. The diary records the wounding of janizaris in the trenches and cannon balls from the walls falling in the tents near Suleiman. The Austrians detect the mine shafts and blow them in; others are started at once toward the gate. Salm sends out a message to the Turks: "Your breakfast is getting cold by now."

October 6. "Attack by the besieged. Five hundred of our men are killed, the Alaibey of Gustendil among them."

(This is a major attack by the Austrians, 8000 strong, emerging on the river side and sweeping around more than half the circuit of Vienna, to demolish the Turkish works; but this time it is caught by a counterattack and pinned against the Kärtnertor where the rearmost Austrian regiments, unable to make their way through the narrow entry, fall into disorder and are cut up. The garrison does not risk another sally.)

128

October 7. "Mining and cannonading continue. We hear that all the grandees of the kingdom are united inside the walls."

October 8. "Arrival of several fugitives from the city. All pashas and commanders remain afoot that night, expecting another sortie."

October 9. "Our two mines are exploded. Assaults fail at the two breaches. Heavy fighting, especially on the sector of the Pasha of Semendria."

(This is the attempt of the Turks to break through the wall to get at the army inside. The Austrians, prepared for it, have inner defenses of beams and wooden shields ready to set in place, and they hold the breaks in the wall.)

October 10. "The Vizir presents himself before the Sultan. At his departure all the commanders accompany him."

(Suleiman does not record it, but at this conference of commanders he gave the order to retire from Vienna and begin the long march of more than seven hundred miles back to Constantinople. Autumn cold is setting in, forage is scanty for the vital horse herds which must be preserved during the march homeward, the foraging akinjis are coming in with what they could glean from the countryside. Only too clearly, Suleiman remembers the cold, the sickness and hunger of the months of the siege of Rhodes. Here in the heart of Europe, he will not risk a repetition of the ordeal. Apparently many commanders agree, but Ibrahim does not, and others support the new Serasker. They have the viewpoint of field commanders, that an action begun must be carried out; they have the superior force, and it can only be a matter of time before the old-fashioned wall of Vienna is demolished. . . . Certainly this wall cannot hold as long as the great ramparts of Rhodes. . . . Against such arguments the officers who favor breaking off the engagement point out that the Viennese have an earth rampart raised inside the brittle outer wall—that the fugitives from the city have given definite information that the Archduke is not in his city—that winter will set in within a few days, blocking the mountain

129

passes with snow, and endangering the flotilla on the river . . . they have stayed too long as it is.)

Suleiman makes the decision to retreat. But as often happens in such situations, he agrees to a compromise. One more assault will be tried, before leaving.

Probably the pashas and aghas at the conference are ordered not to speak of the decision to withdraw from Vienna; but the news leaks out, or the veteran troops sense that they are pulling out.

For two days work is pushed on new mine shafts. The Albanian regiments probe at a fresh narrow breach, losing two hundred men. Suleiman and Ibrahim go up to inspect the wall, discarding their distinctive head ornaments and putting on woolen kaftan hoods to do so. The janizaris are promised a bonus of about twenty ducats each—a rich fief and promotion to the soldier first over the defenses.

On October 13 the trial assault is made, and fails completely. Nicholas of Salm and Rogendorf are ready for it with cannon placed at a barrier of wine tuns filled with earth and stones. The German professional infantry holds confidently and well. On the other hand, the storming forces have no heart; officers are seen beating men with the flat of sabers. By three o'clock in the afternoon the last efforts are at an end. The Turkish askeris, who know the army is to retreat, will not go forward with the officers. At midnight great fires rise along the Turkish lines where surplus stores and huts are burned.

The defenders on the walls of Vienna hear long-drawn outcry where adult captives are being killed—the younger ones are spared to be taken off.

Retreat

Volleys of cannon and a tocsin of church bells sounded in rejoicing from the walls of Vienna. Hearing it, Ibrahim asked a prisoner of war, the standard-bearer Zedlitz, what the noise meant. The Austrian explained that it was rejoicing. After being given a silk robe of honor, he was sent in to arrange for the exchange of prisoners, as the Turks began their march out the next day. Oddly enough some of the Christian soldiers who were sent back caused suspicion in the excited town because they had been given money by the Turks, which they proceeded to spend promptly in the taverns. For a while they were in danger of hanging as renegades or spies. Only three Turks were returned from the town.

The letter given Zedlitz to take in (written by Ibrahim in bad Italian) had in it an explanation of their leaving. "I, Ibrahim Pasha . . . generalissimo of the army, to you, noble and spirited captains . . . Know that we did not come here to capture your town but to give battle to your Archduke. That is what made us lose so many days here, without being able to come up with him. . . ."

Although the Turks had been seen to load their artillery and heavy stores on their Danube flotilla, and to evacuate their lines after the exchange of prisoners of war, there seems to have been doubt in Vienna as to whether they were not waiting in ambush behind the Wiener Wald. Some of the returned prisoners were actually tortured to discover if that were not the case. Naturally, under torture, they confessed that it was.

The next day, October 17, snow began to fall. Cavalry detachments brought back word that the Turks had gone. Whereupon the soldiery, the arquebusiers and Landsknechts, who had defended the wall so stoutly, took over the town, ignoring their officers and threatening to loot Vienna if they were not paid a "threefold gratuity."

For the first time the official commander of the city, the Count Palatine, appears in the records. He appeased the German infantry by pledging payment of a "twofold gratuity" as soon as the money could be raised by the Archduke and the Emperor.

The forays of the Turkish light horse caused consternation

throughout the Empire. The flying columns had cut a wide swath during the twenty days that the army had been across the border. They had reached the environs of Ratisbon, and gained the river Inn. From the foot of the Khalenberg to the castle of Lichtenstein, the countryside had burned The fords of the river Inn had been held by John Starhemberg, but the speeding horsemen had overrun Brunn, Enzersdorf, Baden and Klosterneuburg. Here and there German troops had defended themselves in mills and castles; the length of the Danube had become a swift-moving battlefield, the Styrian mountains had been devastated. Captives had been taken by the thousand. No count was ever made of the victims, but the chroniclers speak of ten to twenty thousand.

In Cologne the chronicle of *Brief World Happenings* relates of 1529 that it was a year "most grievous and full of calamity for the Germans. The Turks broke in savagely. . . ."

Perhaps Hobordanacz and his lord, Ferdinand, had reason to remember at the end of it what Suleiman had promised to do the year before. As he said he would, he had given back to Hungary the twenty-seven fortified towns that Ferdinand had named as a condition of peace; he had installed another ruler in Ferdinand's place; he had visited Austria in person. He had tried for fourteen days to break into Vienna, to get at the army inside.

He had been turned back at Vienna only by the skill and courage of two men, Nicholas of Salm and William von Rogendorf, as Ibrahim acknowledged. Nonetheless, he had been defeated. The Osmanli armies, victorious for seventeen years, had been checked. It is doubtful if Suleiman was much concerned about the battle of Vienna. But as Sultan and son of Selim, he felt the loss of prestige keenly.

He rewarded the janizaris as he had promised, and made a gift to two thousand ducats to "the son of the Doge of Venice" (Gritti). And he sent Gritti with the Hungarian officers to crown Johnny ("Yanush"), as they began to call John Zapolya, with the iron crown of Hungary. Then they raced home against the coming of winter.

His diary, casual at Vienna, shows distress during that six-hundred-mile march over mountain passes and flooding rivers under the lash of snow and hail. "Today, again the army loses a quantity of baggage . . . we leave behind a great number of horses in the swamps; many men die . . . the Sultan, angry at the Agha of Messengers and the Chief of Supply, reduces their fiefs; many soldiers are dying of hunger . . . forced march . . . many transport animals lost . . . a measure of grain sells for five thousand aspers . . . forced march with horses dying as before . . . a great portion of the baggage lost in crossing the Danube . . . severe rains . . . we enter into deep snow. . . ."

Although the armies scattered to take different routes, once the Danube was left behind, Suleiman remained with his own troops. Reading between the lines of the diary, we realize that he stormed at commanding officers, issued grain to the men in the ranks, coaxed the immense column along, and brought it safely in mid-December to Constantinople.

As at Rhodes, this winter march home through the Balkans left an indelible impression on him. After Rhodes he no longer believed in war as a weapon to be used; after the retreat from Vienna, he revolted against the pageantry of warfare.

Only once thereafter did he lead the Turkish *asker* to the prolonged siege of a city, and that was when he was dying.

The attack on Vienna aroused the European courts as nothing else had done. Luther prayed publicly for deliverance from the "terror of the Turks." Suspending his polemics against the papacy, he wrote as in duty bound his *De Bello Turcica*, acknowledging the Turks to be the true enemies of God.

Suleiman had been gone for months when Charles V visited the German portion of his inchoate Empire for the first time in nine years. After paying the ransom of Vienna to the troops that had defended it, he learned the price the Austrian countryside had paid the ravaging Turkish horsemen. He had just been crowned as Emperor by the Pope at Bologna, he was expected to play the role of defender of Christendom, and that particular part of Christendom fully expected the Turks to return in the next year.

Behind this greatest of the Hapsburgs his archantagonist Francis I—while muting down his own accord with the Turks— gave money and aid to the league of German nobles supporting the Reformation against Charles. Francis even tried to strike up an alliance with John Zapolya, friend of the Turks in eastern Hungary, while Ferdinand nagged his brother for money and troops to carry the war against Suleiman into Hungary. (Ferdinand had just been given a new title, "King of the Romans.") The Reformation was spreading. In Bavaria the Wittelsbachs prayed openly for the victory of Zapolya.

Thus bedeviled, Charles saw very clearly the only way out of his troubles. Since he could have no truce with the forces of the Reformation, he must have a truce with the Turk.

So early in 1530 Europe witnessed the strange spectacle of the victors at Vienna sending envoys to the man who by all official accounts had been vanquished, to ask for terms. Charles acted wisely. Unfortunately his prestige as Emperor would suffer if he—the defender of the Christian Commonwealth— should sue for peace with the Turks. The envoys, then, were sent by Ferdinand, and the younger Hapsburg had an amazing knack of doing the wrong thing at the most critical time. His envoys had been ordered to speak only in German in presenting Ferdinand's conditions, which were: recognition as King of Hungary, possession of Buda (then held for Zapolya by a Turkish garrison) and the other large towns. In return the emissaries were to offer to bribe Ibrahim, and to pay Suleiman a "pension."

Nothing could have been better calculated to defeat the purpose of the elder Hapsburg, and to anger the Turks. These had by then a new name for the King of the Romans. It was simply Ferdinand.

When Ferdinand's spokesmen had been conducted past a line of tame, roaring lions and a full turnout of the janizaris, Ibrahim gave them a display of his virtuosity. "You say that your masters," he retorted, laughing, "the King of Spain and Ferdinand, have come to a truce with the Pope. It does not seem to us to be such a sincere truce, after your armies pillaged the Holy City and made the Pope himself a prisoner . . . as to Ferdinand, who would like to be King of Hungary, when we came to seek him at Buda, we did not find him. We went on to Vienna. It is a beautiful city, well worthy of being the capital of an empire, but we did not find its Archduke there. The Sultan, my master, left marks upon the walls as evidence that he had visited it. We did not come to conquer but to overrun the country of Austria. The akinjis galloped through it to show that the real emperor had appeared. . . . Where does Ferdinand keep himself? . . . You say he will return to Hungary, but that is not likely when his own troops like the Bavarians refuse to follow him thither— they prefer Johnny Zapolya as King. No, Ferdinand knows tricks enough, yet he does not show the qualities of a king. How can a man be king unless he keeps his word?"

Anxious as he was to come to agreement with Charles, Suleiman refused to disown Johnny Zapolya, or to give up Buda. The Hungarians did not belong to the Hapsburg empire. He would hear no argument about that.

The odd thing about this peace mission is that the Europeans sought for Suleiman's word, which they knew would guarantee a truce. The vital thing is that Suleiman and Charles were kept at a war they both wished to avoid. The duel imposed on them was to last until the death of Charles in a Spanish monastery near a coast terrorized by Turkish raids.

The mission from the Hapsburgs had one effect. It restored the prestige of the Turkish Sultan. The Hapsburgs had sued for peace after Vienna and had been refused.

SULEIMAN THE MAGNIFICENT

Evidence of the Hippodrome

Unmistakably the Sultan of the Osmanlis was glad to return from the European war to his family and his people. As he had seized three years of quiet after Mohács, he surprised the Europeans by doing the same after Vienna. Not without much truth had Ibrahim declared to the objectionable Hobordanacz, "The Lord of the Two Worlds has more important matters to attend to than you."

At the beginning of summer, 1530, when the judas trees and magnolias flamed along the Bosphorus, Suleiman staged his second festival of the new Constantinople. This time he thought —or Ibrahim did—of some displays, which the European spectators found grotesque, but which pleased the Turks. Trophies, including the three notorious statues from the Buda palace, were paraded around the Hippodrome.

The gifts brought to Suleiman, as he sat on his gold throne of ceremony, were costly enough, but were also products of his vast country—cotton stuffs from Egypt, "damask" cloth from Damascus in Syria, "muslins" from Mosul workshops, along with silver plate and cloth of gold set with jewels, crystal bowls and basins of lapis lazuli.

There were imports too. Suleiman's favorite Chinese porcelain, furs from Muscovy and the Krim Tatars, Arabian pacing horses, Turkoman mustangs, "mameluke" slaves from upper Egypt, black boys from Ethiopia.

Each day of the festival revealed a different spectacle to the watching throngs. Battle exercises staged the storming of wooden forts and the jousting of Mameluke and Turkish riders; acrobats swarmed up the ancient obelisk and walked tightropes stretched from the summit of the obelisk. Melody swept the arena, from the skirling bagpipes of the Croats, from gypsy flutes and the cymbals and bell-staffs of the janizaris.

One day they brought Piri Pasha out from his garden to sit beside the Sultan, now in the prime of life.

"Do you think," Suleiman asked his former Vizir, "that the hope you had ten years since has become reality?"

The aged recluse was confused by the crowd and the sight of such great riches. "Your father Selim, upon whom be the blessing of the Almighty, never beheld such splendor in his camps. It is well. Here you receive the gifts of the world, and in turn you make gifts to all the world."

The weak eyes of the old courtier caught only the colors of pavilions, the flutter of banners, the gleam of cloth of gold spread beneath the Throne of Felicity by which he sat. He did not see the two foreigners who sat apart in drab garments—for the green of the Moslem faith, the white of the Sultan's rank, the blue and yellow of the janizaris, and the red in the pantaloons of the spahis were all forbidden to foreigners, whether Christians or Jews.

Suleiman noticed them, because they were only two, Luigi Gritti and Mocenigo. To this festival he had invited Francis I and the Doge of the Illustrious Signory to come in person; yet Francis had excused himself, promising that some other time when he made a pilgrimage to the Holy Land he would visit the court of the great Sultan (a promise he never kept). The Doge, Andrea Gritti, father of Luigi, had sent gifts by the hand of an envoy extraordinary, Mocenigo. It hurt Suleiman's pride that of all the reigning princes of Europe who sought aid or alliance from him, not one had been willing to be his guest. In truth, he had not been taken into their brotherhood. The reason for that he could suspect. In their eyes he stood alone, a pagan. In him, the Grand Turk, they believed the teaching of the Prophet to be centered, and accordingly the wiles of Satan. Sometimes he wondered if Francis or Charles had ever spoken face to face with a Moslem, as he had done with so many Christians——

Lifting his eyes, he watched sails moving over the blue water of Marmora. Greek fishing luggers coming in, Venetian galleons

137

anchored where some boys swam and a fast caique speeding by —they were all at home in his waters. Beside him the robed Mufti listened with closed eyes to the vibrant voice of a Koran reciter. The voice sang and rose in ecstasy, echoing through the arena. The young reciter, sweating in his effort, lifted his clasped hands. Then he caught at his chest and fell to his knees, his voice failing.

"*Corpo di Dio*—what struck him down?" Mocenigo asked softly. "A dagger thrown?"

Gritti shook his head. "His own effort. Probably the boy fasted the night to gain intensity for this hour. It is their Pater Noster he was chanting."

Gritti had managed to reward himself richly by his service to Ibrahim, who in turn seemed to have the gift of coining into gold every transaction that passed under his hand. While Ibrahim's choice of display ran to liveried servants, splendid stables, jewels and gold embroidery worked into saddlery, and costumes that copied Suleiman's ("His master refuses him nothing," Gritti assured his companion), Gritti had enlarged his mansion and his stock of the finest precious stones, which could be packed into a girdle wallet and sold on any market. In spite of the power he wielded now, the son of the Doge had an uneasy feeling that he tempted fate with each year that he stayed serving Venetians and Turks as go-between. "Their dervishes dance and pray, both," he mused. "At least, they do so when the spirit seizes them. . . . Has Your Magnificence noticed this intensity in them?"

"I have been more struck by their silence. In their mosques a silence falls on them like a plague of meditation."

"Silence can mask the fever heat of thought. A panther moves silently until it strikes. It is your garrulous man who is harmless as a braying donkey. And their new mosques, each huger than the last, with giant columns of stone thrusting up through the dimness of light from colored glass, to the golden circle of the dome—are they not prayers in stone, speaking ever louder?"

Murmuring polite assent, Mocenigo wondered. It was strange that these Turks should erect great buildings only for the dead or for prayer. "Is there then a cult of the dead here, that they serve it in such fashion?" What concerned him at the moment was that these same mystical Turks had put a tax of ten percentum on Venetian imports—for the Mocenigos, like the equally noted Cornaros and Grittis, were deeply involved in Venetian trade as well as policy. What disturbed him was that Luigi Gritti had only skepticism for the latest overture from Paris—Francis had urged that the Serene Republic join the alliance against the Hapsburgs' empire, and had guaranteed in that event the good will of the Turks, through his own offices. That and the city of Cremona, which had once been a possession of the Mocenigos. Cremona and the Po Valley—a tempting price. Very tempting, and safe to take. Yet Gritti's warped mind perceived danger in it, because—said he—the Turks now distrusted Francis whom they praised, and held in regard Charles whom they mocked. Of course a truce between the Emperor and the Turk would be disastrous to the French alliance——

"Haven't we Venetians our own cult of the dead?" Gritti demanded suddenly. "Our palaces and pageantry, our paintings—are they not memories of what is dead, that we would restore? Can we bring back a grandeur that is lost? We who have become merchants, carrying trade in our ships?" With sudden feeling, he cried, "We must remain merchants and Venetians, nothing else."

Silently the envoy decided that the renegade sought to keep Venice neutral in the coming war. Idly he echoed, "Nothing? The word falls strangely upon my ear, spoken by the Dragoman of the Porte!"

Gritti grew pale with anger, and restrained himself when he caught the flicker of the other's smile. "Then will Your Magnificence hear another word? Our city," he said slowly, "must never be drawn into war against the Turk."

Mocenigo nodded, understanding perfectly that conflict between the Republic and the Sultan would be the downfall of Luigi Gritti, who had feathered his nest so nicely here. "It will be my privilege to bear your message to your illustrious father. *Corpo di Dio*, are we such fools as to oppose the will of your Sultan?" Curiously he glanced at the bizarre tent where a handsome, silent man waited patiently for a boy reader to recover from a faint and go on with the infidel chant. "I shall tell your father of Suleiman's—magnificence."

Gritti had wanted to journey back with Mocenigo to the embarcadero of Venice. By now he had jewels worth a quarter of a million ducats hoarded away. But the other's amused contempt made it impossible for him to do so——

Again the boy's voice rose in the chant from the Koran: "... *and say not with a lie upon your tongue, this is lawful and that is forbidden, for so will ye invent a lie concerning God. And they who invent a lie upon God shall not prosper. ...*"

The voice drew Suleiman's mind toward it. He shared in it, and in the meditation of the Mufti at his side; he did not sit apart from them as from the Europeans, who said one thing and willed another. How long had he tried with Ibrahim's aid to educate the best of his people to become part of the brotherhood of Europe? Yet wherein lay that brotherhood?

Although he showed no sign of it, the slow-reasoning Osmanli was losing faith in the Europeans, who came to him only with words of war or prices of trade. He had agreed readily to what his friends asked. But were they truly his friends? And could he trust even Ibrahim?

He gave no sign of it but from that time he began to put his confidence in a woman who was also a foreigner born.

End of the Three Gentle Souls

Suleiman's excuse for the festival had been the circumcision of Roxelana's two sons, growing from childhood to boyhood,

Selim and Bayazid. For those few days the shy boys joined their
father, becoming the center of the rejoicing of the people.

After that the Ayin required them to be confined with tutors
in the harem of the old palace. There they played around the
fountain in the courtyard of the Sultan Valideh. Although ailing to death, Suleiman's mother still dominated her world of
women. Confined to her sleeping mattress of velvet, hung about
with tissue of gold, Hafiza gave her orders after sunrise daily
to the Captain of the Girls, the Mistress of the Rooms, and the
Head Nurse. Roxelana she almost never saw. Yet she had formed
her own opinion about the two sons of the Russian woman.
"Selim snares birds with lime, and he is secretive, hiding things
from me He is slight but pudgy, silent but willful."

Feeling death near her, Hafiza dared speak openly to Suleiman. "In acts as in looks, he resembles his mother the Khasseki
Khurrem. Now Bayazid is both gentle and clever. His face and
his spirit bear your image."

As usual, Suleiman listened without comment. "Paradise lies
at a mother's feet."

Hafiza, however, was not to be diverted. "*Ai*, you say nothing
of a mother's sharp tongue. Well, I will warn you. Do not forget
my words. Trust Bayazid. Be kind to Selim, and take care that
he does not fear you—as I think he does now. But never trust
him."

Evidently Hafiza assumed that Suleiman's sons would grow
to maturity unharmed. Because the eldest was Mustafa, her
favorite, who had been taken from the harem for training, she
did not mention him.

Hafiza as well as Suleiman knew that Gulbehar's boy had
grown in popular favor. Mustafa seldom looked at his books;
he liked better to talk with his elders, and he made friends
readily. He had his father's instinctive skill with sword or horse
or in the water. Often enough he came into his camp with his
head bruised from the wooden javelins thrown in sport on horseback. Tall and active himself, he never shirked injury. The men

141

of the pen who taught Mustafa logic reported that he showed the true Osmanli traits of endurance, and leadership in strife.

It pleased Hafiza that Mustafa had been given the government of Magnisiya, which had been Suleiman's before he came to the throne. This seemed to make certain that Mustafa would be his father's heir, by Suleiman's determination as well as by old custom. Hitherto nothing had been able to alter what the Sultan had determined to be.

Like a shadow Roxelana's youngest son drifted between Mustafa's court at Magnisiya and the palace at Constantinople. Sickly and a hunchback, Jahangir was morbidly attached to the healthy Mustafa. And of all the boys, he was Suleiman's favorite.

Then the Sultan Valideh died. For three days Suleiman mourned, clad in dark garments torn from throat to skirt, fasting, commanding the splendid rugs of his palace to be taken up, and the ornaments turned to the walls. No music was heard in the streets of the city.

Suleiman was thirty-nine years old, in the fullness of his strength. Probably, so deeply was he obsessed with Roxelana, he could not perceive how greatly his household changed. For one thing his mother had been the last member of the trio that held to the old ways—with the gentle Piri Pasha, and the unthinking Gulbehar. Then, too, Gulbehar should have occupied the apartment of the Sultan Valideh. But she chose to stay with Mustafa at Magnisiya. That left Suleiman to the companionship of his two intimates, the dynamic Ibrahim and the resourceful Roxelana.

Outwardly the Russian woman made no attempt to influence Suleiman, or to challenge the primacy of Gulbehar, his first love. She seemed to take Mustafa's right to inherit for granted. For Suleiman, sensitive to influence, was adamant in matters of justice. Surprisingly to the black Captain of the Girls and the observant attendants, Roxelana gave little heed to her own boys, devoting herself to Suleiman.

Yet by degrees she managed to accompany him out of the cloistered harem, sometimes following his horse to reviews and to Friday prayers in her closed carriage, sometimes joining him disguised when he ventured out in the excursions he enjoyed so much on the water. Suleiman would let the loose folds of his turban down over his forehead, to sit by her in the cabined stern of the swift rowing barge. In this fashion they went up the Bosphorus to the Sweet Waters, or across to the cedar-grown cemeteries of the Chamlija.

Within the harem also a change took place. Roxelana's temper showed when, as happened rarely now, a new girl came into the eye of the Sultan. Then the Khasseki Khurrem had a way of taking such an attractive woman into her own service, so that Suleiman would meet the other only in her presence. By degrees the eunuch was certain that his master took enjoyment from no other woman.

Hitherto Hafiza had watched over every member of her confined world. Now there was no mistress of the harem. Roxelana, still Second Kadin, might be the favorite, but she had authority only when Suleiman spoke for her.

Since he did not call the other kadins to him, they remained in their quarters as pensioners, still clad in the special garments of those chosen for the Sultan's bed. Since Roxelana disliked them, they were friendless. It was not hard for the Russian to persuade him, as if in kindness, to give them away in marriage to deserving officers of the spahis or the palace guard.

When that happened Roxelana reminded Suleiman that her own position was becoming unendurable. Those others had become wives, with privileges and property of their own. She, virtually the wife of the Sultan, remained in the eyes of her own servitors no more than a slave. Was not that unjust?

The careful Venetians, who had begun to pay close attention to rumors about Roxelana in the harem, took note of her new influence over Suleiman. "He loves her so much and keeps faith so with her that it astonishes his people. They say that she has become a witch, using her power over him. Because of that the army and the court also hate her and her children; but because he loves her so greatly, no one dares protest."

By tradition, for six generations, no Osmanli sultan had taken an acknowledged wife. But Roxelana knew that Suleiman would not hesitate to break with tradition. In the end he did so.

It was done quietly, in the palace. Before a judge of the Law, Suleiman touched the hand of the veiled Roxelana, and testified, "This woman, Khurrem, I set free from slavery, and make her a wife. All that belongs to her shall be her property."

Apparently those close to Suleiman would not speak of the marriage to foreigners. But he gave a feast afterward, and observers of the bank of St. George, of Genoa, have left this record of it. "This week took place in the city an event without precedent in the annals of previous sultans. The Grand Signior took to himself as Empress a slave woman from Russia called Roxelana, and great feasting followed . . . at night the streets are illuminated, with music played, and wreaths hung from balconies. In the old Hippodrome a stand was set up with gilded latticework to screen the Empress and her ladies while they watched riding and tournament of riders, both Christian and Moslem, as well as jugglers and trained beasts including giraffes with necks that reached to the sky."

So while the absent Gulbehar remained the Sultan Valideh-to-be, Roxelana had made herself Suleiman's acknowledged consort. Again, she exerted herself to draw Suleiman's attention toward her old homeland of the north, in the mountains of Hungary.

The Utopia of 1531

Suleiman had no least desire to return to Hungary, where the embers of war smoldered. Yet precisely at this time the Europeans expected him to do so. More and more they kept their eyes on him—through the eyes of their spies—and in their thoughts he appeared to be the dangerous and dynamic head of the Moslem east. Was he not successor to the kalifs, armed champions of that archfiend *Mahomet?* Were not his Turks a new incarnation of the *Saracens* who had captured Jerusalem from the crusaders? Even Luther said so, now.

Did not ambassadors who had stood before his throne return home to repeat what they had heard: "Where the hoofs of the Sultan's horse have trod, there the land is his forever?"

In the bitterness of religious antagonism the European courts and universities conceived of the Grand Turk only as a conqueror riding forever against them. Unlike the Croats and Hungarians, they had never met with Turks in the flesh. There was no Raymond Lull at that time, to tell them what the Turks were like The mingled culture of Moslem Spain, of Andalusia, that had created the beautiful Granada, was being obliterated. The Moors were being driven out, across the sea to Africa. Some took refuge under Suleiman.

His dream, that where the hoofs of his horse had trod there could be peace, was becoming impossible to realize. He still had hope for it.

Perhaps there was no way to blend the cultures of the east and west in his generation of Turks. But could there not be a *Turkish* culture, standing alone yet respected by Europeans and Asiatics alike? His city at the junction of the seas and the lands —could it not be filled with a population of uprooted people who would owe nothing to and claim nothing from the other peoples of east and west? Like the queen city of Alexandria planned and built by the great Alexander?

Suleiman thought only of finished practical things. A dwelling was a shelter against rain and cold, for a family. He ordered his architects to tear down fortification walls to build aqueducts. He desired a new, *Turkish* design. Must mosques always be built as the Byzantines had designed the Aya Sofia? Must the practice of religion always follow the rules of the Koraish, the Arab clan that had once followed Muhammad the Prophet? Must literature always be Persian?

In those years of his glory he was called Suleiman the Magnificent, and the Grand Turk. Visitors caught the flash of jewels in the floss silk of his turbans, and harkened to Ibrahim's boasts of treasure piled up in the Seven Towers. Yet what he was striving for with silent determination, few of them saw.

It was not much of a utopia. It had no visible acropolis, or any favored class of nobility. It protected only the home dwellers. One of them might own a stone hut, a field of grapevines or cherry trees with a small sheep herd. Such a family man paid in taxes the value of one ducat each year for his house, and one asper for each two head of sheep. (The rough equivalent in modern money of five dollars for his real estate, and one dime for two sheep.) He sent his children to the mosque school to learn to read the Koran, and he took cases for judgment to the village *kadi* or religious judge.

From that moderate household tax came the chief revenue of Suleiman's Treasury. Beyond that, there was also a regular tax on undertakings, such as metal mines and salt mines, customs paid by foreign merchants, and fees for drawing documents.

Some tribute came in from the outer provinces like Greece proper or Syria, and especially Egypt. Even the Venetians paid a token tribute of 30,000 ducats. All in all the revenues totaled 4,100,000 ducats according to Yunis Bey, the head interpreter of the Serai, or 6,000,000 in the opinion of the merchant Zeno. Gritti said they were 4,000,000, but both he and Yunis Bey may have meant the yearly expenditures of the Treasury. Certainly all agree that Suleiman's Treasury took in more each year than it paid out—perhaps 6,000,000 as against 4,000,000.

That was a very small revenue for a dominion as large as western Europe beyond Venice. Moreover, it was fixed, by custom. "What has been, will be," the saying ran. When Europeans saw the Sultan ride forth with the splendor of his entourage, they imagined vast riches under the hand of the Grand Signior which did not exist. Suleiman protected first of all the Turkish hearth.

"In all things the Turks are so great lovers of Order," a Frenchman related long afterward, "that they omit nothing to observe it. Because economy and the regulation of provisions is one of the chief things that serve to maintain it, they take a special care of that, so all things are to be had in plenty and at reasonable rates. They never sell cherries or other fruits when they first come in at the weight of gold, as is done in this country. . . . If their officers who go the daily rounds find any man with weights that are too light, or selling his goods too dear, he would be soundly drubbed or else brought to Justice. So a child may be sent to Market, for none dares cheat the child; and sometimes the officers of the Market meeting a child will ask what it paid for so much goods, and will weigh them to see if the poor thing be cheated. I saw a man who sold ice at five deniers the pound receive blows upon the soles of his feet. . . . A man who sells at false weights may have his neck put into a Pillory which he carries on his shoulders, being hung with little bells—to be laughed at by all who see and know him. . . .

"As to disorders and quarrels that happen in the streets, everyone is obliged to hinder them. To prevent accidents in the night-time all persons whatsoever are prohibited to be abroad in the streets after dark, except it be in Ramadan."

This sense of order and of responsibility for the individual stemmed' down from Suleiman to a chief of the watch in a frontier village. It was the peculiarity of his utopia that he made moral law supersede kanun law. He could do this only by a spoken decision, urf, which, being accepted, became a kanun in time. At this time he was working with Ibrahim on a revision of the Book of the Law of Egypt—the most important of the Asiatic territories. When the annual revenue from Egypt increased to 800,000 dinars, exceeding the established figure, Suleiman directed that the increase be spent within Egypt, on irrigation works.

For these few years he achieved something extraordinary. Under him—more than with any previous sultan or monarch of Europe—his few servants in the Organization managed to bring about the well-being of the multitudes whom he "fed and led."

Suleiman, in spite of the magnificent appearance he presented, kept up no costly establishment. The clothing he wore, the thoroughbred horses he stabled and the festivals he gave made up the bulk of his expenses. Otherwise, the very pages who served him drew sustenance pay, and were in training for posts of higher responsibility. The gifts he made to all who sought him were compensated by gifts to him; the wealth acquired by beylerbeys and aghas escheated to the common Treasury at their death.

Perhaps the most favored group beneath him were the *spahi-oghlans* or Young Riders, three thousand of them, who marched always at his right hand. The Young Riders were given small land holdings from which they had to provide five or six horses and as many followers in time of war. They also were in training for command. "They are great people," an observer relates. "From them the Signor is wont to choose his chief men."

But the Young Riders were growing in number, as was Suleiman's personal establishment. Beylerbeys and aghas began to imitate the lavishness of their master, as well as the splendor of his attire. To do so, they tended to draw more than sustenance, especially from those beneath them.

Perhaps they envied Ibrahim too much. Elder men, men of the pen, and judges of the religious Law complained that the Vizir was taking to himself the authority of a second sultan. They distrusted Ibrahim not so much because he had been a Greek and a Christian—most of the Organization had come from Christian families—as because he kept the Greek statues of Buda and took their Sultan to the home of an infidel, Gritti, and because he went about in garments copied from the Sultan's.

Such complaints Suleiman would not hear. He did hear the frank acknowledgment of most Moslems: "Never had the Turks such a sultan, or a sultan such a vizir."

Then came the case of Kabiz.

It was almost without precedent, for Kabiz had been a member of the *ulema* or interpreters of the sacred Law. By degrees he had become convinced that the teachings of Jesus were superior to those of Muhammad. (Moslem tradition held that Jesus had taught the Word of God, as a Prophet; but to a lesser extent than Muhammad, who came after him.)

Summoned to trial for disbelief, Kabiz had been sentenced to death by the judges of the army, on his own testimony, without argument as to whether he might be right or wrong in his doctrine. Ibrahim, not satisfied with the sentence, had called Kabiz before the Divan for a rehearing. In this hearing Ibrahim argued—and Suleiman listened to the argument—that heresy was not a crime in itself; it could only be tried as a doctrine allowable or not, according to law.

Suleiman did not agree. "How is this?" he demanded of his Vizir in public. "The offender against the Prophet is allowed to go without punishment, and without an attempt to convince him of his error."

Kabiz was brought before the Mufti and his old companions of the ulema. After his new belief was argued in full, he was sentenced to death by these judges of the religious Law.

Never throughout his life did Suleiman escape this conflict between the civil rights of his people and the old Islamic tradition. As supreme head of the religion he was called upon to uphold the tradition, almost rigid, formed in the tribal stage of the Arabs. As head of the administrative Organization he had to decide upon the rights of individuals. And more than a third of his people were Christians—Armenians, Greeks, Georgians, and many others. Kabiz's guilt lay not in affirming the teaching of Jesus but in denying the base of Moslem tradition, when he had been an interpreter of that tradition.

A greater matter Suleiman decided against himself. His early triumphs in war, at Belgrade, Rhodes and Mohács, had been gained at a cost to his people. Iskander Chelebi, the Chief Treasurer, informed him that a war levy had been laid during those three years, of a piece of silver for every head of livestock and measure of grain. So those years of war had been a drain on the country. The ensuing years of peace had repaired the damage.

Suleiman gave his decision that no added taxes for war should be levied henceforth. In his Vienna campaign the army gleaned enough from Austria to pay the cost. The damage during the retreat Suleiman made good from his personal funds.

Yet after three years, in the spring of 1532, he had to lead the *asker* north again, this time against the Christian Emperor.

March of the Phantom Army

Ferdinand made it inevitable. Although the would-be King of Hungary had not been able to rally a following among the Hungarians, he had hired soldiery and gleaned forces from Charles, and re-entered the country. He had laid siege to Buda and had only been driven from the citadel by the Turkish garrison Suleiman had left there to hold it.

With intermittent warfare breaking out along the Danube, Charles had gathered a large army around Vienna. To enable him to do so he had agreed on a truce with the Lutherans (June 1532) dismissing all charges against them before the imperial court. This is known as the religious truce of Nuremberg, and was a triumph for Luther. To face the Turk, it was necessary for Charles to have the German cities quiet behind him.

The army at Vienna that June was perhaps the largest mobilized within the Empire during that generation, for the German city troops as well as the professional soldiery marched at the

Emperor's command, and Charles drew in his veteran Spanish tercios from Italy and the Netherlands.

Good Richard Knolles, three generations later, described the Christian muster enthusiastically:

". . . old, expert soldiers, and of them many whole companies . . . officers and men of mark in other armies now were content to serve as private men. It was thought that so many worthy captains and valiant soldiers were never before in the memory of man assembled together into one camp. For the princes and free cities had sent thither chosen and approved men, striving as it were among themselves who should send the best. All the flower and strength of Germany, from the river Vistula to the Rhine, and from the Ocean to the Alps, was sent . . . or of themselves voluntarily came thither. A thing never before heard of, that all Germany should as it were with one consent be glad to take up arms for their common safety."

Charles, however, remained two hundred miles away, at Ratisbon on the headwaters of the Danube.

What befell this excellent army during the critical months from June to October was entirely unexpected. It mystified the Germans at the time, and it has puzzled Europeans ever since.

Knowing that the Turkish host with its Sultan was approaching swiftly from the south, the Germans prepared to defend the upper Danube, basing themselves on Vienna. There they stayed, steadfastly enough. They never saw Suleiman, or his main army.

They heard tidings enough of the Turks. In the mountains south of them, towns fell before Turkish assaults; refugees began to come in, from farther west. The Turks were seen where no one expected them to be, between Vienna and Europe proper. Other, terrible horsemen who were not Turks drove through the upland valleys, turning to sweep through undefended villages, bridging rivers, or swimming them. These mysterious riders proved to be Tatars from Asia.

151

The flying columns appeared at Steyr and along the Enns, a hundred miles west of Vienna.

About that time, in the first week of August, messengers arrived from the Tauern range. They said the main Turkish army was besieging the small town of Güns, sixty miles south. Very soon after that the baffled commanders at Vienna received orders from Charles to hold their position and not to move beyond the mountains to the relief of Güns.

That small citadel held out valiantly, yet the great German army did not attempt to aid it. Its garrison consisted of no more than 700, most of whom had been caught there while on their way to the rendezvous at Vienna. For twenty days Suleiman remained at Güns, laying siege to it in desultory fashion. Then, on August 28, he accepted the surrender of the place in a mystifying manner He demanded only the keys of the demolished gates, gave the brave garrison immunity, and contented himself with stationing detachments of janizaris in the breaches, to act as guards to keep the rest of the army out, while he withdrew.

The commanders at Vienna were still puzzling over the token surrender of the mountain hamlet when speeding columns of riders appeared *behind* them, pushing past them toward Suleiman, crossing the Danube and laying waste the forested valleys. They came so close that some of them felt their way through the adjacent Wiener Wald, and the Germans were able to about-face and block many ravines, cutting off the horsemen, inflicting heavy loss on them.

But most of the columns found their way back to lower Austria, where Suleiman was circling through the mountains, storming some towns, yet passing by largish cities like Graz and Marburg. His host threaded the rough Alpine region, getting across the swift Mur River and bridging the Drave. In his path there was no army to oppose him.

By October 9, when the autumn storms began, he was out of the Austrian uplands, safely back on the lower Danube, marching down by easy stages to Belgrade.

Not until September 23, when the Turks were far away, crossing the river Drave, did Charles appear in Vienna, to stay a few days. By early October he also was returning home, crossing Italy on his way to Barcelona.

So ended one of the strangest campaigns of history. The anticipated duel between the Sultan of the east and the Emperor of the west had never taken place. The mighty host Charles had gathered to defend middle Europe had stayed passively in camp at Vienna; the formidable Turkish *asker* had avoided it, while indulging in a great raid through most of Austria. The dreaded Suleiman himself had played at war for nearly a month at little Güns.

All this made no sense from a European point of view; it made sense very clearly, when the actual happenings are understood, from the Turkish viewpoint. The answer to the riddle of 1532 lies in Suleiman himself.

He had never intended to invade *Almanya*, as the Turks called Germany proper. Regardless of the speculations and the fears of western Europe, he had no thought of extending the Turkish conquests beyond western Hungary, where he did retake with ease the area necessary to protect Buda, which he now claimed as part of his dominion. To the *Almanya* beyond—tiny Austria, encircled within its hills, and the bastion of Bohemia—he had never made claim. Whatever his intentions had been regarding Vienna three years before, he relinquished that capital city now. The brothers Hapsburg could rule *Viyana*.

Suleiman, always reticent, seldom allowed his plans to be known. Ten years before he had followed out the Moslem custom of sending in advance to an enemy an offer of peace, against the alternative of attack upon a Land of War. In ten years conditions had changed; he was now in direct discussion with the envoys of the Hapsburgs. And the Sultan's character had undergone a change. He no longer trusted in the efficacy of a war of conquest. Yet he was obliged to journey forth at least every three years with the heads of his Organization, and the Turkish muster for war. In spite of his efforts to substitute another leader, Ibrahim for example, the army would accept no substitute for the presence of the Sultan himself. The Turkish state was still based upon the army. Even Suleiman had no thought of disbanding the military organization of which he was the head. Instead, he was working very quietly to change its nature, and its functions. The Ferhad Pashas had disappeared from its command, and Ibrahim, nominally Serasker (Generalissimo), was not a natural soldier.

In his diary Suleiman noted the campaign cryptically as being against "the King of Spain."

In the make-up of that particular army, however, there is a clue. While the regular contingents, the janizaris, spahis and the feudal cavalry of Europe and Asia, remained as usual in strength—45,000 to 48,000, which was about the force of the Germans at Vienna—the light horsemen had been increased to more than 50,000 and the Krim Khan summoned from the steppes with 15,000 Tatars. These Tatars, formidable in surprise raids, were not accustomed to attacking fortified positions. (Although a half dozen years before they had broken into the distant city of Moscow.)

Suleiman, then, moved north with forces adapted to swift inroads rather than to siege operations. He had no heavy artillery with him.

Remember that he was adamant in refusing to be drawn into the siege of a citadel like Rhodes; he had tested the resistance of Vienna when held by a much smaller force of Europeans; and he was determined to avoid another winter march like that of three years before, with its loss of valuable horses.

Yet his supremacy had been challenged by the mobilization of the Europeans at Vienna.

What he attempted to do, and failed to do, is clear. He wanted to draw the German army out of its lines at Vienna, into the open plains. When his flying columns of Tatars and akinjis (Sackmann, the Germans called them) did not bring out the Germans to defend the Austrian countryside, Suleiman moved to Güns. From Güns to Vienna there is a clear corridor of high prairie land, between the great lake, the Neusiedler See, and the eastern end of the Tauern mountain chains.

If the Germans had moved south into that corridor to relieve Güns, their infantry would have been out in open country, infested on all sides by the Turkish horsemen. If a battle had ensued under those conditions, there might have been a second Mohács and an end to the Hapsburg challenge to Hungary.

Charles was wise in avoiding such a battle.

Evidently as soon as Suleiman realized that the Germans would not be tricked, he abandoned his staged performance of the siege of Güns and accepted the keys of the castle in the comedy of surrender.

There is another clue in the cryptic entries in his diary.

"We camp by Graz, a great town lying under the rule of the King of Spain . . . surrender of the castle of Posega . . . we burn the outer town of the castle of *Kobasch* . . . the castle of *Ghouriani* belonging to the son of the despot makes its submission . . . the army camps by the castle of *Altakh* on the bank of the Bozut River; surrender of the castle of Pancova, belonging to King Ferdinand . . ."

Suleiman's army appears to have gathered in the feudal possessions of Ferdinand while making its sweep through the Styrian mountains. Other cities were not molested in that way.

A German chronicle relates: "The rage of the invaders took them into Lincium, a town in which Ferdinand was at the time."

Whether Ferdinand was present in Austria or not, his possessions suffered—"through the length and breadth of his lands."

And the Turkish army repaid the cost of the campaign.

Whether Suleiman regretted that the absent Charles had not ventured out to meet him, we cannot know. Publicly, of course, Ibrahim made claim that although the Sultan had gone to meet him, the Emperor as usual had not been found. The diary itself dismisses the war indifferently.

November 13. "Death of the former Grand Vizir, Piri Pasha."

November 21. "The Sultan returns to the Serai at Constantinople; five days of festival and illumination in the city and its suburbs of Ayub, Galata and Scutari. The bazaars remain open at night and Suleiman goes to visit them incognito."

For the first time Suleiman ventured out among the crowds to hear their talk, after his absence. He was trying, in his slow, methodical way, to make a difficult decision without the aid of Ibrahim.

Truce on the Danube

Suleiman meant to end the Turkish penetration by land into Europe.

At the same time realization seemed to grow upon him that he would never find the friendship he had sought in the west. Francis, who had appealed to him, had tried to use him as a weapon against Charles, to be discarded when not needed. For the nearest of them, Ferdinand of Austria, he had gained only contempt. He had been willing to meet the western princes more than halfway—they had never understood how far he had gone to meet them. In their society he would find no place. He would be alone, a Turk.

With this realization came the certainty that he could rely on no one except himself. He would turn his back on the west. Perhaps he still clung to the idea that his state could be a bridge between the Bible and the Koran, but it would be Turkish, and alone. It would have no Ibrahim as his second self; from it he would send the tricky Gritti. And he himself would venture where he had not set foot in twelve years, into Asia. (Only once had he journeyed across Anatolia, to embark for Rhodes.) There he would follow after his father, but not as Selim had done; he would seek the Moslem lands of peace, of the Koran.

156

Yet by those years of change, from 1533 to 1536 (in which time he married Roxelana), Suleiman had rounded out a wide dominion for the Osmanlis in Europe. His new frontiers lay close to Venice on the Adriatic, some nine hundred miles from Constantinople, and in northern Hungary, seven hundred miles distant, northeasterly they extended through the tributary steppes of the Krim Tatars to Azov by the mouth of the river Don, eight hundred miles away. It was a journey of twelve hundred miles or more from Azov on its inland sea to Zara on the Adriatic. These inner sea borders of his European state were held by the allied Tatars and the friendly Venetians. The Balkan peoples, from Greeks to Hungarians, formed the inner nations of his hegemony. Beyond lay the aliens, Italians, Germans, Slovaks, Poles and the Slavs of Muscovy.

At this line of demarcation, by Suleiman's decision, the landward expansion of the Turks into Europe ceased. This northern frontier was to remain little changed for a century and a half. Nearly at the end of the seventeenth century an ambitious Turkish vizir was to attempt an actual siege of Vienna, and the young Peter Alexeivich (Peter the Great) was to march down the Don against the Turks in Azov.

The dominion bounded and set by Suleiman was no transitory conquest. What cemented it together was the nature of the Osmanli's rule. For the remaining years of his life migrants would flee from war and hunger, coming over the Russian and Austrian frontiers, seeking food and the toleration of their churches, whether Eastern Orthodox, Greek Orthodox, the Armenian rite, the Moslem faith, or the Jewish. It was his *pax Turcica* that gave substance to his hegemony of the Danube.

Again, as after Vienna, the brothers Hapsburg sued for a truce. Nothing could have suited Suleiman better, now that he intended to depart into Asia. This time he himself needed a truce with the Europeans, and he welcomed the envoys cordially.

157

In their new amiability, Suleiman and Ibrahim devised a new status for the brothers Hapsburg. The two ceased to be "Ferdinand and the King of Spain," and became friendly suppliants to be taken into Suleiman's growing family, Charles as a brother, Ferdinand as a son.

This very informal title the envoy from Vienna was obliged to request publicly, with no little humiliation, after making a token surrender of the city of Gran by handing over the keys. From dictation he repeated: "King Ferdinand, your son, holds all things belonging to him as belonging to you, his father . . . he did not know you wanted to possess Hungary, and if he had known it, he would never have gone to war over it. . . ."

And a special representative arrived from Charles, one Cornelius Schepper, who brought a letter with him. Suleiman, in his new role as a head of the European family, assured the gentlemen from Vienna that Ferdinand could have a truce. "Not only a truce, but a peace; not for seven years or a century but for all time—as long as Ferdinand keeps it."

Under the whimsicality and the dig at Ferdinand, the Sultan was expressing an earnest wish.

Ibrahim received Charles's letter with all formality, rising and pressing it to his forehead (to make the most of this first missive from Suleiman's rival). "He is truly a mighty lord, and so we honor him."

But the letter itself caused trouble. "This is not written by a prudent prince or a wise one. Why does he set forth titles that are not his? How dares he style himself, to my lord, King of Jerusalem? Does he not know that my mighty emperor and not he—Charles—is lord of Jerusalem? Why, here he calls himself Duke of Athens, which is now Sethine, a small town belonging to us! . . . My master has no need to steal titles from others— he has enough that are truly his own!"

Whereupon Ibrahim treated the German envoys to one of his dissertations on the state of Europe, this time with Charles as subject: ". . . in Italy he threatened us with war, and promised the Lutheran followers peace; he came to Germany, and there did nothing for the Lutherans or against us. A great ruler should not begin what he cannot finish . . . he announced publicly that he would have a council [to bring the Lutherans into the old religion]. He has not had one. We are not like that. . . . If I chose to do so, I could summon that council, putting Luther on one side and the Pope on the other, and making them agree."

Of the two Hapsburgs, only Ferdinand got his truce, and acknowledgment as King of the northern mountains of Hungary that he already held.

With Charles, Suleiman refused to come to any agreement . . . "until he first makes peace with my friend and ally the King of France, and restores to him the lands he has taken from him."

Was Suleiman overscrupulous in keeping his word to Francis? Or was he mocking Charles and ridiculing Francis' broken pledges?

During the negotiations, however, Ibrahim made an extraordinary statement to the Europeans, who, like others before them, had learned to flatter the Vizir, and to make him costly gifts as the unacknowledged head of the Turkish state. Ibrahim exclaimed: "It is true that I govern this vast empire . . . whatever I do is accomplished. If I wished I could make a stableboy into a pasha. What I wish to give is given, and cannot be taken away. My lord will say nothing against it. If the great Sultan gives something and I do not wish it given, then it is taken away. The making of war, the granting of peace, the disposal of treasure—all is in my hands. The Sultan is not better clad than I. His powers he entrusts to my hands. . . . I do not say these things idly, but to give you courage to speak to me freely."

Whether this was sheer nervous exhaustion, or insane confidence, is hard to say. Ibrahim was not boasting entirely, because he held power and privilege, as he described. His most bitter enemy, Iskander Chelebi, dared complain to the Sultan that the Greek who had been a Christian was taking wealth from all his transactions. Suleiman paid little attention He had given his word not to remove the Vizir in disgrace while they both lived. And Ibrahim's fortune would return to the Treasury at his death. In a sense it was only borrowed.

Gritti, anxious now, shook his head at the self-intoxication of the great Vizir. "If Suleiman," he said, "should send one of his cooks to kill Ibrahim, nobody would prevent it."

The adroit son of the Doge survived only a year. Sent by Suleiman into northern Hungary to arbitrate the limits of the frontier—a task that the Sultan knew would take him years—Gritti lost his nerve or tried to reap a new fortune out of the assignment. (Ibrahim had given him very different instructions from Suleiman, who wished none of Zapolya's territory given up.) In either case, he tried to convince the Austrians that he could gain for them the cities of the great Hungarian plain.

By so doing he roused the Hungarians of the countryside against him. They hunted him down and beheaded him at once. When they stripped his body they found a small casket strapped to his inner thigh, within it jewels worth four hundred thousand gold pieces.

And Ibrahim never gave another audience to European ambassadors. He was sent ahead of Suleiman into Asia.

So Suleiman tried to close the book of *Almanya* and *Viyana*. He meant to depart from Europe for years. Yet, putting no trust in a truce with a Hapsburg, he looked for something to occupy all the Europeans while he was gone. He found it to be a venture out to sea.

In turning to the sea as an expedient, he launched the fortune of the Osmanlis in a new direction, and by so doing he was to shift the kaleidoscope of Europe for more than thirty years.

He might not have found the way to the sea if it had not been for one man, Barbarossa.

III

The Sea

The Impelling Forces

NOW it was strange that the greatest of the Osmanlis should go out, day after day, to his garden path to watch for the coming of one man from the sea. Yet invisible forces drove him to send for Barbarossa, and other forces impelled this Redbeard to shape his course to Serai Point, albeit reluctantly.

The same intelligent Frenchman who had observed children buying cherries in the bazaar saw the significance of this Serai Point—"a point of the main land jutting out toward the Bosphorus, and from it the passage over to Asia takes only a half hour. On the right hand it hath the White Sea [Marmora] by which there is easy passage to Egypt and Africa—whereby it is supplied with all the commodities of those places. On the left hand it hath the Black or *Euxine* Sea and the *Palus Maeotis* [Sea of Azov]. This last, receiving a vast number of rivers and having many bordering peoples, furnishes this city with all the commodities of the North. So there is nothing pleasant, useful, or necessary which is not brought in plenty from all sides by sea to Constantinople. When the wind hinders vessels from coming by the one channel, it helps them in from the other . . . the entry of the port is the loveliest in the world."

So Suleiman had behind him the waterways that carried the

trade of nearer Asia. Ahead of him, beyond the stone castles of the Dardanelles, stretched the tranquil Aegean sprinkled with the islands that had once been Greek and were now Turkish—even to Rhodes.

For the Mediterranean, the Middle Sea as some called it, was no single thoroughfare of water like the mighty ocean beyond. It had its barriers of islands, and its arms stretching far inland, and all these were claimed by somebody or other. Before Suleiman's time Mehmed the Conqueror had launched Turkish ships upon the Aegean, while Selim had sent forth fleets of galleys to hold this eastern arm of the sea. Beyond, past bare Zante and flowering Corfu, the Venetians still claimed the long arm of the Adriatic, swept by blasts of the *Borro*, the north wind.

Westward lay the narrow gut where Malta and Sicily made steppingstones, as it were, between Cape Bona and the toe of Italy. Beyond this barrier the western half of the sea, with rocky Sardinia and Corsica and the chain of the Balearics, was claimed by Charles for the Empire, and especially for Spain. It was to all purposes a Spanish sea to the mighty rock of Gibraltar.

No Turkish ships had ventured that far, and it seemed impossible for them to do so. But there was a way thither by land as well, along the African coast. And as Monsieur de Thévenot had noted, the passage from the Golden Horn to Africa was an easy one.

Moreover, along the African coast smoldered age-old antagonism to the Europeans north of the sea. The desert folk who migrated to this southern coast, whether Phoenicians, Berbers or Arabs, had always found enemies beyond the barrier of the sea, whether Romans or Normans. In the early ages the more cultured people had occupied the southern shore, where St. Augustine had written his *City of God* in the small city of Hippo (Bona) and philosophers had clung to the library in Alexandria. Then the wave of Arabs had swept the flotsam and jetsam of this ancient culture across the Strait of Gibraltar

162

into the Spanish peninsula, bringing Aristotle as well as the kalifate to Spain, pouring the resources of Asia into the barbaric European coast, thus stimulating there the revival of the thirteenth century.

Drawn to these resources or simply pirating at sea, the Europeans had reacted during the crusades, the Italian cities, Pisa, Genoa the Proud, and the Serene Republic of Venice, sending south their armed fleets. St. Louis died by the ruins of Carthage, besieging the port of Tunis. The cruelty of Normans and Italians was fed by the bitterness of religious war that left to the Mediterranean a heritage of pirating and the passage of armed fleets to loot and seize captives for the oar benches of their galleys.

In the lull that followed, the African coast lay under a lotus-eating quiet, the once powerful kalifates broken down into pacific family dynasties that ruled the small garden ports. Arabs or Berbers, they traded along the sea or wandered with the tribes back of the barrier mountains, following preaching marabouts into the sandy desert or making pilgrimage to the holy city of Kairouan.

Upon such a heritage of drowsiness and bitter memories came the thrust of the Europeans outward across the oceans. It glanced against the African coast. The year that the Genoese Cristoforo Colombo returned from his discovery of islands beyond the ocean, the two monarchs of a Spain-to-be, Ferdinand and Isabella, celebrated the conquest of Granada. Moorish refugees fleeing across the water to Ceuta and Mars El Kabir were followed by armored Spaniards who planted their flag over the nearest African ports. Isabella's confessor, Cardinal Ximenes, looked toward a new dominion in Africa as in the New World, to be Spanish and Christian. From their caravels and galleons the conquistadors landed their horses and cannon, to fortify themselves along the infidel coast, particularly in the Island (Algiers). Against such invaders the fugitive Moors and the native Berbers could fling only their anger, being powerless in their light sailing feluccas and fregatas to do more than stab and snatch at the Spanish convoys.

Then like eagles sighting strife on the land appeared the first of the sea rovers from the east. Ruthless as eagles, obedient to no laws, these looters of the sea had no kinship with the distressed Arab and Berber population except the tie of religion and a mutual hatred of the wealth-ridden Spaniards who covered their bodies with steel and slew human beings in their path with powder and lead.

These adventurers of the sea had the ships and the sagacity to meet the Spaniards in combat. The one who made himself most feared was Khair ad-Dın Barbarossa, who, called to the aid of Algiers, seized Algiers for himself.

(Do not think of these men as pirates, corsairs of the Barbary Coast, or even as "Algerine corsairs, from a pirates' nest." Those words did not exist at the time; they were coined later, to fit explanations in European histories. Think instead of the forces that met upon that sea, of the spread of two religions, the outward thrust of two continents upon the coast of a third, and the conflict that ensued between two empires, the Holy Roman and the Osmanli Turkish.)

Khair ad-Din Barbarossa

Suleiman was calling to him this man's bitter anger.

They say he was stout as a wrestler, and he trimmed his red beard close under his beak of a nose. They say he was good-natured but cruel when enraged. He was a seaman, he could sense the coming of a Borro, and he could pick his way through the sandy shallows of the Syrtes, and hide his vessels inside an island, in the hidden lagoon of Yerba. He had been afloat since he left his potter's wheel as a boy, one of the four sons of Jacob the Albanian, on Mitylene Island. One of his brothers had been killed at sea by the Europeans. Another, the older Uruj, with a beard like flame and a generous nature to hold to, had fought the invading Spaniards west from Tunis, as far as the Balearics, losing first an arm and then his life in so doing. Whereupon the youngest, Khair ad-Dın, had led his brother's ships westward again in the same reckless course. His crews had given him the nickname of the dead Uruj, Redbeard.

Grim Sultan Selim, pausing in his conquest of Egypt, heard the legend growing around the name of Barbarossa, and gave him the horsetail standard of a beylerbey, with a horse and sword added. From the Nile, Africa stretched westward before the eyes of the Turks, a new continent to be explored as the Europeans were exploring the Americas. Barbarossa found more use in the regiment of janizaris and the battery of heavy cannon Selim added to his gift.

The legend of Barbarossa continued to grow among the Europeans. He could not be found, yet he appeared everywhere. Spanish galleys caught him ferrying exiled Moors—who had no place to go by themselves—from Andalusia to Africa. Barbarossa added those galleys to his small fleet of thirty-five galliots. He collected papal royal galleys as well, and forced the crews to row them.

When Charles V, as King of Spain, ordered a purge of the remaining Moors (having first been released from his coronation oath to convert no person by force), Barbarossa raided his coast, guided by Moslems in Spain toward churches and garrisons inland. Getting clear with his spoil, he took off the Moslems as passengers. He ferried away seventy thousand in all, and these Moors, eaten by anger as deep as his own, made up the bulk of his crews.

Charles could not tolerate such vagabonds in the western Mediterranean. With Barbarossa there were Sinan, a Jew of Smyrna who could take the elevation of the sun by the butt of a crossbow, and *Cacca-diabolo*, Beat-the-Devil, with Salih Reis, a fat Arab of the Nile who steered Barbarossa's barge. The difficulty was to get the sea rovers out of there. Scorched from

Bujeya, they turned up in Algiers. The Spaniards held the Island, the *Peñón de Alger*, guarding the entrance to the scanty harbor. Tired of dodging past the island, which gave the city its name, Barbarossa pounded its fortifications down with captured cannon, and put its garrison to work building a serviceable breakwater out to sea.

What happened then at Algiers sent laughter far down the African coast. A Spanish relief fleet searching for the garrison on the island failed to recognize the changed shape of the island without its fort, or the city with a breakwater moving out to sea. So the Spaniards went on searching until they were hemmed in by Barbarossa's flotilla and captured entire. So a Spanish *capitana* ship joined the rover's fleet.

Barbarossa's luck, they called it. But it was more than luck he had. For one thing he intended to stay in Algiers where Charles least wanted him to be—within reach of the strait where the treasure fleets came in from the New World, and across from the coast of Spain itself. The rover had conceived a fondness for the town that straggled up a sunny hillside between defending walls. The palace of its late prince had pleasant palm gardens, an attractive home for a seaman. Around that home he settled Moorish artisans rescued from Spain. Around Algiers he scattered colonies of such industrious glassblowers, builders and metalworkers. They helped him set up foundries and dockyards in the enlarged harbor. After his fashion, Barbarossa was building a New Spain across from Barcelona.

This could not be tolerated. Charles gave the task of eliminating Barbarossa from the Spanish beachheads in Africa to the celebrated Andrea Doria, his Genoese admiral (a veteran of politics ashore more than of service at sea). How the rover would have fared alone against such a dominant empire will never be known. After the sailing season was ended by autumn storms in 1532, he received a message from Suleiman at Constantinople. The Sultan asked him to journey thither in person, to take command of the unhandy Turkish fleet.

Barbarossa was in no hurry to do so. In Algiers he was his own master; at sea he had become a match for Doria. Now that he felt old age coming upon him he relished the solace of rare wine, and the most shapely girls. Yet he recalled that Uruj had not lived as long; he wondered what he might accomplish against Charles and Andrea Doria with Osmanli wealth and power behind him. The thought was tempting, and Barbarossa for all his lusts was a devout Moslem. "If God has not appointed the hour of a man's death, how else can he be slain?" he asked, and went.

Unwillingly, he went because only from Suleiman could he gain security for his haven of Algiers. When early summer brought the wind fair astern, with the oar sweeps lashed outboard to catch the wind and the great lateen sail swelling over his loitering crew—Redbeard would have no galley slaves on his own vessel—he led the eighteen galleys of his fighting squadron out to his rendezvous with fate.

The course he followed would have been taken by no one else. North he headed to pick up plunder from the Spanish island of Elba, then sou'east to find and take along a Genoese corn convoy. Wide he swung around Malta with his masthead lookouts searching for a glint of red that might be the dreaded galleys of the Knights on cruise—then over to the Greek shores where Doria had been lurking. Missing Doria (who had heard of his coming and put in to Brindisi), he paused to inspect a Turkish fleet he encountered. Then, not to appear unduly eager, he beached his vessels under Gallipoli light to repaint and refurbish them while he waited for a pressing invitation to enter Turkish waters!

When at last the impatient Suleiman beheld Barbarossa rounding Serai Point, it was with pennons flying over the gleaming dark hulls and cannon firing a salute, and the captured Genoese craft towed behind. When the rover strode into Suleiman's presence in the Hall of Audience, it was as an independent monarch of the sea with eighteen captains rolling after him, and the spoils of Elba to set before the Sultan.

There must have been a moment of mutual examination when the most powerful monarch of the land faced the man who had become a legend on the sea. Suleiman beheld a massive, impatient figure, old and bronzed, with gray in his clipped beard. This impatience jarred upon the careful Turks. Barbarossa wanted no landsmen or soldiery on a vessel; he wanted no vessels ill found, with green wood in them—such as he had seen in the Turkish fleet at sea. He wanted full command, alone.

Suleiman wanted Barbarossa's secret of success. The man from Algiers had no secret; he built ships and he fought them.

Older members of the Divan shook their heads over Barbarossa.

"Have you not experienced pashas enough to serve you," they asked Suleiman, "that you show favor to this outcast son of a Christian potter? How will you trust such a man?"

Unable to decide, Suleiman dispatched Barbarossa inland through Asia to be examined by Ibrahim. The temperamental Vizir approved of the sea rover. "This is the man for us," he wrote his master. "Brave and careful, farsighted in war, enduring at work, steadfast when he meets with misfortune."

On his own account Suleiman reasoned that while the Turkish fleet had been unable to take the sea against Doria, that admiral in turn had been able to accomplish nothing against Barbarossa. Likewise his own adversary the Emperor had proved elusive upon the land but showed every evidence of cherishing his western Spanish half of the Mediterranean. It seemed as if Barbarossa, loosed upon the sea, might be the means of occupying all the attention of the European powers while the Sultan was absent in Asia.

Once he had made up his mind Suleiman gave the adventurer every aid in the great task—a jeweled sword, the rank of Kapu-tan Pasha (Captain of the Sea), the Arsenal, and the Golden Horn to build an entire new fleet to suit him.

From that day Barbarossa's restless energy transformed the Golden Horn, refitting vessels, launching new craft with officers on deck and salutes echoing, initiating Turkish shepherd boys and soldiers into the mysteries of rope and sail. Hugely he demanded, timber and cloth, hemp and tar, bronze cannon, brass astrolabes. Nowhere else could he have obtained all he wanted in that time. The Turks understood that he wanted a new fleet whole and manned, and eighty-four vessels were ready to put to sea in less than a year. Even so Barbarossa was not entirely satisfied. This new armada, he admitted, made a fine appearance, but such vessels with inexperienced crews would be a trouble rather than an aid to him in actual battle.

Perhaps the Sultan suspected the rover of wanting to go off again upon his small raiding ventures in the west, more probably he meant to pin the impetuous Barbarossa down to the command of the great new fleet that might in time be able to hold the eastern waters for the Turks. Certainly he exacted a pledge that his new Kaputan Pasha would not put to sea without all eighty-four sails following him. Barbarossa gave the pledge with mental reservation.

The two of them, however, evolved a plan of action that was startling in its scope. As kaputan of the Sultan, flying the green colors of the Osmanlis, Barbarossa faced potential enemies in papal shipping, in Neapolitan, Genoese, the galleys of the Knights of Malta, of Portugal as well as the sea forces of the Empire. Only the Venetian fleet was neutralized, by treaty, and the French by the inclination of its master, Francis.

Under such circumstances they planned to do four things: to recapture one at a time the European-held ports of Africa; to seize in the same manner the islands that provided Doria with bases at sea; to set up an offshore blockade along the critical Spanish coast; to retaliate for every raid on Africa by a raid on the European coasts.

That was a great task for one man to perform. It would take years. Yet in attempting it, the new Turkish fleet would challenge Charles's command of the Mediterranean. And whatever happened, Algiers would be well safeguarded.

In the spring of 1535 when Suleiman journeyed into Asia, Barbarossa rounded Serai Point with eighty-four sails following.

Charles Sails to Africa

He surprised the Europeans by appearing among them so promptly. He left the ill-found bulk of his new battle fleet behind in the Aegean ports for convoy duty. With a handy striking force, he passed through the tide-torn Messina Strait, storming and stripping Reggio, surprising eighteen galleys at Cetraro, landing elsewhere along the Italian coast as far up as Fondi, where he sent a landing force by night to loot the castle and carry off the lovely Giulia Gonzaga, widow of one of the Colonnas, sister to Joanna of Aragon, whose beauty had been sung by a concourse of Italian poets of love. The equally admired Giulia was awakened by her servants only in time to run from her bed, to mount an unsaddled horse and ride into the night. Some witnesses said Giulia had a nightgown on, others said she had none. However that may be, the one esquire who rode with her to safety was assassinated afterward by the Gonzaga family.

Nothing could have been better calculated to set the European courts by their ears, and to draw their sea commands to the coast at Rome. Whereupon Barbarossa resumed his strategic mission by doubling back to the African coast and taking Tunis, which had been held by one of the neglected Spanish garrisons. Having taken it, as at Algiers, he proceeded to install his own rulers and to use it as a base.

This in turn brought immediate reaction from the Europeans. (Suleiman was far distant in Asia by then.) It was bad enough to have the rover sheltered at Algiers; it was unendurable to have him quartered in the lagoon of Tunis within easy sail of

Sicily, at the African end of the land bridge, where he could intercept merchant fleets passing from the western to the eastern Mediterranean.

The next summer Charles himself embarked with 20,000 Spanish and German veterans and Portuguese volunteers in an armada of 600 sail, convoyed across by Doria with 62 galleys of the Empire, to retake Tunis.

By all the rules of warfare, whether on sea or land, Barbarossa should have withdrawn in his ships before the arrival of the Emperor. Whether he was too stubborn to do so, or whether he carried out the Sultan's behest to keep their European enemies occupied at all cost is not certain. But he stayed to defend Tunis.

Sinan the Jew and Beat-the-Devil were with him. The three brethren of the sea evidently expected that they might fare badly at the hands of the Emperor, because they hid away a dozen or fifteen of their handiest small galleys in the harbor of Bizerta, to the west. This escape fleet was concealed by stripping the masts, oars and cannon from the slender hulls and sinking them along the sandy beach.

These sixteenth-century war galleys, like modern destroyers, had peculiarities. Their great lateen sails were used only in cruising. Driven by fifty or more long oars, they could close an enemy, firing from the heavy cannon on the foredeck, striking with their massive bronze-tipped ram, throwing their force of two hundred or more fighting men across to the enemy's deck.

Built on the lines of modern racing shells (with beam less than one eighth their length), they were speedy enough under oars or sail to overhaul the lofty, tubby sailing galleons or caravels in short spurts; but they could not transport supplies sufficient for more than three or four days at sea, and in a storm they had to run for the nearest shelter. The galley slaves chained to the long oars also presented a problem, requiring food, and warders to guard them. When the crew and soldiers left the deck, in port, the oars had to be unshipped and towed away, to prevent the captive rowers taking the galley out to sea. In battle also the desperate galley slaves had to be watched. On Moslem craft the *Gallienji*, men chained to the ordeal of the oars, were captives from Christian vessels, and vice versa.

Barbarossa would have only Turks on the galleys under his immediate command. That made the handling of his squadron easier, eliminated the useless slave guards, and about doubled his fighting force in action.

Like the Turks, the Venetians still kept to their galleys—galliots being the smaller type, royal galleys the larger—while the Portuguese and Spanish navigators had developed the oceangoing sailing vessel with lofty sides and broadside batteries of guns. In a wind, they were a match for the more manageable war galleys. But the art of tacking was still novel, and in a calm the massive caravel type of vessel became little better than an inflammable drifting fort. A century would pass before it gained supremacy in the Mediterranean.

Charles had several of these broadside-gunned vessels in his armada, and one great carrack of the Knights of Rhodes, at Malta. In their passage to Tunis the Europeans failed to sight the galleys Barbarossa had hidden underwater at Bizerta.

At Tunis he made what preparation he could. Guns taken from his ships were mounted in the Goletta, "The Throat," the towerlike citadel that barred the way from the outer lagoon to the inner harbor. In that harbor he collected all the remaining vessels. Over the Goletta he put the sagacious Sinan in command, giving him the best of the Moorish boat crews and the janizaris. In all Barbarossa had about 5000 trained men and as many Berber tribesmen. To the townsfolk he said, "You've had letters from the unbelievers. I shall go out and fight. What will you do—remain in the city?"

"God forbid," they answered.

For a space until then Tunis, like Yerba, the isle of the "Lotus-eaters" near it, had known tranquillity. Unnoticed, Christian churches had survived by the river gardens. Pilgrims, bound for Kairouan, had paused at its mosques. There was no strength in Tunis to withstand the weapons of the professional soldiers of the Emperor.

For twenty-four days Sinan held the Goletta, while Barbarossa led sallies from the town. Then the great carrack, *St. Ann*, was brought close to the tower, to blast a breach in it, and the Knights spearheaded the attack that drove out Sinan and his men. Barbarossa joined him to make a stand between the Goletta and the town. The Berber tribesmen melted away, refusing to face the pikes and matchlocks of the armored Spaniards and Germans. Three trenches the Turks dug and held for a while, as they were forced back toward the city. With the Goletta they had lost their forty cannon and more than a hundred vessels.

They could not retreat into the town. Led by a captive Knight, the Christian galley slaves prisoned in the Kasaba had broken out and got at weapons in the Arsenal. Several thousand strong, the desperate prisoners held the streets.

From their last trench the surviving Turks disappeared at night. Barbarossa, Sinan and Beat-the-Devil got away with them. When search was made for them after three days they could not be found.

For those three days Charles gave the town over to his soldiers. The armed captives had got into the houses first, and there was fighting between them and the incoming troops over the spoil, while Tunis was stripped and burned. The Spanish and German professionals, loosed in a Moslem community, taught the inhabitants the meaning of savagery. Only remnants of families escaped out into the desert, or threw themselves from the walls.

Muley Hassan, the former prince of Tunis who had invoked the aid of the Emperor, tried to stop the pillaging. An observer relates that when Hassan interfered with soldiers who had caught a Moorish girl, the Moor spat in his face and allowed herself to be carried off.

Outside the walls a court painter, Jan Cornelis Vermeyen, set up the canvas on which he depicted Charles directing the triumphant siege. The operation at Tunis was altogether successful, but Charles did not linger. He arranged a hurried treaty with Hassan by which the prince paid annual tribute to Charles and ceded the Goletta to the Europeans. Thereafter the prince lived in his devastated city as no more than the pensioner of the Spaniards. The pilgrims Kairouan-bound avoided it and Hassan was killed after some years by his own son.

Strangely, Charles made no effort to extend his conquest along the African coast. Instead, he began to withdraw his great expedition toward Sicily. For this withdrawal Barbarossa may have been accountable.

When he disappeared, the old sea rover fled, enraged, straight to his hideaway at Bizerta. There he labored with desperation to get the hulls of his fourteen hidden galleys afloat and equipped again. Doria's cruisers sighted the apparition of a squadron coming up to the surface of the harbor, and a fleet was sent to head Barbarossa off. But he held back the Europeans with cannon at the harbor mouth until he was ready to sail, and when he did come out the European captains could not, or would not, stop him. They contented themselves with sailing in and looting Bizerta after he had gone.

Nursing his rage, Barbarossa headed for his old port of Algiers, expecting the invading armada to be close behind him. Learning at Algiers that it was loafing, instead, homeward by way of Sicily, he took the dozen-odd small galliots of Algiers along with him and disappeared again seaward.

He appeared next where he was least expected. On the island of Minorca at Port Mahon the lookouts were awaiting the return of the imperial fleet, since Charles, sailing from Barcelona, had passed the island on his way out. When they sighted a few galleys bearing in flying Spanish colors and the crew on the foredecks wearing Spanish clothing, they took them for the first of the returning armada. Salutes were fired, and throngs came down to the harbor, only to behold the incoming vessels board and pillage an anchored Portuguese galleon. After the masqueraders came the rest of Barbarossa's squadron, to storm the city and carry fire and sword through the island, as Charles had done at Tunis.

Out of Mahon the rovers sailed with 5700 captives. Before they cleared the island they encountered the first vessels of the armada, laden with spoils from Tunis. These Barbarossa gathered in, adding them to his growing fleet, freeing the Moslems from the rowing benches and chaining Christians in their places.

By the time Doria's battle fleet could reach the scene Barbarossa had disappeared again. Nor could he be found on the route back to Algiers. Instead, he was raiding the Spanish coast. When the exasperated admiral doubled back under orders from Charles to bring Barbarossa to him, dead or living, Barbarossa was back in Algiers with a sizable armada of his own.

When Charles was informed of that, he took measures to rid himself once and for all of the old man of the sea. By a liberal payment to a Levantine, he arranged to have Barbarossa assassinated at Algiers.

Charles returned home with what the *Brief World Happenings* calls "triumph and spoils." Throughout the Empire the triumph of Tunis was broadcast; poets published it in verse; to match Vermeyen's painting, a potter at Urbino burned the scene of the siege into a vase. Charles, as New World crusader and victor over the infidels, commemorated his achievement by creating a new order of chivalry. It had the "Cross of Tunis" as emblem, and the motto of *Barbaria*.

But the official triumph and the Order thereof did not prove convincing. Minorca lay like a blight on the sea, out from Barcelona.

Charles's success had been gained at the cost of something intangible. When he sailed again across the Mediterranean he found that the people of Africa would endure no second Tunis

And when Suleiman returned from Asia with the Turkish *asker* at the end of that year, he heard how the Holy Roman Emperor had gutted a Moslem city that had been under Turkish safeguard. Immediately the Sultan sent for Barbarossa to report with all his force at the Serai in Constantinople.

The seafarer obeyed at once, leaving Algiers in the charge of his son and the loyal eunuch Hassan Agha.

He never saw his city again.

Barbarossa Sells Himself

This time he indulged in no theatricals on the way to Suleiman. He merely spread a report that he was northbound to raid Majorca—this for the benefit of European spies. To provide another false lead he instructed Hassan Agha to raid Sardinia instead. Then, out of sight of land, he changed course and headed due east with all the speed of wind and oar sweeps. It being midwinter, he encountered no hostile sails, for Doria hugged the ports after the storms began.

Driving east through the lash of rain and battering of wind, the aging rover warmed himself with wine. Drunk and moody, he cursed the name of Charles, for Piali told him that Charles had paid good gold to have him assassinated at Tunis—so the assassin had assured Piali, for more gold in hand. He cursed the sap-green young Piali, a school lad of the Osmanlis, forever drawing charts of the coasts they ran down. (This Piali had even turned up in the Arsenal a map drawn by a Turk named Piri copied from one made by a Genoese infidel Colombo. It showed a new land beyond the ocean, and it had been captured on a Spanish galleon. Barbarossa had no interest in the *ocean*, except as treasure fleets hove in from it.)

"The Emperor is a coin-kisser," Barbarossa said. "He bid too mean a sum for my life."

"I will tell him that," Piali agreed, glib.

Barbarossa cursed Andrea Doria, the lord admiral, because he had passed the word that he—Barbarossa—hid himself out of sight. "Doria's a politician," he told his lieutenants, aggrieved. "He is an ignorant man who reads no books. By day my pennon's at the masthead—by night my beacon lanterns are lit. Can I help, if he fails to find me?"

"It might be worth while," suggested Sinan, after considering, "to help him find you."

"By God's eyes—has not Charles offered him reward to do it?"

"Then do you offer more. Who hunts a bargain may trick himself."

Even in drink Barbarossa remembered this. He had sixty-five years of age, and he had nothing to lose except a few years more. It grieved him to leave Algiers behind him. And he felt fear of Suleiman, who had been out of his sight for a year and eight months, in which time—by Barbarossa's reckoning—he had lost Tunis and fled like a goat from the imperial soldiery. No, Barbarossa anticipated no friendly greeting from the Sultan his master. It may have crossed his mind to sheer away from the Dardanelles, and run for it. To what port?

Only Venice lay open to him. For the captains of the Illustrious Signory he had no love. They burned scented oil on their aft decks to sweeten the stench from the slave benches; they lamented their loss after the Turks took from them their Black Sea *fondacos* and made them buy the shipments of silk and spice they had conjured aforetime from the east out of Aden and Malabar . . . their Archipelago made a chain of islands, barring his way to the Dardanelles. . . . Barbarossa would not sell himself to thieving merchants, who mocked his rank of

177

Captain of the Sea. No, he would *be* the captain of their sea, which they married every year, like a new woman, flinging a gold ring into the water. He would never sell himself . . . but he might——

At the Serai Barbarossa hauled his bulk up the stone steps of the landing, his narrowed eyes seeing no one of rank to greet him, only feather-capped gardeners who ushered him to a steward with a staff, who salaamed silently and turned before him, not to the door of the Throne Room Within but to the guards who were like statues before the door of the Divan.

For once afraid, Barbarossa strode in, his hand hooking toward the hilt of his sword in readiness to cut at any man, pasha or swordbearer, who tried to seize him as the commander who had failed, and had lost Tunis. From the couch against the wall three pashas faced him, and Ibrahim, who had been his friend, was not among them. In Ibrahim's place sat Lutfi, a dour soldier.

Scanning them, waiting for their accusation, Barbarossa was at last aware of Suleiman seated alone at the side. The Sultan's face was lined, his gray eyes heavy.

"May God bless and protect the Lord of the Two Worlds"—he muttered the customary words.

"May God give health to my Beylerbey of the Sea."

It took Barbarossa a moment to remember that this was a new word. He did not know what it meant. "What?" he asked bluntly.

Patiently Suleiman explained, his face unchanged. "As Lord of the Sea you will have the rank of pasha, being the fourth commander of my government." Suddenly Suleiman smiled, as if at a pleasant thought. "The sea is no one place; it is not a grant of land, but I think you will know how to make use of it. Perhaps, instead of three horsetails to your standard, you would like to have three stern lanterns."

The three lanterns struck Barbarossa more forcibly than the fact that he was now one of the great commanders. Since Suleiman had said it, it was so. To the listening men of the Divan,

Suleiman said: "The reward is given Khair ad-Din because for one year and eight moons he held in play all the enemies in Europe; he requited the loss of Tunis by the raid on Spain."

The blood warmed in Barbarossa's veins, when he was seated within the Divan. Such a craving seized him for wine that he hardly heard the words of the discussion that followed. But his sharp instinct caught the sense . . . Charles must atone for his act in sacking a Moslem city to which he had no claim . . . in moodiness, Suleiman revealed that war was at hand by land and sea . . . the King of France was moving against the Emperor again, and in alliance with Francis the Turkish *asker* would cross to Italy . . . Barbarossa must lead out a greater fleet to ferry the army, and he could play hide-and-seek no longer around islands.

"Then it will be the Adriatic!" he blurted.

It surprised them that he should think it strange. He was thinking of the Venetians. *They* would be done with marrying the sea, which would become a Turkish sea——

Not until long afterward did he realize that Suleiman had caught him and held him to the command of a hundred and forty vessels, and more than that, to act as escort to the army.

For the rest of that winter flares burned at night along the Arsenal shipways, while Barbarossa stormed the length of the Horn conjuring up a new navy, with long basilisk cannon to throw shot two hands' breadths around, and janizaris to serve for marine guards.

Fair weather came, and it maddened Barbarossa to hear that Doria was at sea with nothing to oppose him. On the plea that the grain fleets were on the way from Egypt unprotected, Barbarossa got permission to go out with forty galleys, claiming the rest would follow when finished. He brought in the grain convoys safely.

Meanwhile, finding it impossible to wait passively, he had got into contact with Doria in unlooked-for fashion. Whose idea it was, and who first attempted to carry it out, remains obscure. But this much is clear. In some way Barbarossa spread the rumor that he was ready to sell himself.

European espionage had diagnosed the preparations in the Golden Horn pretty accurately. Rome, Venice, Vienna and Valladolid realized that the Turkish objective would be the Italian coast. There were rumors as to Barbarossa's disgruntlement, and antagonism to Lutfi Pasha, commander of the land army.

At this point Charles received a message from the Beylerbey of the Sea—that if Tunis were evacuated and left to him, he might see fit to forsake Suleiman and the Turks, and retire peaceably to Africa.

Apparently Charles was too wary to believe that the man he had arranged to assassinate would come over to him; still the message must have been discussed with Doria. The menace of a larger Turkish fleet led by the seaman of Algiers was very great. (And Doria, always a politician first, had at heart only the safeguarding of his native Genoa and his own glory.)

Neither Charles nor Doria could forget the tempting possibilities in the missive of the Beylerbey of the Sea. Doria himself had shifted sides before. Why should not a pirate change his flag? If Doria could remove Barbarossa *and* contrive the destruction of the new Turkish fleet——

Months later Andrea Doria yielded to this irresistible temptation. At the tiny port of Parga, looking out at Corfu, he contrived to meet a spokesman for Barbarossa. Doria had Gonzaga, Viceroy of Sicily, with him, empowered to treat for the Emperor. The discussion at Parga went on for days, Charles at first refusing to give up Tunis, then agreeing—if Barbarossa would first burn the Turkish ships that he could not induce to sail away with him.

Barbarossa would not do that. But the Europeans left Parga with the impression that, soon or late, the Sultan's old man of the sea might be won over. And the effect of that impression was disastrous in turn to Doria and to Charles.

The Instructions of Monsieur de la Forêt

It might not have happened, except for Francis I. Suleiman was then deeply preoccupied with Asia and was building another fleet on the Nile, to be dragged and sailed over the narrow isthmus separating the Mediterranean from the Red Sea, to explore the eastern oceans.

However, Francis, with his strange admixture of sagacity and vainglory, had conceived of a way to cripple his great adversary Charles by striking him in a vital spot, Italy, with the most dangerous of weapons, the Osmanli Turks.

To accomplish this desired end, Francis had sent a cultured and able diplomat, one Jean de la Forêt, to the Gate as his first ambassador to the Turks. To negotiate with the enigmatic Suleiman, De la Forêt was provided with secret instructions. (After calling on Barbarossa, to urge the admiral privately to menace the coasts of Spain "with all manner of war." As reward, Francis promised to ensure the "lord Haradin" full possession of Algiers and Tunis.)

From Suleiman De la Forêt was to obtain "a million of gold, which will be no inconvenience to the Grand Signior." After financing the French King in this fashion, Suleiman was to invade southern Italy with all the strength of the Turkish army and capture Naples, while Francis took up again his periodic march upon northern Italy beyond the Alps.

So much Suleiman was to do for Francis. In return the secret instructions of the Most Christian King offered the Turk the following: a French ambassador, a perpetual treaty of alliance, friendship and trade, as between equals; the pledge of Francis "to hold all Christianity quiet, without war undertaken against him . . . in a universal peace."

This last was to be achieved—and Francis must have known how greatly it would interest Suleiman—by weakening the stubborn Charles until "he can no more resist," and accordingly "will agree to the said universal peace."

So ran Francis' instructions to De la Forêt, who carried them out ably enough. Suleiman, who lacked Ibrahim's clairvoyant grasp of such a situation, wanted the treaty of alliance but deeply distrusted the military venture attached to it. He told De la Forêt, "How can I have trust in him? He has always promised more than he can carry out."

Still it was a great temptation—to draw down Charles where he would have to meet the Turkish army, and thereby to gain peace along the European borderlands. Suleiman agreed, with some mental reservations. But unmistakably he granted wholeheartedly the new treaty of perpetual friendship and commerce to bind the Turks to the cultured French.

By it he granted their merchant fleets freedom from duty and the rights of the Turks themselves to trade throughout his dominions, while they retained the privileges of foreigners. Their churches, their law courts, and all personal affairs would be extraterritorial in Turkey—inviolate under the French flag.

This treaty, known as that of the "capitulations," established the French as the most favored nation. Suleiman had achieved his wish to join in active contact with one of the greatest European nations. It also established the principle of extraterritoriality for Europeans among orientals, and it became a model for future treaties as far distant as China.

It had very vital immediate consequences. Turkish soil became a kind of crown colony of France. It became almost the first French outlet across the seas. (Just then Jacques Cartier was questing along the newly discovered St. Lawrence River in the New World, seeking a passage to Cathay in the Old World.)

Necessarily, other European merchant craft had to come in under French colors, to obtain the capitulations privileges. Since the French had a protectorate over their churches, that protectorate extended—by the wording of the treaty—to the Holy Places in Jerusalem.

To Francis, this treaty of February 1536 served to cover the secret military compact. It was a thin cover, and barely tempered the European condemnation of "the impious alliance" between the Most Christian King of France and the Osmanli Sultan.

To the Venetians it acted like a dagger thrust. Even in Turkish waters they were to be superseded and their profitable oriental trade was to be tapped by another rising nation. They reacted with desperation.

In February 1537 a French army threaded through the mountains to march into Piedmont. Suleiman carried out his part of the bargain. With the Army of Europe he moved toward the Strait of Otranto, at the mouth of the Adriatic. And Barbarossa took to the sea again with his new battle fleet, prepared to make the most of all that came his way.

Foray into Italy

The heel of the boot of Italy lies flat as the sea itself. On the far side of the strait, mountains rise behind the small fishing port of Avlona. Out of these mountains came the Turkish advance, down to Avlona. By early summer Barbarossa's galleys cruised the strait, towing huge flatboats into Avlona.

When Barbarossa's flagship passed a Venetian craft he hailed: "You can have done with marrying the sea; the sea is ours now."

He ferried the advance of the *asker* across—some 10,000 horsemen under Lutfi Pasha. For the first time in fifty-eight years the Turks were on the Italian peninsula. They stormed the small port of Castro, breaking their agreement to let the defenders go free. They spread out swiftly over the flat, marshy heel of the land, throwing screening forces around Otranto and strong Brindisi, striking inland toward the mountains and Naples.

"We will do the choosing of the next Pope in Rome," Lutfi Pasha's riders taunted the countryside. The main force under Suleiman was preparing to follow, in July.

Then the kaleidoscope of European forces shifted abruptly. Word reached Avlona that Francis, who should have been invading Milan, had signed a ten-year truce with his enemy Charles, and had ended hostilities in the north!

For the second time the Sultan's slippery ally had abandoned him in mid-campaign. More than that, the Venetian commanders at sea were in no mood to watch the seizure of the mouth of the Adriatic peaceably. The tensity of the situation exploded in local conflicts. A dozen Turkish galleys were hunted into a nest of islands and destroyed by a Venetian naval force on the pretense that they had been identified as pirates. A great ship bearing Yunis Bey, the long-time ambassador of the Gate to Venice, was fired on and disabled on the excuse that it made no recognition signal.

The French fleet remained invisible. Within these few days Suleiman found himself deserted by Francis and engaged with the full power of the Empire, Venice and the Papacy—the last two Francis had claimed to be friendly to him.

Quickly, early in August, he recalled Lutfi Pasha and the raiding cavalry, which came back burdened with spoil and captives. They had been on Italian soil only sixteen days. When the bulk of them were safe across the strait Suleiman moved to attack the island of Corfu, the key of the strait held by the Venetians.

Both the Venetian fleet and Doria's battle force were converging on the strait. The lord admiral caught a dozen Turkish transports, no more.

By August 18, Barbarossa had his grip on the narrow passage between the lovely island of Corfu lying like a jewel before the bare coast, while the siege train of the Turkish *asker* was ferried over. Turkish horsemen slashed into the fertile hills of the island. Only the citadel of San' Angelo held out on a rock height.

The galleys tried to batter down the strong walls of San' Angelo and were driven off with loss. The defenders, desperate, drove out the inhabitants who were physically unable to man the walls. Heavy Turkish siege guns were hoisted to rock peaks to bear down into the citadel. It held out, as Rhodes had held so long, under the direction of a skilled artillerist.

On September 6, Suleiman halted the attack and ordered a withdrawal from Corfu. Barbarossa argued against it bitterly.

"So much effort and cost need not be lost. Only a little time, and we can take the place."

Suleiman's temper flared. "Such a place as this," he retorted, "is not worth the life of one man of mine!"

He would not keep the pick of his army on the island, while the European fleets were gathering in the offing. He left Corfu desolate after the eighteen days, as Barbarossa had left Minorca.

The withdrawal was accomplished safely September 15. In spite of rain and wind, Barbarossa stretched an effective moving bridge of boats over the half-mile strip of water to the mainland, ferrying across guns, horses and baggage with the masses of prisoners.

Some of the prisoners were released, however, and shipped back to Castro on the Italian shore. Suleiman had learned of the breach of faith by which the Castro garrison had been taken, and he returned them to their city after executing the Turkish officer who had broken his pledge to let them go free.

So far nothing very serious had happened to the Europeans. What befell now, in the late autumn, was terrifying. As soon as the last of the Turkish army landed safely on the Dalmatian coast, Barbarossa was free to go his own way with the battle fleet.

From Corfu at the Adriatic's mouth, the Greek islands lie in a vast semicircle all the way to Rhodes within sight of the Turkish mainland. They rise like the summits of unearthly hills from the blue of the sea. Their very names have inspired poems. Lesbos and Andros—Aegina and Mitylene, where Barbarossa had been born.

He knew them. He saw them now as a barrier flung across his sea, feudal demesnes of Cornaros and Mocenigos who combed them for strong slaves to pull their oars.

Through them he swept that autumn with his amphibious force of galleys and transports filled with the troops of Lutfi Pasha, his rival. Ravaging Cephalonia, the guardian of the Gulf of Corinth, passing by mountainous Zante, rounding Cape Matapan to strike at Aegina, he sailed down the Archipelago. Often the lovely islands where the folk tended olive groves and listened to songs of forgotten times had no thought of war. Their ports were seized, their hill castles battered down, fields and villages stripped and young people herded off as slaves.

Over mighty Crete Barbarossa swept, passing by its stronghold of Candia. On the mainland of Greece the last remaining Venetian ports, Nauplia and Malvasia, defended themselves and weathered the storm.

Doria lacked the force, or perhaps the inclination, to challenge Barbarossa's sweep of the eastern sea.

Hajji Khalifa, the matter-of-fact Turkish historian of the sea, relates that Barbarossa captured twelve islands and plundered thirteen more. Of captives the Turks took 16,000 with spoil appraised in Constantinople at 400,000 gold sequins. By so doing Barbarossa had won the hostile bases at sea near Greece, and—by his own reckoning—had avenged Tunis. Moreover, he had rid himself of the task of guarding the Aegean, which had become a Turkish lake. (Almost a century would pass before European fleets, except for the privileged French, would enter its waters again.)

When Barbarossa came back at last to the Golden Horn, he

led in to Suleiman a parade of two hundred boys in scarlet carrying gold and silver, and as many infidels with purses slung over their shoulders, and as many more with bales of fine cloth. So says Hajji Khalifa.

This bit of theater probably impressed the bystanders more than Suleiman. Yet in the short space of three years he had gained full confidence in his Beylerbey of the Sea. The sagacious son of a Christian potter had proved himself right in the pitiless test of conflict. Barbarossa preferred to have the Venetians open enemies rather than shifty friends. And certainly the old man had drawn down on himself the full energy of the Emperor and the Doge alike. Assuredly now they would have to challenge Barbarossa or lose the command of the Mediterranean.

It suited Suleiman to have the conflict take its course out to sea, away from his land frontier and people.

Very soon he put the newly captured island empire in the name of Barbarossa, thus giving the old man land on the face of the water, to justify his title of Beylerbey, or Governor-Commander of the Sea.

The Lost Army and the Holy League

Already, late that autumn, the two Hapsburgs had tried to strike back at him by land.

Behind the Dalmatian coast, where he had been occupied then, the mountains rise, wave on wave, their upland valleys set with the stone villages of the Serbs and Bosnians. Down the far side of that hinterland—Yugoslavia today—the river Drave winds to the Danube.

Down that river Drave an Austrian army had felt its way far into Turkish territory.

It had started out at command of the Hapsburgs. Charles had wanted his brother to create a diversion by moving against

187

the Turks from Austria. Ferdinand had broken his pledged peace with Suleiman, to send the eastern field army of the Empire down against the Turkish communications. He did the very thing Charles had refused to do five years before when Suleiman had waited for him at Güns. Ferdinand had sent the field army of about 20,000—almost the strength of the Hungarians at Mohács. "Horsemen of Carinthia, and Saxony, and Thuringia," the *Brief World Happenings* relates, "footmen of Franconia, Austria and Bohemia."

It was commanded by John Katzianer and Ludwig Lodron, both veterans of the defense of Vienna eight years before. It descended the Drave, in obedience to orders, and reached Eszék far within the Osmanli lands, where a bridge crossed the Drave, on the main highway from Belgrade to Buda. Apparently unopposed, it settled down to besiege Eszék, in correct military procedure.

Very soon the army perceived that it had camped in the midst of mounted Turkish forces, come from Belgrade way. No more than an easy day's ride distant lay the marshy field of Mohács. The army of Katzianer felt its first privation when supplies ran short because the foragers brought in nothing from the countryside, cleared of grain and cattle by the invisible enemy.

Late in November Katzianer and Lodron began to retreat through the forests of the Drave. The retreat became a march of terror. The road was blocked by felled trees, so that the wagon train had to be abandoned. The Hungarian hussars deserted at night. Cannon were left behind, and powder kegs burned.

Hunger weakened the marching column. The dark forest took hourly toll of the men; flights of arrows swept down from the slopes; charging horsemen cut into the column.

Then panic seized it during a night. Katzianer made his escape alone, leaving his tent standing, with silver plate and servants. A veteran German pikeman taunted Lodron: "I can see easily enough that you will not run away—on that fine racing horse." Lodron dismounted and slashed his sword through the tendons of the charger. "Now you can see that I will stay with you."

"After that," the *Brief Happenings* relates, "it was a pitiful thing how almost every man, whether horsed or foot, who had not fled from the battle was slain by the charging enemy."

The lost army had been trying to reach the citadel of Valpo, where a narrow ravine might have given it a chance to check the pursuing Turks. People throughout the Empire heard of the "rout of Valpo."

The memory was still stark when Richard Knolles wrote: "This shameful overthrow at *Exek* was reported to have exceeded the most grievous overthrows that the Christians had received in any former time—for the flower both of horse and foot was there lost, so that many provinces were filled with heaviness and mourning. For it never chanced before that the Turks got such a victory without some loss."

The unfortunate Katzianer was almost the only survivor to reach Ferdinand's court. Imprisoned by his master there, for cowardice, he escaped and took refuge with the Turks, who treated him with contemptuous indifference. Years later when they captured a peculiarly large cannon from the Austrians, they gave it a name, as they did habitually. It was a Katzianer cannon.

Again in that winter of 1537–38 fear made itself felt in the western courts. No one could be certain whether the Turks would advance in the coming summer by land or sea. Vienna, without an army, called for aid and the Pope, Paul III, declared that a crusade must save Europe; Charles tried to strengthen his defense of Naples, while Venice in desperation levied a tax of five tenths on the capital goods of its merchant families. Out of this mutual need, the Holy League was formed, and signed by the Pope, the Emperor and the Doge, with Ferdinand also a member.

Perhaps the signers of the League placed their hope in an all-powerful armada. For they agreed beforehand on the rewards of victory. Venice was to gain back all her islands, as well as Castel Nuovo and Avlona on the Dalmatian coast; the Emperor all the territory in Europe that had once belonged to the Eastern Roman Empire; the Papacy would receive such lands as it desired.

Now here is something extraordinary. The Holy League, hastily arranged to defend its members, agrees within itself how the spoils are to be divided. After victory, the Osmanli Empire is to be partitioned. The Venetians, that is, shall gain back all that Venice ever held in its glory as far as the Dardanelles; the Empire shall recover the grandeur of ancient Rome, even to Constantinople itself. The Turks, apparently, must be thrust back across the Dardanelles and the Bosphorus into Asia from which they emerged a century before.

Grant that the League expected victory from the superior strength of its armada; concede that Doria hoped just then to buy over Barbarossa, still this concept of conquest after victory remains fantastic. And Charles, then in the prime of his energy, capable of subtle manipulation of thrones, marriages, and feudal claims, was in no respect a fool; the harassed lords of the Illustrious Signory were even more astute.

Jealousy appears here, with distrust. We imagine the once potent sea lords laying down their claims to irredenta. Hearing those claims to lost islands and trading ports at sea, the impatient spokesmen of the Empire raised their own claims to everything on land.

Listen in for a moment to the debate going on between the senators in Venice. One of the Cornaros is speaking—Mark Antony Cornaro. . . . "You have agreed to a League . . . you have felt that there would be more glory, more security in your union with the Christians than in the peace with the Turks.

"Today, after four months, after our armed forces have ravaged certain lands of the Sultan . . . can we renew the negotia-

190

tions with him of which we ourselves broke the binding thread? Can we obtain security by showing hesitation in such a moment? Only by courage can we vanquish danger!"

Another senator rises in rebuttal Francis Foscari is a councilor old and bitter with his experience of adversity. "I do not share either that opinion or that hope. Today . . . I can only take account of circumstances as they actually are, not as our illusions or our pledges make them appear to us. . . . I can't think how this confidence in ourselves is suddenly born, or this blind faith in the promises of princes who have tricked us so often. In these circumstances a mistake would be shameful and its consequences could be cruel.

"I fear that a fatal optimism is drawing us toward ruin . . . we pretend to forget that two days ago one of our army captains complained of the delay in paying his men, and warned us—too outspokenly no doubt—to make peace if we could not pay the expenses of war. Every day it is necessary to increase the charges on our people. It is a great mistake to believe that a war which costs more than two hundred thousand ducats a month can be carried on by imposing extraordinary sacrifice on ordinary citizens."

As for the League itself, Councilor Foscari says, it can only languish as long as undeclared war exists between the King of France and the Emperor. Then he asks what peace with the Turks might mean.

"We are told this peace would be neither assured nor glorious. I do not know how to guarantee that it would be what we desire, but I do believe it would shelter us from the present peril. Such a peace is not impossible. The Grand Vizir has constantly offered it and wanted it. He is at cross-purposes with Barbarossa, who grows in favor through war. Barbarossa himself wishes peace to go off to enjoy his rule in Algiers. As to the distrust that Suleiman has, we are told, of our friendship—I see no evidence of it. He has observed the thirty-year-old treaty of accord between us. Even now, he offers to continue it. If he has committed acts of violence against us, it is only just to recognize that he has not done so without provocation. We have, perhaps, less to complain of him, than he has of us.

"If the Turks had resolved, as some people pretend, on the downfall of our republic, what better opportunity could they have wished than that offered them some years ago, when all the [European] princes were aligned against us,[1] and we had neither resources nor outside aid?

"The empire of the Turks is immense; they are abundantly provided with all that is necessary for war; their military discipline could serve as an example to the Christians. What can be attempted against such an enemy?"

Yet the Senate declares for war. The Emperor will pay one half the cost of a great armada, the Pope one sixth; Venice will contribute 110 galleys, the Knights of Malta 10. Gold and ships arrive slowly; grain fails to come from the Spanish ports after the harvest. The generalissimo of the Serene Republic demands that the fleet put to sea regardless; Doria will not move until he gets the last 50 galleys which in turn wait at Sicily for their contingent of soldiery from Spain.

Then Andrea Doria goes to Parga, not far down the coast, to attempt to buy Barbarossa. He comes back with a thought that Barbarossa *may* betray the Turks.

So it is late in the sailing season, September 7, before the great armada puts out from the shelter of Corfu. But such power has never been seen before in the Mediterranean. The long galleys number 202, the sturdy transports 100, and they carry 2000 cannon; they bear with them 20,000 Italians, as many Germans, and 10,000 armored Spaniards. Even more, a new power lies in five huge sailing galleons with timbered sides proof against ramming, and broadside cannon able to beat off the light galleys of the Turks.

[1]The League of Cambrai, 1508, by which the French King and Maximilian the Emperor with the Pope Julius II expected to partition off Venice.

Seven flags fly over these ships, bearing the eagles of the Empire, the crossed keys of the Papacy, the lion of St. Mark, the castle of Genoa, the cross of Malta, the shield of Spain and the crown of Portugal.

Venetian scouts have tracked the Turkish fleet coming up, around Matapan, passing Santa Maura Island, and turning into the landlocked Gulf of Arta, no more than a half day's sail away.

There Barbarossa is caught.

The Duel off Prevesa

For once Barbarossa had displayed caution. He had sheltered himself in the gulf, oiling the keels of the galleys and refitting while he waited for Salih Reis to join with the last-built squadron of twenty galleys from Constantinople. After these came in, his strength was 120 galleys and some supply vessels. He had no heavy galleons that the Turks called floating castles. By the reports of his scouts he knew that he was outnumbered three to two in vessels, and two to one in guns and men.

Presently the Turkish lookouts could see that for themselves because the European armada came into sight, cruising back and forth with all standards displayed.

The winding Gulf of Arta is spacious as a miniature inland sea. Mountain walls hem it in, except for the narrow entrance where a bar makes passage difficult in a strong surf. The town of Prevesa at the entrance gave further protection. (Off Prevesa in Roman days the fleet of Mark Antony and Cleopatra had gone down to defeat, at Actium.)

Barbarossa had occupied the gulf and the town.

Such was the situation in mid-September 1538, at Prevesa. The Beylerbey of the Sea was holed-in at the great gulf, waiting to discover if his adversary, the lord admiral of the League, would make the mistake of trying to force the treacherous entrance. Doria's five dreadnoughts could not come in over the treacherous bar, and his galleys would be crowded inevitably in the narrow passage, while the Turkish fleet lay in line of battle across the miles of the tranquil gulf. Doria made no such mistake.

Restive and anxious, Barbarossa then took out a portion of his fleet when the sea appeared clear beyond the entrance. He met heavy long-range fire from the Venetian fleet, and turned back at his leisure. His trick—if trick it was—failed to draw the main armada after him in pursuit. Again he was locked up securely behind his mountains. Again Doria waited and watched offshore.

By then the autumn storms that sweep the Adriatic with hurricane force might begin any day. And Barbarossa displayed irresolution. Here he was immobilized with a massive battle fleet, very different from his speedy striking force of a dozen galleys which he had manipulated deftly out of Africa. What was he to do?

He had a heavy responsibility. Lutfi Pasha had been dismissed from command after the failure at Corfu the year before. Suleiman appeared to be thoroughly disgusted with war as waged in Europe and had taken himself off earlier in the summer with his household army to the east—to the steppes above the Black Sea where he was meeting the Krim Khan. Alone, Barbarossa faced the seven standards of Europe. He had never beheld such power at sea before. No doubt he pondered the strength of the floating castles.

The army officers with him urged that the troops be landed from his vessels, with guns, to fortify the land approaches to the gulf. They could hold Prevesa and its mountains, they said, forever. But Barbarossa did not think Doria would attempt a landing.

His sea rovers begged to be led out. Even if outnumbered, they felt their craft to be more weatherly and handier than the European ships. Salih Reis, Sinan, Beat-the-Devil, pleaded to get loose at sea. A newcomer, Torgut, son of an Anatolian peas-

ant who had served as pilot, kept at Barbarossa's side, pointing
seaward. (The Europeans called him Dragut and were to know
him only too well in years to come.)

So the young lieutenants urged. Barbarossa shook his head.
Out there were the new floating castles. He had counted their
guns. Around them Doria's galleys could mass, as an army
stands upon a citadel. The broadside guns of the castles of the
sea could fire over the low-lying galleys. That was what Doria
wanted—for the Turks to sally out against his fortress of ships
at sea. Could Barbarossa risk the loss of the Osmanli battle
fleet?

An old eunuch spoke up, a messenger, acting as observer for
Suleiman. "What words are these?" he demanded. "You are the
Beylerbey of the Sea. Has our master not given you ships
enough, and more men and guns than you asked for? Out there
is the enemy of our master. Why do you wait here as if drunk or
sleeping?"

The taunt must have stung Barbarossa to the heart. At the
first chance he came out, to fight.

In the hope of decoying the Turks out again, Doria had
drawn off his main fleet toward Santa Maura, twenty miles to
the south, leaving only a screening force to watch Prevesa.

But Barbarossa started his squadrons out the entrance at midnight, scattering the screening force. Before the dawn of a
misty day, September 28, he had his fleet safely out and formed,
hugging the coast.

What happened then off Prevesa has been muted down in the
pages of European histories. Doria's vague excuses, the spiteful
resentment of the Venetians, the silence of the chroniclers who
had written down the strength of the armada, and the glory of
the victory to be gained by the Christians, the taciturn com-
ments of the lieutenant of the Grand Master of the Knights of
St. John, of Malta—all these will give you impressions of three
different battles, or of no battle at all. Out of this confusion of

tales modern naval historians have picked one certain outstanding fact—the fight of the great Venetian all-gun carracks against the Turkish galleys. So they have managed to add the semblance of a fourth battle to the others.

Yet what happened is clear enough.

Andrea Doria says, and it is true, that at dawn of that day he was heading offshore, to draw the Turks out of their impregnable gulf. Informed that the entire Turkish fleet had emerged and was hugging the coast, he kept on with his maneuver to decoy them into open sea.

The wind was light and fitful from the west, against Barbarossa. The huge sailing vessels, either unable to clear the coast or left purposely by Doria to engage the Turkish galleys, fell behind, and were becalmed after the first hours.

The masthead lookouts on the Turkish vessels sighted Doria's forest of masts off the island of Santa Maura soon after daybreak. Barbarossa signaled his captains to follow him and went out after the Europeans. He struck the floating castles first, some five of them.

The engagement began around Conduliniero's great carrack. The heavy projectiles of its powerful battery beat off the first wave of galleys. One was struck by a 150-pound shot that raked it from bow to steering platform.

Barbarossa drew off and sent in his speedier galleys to fire their heavy bow guns and veer off behind the smoke. By midmorning the carrack was burning, and in the dead calm the smoke and mist afforded a screen to the galleys, which worked in closer.

Conduliniero's ship became a dismasted drifting hulk, saved by its broadside batteries that aimed at the water, the shot ricocheting among the galleys. Two other sea castles burned to the water and were abandoned. Another, dismasted, drifted off into the mist. By early afternoon the galleons were out of action.

On Doria's flagship, miles away, the commanders of the Roman and Venetian fleets, Cornero and Grimani, appeared. Tense with anger, they demanded that the order be given to close the enemy, now in scattered formation around the hulks of the galleons. "If you think we are afraid," they cried, "then give the order to attack that we would have given before now, if we had held command."

Doria retorted that the other fleets must follow his, and he would signal the proper time for action. If they obeyed orders, they would catch the Turkish armament entire.

Barbarossa was heading after the European array with his battered galleys, the weather thickening. He neared Santa Maura and Doria still withdrew, losing touch with the wings of his disordered formation.

The squadrons that got in Barbarossa's way were driven off the Turkish wedge. Two Christian galleys trying to rejoin their command found themselves in the mass of Turks and hauled down their colors.

So it happened at Prevesa as it happens sometimes at sea through the centuries—the greater fleet, attempting to maneuver under divided, uncertain leadership, was driven by the smaller fleet closing to fight.

Call it a mystery of the sea, say that Doria, an old man, was befuddled by his attempts to maneuver, admit that panic seized the Europeans, as you please. At the end of the afternoon, with wind gusts striking down the Adriatic, driving the mist like smoke, the Corneros, the Condulinieros and the Grimanis ran before Salih Reis, Beat-the-Devil, Sinan and the ruthless Torgut.

At the first rain squall Doria signaled withdrawal and fled north himself before the wind. The lash of rain put out the beacon lights on the admiral's ship.

Following hard after Doria, Barbarossa saw the guide lights go out. And he mocked Andrea Doria for it, saying that the lord admiral had doused his lights, to escape.

Then wind and darkness ended the conflict.

When the two fleets finally met again it was up the Adriatic, four hundred miles north of Prevesa, far above Corfu. Barbarossa held the Adriatic, and Doria's remaining vessels were sheltered in the Gulf of Cattaro, by Castel Nuovo. There they stayed.

Then was when the Borro struck the Adriatic, the hurricane out of the northwest. Caught at sea by the storm, Barbarossa lost thirty galleys. Thereafter Doria claimed that he had preserved his battle fleet while the Turks had lost heavily.

But from Gibraltar to Gallipoli point the word passed from ship to ship and fishing village to port that Barbarossa had won the Mediterranean. The Empire, the Papacy and the Venetians had put forth their utmost effort and had lost.

When the news of Prevesa was carried to Suleiman in the eastern steppes, the Sultan rose at the first words, so that the report was heard with all standing. At the end, he ordered the encampment to be illuminated in rejoicing.

No one realized the consequence of Prevesa better than the Venetians who hastened to sue for peace as Foscari had predicted. It cost the Council of Ten heavily—300,000 ducats to pay the expense of the war to the Turks, with the two ports of Nauplia and Malvasia remaining to them on the mainland. The aged Doge, Andrea Gritti, father of Luigi Gritti, died of grief, refusing to sign the peace of Prevesa which ended the sea empire of Venice.

The Wind of Charles

After Prevesa, Suleiman believed that his long conflict with the Hapsburg brothers had been won. With truce on land and victory upon the sea, surely he had gained equality in Europe with the Emperor and his unpredictable brother. But before long the two Hapsburgs yielded to temptation in different ways.

In Hungary John Zapolya died, who had been supported by

198

Suleiman. And Ferdinand gathered together his forces to besiege Zapolya's widow in Buda. Isabella, who had been the
daughter of the King of Poland before her marriage to the Hungarian, had her infant son with her in that summer of 1541.
Helpless to decide what to do, she longed for nothing more
than to yield to the Austrians and escape from the strife-torn
country.

Before Ferdinand's army could force its way into the city or
Isabella act for herself, the disposal of the country was taken
out of their hands by Suleiman, who came up swiftly from the
south with the Turkish *asker*. As usual the King of the Romans
remained safely behind his own frontier, and Suleiman, after
punishing his army and driving it out, left him there unmolested.

No less decisively the Osmanli Sultan dealt with the young
mother, who was also a queen. His messengers brought gifts to
her and asked if it were true that this child of Johnny's was her
own? For answer Isabella bared her breast and nursed the boy.
Then the Turks explained courteously that by Moslem law their
master could not come into her presence. Instead, he wished
that her young son be sent out to him, that he might see the boy.

There was no refusing. The distraught Isabella let the child
go with his nurses and her ministers, to be carried in his cradle
through the guard of janizaris into Suleiman's tent. There the
Sultan asked his own son Bayazid to hold the child and kiss it.
Before evening Isabella's boy was returned to her, with word
that the Turkish leader had promised that he would be King of
Hungary when he came of age. That night during the popular
rejoicing the janizaris quietly entered Buda.

Isabella was then removed from embattled Buda to a castle
in eastern Hungary. With her she took a letter inscribed in gold
upon purple paper. "It says," she was told, "that the Turkish
Padishah swears by the faith of his fathers and by his sword that
your son will come to the throne of Hungary when he is old
enough."

"A promise!" she told her counselors. "A few words written upon paper."

"It may well be the grant of a kingdom," they assured her.

Buda itself Suleiman kept under Turkish guard. By degrees he turned most of Hungary east of the frontier into Turkish sanjaks. But in doing so he revealed a new harshness. Austrian prisoners were slaughtered. The generosity he had shown at Rhodes twenty years before had changed to a calculating severity. In truth Isabella might fear that in his written promise she held no more than a worthless scrap of paper. Yet the inhabitants of Rhodes still enjoyed the freedom he had granted them; the line of demarcation that he drew across Hungary was to stand for a century and a half, making Vienna the frontier outpost of the Christian west, Buda that of the Moslem east. Vienna still faces west, Buda east.

While Ferdinand was failing to restore the Hapsburg bastion of middle Europe in that eventful summer of 1541 his more gifted brother Charles embarked to regain Spanish mastery of the Mediterranean—at least of the western half, menaced after the collapse of the allied Christian sea power at Prevesa.

In particular Charles sought to break the fantastic spell that the name of Barbarossa had cast over the sea. Twenty years of shuttling through his vast dominion had wearied the versatile Charles; he could influence the councils of Europe by his personal charm, but his craving for tasty foods and rare wines had afflicted him with gout; his lifetime struggle with Martin Luther had embittered him against heresies. Often he talked of retiring to a monastery, there to assuage within comforting walls his religious melancholy.

Yet he still embodied the fading grandeur of empire, dominant, Christian and European. Of him a curious Englishman, John Morgan, wrote later, "I never met with that Spaniard in my whole life who, I am persuaded, would not have bestowed on me at least forty *Boto a Christo's* had I pretended to suspect

Charles V not to have held the whole Universal Globe in a string for four and twenty hours; and then it broke."

Such a monarch could not permit himself to be defied by a Turkish Beylerbey of the Sea. Yet a task force of galleys flying the green banner of Islam raided Gibraltar; another attacked a Spanish convoy off the Balearics. A small sailing craft hailed a fleet of Portuguese barges—"Come in, Barbarossa wants you" —and the Portuguese came in obediently.

There was something fantastic in the omnipresence of Barbarossa A Turkish potmaker's son, fat, winebibbing, assaulting castles to bear off beautiful girls in spite of his sixty years of age—isolating the Spanish garrisons in Africa, presuming to claim a continent for his master the Sultan. Whatever Charles might accomplish on land, the name of Barbarossa haunted his coasts.

That summer, to Barbarossa's chagrin, Suleiman held him in the eastern end of the Mediterranean. Pent up again, he offered himself for sale again. This time he let it be known that he was willing to sell his allegiance to Charles. Probably the sagacious Hapsburg distrusted the offer, aware that Barbarossa received twenty thousand gold ducats a year from his master, and remembering that such a rapprochement had been the overture to the calamity at Prevesa. Still, as Andrea Doria had done, he pondered the possibility.

He gave more belief to a second offer. It came from an old servant of Barbarossa, a certain eunuch, Hassan Agha, who had been left in charge of Algiers. Hassan Agha proposed to surrender Algiers to the Emperor "provided he sends an expedition of such strength that surrender will appear to be a necessity rather than treachery."

Just then Charles was preparing to do exactly that. Algiers had been and was Barbarossa's personal holding; it was, besides, the one strongly fortified Moslem port close to the Spanish coast—always a sensitive point with Charles. By capturing Algiers he could make shift to bar the Turks from the western bastion of the Mediterranean, over which the Knights to whom he had given the rocky islet of Malta stood guard.

With Suleiman occupied at Buda, and Barbarossa absent, with Dragut, his most dangerous lieutenant, temporarily captive, and Hassan Agha willing to sell Algiers, Charles resolved to have it. And he held to his purpose obstinately. Hastily he offered tolerance to the contentious Lutherans (the Book of Regensburg) and hurried down to the Mediterranean.

The armada that awaited him had all the strength Hassan Agha could have wished. Out to sea Doria's battle fleet escorted more than 400 transports, filled with 20,000 Spanish, German and Italian veterans commanded by the Duke of Alva, whose name would be joined forever to bloodshed in the Netherlands. Other peers of the realm embarked among the 3000 volunteers; a few brought their ladies along to watch the spectacle. At sea they were joined by galleys from Malta with 500 of the formidable Knights and their men-at-arms. They had as guest the lowborn but famous Hernando Cortez, conqueror of Mexico.

When autumn winds struck the armada, scattering it among sheltering ports, the cautious Doria warned the obstinate Charles that the stormy season had begun. It seemed absurd to the Emperor to turn back now that his expedition had embarked. Only a short sail separated their port of Minorca from Algiers. No more than a few days would be needed to batter down the slight walls of the Moslem lair—even supposing that the old eunuch did not surrender it. For Hassan Agha had only a force of 900 Turkish janizaris, and several thousand seamen and Moors. No, the Emperor could not withdraw from such an undertaking, wind or no wind.

It was partly Doria's doubt, partly Charles's obstinacy, but more it was the divided command, sailing as if to a military spectacle, that brought about the incredible result on the dark African coast where anger awaited them. In those few days the armada crossed over to a malignant coast where Berber and Arab tribes swarmed down from the heights. There was nothing in that to disturb veteran troops. Easily they disembarked along the level beaches behind the outthrust of Cape Matafu. Without trouble they drove back the restless tribesmen. Not bothering to wait for the main stores of food to be landed, the Spanish tercios led the way overland to the rocky promontory where Algiers rose behind its curtain wall to the round tower at the summit. No heat troubled them, in late October.

Around this small town, glistening in the sun, the expedition dug some trenches and set up its artillery in battery. Three days, and its commanders believed their task would be pleasantly accomplished. Hassan Agha had not surrendered.

The wind came from the west, striking full into the shallow bay behind Matafu. Gusts of rain followed, drenching men whose tents had blown down. The cold ate into them. No supplies came up from the beachhead, where a heavy sea ran. The hungry troops waited for food to reach them after the wind stopped. But it rose to hurricane force. Their wet powder became useless.

Then from the wall of Algiers Hassan Agha attacked. His janizaris could use their bows in the rain; his Moors, who had been driven from Andalusia, carried the steel of their hatred against the Spaniards, their former masters. The fury of this small force started panic in the besiegers' lines.

Charles himself led a counterattack by stolid Germans, and led it too far. Pressing close under the wall, it was decimated by cannon fire, and gave back.

This might not have been serious, if it had not been for the hunger of the soldiers and the greater misfortune at the beaches. There the admiral, Doria, had taken the bulk of his galleys to sea to ride out the gale. Instead of following him, the captains of the transports tried to beach their craft or lost control of them. Of the galleys and transports, 145 foundered in the surf; survivors of their crews escaping ashore were massacred by the tribesmen who thronged down to overpower the guard troops and carry off the stores already landed. The three days' storm seemed to fill the coast with human assailants who had been invisible before.

In the mud of the half-dug trenches by Algiers, Charles and his noblemen, and the Knights of Malta, held back the attacks of the exulting townsmen. Until the commanding officers agreed that they must retreat to the beaches, fifteen miles away, to get at their supplies. The men were weakened by two days of hunger.

Accordingly the siegeworks were abandoned, the transport animals killed for meat, and the retreat through the rain and mud began, with the Knights holding the rear. Only Cortez protested against it.

Once begun, the retreat broke the spirit of the massive expedition. The Germans especially, with their firearms useless, weakened under the near starvation. Encircling tribesmen, mounted on fleet-footed horses, mocked their heavy plodding through mud and swirling freshets. The rear of the laboring column was held firm by the contingent of the Religion. One height where these sworn enemies of the Turks made a stand was named by the native Berbers "The Grave of the Knights."

When the retreating soldiery reached the beaches, only a remnant of supplies was to be found in the shambles of shipwreck and slaughter. Although Charles called a council of war to decide whether they would hold their ground at the beaches until fresh stores could be sent from Europe, there was no possibility of checking the retreat. It was the last day of October, and the angered Doria pointed out that no convoy could be brought to their relief in winter, and that if Barbarossa came up with his battle fleet intact the disaster to the Christians would be complete. The mass of the soldiers had only one thought, to get on board the surviving ships.

So the great expedition retreated to sea. There again fate seemed to turn against it. Because more than a third of the transport vessels had been lost, the human survivors had to be crowded into the seaworthy shipping. There was no room left for the splendid Spanish horses of the expedition. "Caesar [the Emperor] decided that no lives of soldiers must be lost because of their horses." So the *Brief Happenings* relates. "He ordered the animals to be thrown into the sea. This throwing-forth of the horses wrung the hearts of their masters."

Greater evil followed them out to sea. Wind, rising again to a gale, scattered the damaged vessels, driving some back into the port of Algiers where they were seized by Hassan Agha. Doria brought Charles to shelter with some of his galleys in the small port of Bujeya held by a Spanish garrison. There the scant food supply of the garrison did not serve to feed the refugees. The weakened oarsmen of the galleys could not pull the water-logged craft out to sea against the wind.

A secret agent of the French King described the plight of the survivors in Bujeya in his report to Francis thereafter. "Only one carrack [ship] gained the said port of *Bugeya*, and there sank, strange to relate, in the presence of the said emperor without anything being saved from it. And in this place they endured worse hunger than had happened to them before, since they had only dogs, cats and herbs to eat . . . the son-in-law of the emperor escaped in his breeches and shirt . . . a great part of the grandees of Spain in his company were lost."

Relief vessels from Sicily took Charles and his companions from the ill-fated port. The Sicilian captains brought with them the information that Barbarossa had put to sea with 150 sail. (As soon as Suleiman, on the way back to Constantinople, heard that the expedition of the Emperor had started for Africa, he released Barbarossa, to make all speed to Algiers.)

The storms that took such toll of Charles's armada served him well in the end because Barbarossa was pinned down during November in the Greek islands. Portions of the expedition came in along the European coasts, all the way from Trapani in Sicily to Cartagena in Spain. "It has been a greater disaster than people know, or I can write to your Majesty," the spy assured Francis. "He [Charles] will remember it all his life."

The loss of 8000 fighting men and half his warcraft did not signify so much as the deaths of 300 noblemen of the Empire. In one particular the observant spy emphasized the truth: Charles never forgot the hours when, a refugee on the deck of a Sicilian merchantman, he had heard the rumor that Barbarossa had put to sea with the Turkish battle fleet. In the seventeen years of life that remained to him Charles did not venture to go to war at sea again.

At Algiers, where the aged Hassan Agha resumed his caretaker's duties contentedly, a western gale was known for a long time as "the wind of Charles."

The disaster at Algiers, however muted down, had an immediate effect upon the political kaleidoscope of Europe. Convinced by the reports of his agents of what had happened, the volatile French King broke his signed truce with his lifelong antagonist, the Emperor. The Hapsburgs had to face the crisis of their struggle with the Osmanli Sultan, while the Beylerbey of the Sea made the voyage he had longed for into the west, to sweep the Italian and Spanish coasts, to besiege Nice and to winter in Toulon as the guest of the French court.

Whatever else befell, Khair ad-Din Barbarossa had won his conflict with middle Europe. In so doing he had made Suleiman the unacknowledged master of the Mediterranean.

A generation later Miguel de Cervantes, satirizing the armored conquistadors of his time in the deathless personality of Don Quixote, wrote "The world was convinced that the Turks were invincible by sea."

IV

The Quest in Asia

The Secret in the Poem

TURN back seven years, to June of 1534. Suleiman's temper
has not yet hardened against the Europeans. His purpose
has not changed as yet. Something in Asia will draw him to itself and make him more truly an Asiatic.

After nearly fourteen years of struggle in Europe Suleiman
the Magnificent is riding for the first time into the homeland of
his people, in the footsteps of Yavuz Sultan Selim. He has just
tried to close the book of Europe, patching up a truce with the
Hapsburgs to do so. In his household the Sultan Valideh has
died, Gulbehar is in exile, Roxelana married to him. In his
thoughts he has realized that he cannot enter the society of
Europe. He is a Turk, and he will remain a Turk, alone.

What purpose has he now? He will not break his silence to
tell it. The most powerful monarch in Europe, he has hidden
himself from his own council; he has named Ibrahim Serasker
to lead the army—sending the arrogant Greek ahead to reap the
glory of a campaign in the field; behind him, his new fleet—upon
which he never set foot—is made over to an island peasant.

Is he a weakling? Seemingly, that could be. In this same
month Daniello de' Ludovisi says of him that he has "a melancholy temperament, given rather to ease than to business. His
mind, it is said, is not very alert. Nor has he the force and pru-

207

dence which ought to be in so great a prince, for he has given the government of his empire into the hands of another, his Grand Vizir Ibrahim, without whom neither he nor his court undertake important deliberation, while Ibrahim does everything without consulting the Grand Signior."

Now that sounds familiar, and it is in fact what Ibrahim himself has said. Ludovisi tells a part of the truth but only what comes from the gossip of the diplomats. Out on the sea Barbarossa appears to be his own master, yet by a silken thread Suleiman guides him, and in reality until now Ibrahim has done what Suleiman wished. Suleiman has the dangerous force of tempered steel, even though it is sheathed. Perhaps he fears most his own savage temper.

What purpose, then, moves him into Asia? He has confided much in Roxelana, but she is not one to prattle. Nor has he taken her with him on this long journey. Some words of his may reveal the secret. Not in his laconic diary of events but in the awkward poems he wrote for himself, signed He Who Seeks a Friend.

One ghazel holds a human longing.

He who chooses poverty wants no stately house—
Wanting no bread or alms other than the dole of pain.

There is a sense of punishment here. This intensifies in another two lines: a man who scars his breast will take no joy in the sight of a garden. Once Suleiman speaks outright.

"What men call empire is world-wide strife and ceaseless war.
In all the world the only joy lies in a hermit's rest."

Suleiman was trying to express a longing in awkward words. The empire of conflict and power he did not want; there was a fellowship in suffering to which he could belong. He seemed to realize the futility of seeking that, because he invokes the picture of a religious recluse as a man who has no further cares. That refuge was not for him.

With all his stubborn determination he began to search through Asia for this utopia that he had missed in Europe.

What Ogier Busbecq Saw

A kindly Flemish gentleman served as the last Austrian ambassador, and, being held in polite captivity, had a rare opportunity of studying Suleiman in the years of greatest strain.
Being also a philosopher with a craving for botany, Ogier
Ghiselin de Busbecq accumulated strange animals as he journeyed with the Sultan through Asia—among them a friendly
lynx and a crane that attached itself to the soldiers, marching
beside them, and even laying an egg for one. A pet pig served
a special purpose, because the Fleming could send secret messages back and forth in a bag with it, the orthodox Turks refusing to interfere with a pig.

Insatiably curious, Busbecq managed to watch the Sultan
with his people as few other foreigners did. At the great feast of
Bairam after the yearly fast, he contrived to be a spectator.

"I ordered my servants to promise a soldier some money and
so get me a place in his tent, on a mound overlooking Suleiman's
pavilions. Thither I went at sunrise. I saw assembled on the
plain a mighty multitude of turbaned heads, attentively following in deep silence the words of the priest who was leading their
devotions. Each kept his proper place; the lines looked like so
many hedges, near to or far from the spot where the Sultan
stood.

"The scene was charming—the brilliant uniforms under the
snow-white head-dresses. There was no coughing, and no one
moved his head. For the Turks say, 'If you had to talk with
Pashas, you would hold your body in respectful-wise; how
much more are we impelled to the same reverence toward God?'

"When prayers were finished, the serried ranks broke up, and
the whole plain was covered with surging masses. The Sultan's

209

servants appeared with his breakfast, when, behold, the janizaris laid hands on the dishes and devoured the food, amid
much merriment. This freedom is allowed by ancient custom,
as part of the day's festivity."

Being quartered near the camp of this household army, the
careful Fleming took the risk of inspecting it incognito. Moreover, he compared what he saw to the camp of a European
army.

"I put on a dress usually worn by Christians in these parts
and sallied out with a companion or two. The first thing that
struck me was that each corps had its proper quarters from
which the soldiers were not allowed to move. Everywhere order
prevailed; there was silence, no quarrels, no bullying. Besides
there was cleanliness, no heaps of excrement or refuse. Holes
are dug for the use of the men, which are filled in with fresh
earth.

"Again, I saw no drinking or gambling, which is the greatest
failing of our soldiers. The Turks are unacquainted with the art
of losing their money at cards.

"I had a fancy also to be conducted through the shambles
where the sheep were slaughtered. There I saw but four or five
sheep which had been flayed for—I think—no fewer than four
thousand janizaris. They pointed out to me a janizary who was
eating his dinner off a wooden trencher—a mess of turnips,
onions, garlic and cucumbers seasoned with salt and vinegar.
To all appearances, he enjoyed his vegetables as much as if he
had been dining off pheasants. Water is their only drink.

"I was at the camp just before their fast, or Lent as we should
call it, and was still more struck by the behavior of the men. In
Christian lands at this season even orderly cities ring with
games and the shouting of drunkenness and delirium. But during the days before fast, these men do not allow themselves any
extra indulgence in the way of food or drink. Nay, rather, by
cutting down their usual allowance, they prepare themselves

for the fast, for fear they should not be able to endure the sudden change.

"Such is the result of military discipline, and the stern laws bequeathed them by their ancestors. The Turks allow no crime to go unpunished. The penalties are degradation from office, loss of rank, confiscation of property, the bastinado, and death. Not even the janizaris are exempt from the bastinado. Their lighter faults are punished with this stick, their graver with dismissal from the service or, removal to a different corps, which they consider worse than death."

Ogier Busbecq marveled at the endurance of these men under punishment or privation. He sensed the fact that janizaris would choose to be beaten numb by staffs rather than be sent away from their fellowship. Unwittingly he touched upon a vital weakness of the Turks, in the cherished plumes of the veteran janizaris. They craved some bit of splendor on their bodies. In the same way, aghas spent a year's pay for a silver-worked saddle; sanjakbeys went into debt to gain ceremonial robes of tissue of gold. Did not the illustrious Ibrahim, Bearer of the Burden, and the Sultan himself set this example of personal magnificence?

The Enemy in Asia

Suleiman was going not to the luxurious cities of the Nile or the holy cities of Mecca and Jerusalem—he never laid eyes upon these—but into the hard northeast, to meet a threat to his dominion. He was riding back upon the path of Osmanli migration to solve a problem that was almost impossible to solve.

The growing power of Persia was pressing into his eastern borders, and with the shahs of Persia he neither wished nor could allow a major war. Here in the east grim Sultan Selim had clashed violently with the equally aggressive Shah Ismail, and both nations felt the wounds and the bitterness of that clash, after which it was said that Ismail never smiled.

While absent for fourteen years, Suleiman had tried to preserve a live-and-let-live peace through nearer Asia. His ships on the river Don traded with the frontier posts of the Muscovite grand princes; he sent gifts including janizaris and cannon—to demonstrate his force without using it—to the still distant moghuls of India and the Turkish Uzbeks of Samarkand.

In Tabriz, Shah Ismail—a mystic, follower of the schismatic Shi'a faith—had respected the unwritten truce. Not so his more realistic son Tahmasp. With the Osmanli away from the east, Tahmasp had seized Turkish Bitlis, the stronghold of great Lake Van. His horsemen had appeared at Baghdad on the Tigris River, a holy city. To this Venetian envoys had egged him on, laboring skillfully to loose the power of the Shah in war against the backs of the Osmanlis. Such a war would relieve the pressure against Vienna and the Mediterranean. If it could be brought about! (Busbecq himself would write before long: "'Tis only the Persian stands between us and ruin.")

And here the vastness of his domain handicapped Suleiman. The Austrian frontier lay as far—nearly a thousand miles by road—to the northwest of Constantinople as the Persian border lay to the east. Depending as it did upon grazing, the Turkish army could not move between these frontiers in the same year. Where the army went, it expected the Sultan to go, and with him went the Organization. Ibrahim urged him to finish the task Selim had begun, and crush Persia.

As protector of the holy cities, the Sultan could not allow the loss of Baghdad. Poets invoked his aid as "the friendly, foe-destroying warrior." And as head of the war-born Osmanli state he could not well allow ancient Turkish strongholds to be snatched away under his eyes. "Yavuz Sultan Selim," his aghas reminded him, "would carry fire and sword through the heretical Persians."

This problem Suleiman met as usual with a solution of his

own. While he had remained in Constantinople to watch events, using Barbarossa to amuse the Europeans, he had sent Ibrahim eastward with the bulk of the army, to retake Baghdad.

But Ibrahim had departed from his orders, to turn instead into the mountains around Van, to regain the frontier posts by some brilliant diplomacy and then to push on through the heights to the blue-tiled domes of Tabriz, the capital city of Shah Tahmasp. No great battle had been fought because the Persians would not risk their main strength of horsemen against janizaris and artillery. Only raids had been flung against the advancing Turkish *asker*. Detachments of Turks going out against the raiders were cut off and destroyed, while the army at Tabriz faced the coming of winter in the mountains. More, it complained bitterly of the absence of its Sultan.

"The Vizir at Tabriz," messengers related to Suleiman, "is like one drunk with victory. He swears that he alone gains the victories which the Lord of the Two Worlds can no longer achieve."

Then a courier showed Suleiman an order of the day for the army. Ibrahim had signed it as Serasker *Sultan*.

There could not be two sultans. At sight of the signature Suleiman started east, to take command of the army.

Journey into the Past

In doing so he followed a strange route. He was meeting the Asiatics in their homelands for the first time. And he was also opposing himself to a force that could not be checked by janizaris and guns.

The new shahs of Persia were Sufis, Wool-wearers, men who followed after dreams. The Shi'a, their religious faith, had become the creed of Persia. They mocked the orthodox Osmanli imams—who castigated them as heretics. In their memory the wild Ismail had become a saint, performing miracles. This tide

213

of the enthusiasm of the Shi'ites had swept far into Anatolia. There the dervish orders were caught up in it. In venturing among them, Suleiman faced a rising fanaticism as intangible as the night wind that swept his encampment.

He met this religious unrest by journeying as a pilgrim, with a small following. Swinging south, he paused at Koniah where the Seljuk sultans had dwelt, to pay honor to the tomb of the greatest of the poets and mystics, Jallal ad-Din Rumi. At this shrine where towers soared against the night sky, his coming must have pleased the Mevlevi dervishes who flocked around him. To the wild summons of their drums and flutes they danced before him, whirling as spirit seized upon them, emerging from their trance to tell him that the Sultan of Spiritland had spoken to them, predicting success for Suleiman in Persia.

The farther he went, the more the ties of Constantinople fell away from him. Around him gathered human beings who lacked both education and fear.

Skullcapped dervishes, monks from the monastery of Hajji Bektash, Kalendars striding up with their long staffs, they thronged his sitting place in caravan serais, or watched at his tent entrance until he slept. Lean brown men called to him plaintively, "Lawgiver, Conqueror—Sultan Suleiman Khan!" They voiced their merriment. "So you are alive. You are not merely a name. We can see you! You eat rice with saffron. Well, what have you in mind for us beggars?"

Peasants, walking wide-legged, brought him fruit to eat, and their children to care for, chanting, *"Chelebi, biza onutma!* Lord, forget us not!"

Over the red clay plain Suleiman rode to the granite upthrust of the mountains. Bektashi babas ran with his troops, performing small miracles at night, by the fires. They peered at him and they challenged him. "Say, Sultan Khan, what do you in the far city?"

"I bring water in, by aqueducts."

"Water is clean only in the channels made by God. What

good is it to build walls that will tumble into clay and stones in another age?"

Suleiman thought of the ruins of Byzantine palaces, the blackened column raised by the Romans. "What, then?" he asked.

"The Lord of the Two Worlds comes with an army, and with money. Why do you bring money? The infidel Feringhis must have money, to eat, but you have only to ask and we shall give you food. You bring an army, but the Shi'ite Shah wrote poems urging us to rebel. Nay, we did not rebel, but the poems were fine to read, saying that he came with the rain and shone with the sun, and soon he would be master of *Rum*."

By *Rum* they meant the Turkish land, which ignorant folk knew only as Rome. Their minds had changed no more than their fields and forests. The scent of fir wood burning, the dry sweet smell of the desert, caught at Suleiman.

"Such poems are like wine, the red mad thing." He wished that he could write winged words, or hold these listeners as the babas did by the spell of his voice.

"Not wine of the flesh—wine of the spirit!"

Past the headwaters of the Euphrates Suleiman rode, past stone villages of ancient folk where women gathered in wheat unveiled. Still the strange inquisitors came to his knee, asking his answers to the mysteries of their life "These days are evil. Did God create evil to mislead men?"

"Whom he wills he misleadeth, whom he wills he guideth."

"In what way? By what sign will we know his guidance? Say, Lord of the Two Worlds, by what sign do you draw your reins to the east?"

By what sign? By the sickness in the mind of the arrogant Ibrahim.

Above him echoed the bells of domed Armenian churches. Above the dark forest mesh rose the snow peaks that marked his way. For days he watched one of the sentinel peaks, shining at sunrise, and glowing again when the first stars showed. At

Akhlat he dismounted to go to the tomb of Osman, the first of the ten sultans his ancestors. "By this sign I go," he said.

On the rock pinnacles around him beacon fires made points of flame, lighted by the wild Kurdish tribes. Their chieftains rode down in splendor to behold the Sultan who had been only a name to them.

Greeting them, Suleiman thought: Ibrahim will never yield up his rank and responsibility, and I cannot. He thought fleetingly of putting aside his sword and departing forever from his place in the Divan and his care, going on foot—which he had never done—to the monastery of the Bektashis, to rest his body and meditate. So had his grandfather departed from Constantinople to go to his home, and had died on the way. . . .

Early in the autumn he reached the Turkish army waiting at Tabriz in the mountains. He took the command from Ibrahim. He would not listen to the officers who came to his stirrup to complain that the askeris were starving in the winter cold.

Strangely, once they had seen Suleiman's standard with the seven white horsetails, the men of the *asker* recovered their spirits. Through mud and snow he brought them down to the desert of the twin rivers, Tigris and Euphrates. Transport horses died of starvation, and the heavier cannon were abandoned, buried in the mud where the elusive enemy could not find them.

Once safely in the desert, the army was free of the cold and the harassing attacks of the Persian horsemen. Suleiman followed the Tigris down, to capture Baghdad and winter there. Entering the city of the illustrious kalifs, he allowed no looting or injury to the inhabitants. The place had become a shell, touched with the fading splendor of Harun the Blessed.

Yet the army took vast encouragement from Baghdad. Its Sultan had brought it to the city protected by God; now in reality Sultan Suleiman would take the place of the kalifs dead in their graves. The mantle of the Protector of the Faithful would fall upon him.

A dervish who tended the shrines chanted a prophecy. "I see

in him the aspect of the Prophet—knowledge mingled with mercy. . . . I see again the White Hand of Moses taking up the sword. . . . I behold the Leader of our time in the rose garden of Faith!"

There was even a miracle in the cemetery across the river. A caretaker of the tombs professed to have found the bones of a vanished saint under a grave slab without marking. Summoned to the spot, Suleiman entered the grave below the slab —well aware that the marvelous discovery had much to do with his arrival in Baghdad. Descending a ladder, he found beneath him a skeleton wrapped in linen scented with musk, lying toward Mecca. By certain signs known to the tenders of the tombs, the bones were proclaimed to be those of the sainted imam, Abu Hanifa.

The army took this to be a sign that the Sultan verily had been guided by God.

So intangible a thing is faith. A featherweight of fact, slight as the memory of a dream, yet drawing human beings where whips cannot drive them. The heretic Persians had thrown off shields and armor, to go against Turkish steel with their bodies bared. . . .

The Case of Iskander Chelebi

In Baghdad that winter he had to judge his other self, Ibrahim. There was no escaping it. He held in his hand a sheet of paper with a few words written in Iskander Chelebi's familiar calligraphy. These words forced him to sit alone in judgment upon the oblivious Ibrahim. "In the name of God the all-pitying and compassionate, in the hour of death I testify that I, Chelebi the Defterdar, conspired to mulct money from the army supplies, and entered into treacherous agreement with the heretical Persians to defeat my master the Sultan. Also I swear that Ibrahim the First Vizir was joined with me in this treachery, and besides paid assassins to take the life of the Sultan."

217

All of it was, Suleiman knew, a lie. Yet many people knew that he had it, who held the word of a dying man to be inviolable.

Carefully Suleiman reviewed the case of the great Treasurer. A Turk, bound by old customs, Chelebi had long been a rival of the brilliant Ibrahim. They had vied with each other in the size of their following and the splendor of their uniforms. Unfortunately Suleiman had sent Chelebi as lieutenant to Ibrahim with the army.

After that their feud became deadly. When Chelebi packed the money chests on camels for one day's march, Ibrahim's guards seized his men, swearing that the gold was being stolen. A foolish trick. Probably in revenge Chelebi persuaded Ibrahim to move on Tabriz, to enhance his glory. And, obliviously, the Vizir did so . . . claiming that the army failed against the Persians because Chelebi had not kept up the service of supply. . . .

Then Ibrahim brought these charges against the elderly Turk, and had him executed. So greatly Chelebi hated the Vizir that he signed this confession, implicating Ibrahim.

No, there was no truth in the words, except what they implied—that the wealthy Treasurer had been no more guilty than the Vizir who put him to death. Ibrahim had been the one to urge the Persian war on Suleiman. In his self-intoxication Ibrahim had signed himself *Sultan*. Never intending to assassinate Suleiman, he had thought himself to be greater than the man who had raised him up . . . from the night, thirteen years before, when Suleiman had pledged his word that he would never dismiss his friend in disgrace from the vizirate . . . how many times the Christian apprentice had shown contempt for the dull mind of his Turkish master . . . yet the only thing that could not be forgiven was the death of Chelebi.

Suleiman decided that Ibrahim must have the same fate as Chelebi, when they returned to Constantinople.

But he could not turn his back on his antagonist, the Shah, who had recaptured Tabriz and seized the mountain passes during his absence in Baghdad. In bleak anger Suleiman took his Turks up to the heights again, thrusting deep into Persia, sighting the oil-flecked waters of the inland sea, the Caspian. He stormed and sacked Ardibil, the old home of the shahs. Before him the enemy withdrew again. The land had been devastated, the pasturage consumed.

If Suleiman detached forces from his main array, they were cut off and annihilated. Under such conditions he knew it to be useless to try to hold any portion of Persian land. Turning back to Tabriz, he stripped the city, and burned the palaces. Then he led his army homeward, toward grazing land and untouched crops.

With Ibrahim and his personal escort he went on swiftly to the Serai at Constantinople.

There he threw himself into the daily hearings of the Divan, keeping Ibrahim at his side, and sleeping little. Until the evening when, the last reports put away in the folders, he ordered food brought to the two of them in his private audience hall. Often they had shared this last meal during the years that Ibrahim had been Vizir of the empire. That night, sitting in his accustomed place, Ibrahim no longer thought it strange to be eating from the same dishes as the Osmanli. He was rather annoyed that he had not been freed to go to his own palace, where he had the count of the day's gifts to take.

Aware that Suleiman was brooding as usual, he said carelessly, "You have given a lashing to the Persian dogs. They will lick their wounds for a long time."

"Yes," Suleiman acknowledged. Then suddenly he said, "The war was not well advised."

When he left to go to his own sleeping chamber, he asked Ibrahim to remain. As usual, Ibrahim sought the mattress placed for him in the alcove.

The next morning the walls of the alcove were streaked with

blood. The body of the First Vizir who had been Suleiman's favorite was found outside the entrance to the Divan, with an executioner's bowstring knotted around the throat.

Of Ibrahim the Moslems said: "He was caught in the net of imagination of power." The Venetians said, "He loved himself better than his lord."

The Power and the Glory

The stains of Ibrahim's lifeblood were allowed to remain on the alcove walls. When young ajem-oghlans—foreign boys who served in the palace gardens—started to wash away the brown streaks the next day Suleiman forbade them to do it. Years later attendants swore that the stains had been left, as a lesson. But to whom?

Suleiman never explained. His silence now became notable, and older servants fancied that his eyes and mouth grew to resemble those of the Yavuz Sultan, his father. "It is the suffering of responsibility," they said. "From it there is no moment's rest until the hours of sleep."

Having killed Ibrahim, Suleiman had to assume all the burden of government. He went himself to the Treasury when the secretaries had collected there the vast stock of valuables of the great Vizir. Among them he found a drinking bowl of lapis lazuli, his own gift, and the ruby signet ring of the French King, Francis . . . he had tried to give all credit for their mutual accomplishments to Ibrahim, from that first battle of Mohács. . . .

Now he was alone. As First Vizir he named an old Turk, Ayas Pasha, heavy with good eating, the father of uncounted children. Ayas Pasha laughed at the story that he kept forty cradles filled at a time in his harem. No title of Serasker went to this obedient servant who enjoyed an afternoon row on the Bosphorus more than a session at the Divan. Ayas Pasha merely said, "It will be as God wills." Suleiman read the petitions and signed the orders alone. But the merriment of the old Turk eased the Sultan's brooding.

For five years from Ibrahim's death in 1536, the cautious care of the Osmanli brought his people to their greatest glory. (The first treaty with the French had been signed; then followed the foray into Italy, the defeat of the Holy League at Prevesa, the surrender of Venice, the promise to Isabella's son, the disaster to Charles at Algiers, and new victories over the Austrians in the perennial conflict of Hungary.)

Suleiman led the *asker* himself. Neither the feudal armies nor his household janizaris and spahis would follow an Ayas Pasha. Old custom, in this particular case, was stronger than the will of the Sultan. Suleiman tried a new experiment, to increase the number of the janizaris and spahis, who would have to obey his personal orders.

The janizaris rose from 12,000 to some 18,000 and the elite horsemen accordingly. By strengthening the two corps subject to his immediate command, Suleiman increased the danger to himself, if the household troops should turn against him.

Such danger appeared slight, in the flood tide of the Sultan's achievement and popularity. Moreover, final authority did not rest in the hands of the Sultan himself. The Mufti, arbiter of the religious Law, could write a few words declaring that the master of the Serai had offended the Law, and Suleiman would no longer be Sultan. So, at least, tradition had it.

There was small chance of that. The judges of the Law realized that to the tireless Suleiman would succeed his popular son, the well-loved Mustafa. No sane judge of Islam would interfere with such auspicious leadership.

Nonetheless, Suleiman was very conscious of the cleavage widening between the Law and his Organization. It was like the rift between Church and State among European nations. The earth was God's. The Sultan merely served as caretaker of the Osmanli portion. His School studied new sciences; his officers, from Vizir to the youngest ajem-oghlan seeding flower beds and the lowliest *defter* balancing accounts, all served the everlasting interest of God. The Law endured, while sultans abode only their destined hour. The religious Law held fast to its properties; it remained traditional, Turkish. Families administering the unchanging Law kept their libraries, their beliefs and their estates. The orthodox Turkish Law stood still, while the young, foreign and Christian-bred Organization progressed.

Until now Suleiman had thrown his support to the Organization. To do so, he had disregarded the criticism of individual Turkish judges—that he was being guided more by European ideas than by the precepts of the Koran. Now, after his journey to the shrines of Asia, he turned more to the Koran.

So for a few years the educated Organization remained in balance with the ritualistic Law. Such a balance seldom endures for long within a growing dominion.

During the twelve years after Ibrahim's fall Suleiman led his army out only twice, in vast parades to restore his frontier line, as when he pledged Isabella that her son would be King.

On the Steppes of Asia

Suleiman loved the prairies. If the Hungarian plain was to be his purgatory, the steppe of the Vlakhs (Wallachians) to the east of the great circle of the Carpathians was his paradise.

For one thing he was journeying at ease through fine grasslands around the sea that had become a Turkish lake (and Suleiman fully intended to keep it so). *Karadeniz*, the Black Sea, was quite as important to the Osmanlis as the Mediterranean. Suleiman himself held the title of Lord of the Two Seas (the White and the Black). True, Italian shipping had monopolized it as late as the time of the Golden Horde when the brothers Polo did business there, in lovely ports like Kaffa and

Trebizond. All such ports with their fondacos had fallen to the Turks, as far as the dim heights of the Caucasus at the distant end of the sea. Even through the Caucasus, Suleiman's command was heeded attentively, even if not always obeyed.

The Venetian merchants who carried the bulk of the Black Sea trade, however, obeyed Suleiman of necessity. Being hopelessly inept as traders, the Osmanli Turks were quite content to let the merchants of San Marco carry on business as usual, paying tribute for the privilege of bearing away the wines and wax, the cattle and grain of this tranquil sea.

The question of the traffic by sea being so easily disposed of, Suleiman devoted himself to keeping order along the shores, and he found this a most pleasant task. His heart inclined to it, for he had spent his youthful years of dreaming at Kaffa; his mother and Gulbehar had come from these shores.

In a very true sense, at such a time, the son of Selim was returning home. The folk of the countryside spoke Turkish; they bred the finest horses, and they looked to him as the arbiter of their fate. They brought him gifts of milk and horses and gold strained from running streams by gypsies, and they went from his presence joyfully.

Here he was more truly Suleiman Khan than the Osmanli Sultan. More than that, he was the king of the nomads who had mastered city life and returned accoutered in splendor, still dwelling in a tent—a pavilion of dream stuff—with such power in his hand and word as the nomad princes had never conceived. With a single command he could invoke the thunder of massed siege guns, or the terrifying tread of ranked janizaris.

So long as he lived Suleiman never made use of those guns or that soldiery along the shores of the Black Sea.

The familiar road to the steppes was in itself a joy to him. (No Roxelana accompanied him.) It led over the mightiest rivers, the Danube where the dwellings of the Vlakhs were scented with sweet herbs, where those Christian folk drank white wine and red and danced to their gypsy flutes at horse fairs. Then through the cypress forests of the Transylvanians, with the snow peaks of the Carpathians against the sky line—past the vestiges of Roman baths, and gleaming sand beaches, to the river Pruth—where he had heard the tidings of Prevesa—and the prairies of the Dniester. The Christian folk here still cherished legends of Rome, calling themselves "Rumans" and their land Rumania. Like the Transylvanians, they were free of the rule of Turkish sanjakbeys, but they paid a light tribute.

Among this Christian folk of his kingdom by the sea there were children of Greeks who had learned tricks from the Venetians. They could blow molten glass into vessels of different kinds; they had made printing types and with these they printed crude books.

Beyond these stoneless prairies stretched the true steppe, of dry grass so high that it reached a rider's girdle. On this dry sandy steppe where mighty Father Dnieper swirled to the sea, the folk moved as nomads, following the water. Out of the steppe grass the round summits of Islamic tombs and mosques arose. Here Suleiman gained a new attribute, as a leader of the faith. The steppe folk who dismounted at their whitewashed shrines felt awe of the man who could speak a word and have it obeyed as far as a rider could speed in a month.

Suleiman camped where salt marshes gleamed in the starlight. Far in the north lay the frontiers of two Christian monarchs, both friendly. The King of Poland bore him good will because they had enemies in common; the Grand Prince of Moscow conciliated him with gifts of sables because the Tatar khans, the old antagonists of Moscow, obeyed him.

Scarcely heeded by Suleiman, certain refugees from Polish and Muscovite lands were drifting down the rivers into the free steppe. In the reed-grown islands of Father Dnieper they hid their dwellings, they pushed down the river current in their long boats. In the steppe itself their villages sprang up in the space between Muscovite guard posts and the paths of the Tatars. They became wanderers, settlers and fighters, known to the elder steppe dwellers as Cherkasks, or Kazaks, Wanderers. Along the tranquil-flowing Don, in the fertile black earth region these "Cossacks" thrived.

Another refuge of peoples on the Black Sea Suleiman knew well. In the Crimea, joined to the great plain only by a narrow neck of land, remained vestiges of all who had passed that way, survivors of Goths who still spoke their Germanic tongue, holed up in the stone height of Mankoup Kalé, Greek artisans, Jews who had crossed the steppe, and chiefly the Tatars who were still ruled by descendants of Genghis Khan. These dwelt in crude blue-tiled palaces in the gardens of Bagche Serai, as masters of the Krim Horde.

Apparently Suleiman never ventured back into the fastness of the Crimea where he had come to know the Krim khans so well; perhaps that same knowledge kept him from doing so. Even now he had fewer Turkish families behind him than there were Tatar yurts in the steppes—as far as Astrakhan on the inland Caspian Sea that he had sighted from the Persian highlands, and Kazan up where the Volga River bent to the south. Here the three hordes numbered their riders, as their sheep, by the tens of thousands. They watched the Osmanli as dogs eye a lone wolf. For some reason payments to the Krim Khan were carried on the books of his treasury as "pay of the dog-keeper."

Sons of the khans had come to dwell in Constantinople to be educated in Turkish ways. For the orderly Turkish government remained a mystery to these surviving nomads, and they respected Suleiman's power as something of a miracle. They were willing to join him in raids into Christian Europe, as when they ravaged Austria with him.

Evidence of Suleiman's influence upon the Krim khans showed in different ways, some of them unexpected. One khan after a visit to Constantinople ordered the *kibitkas* or tent wagons of his people to be broken up, hoping to make them townsdwellers like the prosperous Osmanli Turks. Another spent his "dog-keeper's pay" at Bagche Serai in building public baths, water channels and small palaces in Turkish fashion. Meanwhile Suleiman named the successors to the khans, and supplied them with a token force of janizaris—who helped to see that his commands were carried out—and an imposing battery of heavy cannon.

These last the Krim Tatars promptly transported in wagons over the steppe, to aid them in battering at the fortified height of the Muscovite Kremlin. Sahib Ghirei, who conceived this notion, also sent the regiment of janizaris to see that the guns were cared for. Afterward he explained by letter to Vasily, who was then Grand Prince of Moscow, that this invasion had been a mistake, because he had sent his people to fight Lithuanians and of their own accord they had taken the road to Moscow instead. His captains felt aggrieved, it seemed, because they took in so little tribute from the Russians and they complained, "What good do you have from any friendly exchange with the Russians? Hardly one sable skin a year, while war gets us thousands." "This," added Sahib Ghirei, "shuts my mouth. As for you, you can make your choice, but if we are to remain friends your presents to me must equal in value at least three or four hundred prisoners. To that you had better add a gift of gold and silver money, and well-trained falcons, with a baker to make bread and a cook also."

In such carefree fashion did the Turks have their first contact with the Russians who were to become their most persistent enemies. Suleiman himself was careful to keep aloof from the conflicts that swept over the steppes and passed on like storm clouds. He dignified the Krim khans by announcing his victories elsewhere to them as he did to his outer friends (whether tribute-paying or not), the doges of Venice, the sherifs of Mecca, the Mameluke princes of Egypt, and the Council of the free city of Ragusa.

Yet he made one move to control the Tatars who hemmed in the Russians. It was very remote and quiet control; he explained that as he helped the Krim Tatars to choose new leaders, he would aid also those of the khanates of Kazan and Astrakhan. As it happened, this was only a few years before a boy with strange fancies came to the throne of Moscow, as Ivan IV. This prince insisted on calling himself the Tsar, and he became widely known as Ivan the Terrible. Almost his first move toward greater power was to be against the Moslem Tatars of Kazan and Astrakhan.

Meanwhile in 1543 Suleiman called the son of Sahib Ghirei to accompany him on another march around Hungary, at a time when a drama was being played on another stage of conflict, the Mediterranean, with Khair ad-Din Barbarossa as chief actor.

Barbarossa's Last Jest

Of late years Suleiman had let the stalwart Beylerbey of the Sea have his way upon the Mediterranean for several reasons. Barbarossa was pulling off miracles at no expense but an actual profit to the Treasury. In so doing he required nothing but timber, sailcloth and powder and twenty to thirty thousand men, half of them captive Europeans, to pull the oars. Of all these ingredients Suleiman had a superabundance, and Barbarossa had a habit of bringing back more than he took out. Moreover, this energy of the old man of the sea exactly fitted the Sultan's new determination to risk not the life of one janizary beyond his frontiers in Europe, while frustrating the Christian monarchs by sea.

In the spring of 1543, however, Barbarossa asked a great favor. As admiral of the Osmanli Empire, he wanted to take his fleet across to France.

The kaleidoscope of the European courts had fallen into a new pattern after Charles's debacle at Algiers. The English Henry VIII had forsaken the French to espouse the cause of the Emperor. At the same time the aging Francis returned to the attack upon northern Italy which had been the dream of his youth and the nostalgia of his old age—whether or not encouraged by his Italian daughter-in-law, Catherine, who had been a Medici. Again he besought his unacknowledged allies the Turks to aid him by invading the Empire, Suleiman with the army by land, Barbarossa with the fleet by sea, this time in junction with the French fleet.

Formidable as such an attack may have seemed to Francis—and it worried Charles greatly—it came to little. Suleiman, who no longer had any interest in joining the concert of Europe as friend or foe, merely made one of his marches around the Hungarian plain where neither Ferdinand nor the German armies cared to meet him, after the rout at Valpo. In doing so he gathered back the towns Ferdinand had seized beyond the Austrian frontier. It was very different with Barbarossa.

He begged for permission to sail to the far west, there to end his duel with Doria and the Emperor as the guest of the Most Christian King of France. Only after long hesitation did Suleiman allow his admiral to depart with the main force of 110 galleys and 40 auxiliaries, manned by some 30,000 souls. It was a great stake to risk entire. But Suleiman remembered Prevesa and let the old seafarer go.

Barbarossa sailed happily from Gallipoli Point. What he did thereafter has been nearly deleted from the European historical record; but it is a story worth restoring, from Barbarossa's point of view.

Entering the tricky tides of Messina Strait, his ships are fired on by the castle at Reggio. Unexpectedly to the castle folk, Barbarossa puts back at the shots. Storming the castle, he finds within it a striking girl, daughter of the commandant, a certain Don Diego. Appropriating the girl, he bestows Turkish rank on her parents, as his new in-laws.

Up the coast he puts in to Civita Vecchia and terrifies the people of that seaside resort by simulating an attack (French liaison officers with him persuade him that the port, belonging to the Papal State, is now friendly to France). Heading out to sea unmolested, he arrives at the rendezvous in the Gulf of Lyons with his co-commander, François Bourbon, Duc d'Enghien, who salutes him with all ceremony. But D'Enghien has very little force with him, only 22 galleys and a baker's dozen of broadside-firing galleons. Barbarossa is not content until the junior officer with the lesser fleet hauls down his banner and hoists the green flag with the crescent.

The French prove to be less desirous than the Turks of seeking a battle at sea. Barbarossa cannot see the sense of gathering a fleet of more than 200 sail and doing nothing with it. He stipulates for the capture of Genoa where Andrea Doria has sheltered the remainder of the imperial fleet. The French object. D'Enghien complains of lack of powder. Barbarossa vents his anger: "Are you seamen, to fill your casks with wine instead of powder?"

He lends powder to the French, who agree to allow him to take Nice The Turks beset the town, which surrenders, except for the citadel where a Knight of Malta rallies a defense. Before the Turks can batter their way into the citadel they hear that an imperial army is advancing on Nice, and they re-embark, after ravaging and burning the town.

With the sailing season ending, Francis offers his guests the port of Toulon for winter quarters. He instructs his lord lieutenant of Provence "to lodge the lord Barbarossa sent to the king by the Grand Turk, with his Turkish army and grand seigneurs to the number of 30,000 combatants during the winter in his town and port of Toulon . . . for the accommodation of the said army as much as for the well-being of all this coast, it will not be suitable for the inhabitants of Toulon to remain and mingle with the Turkish nation, because of difficulties which might arise."

When the lord lieutenant removed the bulk of the population of Toulon to Marseille, he prudently took away the cannon also. However, the dreaded Turks, moving into Toulon for the winter, merely demanded that food be supplied them, and the church bells be not rung.

Such inaction, comfortable though it might be, grieved the Turkish brotherhood of the sea. Before the winter storms ended, Salih Reis was off raiding down the adjacent coast of Spain. Their galleys combed through the Balearics. Captives fetched back were sold in the markets of Marseille. Francis began to fear that Barbarossa might sell Toulon itself to Charles.

Barbarossa proved to be deaf to any suggestion that the campaign was ended and he should return home now that the sailing season was at hand. At Toulon he had a splendid base, next door to the Emperor's homeland of Spain, and to Doria's native city of Genoa. Thence he could operate at the expense of the King of France. The lord lieutenant complained that he "takes his ease while emptying the coffers of France."

If the French were not minded to put to sea to carry on the war to which they had summoned him, Barbarossa did not share their inclination. Why should he? His crews were not raiding Spain; they were returning to the homeland from which, as Andalusians, most of them had been driven by order of Charles. And as admiral of the fleet of the Grand Turk, ally of Francis, was he not expected to maintain an offshore blockade of the imperial coasts, and take in what merchantmen he could find?

Having put a stop to navigation in the western Mediterranean other than his own, Barbarossa refitted his vessels at Francis' expense in the dockyards, and from the comfortable terrace of the lord lieutenant's palace surveyed the distant blue Mediterranean with the pleasant certainty that his own port of Algiers was now secure.

The French had no way of removing him. Evidently Suleiman refused to summon him home.

At more than seventy years of age, Barbarossa may have lacked the fiery energy of his African days, but his presence hovers over the interplay of secret negotiations of those months

—Francis negotiating with Doria, and agreeing to a new peace with Charles, the Peace of Crépy.

When it was all over, Barbarossa abandoned Toulon to Francis and secured for himself the release of one of his captured lieutenants, Dragut, from Doria, the release of 400 Moslem captives, pay and rations for all his crews up to the hour of their re-entry of the Golden Horn, and a personal gift from Francis to himself of robes and jewels.

Voyaging home, he carried terror to the remaining imperial coasts. Passing Genoa with all banners displayed, he swept over Elba and in to the Tuscany coast, capturing the Isle of Giglio, plundering Porto Ercole. Skirting papal territory, he brought his fleet into the Bay of Naples, stripping the islands, landing at Pozzuoli, marching to the gates of Naples. Before seeking Messina he swept up the population of the Lipari Islands.

When he rounded Serai Point, Barbarossa brought with him many more ships, chests of gold and men than he had taken away.

It is said that Suleiman came down from the kiosk of the Serai garden to greet him at the landing stage. Of what was said between them, as Barbarossa related his experience as guest of the French King, there is no record.

Barbarossa did not put to sea again. Two years later he died. Suleiman built for him the kind of tomb he had wanted, plain and small, of enduring gray granite, so close to the water of the Bosphorus that passing ships had it in full view. For many generations thereafter no fleet cleared Serai Point without turning first to fire a salute at Barbarossa's tomb.

It had carved upon it a legend of three Arabic words: *Ma'at rais al bahr.* Dead is the Captain of the Sea.

Dragut

Barbarossa bequeathed to his master a brood of sea rovers. The task he had begun, of bedeviling the Mediterranean and of making the Turkish flag supreme, they carried out to the full.

Crafty Sinan, although getting on in years, served as Kaputan Pasha, spending most of his time ashore at the Arsenal. Salih Reis, the fat Arab from the Nile, disappeared from the brotherhood, but Piali, the studious Croat from the School, rose to command. He was liked and trusted by Suleiman.

Torgut, already known only too well by the Spaniards as Dragut, had Barbarossa's knack of surviving defeat, and of accomplishing the seemingly impossible. Oddly, he was the only Turk by birth among the lieutenants, being the son of an Anatolian peasant. Dragut had always craved to be on the sea, and with the money he made as a wrestler he bought a small galliot, attracting Barbarossa's attention by his skill as a pilot.

Generous and reckless, Dragut fared best when in command of a few vessels, alone. Headstrong, he could not accustom himself to carrying out orders, and Barbarossa had never entrusted many sails to him. And Dragut had been caught by Giovanetto Doria—the nephew of the celebrated admiral—on a beach at Sardinia while he was landing spoils to divide them among his officers.

While chained to the oar of an Italian galley, Dragut had been seen and recognized by De La Valette, a Knight of Malta who in turn had served as oarsman captive of the Moslems.

"*Señor Dragut,*" the Knight exclaimed, "*usanza de guerra* [Sir Dragut, 'tis the way of war]!"

Dragut also remembered De La Valette as an oarsman. "*Y mudanza de fortuna* [well, a turn of luck]," he corrected, cheerfully.

Barbarossa did not rest content until he had ransomed his

audacious lieutenant from Doria, paying the high price of three thousand gold pieces—a bargain that Doria had every reason to regret thereafter.

For, like the specter of the dead Captain of the Sea, Dragut haunted the mid-Mediterranean. Having studied European routine while a captive, he took toll of European commerce —once taking in a Malta-bound treasure ship with seventy thousand ducats, and again overrunning Sicily under the eyes of its Viceroy. Even Dragut's mishaps had a way of turning out to his advantage.

He was cruising off Genoa when his favorite castle in Africa, Mahdiya, was captured by Garcia de Toledo, son of the discomfited Viceroy of Sicily. This annoyed Suleiman, who had made his final peace with the Europeans by then, and he protested the attack on a Moslem port by a force of the Empire.

In answer, Charles called it no act of war but an attack on brigands. Suleiman retorted that in his eyes the sea captains were no more brigands than those of the Empire. And he recompensed Dragut with the gift of twenty galleys and their crews.

Straightway Dragut managed to have his enlarged fleet trapped by no less a sea lord than Andrea Doria. Again, his mishap came from carelessness. Evicted from Mahdiya, he had settled on the marshy fertile isle of Yerba—the drowsy isle of legendary lotus-eaters. There he occupied a castle raised by a Doria of an earlier time, while he quartered his fleet in its shallow lagoon. He was greasing the galley keels when the living Doria appeared with a small armada off the narrow entrance of the lagoon.

Certain that he had Dragut with all his fleet, the Genoese sent a courier vessel back to Naples with the message: "Dragut is trapped in Yerba, without escape."

As he had hesitated off Prevesa, Doria took his time about forcing the entrance to the lagoon. Hastily the Turks threw up a breastwork on either side the narrow strip of water, and mounted cannon to blaze away at the imperial fleet without result except to make Doria hesitate the more.

At last, when he observed that the cannon were missing from the entry, Doria pushed into the lagoon, to find Dragut vanished with his fleet. The elusive Turk assuredly had not come out the entrance, yet he was no longer in the lagoon.

It took the Christians quite a while to solve the riddle. While they had delayed, the Turks had dug a canal through the low shore on the far side, hauling their vessels through and over the swamps to the sea.

There Dragut had the sheer luck to capture the galley sent from Sicily with tidings of reinforcements on the way to aid Doria to gather in the Turks.

"Torgut," Turkish chroniclers related, "is the drawn sword of Islam."

These sea captains of Suleiman, for all their eccentricity, were carrying out the plan of Barbarossa, maintaining an offshore blockade of the northern, European coasts, while driving the Spanish garrisons out of their fortified points on the African coast. Bujeya followed Mahdiya into Turkish rule. Distinguished commanders like the French Duc de Bourbon and the English Henry of Beaufort set sail blithely for Africa, to come back frustrated.

Something important was taking place. The Spanish attempt to make North Africa a New Spain was failing as decisively as their conquest of the New World beyond the Atlantic was succeeding. The Mediterranean, unlike the Caribbean, never became a Spanish Main.

Suleiman saw to that. As he aged and turned more and more to the reading of the Koran at night before sleep, the hope grew in him that he could see the last of the Christian garrisons driven out of Moslem Africa.

At the same time in Spain itself, in the portrait-lined halls of Tolédo, the son of Charles held more stubbornly to a different hope. Don Philip—who was to be Philip II of Spain—had been tutored in the grandeur of empire. No warrior himself, Philip resembled Suleiman in being withdrawn from the people who served him, and in looking ever to the consequences of his actions.

When Don Philip put to sea, to his first marriage, it was on the deck of Andrea Doria's capitana galley, carpeted and gay with banners and music, surrounded by the caravels of Spain. (The voyage hugged the coast to Genoa, well away from the orbit of the Turkish fleets.) The young Philip, then, sensed the reality of sea power, and the pageantry of empire. Yet when the electors of the Empire failed to name him to succeed his father—choosing instead the Austrian Hapsburg, Ferdinand—Philip awakened from his dream of world authority to find himself master of Spain alone. Driven inward, as it were, he still looked to Spain to become a dominant state. He still thought of himself as the successor to his father.

Inflexible in his devotion to the Catholic Church, Philip determined to purge his kingdom of the minority of infidel Moors. More than that, he would restore the Spanish dominion upon the African coast.

In attempting to do so, the stubborn and methodical Philip found himself opposed by the elusive and invincible Dragut. It was a case of Barbarossa over again.

Dragut's luck seemed to be pure happenchance. Once, when he and Sinan landed on Malta itself, only to decide against besieging that stronghold of the Knights, they turned aside to Tripoli instead. If they could not bring back to Suleiman the trophies of Malta, they would announce the capture of Tripoli from those same Knights. As it happened, they did so. Sinan showed less courtesy to these sworn enemies of Islam than the Sultan had shown at Rhodes—they were chained and exhibited at the Serai as captives.

Years later when Philip launched his first expedition against Africa it went to Tripoli. As usual it had great strength, under the varied flags of Europe, with distinguished commanders—the Duke of Medina-Celi and Giovanni Doria, grandnephew of Andrea—and being thus made up mostly of soldiery, it fared badly at sea. Unseen devils of storms and plague beset it When at last it sighted the sands of Tripoli the commanders decided it had been weakened too greatly to risk a siege of that strong citadel.

They resolved instead to take Dragut's cherished isle of Yerba only a few days' sail along the coast. This they did easily enough, in Dragut's absence. The peasantry of the drowsy place did not try to stand against the armored Spaniards.

Thereupon the ancient spell of the lotus-eaters seemed to fall upon Philip's crusaders. They lingered, feasting on pomegranates and melons. Between whiles they built a new castle to enable them to hold this strategic spot. They lingered on to do it.

They delayed too long. In the winter storms the tranquil lagoon made a pleasant haven. Then Dragut's sails were sighted coming home. In a day the aspect of the lagoon changed. Its narrow, shallow entry transformed it into a trap. Medina-Celi and young Doria tried to embark their forces. Panic threw the lagoon into a turmoil of colliding galleys and galleons running aground.

Into that confusion Dragut and Piali Pasha brought their fleets. They had had long experience with the shallows of Yerba and their crews had been at sea during the months the Spaniards had idled ashore.

Philip's two commanders escaped, but the rest of the armada remained, to surrender to the Turks. Fifty-six vessels and more than fourteen thousand men fell into Dragut's hands, with the excellent new castle to guard the entrance thereafter.

They called it Dragut's luck. At Genoa, when the news of the disaster was brought him, the aged Andrea Doria asked to be carried to church. He died after this last Mass.

At Constantinople, Ogier Busbecq was to witness the final debarkation of Philip's expedition.

The retreat of the Europeans toward the Gibraltar end of the Mediterranean left one stronghold exposed to face the Turks. The islet of Malta had been fortified by the Knights. The Religion had no intention of retreating again before Suleiman. And there Dragut and De La Valette were to meet in final conflict.

With the Turks holding the Mediterranean, the sea captains of Spain and Portugal had to find their way to the Orient around the Cape of Good Hope. In Africa their traders were detoured southward, to search for gold, elephant ivory and Ethiopian slaves.

Of these voyages through the outer oceans Suleiman was informed by prisoners who had coasted the shores of India. Piri Reis had drawn maps of the outer world to show how the Portuguese by circling Africa were draining the trade of the far east. As overlord of Egypt Suleiman had an interest in that trade, and he wanted to protect the Moslem shores of India.

His idea of course was fantastic—that he could challenge the galleons of Portugal on the far seas where he had no ships. But as usual he saw it carried out. His seamen performed one of their feats of moving vessels over dry land—in this case timber and cannon only, hauled and floated across the Suez isthmus, to be turned into seventy galleys upon the Red Sea, and given to the care of an aged but versatile eunuch, Suleiman Pasha.

This unusual commander managed to sail his improvised fleet down the Red Sea, to take Aden for the Sultan, and Massawa under the Abyssinian hills. Somehow he coasted along the Yemen and found his way across the waste of the hot ocean to the port of Diu, off a river mouth of India. There he battered at the proud Portuguese by land, not by sea. Not faring too well in his venture, the pasha navigated back, taking care to make the pilgrimage to the Ka'aba at Mecca, to bring to Suleiman the account of his pilgrimage instead of a victory off India. Where-upon the Sultan ordered transports to be built on the Red Sea, to carry pilgrims across to Jiddah.

Soon after that the stout and cheery Ayas Pasha died of the plague. When his children were counted, they were found to number one hundred and twenty. The vizirate Suleiman gave to the aged navigator of the Indian Ocean.

A Peace Is Won

At that time Suleiman asked no more of his vizirs than that they should be faithful servants. Still trying to carry the burden of administration alone, he seemed to turn to elder Turks of simple mind, and to old friends of the School. The three who became his closest companions in work were utterly unlike Ibrahim. Yet each was a genius in his way.

Sinan Agha—known everywhere as "the Architect"—had come up from the boy levy, to serve in the campaigns from Belgrade to Vienna, where he accomplished a miracle in engineering. He had an amazing knack of building whatever was needed. Moreover, he had the Turkish knack—of Suleiman's time—of doing the more difficult things swiftly; the seemingly impossible took the Architect a little longer. After finishing new bath chambers in gray marble next the Sultan's sleeping room in the Serai, Sinan threw an aqueduct across the desert to waterless Mecca.

Rustem, an Albanian who had risen to the top in the Organization, had a gift for management. It was said of him that he never smiled and never spoke unless giving an order. Evidently Suleiman hoped for much from him, bestowing his favorite daughter Mihrmah on him as a bride.

The third, Ibn Sa'ud, was remarkable. By descent a Kurd, by birth a Moslem, by education a doctor of the Law, he could write a poem vibrant with grief after the death of a child. In

Ibn Sa'ud Suleiman had found a legalist who could place personality above the Law. He named Ibn Sa'ud Mufti.

Upon two of this triumvirate he would rely greatly in the twenty years of life remaining to him; one would carry out his ideas after Suleiman's death. Yet to none of them at this point did he grant a portion of the overriding authority that had been Ibrahim's undoing. It was as if he tried to say to them: *The responsibility we will share; the rewards must go to no one.* But the Osmanli remained inarticulate as always. He could only show what he meant by an example, or judge a case where a man had erred. Much as he loved the winsome Mihrmah, he was to earn her hatred and to hear of her death in bleak silence.

Small wonder, then, that at fifty years of age Suleiman was still an enigma to European minds. His likeness they knew because even Dürer had sketched it; his fame had spread through all their courts. Titian painted him as one of the enemies of Christ in the great canvas of the *Ecce Homo.* Paul Veronese was to place his likeness beside Francis and Charles V in the *Marriage at Cana.* The aged historian Paolo Giovio, who had written so often of "the Turkish terror," sent a copy of his *Commentary on Turkish Affairs* to Suleiman, and received back— so rumor relates—a miniature portrait of the Sultan.

An Italian, Navagero, described him as "tall and thin with an expression of gentleness and majesty. He now drinks no wine as they say he did in Ibrahim's time. Almost daily he leaves the city in his barge to walk in his gardens or hunt on the Asia shore. I am told he is very just, and when he understands the facts of a case, he never wrongs any man. He asserts that he will never break his word."

In those years, 1544–47, Suleiman won from the Europeans what he had sought with unquenchable determination for a dozen years—a signed peace with the concert of Europe. Perhaps Barbarossa's final ravaging of the Mediterranean in 1543 paved the way to this; perhaps Suleiman had made it clear even to the Hapsburgs that he would stay in the Hungarian plain and would not go beyond it. Whatever the reason, the perseverance of this one man obtained his *pax Turcica*. "One man and one purpose."

When new envoys came from the Austrians bringing a rare gift, a great gilded clock with miniature sun, moon and planets that moved in time with the passing of the hours, Suleiman was pleased. He did not need the explanatory booklet they offered him because he had spent many hours in his House of Time where observers worked with astrolobes to check the hours by the rising of the stars. But when, with their compliments, they offered only the old plea of Ferdinand, for Buda in return for 100,000 ducats, Suleiman stormed at them through the mouth of his Vizir. "Do they think the Padishah has lost his mind? Do they think that he will yield up for money what he has conquered and won back twice with his sword?"

One of the envoys, Sigismund, Baron von Herberstein, who had gained experience at the court of Moscow, left the Turkish border in a thoughtful mood. "I have seen the strength," he said, "of a great and powerful monarch."

The treaty of 1547 had two remarkable points in it. Although drawn with the Hapsburgs, it included the French King, the Pope, and the Signory of Venice. The Osmanli was making his point clear here. He rested on his arms, apart from the westerners, to preserve peace with *all* of them.

Yet he made a second point, just as clearly. His sea captains were not to be bound by the treaty. (He intended to journey into Asia again and Barbarossa had taught him how his fleets in the Mediterranean could mystify the courts from Tolédo to Vienna. And Dragut saw to it that they did so.)

Suleiman insisted on one thing more. Ferdinand, King of the Romans, was to pay 30,000 ducats every year for the mountains in northern Hungary that remained to him. The Austrians called this an honorary pension, but Suleiman understood it to be, as it was, a payment of tribute to him from the House of Hapsburg.

The money he hardly needed. As in the case of the small yearly payment from the Venetians, it was simply a point of pride.

Then in the full tide of triumph, terror struck at him.

The First Conspiracy of the Harem

It began in his own household so gradually that at first he did not notice it. The fire, of course, set it going.

Roxelana, now his acknowledged wife, had hoped for Ibrahim's downfall. The brilliant Greek had been the third person in the way of her supremacy within the household. Aware of Ibrahim's megalomania, the Favorite Laughing One may have used her influence against him, but it was little needed.

Suleiman's distrust of advisers after Ibrahim's death had played into her hands. She had no other woman to fear. Yet the Sultan's absorption in duties kept him away from her except for occasional hours—she being penned in the old palace while he worked and often slept in the Serai on the point. When Roxelana begged to be allowed to quarter herself near him within the Serai he refused. By order of the Conqueror, no woman had been allowed to sleep the night where the Divan carried on the business of the dominion.

The great fire, however, moved Roxelana to the Serai temporarily. It swept the water front, rising to the ramshackle buildings of the old palace, destroying the women's wardrobes and treasures. Necessarily, the wife and favorite was hurried to shelter, and Suleiman gave her the rooms behind his own within the third court.

Now from the Conqueror's day the Serai had been a work place. Suleiman himself ate, slept and received his intimate visitors in cramped quarters between the room of his Chief Squire, who happened to be Rustem, and the hospital of the School.

241

Even the Sultan was not prepared for the following that Roxelana brought with her for shelter, nearly a hundred servants, robe makers, black eunuchs and messengers. Since Roxelana did not seem to be able to manage without this entourage, Suleiman quartered it also in the chambers around the inner courtyard of the Serai.

There it stayed, as his harem. Somehow the work of rebuilding the uncomfortable old palace lagged. Roxelana wondered why it should be rebuilt at all. Besides herself, who was to occupy it now that Gulbehar had died? Only a few old women pensioners who were happier in any case elsewhere with their relatives.

So Roxelana remained in the Serai of the administration, as the single wife of the Osmanli Sultan. Thereby she broke a kanun of the Conqueror. Since the old law of the harem of course prevailed as before, all her section of the Serai became closed to outsiders. Within it, as the Sultan Valideh had ruled the old building, Roxelana ruled, although she was not and apparently could not be a Sultan Valideh.

A private door was cut between her labyrinth of chambers and the Sultan's small two-room apartment. There was nothing luxurious about either suite. But slaves began to speak of her reception room with the dome looking out into the wooded garden from latticed openings as the Throne Room Within. There Suleiman came to spend much of his leisure.

He could not or would not order his wife to be taken bodily from the Serai. Where would she go? Installed at his side in this manner, the Russian woman could venture veiled out into the corridor called the Golden Road that led to the Divan. Who was to turn back the wife and favorite of the Padishah? Beyond the Golden Road another corridor led to the stair of the small tower which in turn gave access to the hidden window where Suleiman listened at times to the never-ending discussion of the Divan below. Roxelana could not venture as far as the window, but reports were brought her by those who did.

Restless anxiety drove her to weigh every word of her spies. It came from the Osmanli law of fratricide. Although Gulbehar had died, Mustafa, the son of the Circassian woman, would be the next Sultan. What if Mustafa chose to invoke the ancient law, and to put to death his stepbrothers who were her own sons, Selim, Bayazid and Jahangir?

Impetuously the Russian woman urged this danger upon Suleiman, only to be met by his calm assurance. Mustafa *was* the heir, he repeated over and over. The family had stepped beyond barbarity. Mustafa, amiable and untroubled, would never demand the lives of his younger brothers. She could be certain of that.

Roxelana had the clear-eyed realism of a peasant girl who had been captive in this strange court. Having courage as well, she never argued for herself, although she would become no more than a widowed woman, solitary at the Sultan's death. Yet her tense emotion broke out in protest. "Lord of my life, the truth of your words heals my heart. Mustafa's good feeling will not change. I fear others than him. What will be the thought of the one who is Vizir? Would a dried-up monkey like the eunuch Vizir have love for the afflicted Jahangir? Could even the astrologers of the House of Time foretell what plans an Agha of Janizaris might hatch, or the brotherhood of the janizaris be moved to do to our sons? Already they follow Mustafa about like faithful dogs. Can you read the minds of servants?"

Suleiman, in justice, could not deny the danger she feared. He could not provide for what would happen one minute after he ceased to live.

It was not devotion to Roxelana alone that troubled him. His fondness for the crippled Jahangir and the slender, winsome Mihrmah pressed upon him. Upon this Roxelana played. If Rustem, the husband of Mihrmah, could only be given authority! Inflexible and just, Rustem could protect the others of the family. If he were Vizir.

Suleiman could appreciate that. Not that he anticipated his

own death—Roxelana had shown great daring to mention it—but he felt that his children should be safeguarded before it. What he did at the time was to send Mustafa from the administration of fertile Magnisiya—the training ground of a Sultan-to-be—to a government far from the city, in the east. Rustem he appointed Beylerbey of Diyarbekr, even further away.

Rustem resembled his father-in-law the Sultan in his silence and tireless energy at a task; he had more than Ibrahim's skill with finances. No one questioned the Albanian's integrity, but no one knew how avaricious he would prove to be, or how Roxelana could twist his will to her advantage.

Her opportunity came with the growing incapacity of the aged eunuch Vizir, who could do little more than sit as a figurehead in the Divan. Suleiman retired him and named Rustem in his place. Thereby he violated another kanun of the Conqueror—that appointment should be by ability alone, and no Sultan might name a relative to an office near him.

Very deftly Roxelana had intrigued to gain her purpose. Only one thing stood now between her sons and the throne, the life of Mustafa. If Mustafa could be removed, she could abide in the Serai as the Sultan Valideh-to-be, with a sure hold upon the vizirate through Rustem.

Yet the able and popular prince could be executed only by command of Suleiman, who had never dreamed of the death of his son. Roxelana had a slight circumstance to aid her. Off at the far frontier Mustafa was becoming a favorite with the troops. Her spies brought her certain evidence of that, without, however, any proof against Mustafa's loyalty to his father. They merely had the talk of the camps. "The young Sultan is born to the saddle . . . even now he can lead the standards to the Lands of War more swiftly than the Padishah . . . when he makes gifts, he gives with both hands . . . may God lengthen his years and preserve him to become our Padishah."

A little of this, carefully selected, Roxelana contrived to bring before the eyes of Suleiman. She knew his mind, and remembered how long he had brooded on the rising of the Young Troops against his aging grandfather. If he had not confided that to the woman he loved, she might not have succeeded.

It took years to accomplish.

Unceasingly Roxelana studied the mind of her husband. She had the choir of boys from the Enclosed School across the way brought to her Throne Room Within, blindfolded, that she might sit behind her lattice screen and watch Suleiman's face as he listened, relaxed by the songs. She sensed something withdrawn in him, beyond her touch. In that depth lurked cruelty, and suspicion of what he did not understand, and a yearning for more than the Khasseki Khurrem, with all her intuition, could realize.

It would be dangerous to plot against him; even the oblivious Ibrahim had not attempted that. To rouse his suspicion, by apparent chance—that was the utmost she could do . . . when he rode past the barracks of the janizaris at the outer court, he still glanced at their great soup kettles, from habit. If it could become a habit with him, to watch for what she had made him suspect!

Roxelana praised the virile strength of the son of Gulbehar. Soon, she agreed, with the Army of Asia, Mustafa could end the suspense in the east caused by the fanatical Persians. Even the janizaris would follow him, although they would suffer no one else to command them, except of course the Ruler of the Two Worlds. Suleiman need not go again to the east.

Yet he did go after making peace with the Europeans. Perhaps he hoped to end the Persian conflict himself, because a brother of the Shah had fled to sanctuary at his court of Constantinople. Suleiman endured the disapproval of his own officers in taking this heretical Shi'ite eastward with him. If he could divide the rule in Persia between the Shah, Tahmasp, and his rebel brother, his own frontier would be left untroubled.

Suleiman was gone with the great army for the winter of

1548–49. Roxelana heard there had been no battle, for the Shi'ites retired before his army. His diary, which she contrived to read, was more curt than ever. Although he must have climbed through mountain chains and sent his horsemen flying down to the gates of Isfahan, he had written only the names of places in his diary. Although, as before, he had sent a sea commander, Piri Reis, out to the far east, to seize Muscat and hold the Persian Gulf against the infidel Portuguese, he took no pride in that. He said only that Piri Reis had escaped with two galleys after his fleet had been shipwrecked on the Bahrein Islands. In Egypt, Piri Reis had been tried for losing his vessels, and condemned to die.

By that Suleiman had revealed the anger he restrained so carefully. Roxelana took heed of it, noticing how Rustem confined himself to the affairs of the Treasury, avoiding any pretense of the political power that Ibrahim had abused. Rustem, too, feared the Sultan.

As before, after returning from Asia, Suleiman devoted himself more to religion. Often he read commentaries on the Koran from the pen of the Mufti. Roxelana urged that he ease the weariness of his mind by appealing to the Mufti to make vital decisions for him.

But Suleiman did not agree. "In matters of faith, yes," he responded. "There the Law decides. In matters of obedience or loyalty, how can the will of God be known? There judgment must be given upon the evidence."

So cold his mind was, so stubborn to hold to facts. The woman could not realize how, standing stooped and tall, his gray eyes heavy with lack of sleep, he was trying to shoulder the needs of millions of human beings, and feeling with the ache of a wound his inability to do so. "Piri Reis should not have left his crews," he muttered.

Curiously she observed his own longing to build the *Suleimaniye*. Out from her windows, across the curve of the city, another height overgrown with cypress rose above the cluster of masts along the Golden Horn. Instead of rebuilding the old palace, Suleiman had resolved to take this height entire and build a place of his own on it. Not in the least resembling a palace, the Suleimaniye would have such things as a hostel for wayfarers, religious schools, a soup kitchen, a home for aged and twisted minds, all centered about a mosque that would surpass the Aya Sofia in beauty.

He had the architect to do it, now, in Sinan Agha, Rustem's brother, who had restored Baghdad. Sinan had drawn plans for a dome larger than any in the city, and he was certain it could be upheld on four columns, although that seemed incredible.

And there was something incredible to Roxelana in the way Suleiman drove the brilliant minds about him now—Sinan's to the task of imagining bridges of stone and wayside shrines, Rustem's to the eternal problem of gleaning enough but not too much in head tax from the people, eked out with tribute from foreign lands, Sokolli's to the care of the ships left by Barbarossa. Like Suleiman, their good will could not be bought, or their minds distracted from daily duties. . . .

The Three Mutes of the Bowstring

Mustafa's life appeared as secure as that of the Mufti himself when a slight misfortune drew attention to the eastern frontier in the summer of 1553. There the Persians advanced through the mountains to take Erzerum, the stronghold that defended the main east-west pass. Instead of going east himself Suleiman, who was then nearing his sixtieth birthday, sent Rustem in command of the field army.

Almost at once disturbing reports came back to the Serai. The veterans of the army, displeased because the Sultan had not come with them, were causing Rustem trouble. Unaccountably the army delayed its march near Mustafa's government of Amasiya. Then the reports spoke of rebellion. The troops demanded, if the Sultan were too old to ride with the *asker*, that the prince, Mustafa, lead them. "Let it be done," they said. "Only the First Vizir objects to yielding his place to the Sultan-to-be. This Rustem is not of the blood of the Osmanli. By slaying him and sending the old Sultan to rest in retirement, we may have at our head the man who should lead us to war."

Such talk had been heard before. Now it came from the main Turkish army in the field. Rustem's private report stirred Suleiman to suspicion and immediate action. Mustafa, the Vizir maintained, had listened willingly to the rebels. Rustem could no longer control the army. Suleiman must journey east swiftly, or lose his throne.

Not doubting Rustem, Suleiman prepared to march at once, then hesitated. What would happen upon his arrival? He could compel the obedience of most of the army, but there might be conflict, and certainly execution of the dissidents. In such a case Osmanli Law required the taking of one life, if it would save thousands.

Probably Suleiman had no fear of an outbreak of rebellion. He had to decide the question, what wrong had his son committed, by what right could Mustafa be judged? Unable to decide himself, he ventured to put the question to the supreme judge of Islam, giving no names.

"A well-known merchant of this city, leaving his home, placed all that belonged to him there in the care of the slave he most favored. This slave, in the master's absence, began to steal his goods and to plan to take his life. In such a case, what sentence does the Law impose upon the slave?"

This was given the Mufti, Ibn Sa'ud, without comment. But the messenger who followed it from the Serai let the Mufti understand that the question concerned the Sultan in person. This secret admonition must have come from Roxelana's clique.

The Mufti replied bluntly, "In my judgment the punishment of the slave should be death by torture."

The advice of Ibn Sa'ud, Rustem's warning, the ominous

rumors that met Suleiman in his audience hall and the Divan, all had taken shape by Roxelana's contriving.

Suleiman recalled Rustem from command, turned over the rule of the city to his favored third son, Bayazid, and started with his household regiments on the long ride across the ferry to Scutari, and the foothills of the east. As he did so he wrote to Mustafa to come in person to his camp to answer the accusations against him.

To Roxelana, waiting for word of Suleiman's arrival at the army, it seemed that Gulbehar's son would not be foolish enough to obey his father's command. Yet the alternative of flight in Mustafa's case would be a confession of guilt. She hardly believed the report that the prince was riding to meet the Sultan, although warned against doing so. "He said," her spies insisted, "that if he had to die it could not be in a better way than by his father's hand"

Yet Mustafa came into Suleiman's camp, splendidly mounted, taking the salutes of the enthusiastic janizaris. He dared place his own tent close to that of the Sultan.

Across the space between the tents he rode with only two followers. At the entrance of the Sultan's he paused because the janizaris on guard flocked around him. He went in alone to meet his father. In the reception space three deaf mutes waited, holding a bowstring.

The spies said that Suleiman watched the death of Mustafa from behind a transparent curtain. Assuredly Mustafa's two followers were killed outside the entrance with swords. His body was placed there on a carpet, for the men of the *asker* to see as they filed by.

Roxelana paid little attention to reports that followed—of the mourning and outcry of the janizaris. No one else was punished. But that day the janizaris would take no food. They demanded the life of Rustem, who was safe on his way back to the city by then.

Worse happened in the old city of Brusa. There Mustafa's

widow feared for the life of his four-year-old son, when a
eunuch appeared as messenger from the court, to summon her
to the Serai. The eunuch contrived to get the boy out of her
sight and kill him. When the death was known in Brusa, townspeople ran out to hunt the murderer, who escaped.

Mustafa had been innocent of treachery. In the crisis he had
shown great courage and had been met with conspiracy, for
which the Russian woman was responsible.

It had seemed a simple thing, to remove the elder stepson
from the path of her own sons; but it was to have consequences
unsuspected by her and decisive for the future of the Osmanli
dominion. What the future might have been, along the direction
laid down by Suleiman, carried forward by leaders like Mustafa,
can only be imagined.

The first consequence was the anger in the city, not against
Suleiman who—in popular opinion—had merely condemned his
own son with cruelty, but against the two conspirators of the
palace, Rustem and Roxelana. Since the woman could not be
mentioned publicly or touched, the restrained anger turned
against the Vizir, her son-in-law. A poet of the day, a certain
Yahya, wrote and passed from hand to hand a lament for his
hero, the young Osmanli. Yahya, who had been a Christian and
an Albanian, seemed to have no fear of consequences.

Rustem, aware of the feeling against him, had Yahya brought
before the Divan. "How have you dared," he asked, "write
that I live on like Satan, while Mustafa is lost to Suleiman's
throne?"

With quick wit the poet answered, "Like everyone else, I
bowed to the justice of my lord the Sultan. Like everyone, I
cannot refrain from weeping at the sad consequence."

Angered, Rustem would have had Yahya executed, but Suleiman refused to punish the poet. Instead he removed Rustem
from office. His messenger, the Treasurer of the realm, appeared
before the Divan to demand the Osmanli seal from Rustem in

the name of the Sultan. Rustem was ordered to his quarters, and the seal given to the Second Vizir.

Then Jahangir died. The neurotic cripple, Suleiman's companion, grieved incurably after the loss of Mustafa. The court physicians could not save him with their medicine.

All Roxelana's ingenuity could not prevent immediate rivalry between her two surviving sons. Her devotion went to Selim, the elder, ungainly and unliked. Selim was subject to fits of terror, and took to wine drinking to quiet himself, gaining other oblivion from slave girls. His mother tried to persuade Suleiman to name Selim as Sultan-to-be, and failed. Suleiman favored Bayazid, the younger, who had Mustafa's qualities and quick sensitivity and foresight.

In these circumstances the dark, gray-eyed Bayazid kept on with his training without misgiving; the florid Selim began to assemble followers of his own, to strike at his brother secretly.

Suleiman might have been able to control Roxelana's sons, if it had not been for the ghost of Mustafa. It was no more than an impostor, taking the name of the dead prince to gather a following about him. In the desert regions of Anatolia he stirred up the tribes with the aid of dervishes who had grievances. Even army officers who had known the dead prince swore that this was Mustafa in the flesh.

Very soon the false Mustafa was identified and caught. But the unrest that had gathered around him spread to the camps of the two living sons. Slight as it was, the fearful Selim fostered it.

Alone, riding through the Great Gate, alone when the wardrobe page bowed and left him after the last prayer to lie on his quilt on the tiled flooring, watching through the narrow window as the pattern of stars moved above the cypress trees, Suleiman remembered the face of his son. He did not speak of it. By the night lamp that he kept burning now he would look at the page of the poem of Yahya the Albanian who had loved

Mustafa. *The hidden hate of the liar . . . made our tears to flow . . . what had death itself brought to Mustafa? He started like a stranger on that journey, all alone.*

He rode now with the pain of gout in his legs and his breathing labored as he tired. Unless he, the Sultan, could go to the place of trouble with his officers, he could not know the root of the trouble. Nearly sixty years of age, he found it more difficult——

He did not go to Egypt, where he had sent Ibrahim so often, when the feud flared there between the governor and the new Vizir Ahmed. Suleiman had thought Ahmed to be honest, and the governor to be honest, yet the trouble came from one of them raising revenues for his own enrichment. Again a letter came into Suleiman's hands written by Ahmed, bidding his agents increase the revenues, to disgrace the governor. Ali the Fat they called the governor.

In sudden rage, because he had seen the letter, Suleiman ordered the execution of Ahmed. Only after that did he hear that Ahmed had been afraid not to increase the Egyptian revenue, as the capable Rustem had done. Roxelana had contrived the proof against Ahmed.

In the Serai his daughter Mihrmah pleaded with him, and Roxelana urged him to give the vizirate back to Rustem, upon whom he could rely. After another year he did so.

Rustem, moving cautiously, relieved the Sultan of no responsibility except the accounting of money taken in and given out. By now Suleiman understood that no one could share greater responsibility with him. The Mufti might pronounce the Law of the Koran but the judging of the Law rested with Suleiman. The canker within his household could be cured by no one but himself.

He could not suspect that the intrigues of Roxelana and Mihrmah in his harem had opened up a fatal weakness in the Organization. If secluded women could influence the Divan, they could in time manage the affairs of the empire, because they remained invisible and unheard by those outside the Throne Room Within.

Rustem was the first of many vizirs to be created by the harem.

The Refuge on the Hill

It was Suleiman's failing that he tried to project ideas beyond the ability of human servants to carry them out. Justice remained, in his thought, an unalterable law; he would keep to his given word, even when the consequences were harmful; the gleaming rubies and amethysts set into his sword hilt were not precious stones in which he took pride—they were tokens of the dignity of the Osmanli. Along with the shimmering cloth of gold that covered his body, they were part of the ritual of his life. Rarely did he reveal human fondness for things close to him, pet horses among the thoroughbreds of his stables, a gold goblet wrought by the hand of a Cellini, or a remarkable clock.

"Someone found fault with him," Ogier Busbecq recalled, "for eating off silver plate, so he has used nothing but earthenware since."

This duality of the Turks and their Sultan was forever puzzling the Europeans who had begun to come to the Gate. They decided that the Turks were brutal mystics. One said, "They are in truth grand seigneurs in great affairs, marauders in little." Busbecq discovered that the inexplicable Turks picked up scraps of old paper from the ground to tuck into walls or shrubs because any fragment might have the name of God written on it; they picked up fallen rose petals because, superstitiously, they believed that such petals were the tears of Muhammad the Prophet.

Usually the casual Europeans could adapt their ideas to their personal needs and desires. Suleiman could not. He had never claimed, for instance, that he was Protector of the Faithful, like the earlier kalifs; instead he had sought to make Constantinople an international refuge, where the inner seas and the great continents met. He had failed because he could not give natural life to the great city. To Rome across the waters multitudes flocked because they sought its shrines, its workshops of artisans, its markets or streets of prostitutes.

Constantinople remained, as it had been, a city of refugees, sprinkled with the markets and the abodes of the inner peoples, with Greek churches, and Jewish synagogues, and the multitudinous baths and tombs of the Turks. It remained like a huge caravan serai, lifeless except for the throngs that came and went.

Suleiman did not easily give up an idea Realizing that he had failed to create a metropolis of peoples, he had ordered Sinan the Architect to erect a Sultan's sanctuary back of the wreckage of the old palace. If he could not make Constantinople into another eastern Rome, he would give to his people an inner city, the realization of his dream. It would be complete in itself, somewhat like the city of the Vatican—as Europeans had begun to call the residence of the Christian Pope.

In six years he built the Suleimaniye, he and the tireless Sinan. Suleiman gave to his architect the fine marbles and porphyry from abandoned churches and the still standing palace of Belisarius. It was an amazing accomplishment to erect and furnish a religious center in that time. Over in Rome, the aged Michelangelo was laboring to raise the dome of St. Peter's, from the plans of Bramante, with the aid of Nanni and the assistance of two popes. Under Suleiman's insistence, the Turkish workmen went at their task with the energy that had put together a fleet for the impatient Barbarossa in a year and a half.

Neither the Mufti nor Suleiman, however, occupied the Suleimaniye, the only place to which the Sultan gave his name. (In Paris Francis had begun to rebuild the Louvre as a new royal residence, and Catherine de' Medici would soon order a Palais des Tuileries for herself.) The structures on the hill were for the use of all people in the city, without cost. A reservoir supplied two necessities of Moslem life, clean drinking fountains and water for the baths. A primary school taught young children the essentials of reading the Koran and simple arithmetic; four small academies gave classes in rudimentary sciences, along with such unusual matters as metaphysics, music and astronomy. Savants in the House of Time kept track of stellar time. Mullahs in a Hall of Reading took turns in maintaining a continuous recitation of the verses of the Koran.

For the sick, there was a crude hospital with a medical school attached. (Islamic teaching, however, refused to recognize prevention in cases of epidemics, so that plague in the city always took a heavy toll of lives.) For the non-Moslem sick, there was also a smaller hospital where patients could be treated in accordance with their various religions. Christians, native or foreign, could also stay for three days at a hostel of their own, provided with soup, barley and meat at no cost to them.

For students there was the inevitable library in the vast galleries of the mosque itself. The books were manuscripts, written, illustrated and decorated by the hands of calligraphers, because the Turks did not like and could not master the new European art of printing with metal type. Although most of these volumes dealt with religious Law and tradition, the curious student could find geographies and fables of animals among them, along with the great Persian poets like Jami and Rumi. The upper galleries of the mosque served another need; personal valuables could be stored there under seal. Whether jewels, gold coin, silverwork or simple keepsakes, a man could bring his trove to this treasury of the Suleimaniye and deposit it with caretakers, out of the reach of thieves and tax collectors.

From this height, the great mosque of Suleiman rose. Outwardly it was no more than another Turkish copy of the majestic Aya Sofia, except that its courtyards had the spaciousness of parks. Only in the interior did Sinan create something unique.

A man enters this place of prayer of Suleiman and stops,

instantly aware of space and silence, of shadow and light. He feels the impact of challenge from the coloring of walls and four immense square columns inlaid with vari-hued marble. There is nothing more. Not a statue or projection breaks the surfaces around him. Light glows through stained glass—Ibrahim the Drunken made those paintings on glass—and overhead there is the immense vault of the dome.

In measurement, the dome is five meters wider than the Aya Sofia's, and about as much less than the diameter of St. Peter's.

But probably no other structure in the world resembles less the interior of a building. Within it, there is the feeling of the evening sky.

The driving energy of the aging Sultan besprinkled the land with bits of Suleimaniyes. Only a Sinan, aided by skilled constructors, could have designed all that Suleiman demanded of him.

Private buildings made up the smallest third of the great total—27 residences, 18 tombs, 5 treasure storage places. Public welfare invoked a larger third—18 caravan serais, for travelers on the roads, 31 public baths, 7 bridges and as many viaducts, 17 soup kitchens, and 3 hospitals.

Religion benefited by the largest third of the Sultan's gifts to his people—75 great mosques, 49 small mosques with as many religious schools attached, to become centers of outlying villages, and 7 institutes for advanced Koran study.

Most of these buildings were stone, or stone and brick, within walled gardens. In distant Jerusalem, Suleiman's design stands today, in the granite wall enclosing the old city with the bastion gate called the Tower of David. Especially on the east side, he had the half-ruined sanctuaries rebuilt, around the Dome of the Rock and the El Aksa mosque. This enclosure of the sites sacred to Islam was named the *Haram*, the Sanctuary. From it Suleiman had the abode of the Franciscans removed, as being out of place within the Haram. But in return he made over to that brotherhood of the Religion a site close to the Sepulchre of the Christians.

It was not remarkable that Suleiman should use his growing wealth for such building. To his thinking that wealth was not his personal property. Like the vast surface of the earth he ruled, it belonged to God. He could benefit only from the use he made of it.

The one residence he erected for himself was the summer place across the Bosphorus, where he had himself rowed more and more often to rest.

By its very extent, however, his grant of buildings and ground aided the Moslem She'ri. Such property, ceded to the Law, became *Wakf*, a permanent endowment to religion. Slowly Suleiman himself was helping to swing the balance between the Law and the Organization. Paradoxically, he was weakening the Organization of which he was head, to add to the wealth and influence of the religious Law. He was turning from innovation, from the thought of Christian Europe, to the unchanging refuge of religion. Only God's mercy could alleviate the guilt of the murder of Mustafa.

The Danger of Peace and Wealth

And it seemed as if God's anger had fallen upon Suleiman's family. Roxelana was sickening; his two surviving sons were drawing close to open war. Roxelana still besought him to support the weak Selim against the brilliantly able Bayazid. To Suleiman it was clear that Bayazid must succeed him. There was no one else able to lead the Turkish people.

Then Roxelana died in her chamber next the Throne Room Within. Being a woman, her death occurred almost without notice outside the Serai.

Suleiman of course gave no evidence of his grief. He had loved this one woman for half his lifetime; he had granted too much to her influence and at least twice had been tricked by her. Yet he had never willingly allowed her to affect the rule of the empire. After Ibrahim no one had been able to do that.

So her death made no perceptible difference in outward events. Years before the Russian had been hated by orthodox Turks, because of the favor shown her. Now there was no feeling against her. Throngs going to pray in Suleiman's new mosque did not think it strange or untoward that Roxelana's body should be in a tomb close behind the mosque, or that the Sultan should order another small mosque to be built in the name of Khasseki Khurrem near the women's market. To this mosque he added the endowment of a school and a hospital for the mad—where turbaned priests might minister to helpless folk who babbled.

No more than that remained of Roxelana, who had stirred him by her woman's will, never yielding what once she had gained. He never spoke of her. Perhaps he wondered what would have become of the domain if he had sickened and died instead, leaving Roxelana to urge on Selim as Sultan, she the Sultan Valideh. That, he must have known, would have meant misfortune for the years to come.

In fact new troubles seemed to be afflicting his people.

His instinct could sense danger to the nation. Even Rustem, absorbed in the accumulation of a private fortune, assumed that as the Osmanli power and wealth increased so would the Osmanli rule continue, unchallenged. No visible force, in Rustem's eyes, could now defeat the Turkish army or fleet; no drought could seriously curtail the abundant crops and herds of their agriculture. What, then, had they to fear?

Brooding in his habitual silence, the old Sultan found it hard to explain what he himself feared. "A house of wood will burn down," he said. "A house of mud bricks will weaken in a storm, or it will fall in an earthquake. Stone endures."

"Well," Rustem commented, "you have built enough out of hewn stone, in spite of the cost."

To Rustem's calculating mind, it was sufficient to get in more money than they needed for a year's expenses. But when he showed Suleiman how the revenue from grain-producing Egypt had been doubled, the Sultan fell into one of his fits of anger. The exaction of so much money would be a hardship for the Egyptian peasantry. Harm to the peasantry would affect the next year's growth of rice, lentils and grains——

"Reduce the payment of Egypt to the old sum," he ordered.

Rustem almost smiled. How could revenue, once established, be reduced? And what would happen if that were done? The Sultan's personal income had risen, under Rustem's management, to 2,000,000 Venetian ducats, leaving a balance to the Treasury of 7,100,000 yearly. Yet still more was needed to meet rising expenses. Since no new wars were undertaken, outer tribute and the kharaj from subject peoples did not increase. Since no customs dues to speak of were taken from foreign merchants, especially the French, under the new treaties, nothing more was to be looked for there. What remained, except the old taxes on farms and animals, on metal mines and salt mining, and perhaps—here Rustem passed lightly over details—the fees collected from new officers of the Organization? If such taxes and fees were not increased, how could they enlarge the yearly revenue of the Treasury?

Suleiman would not take more than the old taxes from the people at large. Yet he allowed Rustem to exact fees from men appointed to office. And very rapidly such fees seemed to transform themselves into heavy payments to the Vizir and his underlings, down to the gatekeepers.

That speedily was to become simple bribery. It followed naturally that the applicant who would pay the most usually got the office. That, in turn, tended to make the new officeholder reimburse himself from those beneath him.

It was impossible to defeat the human craving of servants

of the Organization to keep something for themselves of all that passed through their hands. Beylerbeys far distant from the scrutiny of those behind the Gate managed to bestow feudal grants on their own henchmen. Suleiman tried to check this by requiring them to obtain permission for each grant from the Vizir's office. Yet the office in Constantinople found it very difficult to ascertain just who was receiving what in the vast provincial areas. Also, well-placed bribes helped get the necessary "tickets" from the office. Once the simple human honesty of the elder Turks broke down, it did little good to pass laws to remedy matters.

Suleiman started to register all lands and their holders. The work went on for years without being completed.

The old Osmanli system had worked well. The Turkish people farmed the land or produced goods, and paid a small tax. The members of the Organization that managed things and manned the permanent army paid no tax; instead, they were nourished and clothed out of the tax money. So it had been, more or less, in the time of the Conqueror when the domain had been small, and Turkish peasantry and School-educated managers alike engaged in constant wars and construction. Now in the quiet of peace, with food abundant, the workers of the Organization found themselves left with a pittance. The native farmers increased their herds and possessions and families. Naturally the unpaid servants of the Organization tended to seize what they could illegally and surreptitiously. "Gifts" to many of those in power multiplied amazingly.

"Unless you have a gift in your hand," foreigners were beginning to say, "it is useless to try to gain a hearing from these people."

Suleiman himself enjoyed a rare porcelain dish or a jewel glowing with fresh color as a gift. The feel of a smooth-paced Arab horse between his knees or the touch of cool silk against his throat had become necessary to him. No longer did he think of the sheepskins of his ancestors hanging in the Treasury.

THE QUEST IN ASIA

When an inventory of Rustem's possessions was made at last it revealed some strange hoards. Besides the accustomed farms, animals, water mills, slaves and coined money, the Vizir had gathered somehow 800 Korans, many with jewels set into their bindings, 1100 skullcaps of cloth of gold, 600 saddles, much ornamented with silverwork. Although Rustem, unlike Ibrahim and Iskander Chelebi, kept no personal army, he had quite a store of weapons—2900 trained war horses, and as many shirts of mail; helmets plated with gold, and scores of pairs of gold-worked stirrups. These were all valuables, easily sold. Great diamonds and moonstones, emeralds—32 in all—had the worth of a fortune.

Ogier Busbecq said that the avaricious Rustem sold off even the vegetables grown in the Serai gardens.

Against such human greed and the forces of disintegration, Suleiman set the impersonal ideal of the School, with its intensive education and doctrine of service. "These Turks," Busbecq admitted, "do not measure even their own people by any other rule than that of personal merit."

Against Turkish jealously of the foreigners, who were above Turkish law, he invoked the lessons and advantages to be obtained from the visitors. Feeling rose at times, to challenge the rights of the inner nations—the Armenians, Jews, Greeks, Serbs. Suleiman invoked the old agreements, that these encircled peoples were to preserve their own customs so long as they did not interfere with the Turks. The Mufti, Ibn Sa'ud, supported him, announcing, "If an unbeliever pays the kharaj, by such payment he secures the privileges agreed upon in the first place."

Even Rustem admitted the possible spiritual equality of the Christians. "A Moslem who does not carry out the requirements of his faith is less sure of salvation than a Christian who does."

For a space Suleiman welded together the integrity of the religious Law and the hope of the young graduates of the

School. He insisted on going himself to speed the grown apprentices out of the Gate of Felicity, which they could not enter again—giving each graduate a horse from his own stable, a robe of honor and money for the journey. An Italian, observing him, said, "He sows sure hope of reward in all sorts of men."

The Approach of Ivan the Terrible

Rapidly as he journeyed now, Suleiman could not be in two places at the same time. The weakness of the Osmanli system lay in the fact that only one man, the Sultan, could cope with a crisis.

For some time one had been preparing in the steppes north of the Black Sea, where Suleiman's dependent, Sahib Ghirei, ruled the Tatars of the Crimea in savage fashion. Over those steppes the Sultan held only remote control. Both Tatars and Russians feared his power, perhaps the more because he had refrained from sending a Turkish army to interfere with them.

When Ivan the Terrible advanced his own army from Moscow against Kazan, the nearest stronghold of the Moslems and Tatars on the upper Volga, Suleiman had been content to advise Sahib Ghirei to send a strong leader, one Idiger Khan, from the southern steppes to take command of the defense of Kazan.

It fell to the Russian siege in 1552—a landmark in Russian history, the breaking of the yoke of the hitherto dreaded Tatars.

Suleiman had also sent a young Tatar from Constantinople to take command of Astrakhan, at the far-off mouth of the Volga.

Then, on the other side of the Black Sea, he was drawn to the crisis that ended with the death of his son Mustafa, and Rustem's dismissal.

That in turn had an effect in the Crimea. There the Khan, Sahib Ghirei, had been the opponent of Rustem, who disliked him. Turkish spahis and janizaris, sent to strengthen the Khan in his conflict with the Russians now advancing down the great rivers into the dry steppes, had quarreled with Sahib Ghirei, telling him, "It is not your bread we eat but that of our master the Sultan." In the Crimea the trouble ended with the assassination of Sahib Ghirei, the last descendant of Genghis Khan to rule the Russian steppes. He had been Suleiman's friend, but the Sultan could not be there to restore order on the northern shore of the Black Sea. For the two critical years of 1553–55 he was kept on the other shore, near Persia.

Very quickly Ivan's forces captured Astrakhan, the key to the Volga and the Caspian Sea.

Inexorably, with increasing numbers, the Russians were pressing south toward the fertile Don basin and the inland seas. Suleiman heard with regret of the loss of the two famous Moslem cities. When a new Russian army appeared in the steppe above the Crimea in 1555, he let it be known that he would not consent to the invasion of the home of the Krim Tatars.

The Russians hesitated. Some of their commanders urged an attack upon the last of the Tatar khanates. Others feared the Krim riders, the barrier of the desert, and the Turks who held all the Black Sea ports, including Kaffa in the Crimea itself. Eventually Ivan turned north instead, toward the Baltic—to make there a new advance in the slow Russian expansion toward the seas.

Whereupon Suleiman sent to Ivan a letter written in gold on purple paper, addressing him—whether in irony or in warning—"Fortunate Tsar and wise Prince . . ."

For a moment Charles V and his allies considered the newly manifest strength of the barbarian Muscovite. Was there not here a power that might be played off against Suleiman? The German and Danish artillerists who had forged cannon for Ivan and had aided him to batter down the ramparts of Kazan said so. But Charles ordered further aid held back from the Muscovite, and stopped the migration to Moscow of German technicians.

Suleiman, who never gave up an idea, had by no means forgotten Kazan and Astrakhan. He would not go to war over them, nor could he venture so far to the northeast himself. Years later he decided on a way to regain the Moslem strongholds. By ships

Turkish fleets could navigate the river Don, beyond Azov. At the point where the Don bends east and the Volga west, a canal might be built. His engineers believed it possible to cut through the intervening land. A fleet could then be brought into the mighty Volga, and could so dominate Kazan to the north and Astrakhan to the south, and possibly the Caspian itself. (It was the old Turkish scheme of moving ships bodily overland.)

Yet he had no one to send to do it. Even Sinan the Architect could not join rivers together in the steppe. Moreover, the new Krim Khan feared to have Turkish power fetched from the sea to the steppe, and put obstacles in Suleiman's way, while secretly informing Ivan of the plan of the Don-Volga canal.

Cossacks were to haul their river vessels across the narrow neck of land, and Russians were to build the forts and attempt the canal that Suleiman planned.

If he had had a Barbarossa in the east, it might have been done as he wished.

Three supremely able men helped Suleiman hold the unstable Osmanli rule in balance at home. Of these, Ibn Sa'ud was at heart a ritualist, Rustem an incipient miser, and Sokolli a ruthless driver. Yet in the years of their service under Suleiman all three developed a tolerance that matched their peculiar abilities.

Such men were not easily led. At sea the headstrong Dragut obeyed orders from the Gate only when he felt like it. When this archfoe of the European courts raided Venetian shipping lanes, he started a healthy feud with Rustem, who did not want the Venetians injured. When the combined sea captains

wrenched the port of Tripoli in Africa from the strong hands of
the Knights, Rustem accordingly awarded the prize to Sinan
Reis as a fief. Whereupon Dragut, enraged, hoisted his red
and white pennon and sailed away westward to seek his own
prizes. Most of the Osmanli battle fleet chose to follow him.

At the Serai, Rustem fitted out a squadron to pursue the
deserter. Suleiman stepped into the feud, sending an honorary
sword and Koran and a written safe-conduct out to the errant
Dragut.

As Rustem's captains prepared to embark on their punitive
expedition, they met Dragut coming in alone. He went straight
to Suleiman's presence and came out pardoned, with Tripoli as
a gift.

The Lost Admiral

Dragut had been willing to trust himself and his case to
Suleiman. Such trust did not spring from devotion alone, or
from religious ardor—the zeal of the Moslem brotherhood for
the well-being of its chosen leader—or from discipline alone.
Rather it came from what Busbecq shrewdly identified as hope.
Dragut had risen from a peasant's field work and roadside
wrestling to the command of a fleet. He owed that rise to no
one's influence, but to his own ability. By the same token he
now had a right to command. As long as he succeeded, he was
sure of rising toward the rank of Kaputan Pasha. If he failed,
then the dour Rustem, son by marriage to the Sultan, could
set him aside. But until then Dragut was a free man, and no
scion of birth or wealth could interfere with him.

So he had gone to Suleiman not to beg for mercy but to argue
his own right.

One sea commander disappeared entirely for three years,
and came back to claim his reward. Sidi Ali was a Turk, son of
a certain Hoseyn who had commanded the Arsenal. They
called him the Writer because he had put together a treatise on

265

.navigation, *The Ocean*, and because he enlivened dinner parties with improvised poems. Sidi Ali had served under Barbarossa and boasted that he knew every inlet of the Mediterranean. Yet when he was given a fleet and a mission to engage the Portuguese along the far coast of India, he found it was easier to describe the outer oceans than to keep a fleet afloat on them.

(Suleiman was still trying to break up the Portuguese traffic by sea with the rich coasts of farther Asia, where the King of Portugal had been proclaimed by papal bull to be "lord of the navigation, conquest and trade of Ethiopia, Arabia, Persia and India." The Portuguese, based on the island of Goa, had beaten off the threat of the Turkish squadrons. With their missionaries backed by the growing power of the Inquisition and their merchant captains by superior cannon, they held the Malabar coast longer than the Spaniards had been able to grip the North African coast.)

Sidi Ali managed to navigate his fleet safely from the familiar Red Sea to the strange India coast where he said the waves made those of the Mediterranean seem like drops of water.

Somehow he and his crews and Egyptian soldiery survived two battles with the Portuguese "Captain of Goa." A monsoon gale put an end to his cruise. The wind, Sidi Ali declared, rose until the bosun's whistle could not be heard over it, and when the sea around his vessel turned white as far as the eye could behold, his Indian pilot told him they were lost. In the shipwreck that followed the Writer got his men to shore alive, and found his ships broken up beyond repair.

"You are our admiral," the crews assured him, "and where you stand the law of our Padishah prevails. It is now almost two years since we have been paid; our goods are lost, and our return is made impossible. What are you going to do about it?"

Sidi Ali promised them they would be paid in full after he got them home again. To make the situation worse for him, he found they were stranded on a portion of India where Portuguese envoys exerted themselves to have the shipwrecked Turks surrendered. On his part Sidi Ali assured the local Indian princes that he and his men served Sultan Suleiman, who would retaliate for any injury done them.

The Portuguese, defeated, swore that the Turks would never see their Sultan again. "Not a bird," they said, "could get back by sea from the ports of India if we do not permit."

"There is a way to leave by land also," Sidi Ali retorted.

That way he set out to find, through countries where Turks had never been seen before. Wonders surrounded them—screaming parrots, grimacing monkeys who carried their young, and wild oxen that could strip the skin from a man with their tongues.

They reached the mighty Indus, where a prince greeted them as a heaven-sent army, and could not be convinced that they were merely shipwrecked seamen. There Sidi Ali's contingent of soldiers elected to try their luck in service with the Indian nabobs. The crews, following Sidi Ali, lost their arms in the local war, and escaped with him in a stolen vessel up the river. Detained as suspicious wanderers by a Sultan Mahmud, the versatile admiral told a tale that he had seen the blessed daughter of the Prophet in a dream, and she had promised they would reach their homes safely. On the strength of that he was given a good horse and a pair of camels, with a tent and money for the journey.

In the domain of the Great Moghul Sidi Ali wangled a ceremonious reception, because the "glorious name of our Padishah" was known there. This courtesy he repaid with two hasty poems, but found himself kept again at the court to calculate eclipses of the sun and moon for the Moghul's calendar.

He protested: "It is my clear duty to return and give an accounting to my Padishah." He tried more "poetic effusions" without result.

When the reigning Moghul died, Sidi Ali saw his chance to get away in the ensuing confusion. Urgently he advised the assembled counselors to conceal the death of their master, and to spread a report that the ailing Moghul was healthy enough to plan starting upon a journey. To aid in this deception, Sidi Ali offered to start north himself with all his men, to give out the story of the journey. He had not got far on his own journey, however, when he was recalled by the new emperor, who happened to be the celebrated Akbar. Brought back to court, Sidi Ali composed a new poem lamenting the death of Akbar's father. On the strength of that, the shipwrecked mariners got permission to depart.

Apparently they followed a river leading to the wild oxen and equally wild Afghans, where they were feasted "with dancing girls in every corner."

Then Sidi Ali must have got off his course, because his next port of call was Samarkand, then under Uzbek rule. Since sailors were unknown in the mountains of mid-Asia, Sidi Ali identified his Turks as pilgrims, and was shown to his edification the tomb, supposedly, of the Prophet Daniel. Asked what city had pleased him most in his pilgrimage, he replied with a two-line verse:

> *"Far from home, no one longs for Paradise,*
> *For to him his own home is more than Baghdad."*

In Samarkand to his joy the homesick admiral found some Turks. A regiment of janizaris had been lent to the Uzbeks by Suleiman, and these identified Sidi Ali as an officer of the great Sultan. Whereupon the Uzbek chieftains urged the crew to join in a war with them, and Sidi Ali to take for himself the government of Bokhara. Sidi Ali complained that as a servant of the Sultan he should bear letters home, instead, from the powerful Uzbek chieftains.

He was warned of lions in the desert, and assured that the way was blocked by another strange folk, Russians, who had appeared on the Caspian inland sea. "Be warned, and go back."

That Sidi Ali would not do. Taking the letters of the Uzbeks, the homesick admiral avoided the unknown Russians by shaping a course southerly across the red sands of the deserts. This way, he entered Persia, a land antagonistic to all that was Turkish. Still, he made a detour to visit the grave of the illustrious poet Firdawsi at the edge of a desert. Brought before Shah Tahmasp in the Caucasus Mountains for questioning, he made a good impression by writing another four-line poem in praise of his host, the Shah. Again he was asked what city he had enjoyed most. "Stambul [Constantinople]," he answered.

"Why Stambul?" Tahmasp wondered.

"Because in all the world there is no city like it; there is no country like the Turkish, no army like the Turkish army, and no sovereign like the Padishah."

Sidi Ali did not find it hard to leave Persia. Descending the mountains, he sighted the blue dome of the mosque of Baghdad, and soon he was sitting on the same carpet with Turks, drinking fruit julep and chilled coffee, listening to the gossip of those who had seen the Golden Horn within a year.

On his way thither he wrote a new book which he called *The Mirror of Many Countries*. This he offered to Suleiman when at last he passed under the plane trees, through the guardian janizaris, into the presence of his lord. To Suleiman he explained how he had lost his fleet, and had difficulty in returning home.

At the Serai they had supposed Sidi Ali to be lost at sea. His post of Captain in Egypt had been given to an officer from Rhodes. But Suleiman ordered three years' back pay to be awarded the admiral and his men, and granted the wanderer an honorary post near the Divan, hence close to the Sultan himself.

That evening when Sidi Ali watched the sunset gleam on the Horn sprinkled with the masts of ships at moorings, he felt deeply content and he wrote, "Not in seeking greatness but in a quiet mind lies the goodness that lasts."

Nothing in Sidi Ali's narrative reveals Suleiman's keen disappointment at the failure of the fleet to dislodge the Portuguese from Goa. It was his last attempt to challenge the Europeans on their ocean route to the east.

Yet within the Mediterranean his irrepressible captains were driving the European flags from the open sea. At the Serai Ogier Busbecq witnessed the triumphal return of one of them, after Dragut and Piali Pasha had caught the Spanish armada in the lagoon of drowsy Yerba.

"Piali sent a galley here with news of this victory," Busbecq relates. "She trailed in the water from her stern a large flag of the Cross [actually the standard of Spain]. When she entered the harbor the Turks began congratulating each other. They gathered in crowds at my door, and asked my men in mockery, had they any kinsmen in the Spanish fleet? 'If so,' said they, 'you will soon have the pleasure of seeing them.' . . ."

When the victorious fleet sighted Serai Point it hove to for the night, to make its entry in all ceremony by day.

"Suleiman had gone down to the colonnade close to the mouth of the harbor, which forms part of his gardens, that he might have a nearer view of his fleet as it entered, and also of the Christian officers who were exhibited on the deck. On the poop of the admiral's galley were Don Alvaro de Sande and the commanders of the Sicilian and the Neapolitan galleys [one of them being Zúñiga y Requeséns who acquired dubious fame later as Viceroy of the Netherlands]. These captured galleys had been stripped of upper works, and towed along as mere hulks.

"Those who saw Suleiman's face in this hour of triumph failed to detect in it the slightest trace of undue elation. I can myself positively declare that when I saw him two days later on his way to the mosque, the expression of his face was unchanged; his stern features had lost nothing of their habitable gloom; one would have thought that the victory concerned him not, and that this startling success of his arms had caused him no surprise. So self-contained was the heart of that grand old man, so schooled to meet each change of Fortune however great, that all the applause and triumph of that day wrung from him no sign of satisfaction. . . .

"The royal standard of the Neapolitan galleys, bearing the arms of the Kings of Spain, quartered with the Imperial Eagle, had fallen into the hands of a Turkish officer with whom I was acquainted. When I heard that he meant to present it to Suleiman, I determined to make an effort to get possession of it. The matter was easily arranged by my sending him a present of two silk robes. Thus I prevented the glorious coat of arms of Charles V from remaining with the enemy as a perpetual memorial of that defeat."

The Ride to the Last Judgment

Suleiman would have cared nothing by then for the captured coat of arms of his great adversary, Charles. In the summer that followed he mounted his horse by the fountain of the third court and rode for the last time to the east.

Before him trotted led horses; beside his stirrup silent runners kept pace, beyond them the plumes of his mounted guardsmen tossed. Past the Chamlija grove where the dead waited. Up the height, where, turning, he could glimpse the blue breast of Marmora. It hurt him to turn, and because of the pain he rode an easy-paced Kabarda.

He rode with the venom of bitterness in him. At the Serai his daughter Mihrmah had pleaded. She cried for mercy for Bayazid. Her voice chimed like Roxelana's in a song; she had learned to play the flute to quiet him when they were alone. No longer could he trust even Mihrmah. A woman could be pleasing as a dove to gain something for herself——

Rustem, her husband, sick and inarticulate, argued that Bayazid was their only hope. But how could there be mercy for Bayazid?

Suleiman tried to think of what was good. So little good remained. By the road the grinding of water wheels and the creaking of wheat-laden carts meant that the land had food. That was well.

If he could find rest. What had the Moor said of the rest of Charles? Far off in a monastery on the coast of Spain, Charles had been weary; he had laid down the burden of his Empire, to carry off with him some chosen paintings and treasured clocks, to listen in the garden of Yuste to the prayers of his monks.

The Moor said that Charles had ordered his servants to wake him if they heard that Turkish fleets were attacking the coast of Spain, but the servants had not done so, fearing to bring grief to a dying man. Suleiman could not understand why Charles kept on stuffing himself with the odd foods he craved, hams and eels and anchovies, and wine as well. By so doing, the physicians said he hastened his death . . . with a flash of pride Suleiman remembered that the new Emperor Ferdinand still paid him tribute each year.

That other monarch Francis, who pledged so much, had gone into the unknown before Charles, leaving the lands of France stripped and blackened by war . . . his son Henry dying by a lance thrust in the mock war of a tournament . . . there must be no war with Shah Tahmasp, now, over Bayazid——

It was strange that he should have outlived all those princes of Europe. Even Isabella, that frightened, dignified princess of Poland, to whom he had made a promise—her son John was past adolescence, ready to take the throne, as Mustafa had been.

John, they said, had a good will toward his Magyars; he welcomed to him refugees of all faiths, even the Lutherans and Calvinists . . . and he, Suleiman, was riding toward Amasiya where Mustafa died.

Yes, John had suffered and so had grown tolerant of others. Well, that. The refugees came down to him on rafts, drifting down the river Save, as they drifted in to the islands Suleiman now held . . . he had written a letter not long ago to the new

Pope, Paul. He had not known how to address the letter properly. How had they worded it, at the secretariat of the Divan? *To the most excellent lord of the imams of the Messiah Jesus, and lord of Rome, may he be in the keeping of God.*

Was that a fitting salutation to the great Pope? Suleiman wondered, because no reply had come for a long time, although the letter had asked only a small thing, the release of some Hebrews who had been oppressed and their goods taken at the port of Ancona which belonged to the great Pope. The Hebrews were of Suleiman's city.

When at last it came the message from Rome had not spoken of the Hebrews. It came by spoken word from a cardinal to an envoy to Rustem's ear. It asked the Sultan to direct all his armed forces, and especially his sea captains, against Sicily and Naples, which belonged to the Spaniards, the enemies of Rome

Once he could have smiled at the irony of that. Now Sicily and Naples with *Almanya* and their thrones had become meaningless as the shadow shapes of hunchback clowns thrown against a far-off screen at the feast of Bairam. Because of the pain that burned his intestines and the pain in his mind, they were shadows.

The image of Ferdinand whom he had never seen stood before his eyes, over his road. Because in some way Suleiman must win a truce from the new Emperor. For a few months, for time enough to trick the Persians into quiet by threatening them with war . . . six months would do. Unless it could be arranged to summon back Bayazid——

Wind struck across the dry road, and the runners at his stirrup turned their faces from the dust. Sudden, insensate anger gripped the Sultan. Digging the points of his stirrups into the flanks of his horse, he plunged ahead of the runners. He could not summon Bayazid back. He called over his shoulder for a runner to summon the Agha of the Messengers.

The man looked up, frightened by the screaming voice, and he ran off like an animal. When the agha reined close to Sulei-

273

man's stirrup, he was told to turn back to the city to fetch the emperor's ambassador, the little man who collected birds and snakes, to Amasiya. To fetch him barely in time to watch the great Persian amirs dismount at Suleiman's tent, so the little Busbecq might have a lesson from the gracious reception of the Persians. Suleiman did not add that then Busbecq would be the more inclined to agree to a truce.

So it happened that Ogier Busbecq did not find it difficult to view the prayers at Bairam, or to wander through the army. When he reached Amasiya in the days that decided Bayazid's fate, he wrote in his own words what passed.

"The Sultan was seated on a very low ottoman which was covered with costly rugs. Near him lay his bow and arrows. His years are just beginning to tell on him, but his bearing is majestic. He has always had the reputation of being a careful and temperate man, nothing worse could be brought against him than his excessive devotion to his wife, and the hurried way in which he was induced to put Mustafa to death by her influence. From the time she became his lawful wife, he had been perfectly faithful to her.

"As an upholder of his religion he is most strict, being quite as anxious to extend his faith as to extend his empire. Considering his years (for he is now getting on for sixty) he enjoys good health, though it may be that his bad complexion arises from some lurking malady. There is a notion going around that he has an incurable ulcher or cancer on his thigh. When he is anxious to impress an ambassador who is going away with a favorable idea of his health, he hides the bad complexion of his face under a coat of rouge—his notion being that foreign powers will fear him more if they think he is strong. I detected this when he gave me a farewell audience and I found his face much changed. . . .

"The Sultan's audience chamber was crowded with people; but there was not in all that great assembly a single man who owed his position to aught save his valor and his merit. No distinction is attached to birth among the Turks. There is no fighting for precedence. . . . Each man in Turkey carries in his own hand his ancestry and his position in life which he may make or mar as he wills.

"For they do not believe that high qualities descend from a father to his son or heir, any more than a talent for music or mathematics. Such qualities are partly the gift of God, partly the result of good training and effort. . . . This is the reason they are successful in their undertakings. . . .

"Take your stand by my side and look at that sea of turbaned heads, each wrapped in twisted folds of the whitest silk; look at those marvellously handsome dresses . . . it was the most beautiful spectacle I ever saw. . . . I was struck with the silence and order that prevailed in this great crowd. There were no cries, no hum of voices, nor jostling . . . apart from the rest a long line of janizaris was drawn up. It was some time before I could make up my mind whether they were human beings or statues; at last I received a hint to salute them, and saw all their heads bending at the same moment to return my bow. . . . On leaving the assembly we had a fresh treat in the sight of the household cavalry returning to their quarters; the men were mounted on splendid horses, excellently groomed and accoutred.

"The Persian ambassador had arrived, bringing with him a number of handsome presents, carpets from famous looms, tents lined with colored tapestries; but the chief present of all was a copy of the Koran. Terms of peace were granted him immediately, with the intention of putting greater pressure on us, who seemed to be the more troublesome. To convince us of the reality of the peace, honors were showered on the representative of the Shah. The Turks run to extremes, in honoring a friend or pouring contempt on a foe. Ali Pasha, the Second Vizir, gave the Persian suite a dinner in his gardens, which we could view from our quarters. Ali Pasha, I must tell you, is by

275

birth a Dalmatian; he is a thorough gentleman and has (what you will be surprised to hear of in a Turk) a kind and feeling heart.

"Peace having been concluded with the Persians, it was impossible for us to obtain any decent terms from the Turk; all we could accomplish was to arrange a six months' truce. Having received the Sultan's letter, which was sealed up in a wrapper of cloth of gold, I took my leave, with little hope of a successful issue to our embassy. . . .

"My journey was marked by evil chance. I met some wagons of boys and girls who were being carried from Hungary to the slave market at Constantinople. This is the commonest kind of Turkish merchandise. The men were either driven in gangs or bound to a chain in a long file, as we take a string of horses to a fair."

Busbecq returned to Constantinople that summer with a sense of the common purpose that was moving the Sultan and his Turks toward a destination unpredictable as yet. Astute enough, Ferdinand's ambassador realized how a display had been put on at Amasiya to influence him. All that he had seen, even to the rouge on Suleiman's sallow cheeks, he had been meant to see. But for what purpose, he did not know. The six months' truce he believed himself fortunate to get.

That stopgap of a little time Suleiman had needed desperately, to make his last judgment upon Bayazid.

V

Malta,

AND THE LAST MARCH OUT

The Impossible Task

IF ROXELANA had not conspired at the death of Gulbehar's
son, and if her own son Selim had not been afraid, it would
not have happened. Selim the Sot, the janizaris called him, well
aware how he got drunk in secret and clung to the companionship of those who bolstered his self-esteem, women and ambitious souls who for good reason had been given no post near the
Sultan, or high in the Organization.

Busbecq heard the talk and reported in his turn that Selim
was singularly unmannerly, and "had never done a kind deed,
and never made a friend."

Three things Selim feared, the anger of his aging father, the
sight of a bowstring in powerful hands that would end his life,
and the lovable personality of his younger brother Bayazid in
whom people beheld the image of Suleiman. To his father Selim
wrote with the shrewdness of a neurotic, "I do not try to curry
popularity which would raise me up in the esteem of the
crowds, to be a rival to my father, the Lord of the Two Worlds."
He had nothing to depend on, he added, except the love of his
father. Everybody else hated him.

In almost these words Roxelana had pleaded for the fat and

277

florid Selim. Replying, Suleiman urged his self-pitying son to stop worrying and try to live as the Koran taught him. Whereupon Selim's letters—carefully written for him by others—voiced a new fear Not for himself, he insisted, did he feel such ceaseless anxiety, he worried for his father's life. Conspirators could so easily enter Constantinople—where Bayazid had been seen to venture, disguised, to talk secretly with the janizaris at the gate of the Serai—to launch arrows at the Sultan when he rode forth from the inner courtyard.

This filial warning Suleiman brushed aside. Sharply he reminded Roxelana's two sons that they had only one obligation, to carry out the duties assigned to them. But he could not forget that Bayazid was gaining popularity with the janizaris, who had found a new nickname for Selim, the Stall-fed Ox. Then, too, there was truth in Selim's complaint that the dour Rustem believed him to be a drunkard, incapable of ever governing the Osmanli state. Rustem, sickening under the strain of overwork, did believe that, and said so.

So tense had grown the rivalry between the two heirs, and so closely were foreign observers watching it, that Suleiman had sent them to governments in opposite directions, away from the talk and plotting in his city. "He was well aware," Busbecq wrote, "that the eyes of the world were on the rivalry between his sons."

Perhaps he had wanted to test Bayazid, perhaps he had merely sent the stronger man to the post of greater danger. But Bayazid objected immediately to such a post, near the eastern frontier and far from the city. Amasiya had been Mustafa's post, and memories of rebellion lingered among its hills. Probably Bayazid's real grievance was not that he had been allotted Amasiya, but that Selim had been given Magnisiya whence Suleiman himself had ridden to the city in four days to be proclaimed Sultan. The memory of that also endured. By his action, Suleiman had seemed to support Selim against Bayazid.

Actually he was doing so. His sons were almost forty years of age; he felt the weariness of nearly seventy years. By keeping them passive and alive for a short space longer, he could count on an impersonal force to maintain the Osmanli rule after him. This was the Organization itself, never more efficient than now. Probably he anticipated that single-minded servants like Rustem and Sokolli would turn to Bayazid immediately, to lead them. Certainly Selim feared that they would do so.

"I will make no change in the government now. Obey me while I live. The one who disobeys will be guilty of treason," Suleiman ordered his sons impartially. "After that, all will be between you as God wills."

Suleiman could not retire to a monastery as Charles had done. Nor could he divide the Osmanli state between two persons. One man and one purpose must rule.

Suleiman's own purpose might have been carried out, if it had not been for the cunning of Lala Mustafa.

Lala Mustafa had tutored each boy in turn, long before, and had an intimate knowledge of their dispositions. Shrewd as he was, he had not been promoted in the Organization, and had been marked by Rustem as a failure, to be thrown out at the first chance. Having nothing much to lose, the tutor worked on Selim's fears. Bayazid, he declared, was the Sultan's favorite, yet he had means of stirring incurable antagonism between Bayazid and his father—the price was that Lala Mustafa should be First Vizir, under Selim.

Patiently and taking great pains to keep his distance from Suleiman, the tutor played on Bayazid's exasperation, convincing the younger brother that Selim, who appeared so innocuous, meant to have his life. That being so, Bayazid's best safeguard was to force the Sot to make an open move against him. That, in turn, might be done by enraging him. Bayazid was sufficiently convinced to send his brother gifts of a woman's cap, with ribbon streamers, and a distaff.

These exhibits Lala Mustafa advised Selim to forward with

a complaint to his father. Knowing that Suleiman would send a message at once to Bayazid, the tutor had the courier waylaid and killed and the letter burned unread—within Bayazid's territory. At this point Suleiman sent two of the highest officers of the Divan, the third and fourth vizirs, to the armed camps now gathering at Magnisiya and Amasiya.

As to Bayazid's mobilization, Busbecq records, "Suleiman regarded these preparations as directed against himself, nevertheless he passed them over for the most part in silence. This cautious old man did not want to render Bayazid desperate and so drive him into open rebellion."

In an effort to prevent armed conflict between the brothers, he sent a stern arbiter, Sokolli (who had caught the impostor Mustafa), with a token force of veteran janizaris and spahis into Selim's district. Sokolli, however, took forty cannons with him. At this Bayazid sent open warning to the Serai. "In everything I will obey the command of the Sultan my father, except in all that lies between Selim and me."

What followed exceeded Lala Mustafa's hopes. Far to the south at Koniah, Bayazid's followers clashed with Selim's forces, stiffened by the Sultan's contingent. Observers related that a hot desert wind blew dust from the Mevlevi monastery near the fighting into the faces of Bayazid's men. So God's will seemed to turn against the younger brother. Sokolli's forty guns beat off the attack. Yet Bayazid carried out of the conflict the admiration of the fighting forces on both sides for his personal daring. And, with a generous impulse, he wrote his father a full admission that he had been wrong; he would take no further action for himself but would rely on the Sultan's judgment.

This might have ended Suleiman's uncertainty and suspicion. But the letter was intercepted and destroyed by Lala Mustafa. Somehow in doing so, he caught the attention of Rustem, and the vigilant Vizir began to trace down the tutor's actions during the crisis. At the same time the anxious Bayazid, getting no answer to his appeal, acted as impulsively as before. He had reined

his horse forward, to give battle to the Osmanli standard. If he
was to be condemned for that, by Selim's trickery, he would
fight in earnest. Swiftly—for he hated indecision—he borrowed
what he could from wealthy merchants and sent word forth that
he was raising an army under his own standard.

Bayazid's failing at this moment was his heritage of courage.
A daring, generous leader, he gathered restless chieftains to
him as a wind pulls rootless brush—Turkomans galloping in
from their sheep herds, marauding Kurds from the mountains,
with followers of the dead Mustafa, and levelheaded officers
who saw in him the true heir of the Osmanli line.

His move to rebel set flame to the dry tinder of the eastern
frontier.

Death of Bayazid

At the Serai, propped up in the garden, Suleiman faced again
the ghost of Mustafa. The grim Rustem, dying slowly as he
labored, unearthed the trickery of Lala Mustafa, who was exiled in spite of Selim's protest.

They hardly heeded Lala Mustafa. Their actual danger lay
in the army. For years Suleiman had sought to change it from
the old feudal mobilization to a disciplined striking force that
would serve the Sultan's need. No panoplied Serasker commanded the new Turkish *asker;* the great drum of conquest had
not sounded for years. The strength of the mounted levies, the
Turkish *Timars,* had thinned away. The formidable Turkish
feudal warriors were changing into cattle-breeding landowners.

There remained the strengthened nucleus of the personal
army, janizaris and spahis now on duty throughout the domain, and—as Sokolli realized so well—the massive artillery
train.

Now around their soup kettles, at the gates, and along the
road to Amasiya these same veterans were disturbed in spirit.
They spoke their minds without fear. "We are commanded to

draw our swords, but against whom? Against the hope of the country itself. Against the one who is the likeness of our Sultan. Why does our Sultan prefer that fat hug-a-girl, who needs to be kicked out of his sleeping robes . . . did *he* gain the victory at Koniah? Nay, by the ninety and nine Holy Names, it was the wind of the dervishes and the cannon of Mehmed Sokolli the Beylerbey. . . .

"What, then, did Bayazid do, that we should march against him? He did no more than Yavuz Sultan Selim, who mounted to the saddle to fight for his right—nay, it was less than that. Bayazid did not draw his sword against his father. He had a good heart toward his father. It is verily a sin if we obey an order to go against Bayazid!"

From the field came reports of units that would not obey a command to march, and of cavalry that trotted off for a day and returned only at leisure, to demonstrate their dislike of a campaign. Suleiman knew these signs.

"Even the Sultan," the ailing Rustem assured Busbecq, "fears a revolt of the janizaris. At a time like this, if he cannot control them, no one is able to do so."

In those hours Suleiman was paying the price of allowing the great field army of the Yavuz Sultan to deteriorate. He had hoped to create such a way of ordered life within the domain that the army would cease to be the instrument of his rule. Now he realized it was impossible. Out in the provinces a vast borderland of warlike peoples kept their spirit of independence, from the mountain Serbs of the Dalmatian coast, who would serve under him only as Christians, through the Wallachian Christians, and the Asiatic Tatars in their stronghold of the Crimea, the Georgians in the Caucasus—valiant Christians—and the wild Kurds and Turkomans of the eastern mountains.

They were bound to him by no more than the fragile thread of loyalty and—some of them—by the tie of religion. Loyalty could change at the appeal of a new voice; it could never be held fast.

Report came in from Koniah that in the combat outside the
monastery the veteran troops had obeyed Sokolli only with
their bodies; their hearts had been with Bayazid. In the cool
shadow of the Throne Room Within, messengers waited with a
writing from Bayazid. It urged his father not to cross the water
to Asia; Bayazid had his quarrel only with Selim, but if his
father came into the field, the land would be laid waste.

Suleiman put the writing aside, in silence. In bitterness he
made his decision. All those who waited and watched for his
next action would see him again as the commander of invincible
troops. He straightened against the stabbing pain in his shoulders. After long brooding he asked three questions with great
care, and a secretary wrote them down on purple paper, while
Rustem pondered them in assenting silence.

"First, how must the Sultan treat the man who, in his own
lifetime, raised money to arm followers and attack towns, and
trouble the peace of the land?

"Second, what should be thought of those who joined him
and assisted him?

"Third, what could be thought of those who justified him and
refused to take up arms against him?"

These questions he sent to the Judge of Islam, anticipating
the opinion returned to him by Ibn Sa'ud—that the man de-
served the utmost punishment, and those who aided him did
evil because they acted against their religion.

It was then that Suleiman crossed the water to Asia and rode
to Amasiya, whither he had Busbecq follow him. He sent
Sokolli ahead with Selim to search for Bayazid's new army. Having gained his brief truce with Europe and his signed peace
with the Shah across the border, Suleiman dispatched urgent
messages to the restless peoples of the borderland, notably the
great Kurdish tribes and the Georgians, announcing a summons to war, and demanding their support for the Sultan who
had taken command of the army himself, to lead it against Bayazid.

Within that brief summer the conflagration along the frontier was checked. The implacable Sokolli caught up with the fugitive army. Bayazid cut himself loose from pursuit, and headed east for Persia with his four sons, and women, his string of baggage camels and best mounted men. In the highland passes they beat back the Sultan's horsemen, and made their way to the court of Tahmasp, who greeted Bayazid with royal honors, gladly enough, swearing that he would be forever safe on Persian soil.

Yet when he crossed the frontier Bayazid had put an end to himself.

At first he felt only the exhilaration of action, riding at the head of his reckless cavaliers, as the royal guest of the sophisticated Shah. He rode in tournaments of mutual celebration where, unfortunately, his Turkish timariots overthrew too many Persian champions. He wrote to Suleiman that he had found another father in the Shah.

For a few months the courts of nearer Europe looked expectantly toward Tabriz, where the son of the great Sultan had taken refuge with Tahmasp "the Sufi." Among the Venetians a faint hope stirred afresh—that these Persians might draw the Turks eastward, into destructive war.

Immediately Tahmasp tried to realize a profit from his hostage. Under cover of routine salutation to Suleiman, suggestions were ventured that Bayazid might be given frontier provinces such as Erzerum in the mountain passageway, or Baghdad by the Tigris and Euphrates waterways (both thereby coming again under Persian rule).

These feelers Suleiman brushed aside. He had made his decision when Bayazid left Turkish soil. From that moment Bayazid ceased to be his son and became a rebel. For those closest to him, the aged ruler had no final tolerance. Moreover, his officers from Sokolli down to the spahis accepted the fact that in sheltering himself at Tabriz, Bayazid had forsaken his heritage, and ceased to be an Osmanli. Oddly, they had not felt that when their favorite rode against the guns at Koniah. By the standard of intractable Turkish loyalty Mustafa remained a martyr, Bayazid a traitor. There was no longer danger of civil war, and Suleiman saw to it that the frontiers around Persia became a menace to the Shah. With the Uzbek power in Samarkand he allied himself.

To Tahmasp the Sultan made two things clear: the price of peace would be the surrender of Bayazid, and for that only money would be paid.

From demanding, Tahmasp's agents turned to bargaining and then to face saving. Suleiman's son had become the guest of their master, and it was unthinkable that Bayazid should be given up to captivity——

Suleiman, implacable in his anger, would neither bargain nor discuss Persian scruples. Four hundred thousand gold coins were sent to Tahmasp by the hand of an executioner. The Persians made excuses to scatter Bayazid's followers among distant villages, there to disarm them, and massacre them as dangerous conspirators. Bayazid himself was seized as he sat at banquet with the Shah, and surrendered under the pretext that he was to be escorted back to his brother, not to Suleiman. He went only a little way before he was put to death with all his sons by the Turkish executioner. Rumor had it that they shaved his face first, in order to identify him beyond doubt as the Bayazid who had held court at Amasiya. The Persians had dressed him in dirty sheepskins girdled with a rope so he would no longer appear to be the Turkish prince, to whom the Shah had pledged protection.

When Suleiman rode back to the Serai, few familiar faces greeted him as he dismounted by the fountain of the third court. He had left Selim in charge of the government at Kutahiya in Anatolia, and he did not summon his surviving son to his presence again. Rustem died the same year Bayazid was put to

death, 1561. Toward the end, the grim Vizir had done as the
Sultan did, giving the bulk of his immense fortune to the Wakf
—so great a gift that he had received back yearly an income of
200,000 sequins from his religious foundations.

Mehmed Sokolli, "the Falcon," was absent from the Serai,
carrying out the duties in the field that Suleiman could no
longer undertake. Only Ibn Sa'ud in the white Mufti's turban
stood by his stirrup. The pages who tended him now, and the
boys of the School waiting across the courtyard under the elms,
seemed like children—so young were they. Suleiman had difficulty in remembering their names. It did not seem important
to remember, now.

He had looked forward to having Mihrmah wait upon him.
But his daughter no longer occupied the chambers around the
Throne Room Within. Devoted to Bayazid, she would not for-
give her father for his death. Mourning for Rustem, her hus-
band, she had moved away with her women and black slaves.
Only when he inquired for her did Suleiman discover that
Mihrmah had moved to the shell of the old palace on the hill.

She had left a message for him, indirectly, by the mouth of
her Captain of the Girls. She wore mourning now for *all* of
her family. No longer would she occupy the chambers of state
that had been Roxelana's.

In this message echoed a woman's anger. It recalled to Suleiman the words of his sister, of years before in the old palace—
she had hoped the time might come when she would wear
mourning for him, her brother. Mihrmah was the only one remaining of his family whom he cherished. And he wondered if
she had not hated her brilliant mother Roxelana, and if she did
not hate him now. . . .

Bayazid's bright face, Jahangir's shy smile, turned up to him
from the crippled shoulders, he had lost them. The life of his
family had fallen into the hungry body of Selim, the wine-
bibber. He could not restore his family to life; he could not
breed new sons from the body of a strange girl. . . .

He ordered the door into Roxelana's chambers sealed up. In his two rooms he slept and ate alone now. Often he limped down the Golden Road past the salaaming slaves who rose from their niches, to the listening window above the heads of the strange young men who sat in the Divan. In Mehmed Sokolli alone he could put trust

When he woke before dawn, to shift his body and ease the gnawing pain, he often heard the fresh strong voice of a boy reading prayers across the courtyard. Sometimes he called to him a gifted boy, Baki, the son of a Turkish muezzin who could write words that pulsed with life. The Khan of Poets, Suleiman called him. Baki was shy, because many people did not believe he actually wrote his poems. They said so much that a boy could hardly know.

Suleiman never asked Baki to read the *kasida*, the ode he had penned for his Sultan. *"Lord of the realm of gracious-ness . . . in thy domain no man weeps beneath a tyrant's vex-ing . . . the fortune of our king . . . upon the throne above all crowned kings . . . the heart-throne is the seat of that high Sovereign."*

Simple, Turkish words Under a boy's hand they reached toward something splendid. How could Baki know that Suleiman, who had failed in so much, had sought for something told in these words, yet had failed in that also?

Ages ago when he had been eager as Baki, he had watched a lovely girl, Gulbehar, embroider a case for his own stupid writings. . . .

Calling the Keeper of the Gate to bring before him fair new girls from the old palace, Suleiman chose one of their number. He bestowed her on Baki as a gift from the Sultan.

"To be a companion to him," he said.

Perhaps when he rode through the courtyard gate of the Suleimaniye mosque on Fridays, young minds like Baki's beheld splendor in the robed horsemen, with plumes sweeping down from their heads, entering the portal of the house of the

Lord . . . between the four lofty minarets, with the seven balconies with the lamps of Ramazan. . . .

When he lowered his weight from the saddle, helped by the hands of the runners at his stirrup, Suleiman felt the searing pain rise from his legs into his body. Dizziness tormented his eyes.

Watching his every move, young Marcantonio Donini, the secretary of the Venetian Bailo, noticed how he had aged in the last year. "Feeble of body, dropsical, with swollen legs and appetite gone, and face of a very bad color. In the month of March last he had four or five fainting fits. According to common opinion, his death must occur soon. . . . May God bring about that which may be of most advantage to all Christendom."

The greatest advantage to Christendom had been the death of Bayazid. Suleiman realized the loss. The leadership of the fearful Selim could never carry forward the Osmanli rule as either of his two favored sons might have done. But he could not have realized how great that loss was to be.

Refuge on the Black Mountain

Suleiman had one great hope remaining. For years he had been winning the quiet conflict of religions. His missionaries had penetrated far beyond the armies that he had held back.

By wandering dervish, Koran reader, and soldier of Islam he had offered conversion to European villagers. Peasants had moved their carts across the Turkish border, where they might keep an unbelievable amount of the grain they harvested; Greek islanders could sell their boatloads of fish at seaside markets and keep the money. Transylvanian foresters and Slavs of the Carpathians were accepting Islam not so much for tangible gain as for the feeling of joining a brotherhood of peoples.

Doors were not barred or watchdogs loosed within this brotherhood. Bread could be had by asking at the gates. Migrating heretics found their Jacobite and Protestant churches building beyond the Turkish borders. At the outer gate of the Serai itself stood the stone washing basin of the Blessed Mother Mary, for all to see. The name of *Issa* (Jesus) was heard in Moslem prayers.

Even the dour Rustem had tried to convert Busbecq, who explained that he was determined to keep the religion in which he was born.

"That is well enough," said Rustem, "but what will become of your soul?"

"For my soul, also," Busbecq replied, "I have good hopes."

After thinking a moment, the Vizir said, "You are right; and I agree that men who live in holiness will survive after death, whatever religion they have followed."

Busbecq could not say the same. He felt the compulsion of the faith that surrounded him, as if he were swimming almost alone against a tide that carried others with it. That tide had engulfed most of the Greek islands by then, and the valleys of the Balkans. It swept far out over the eastern steppes, almost to the walls of Moscow.

Within Suleiman's dominion armed Christianity resisted only on the Black Mountain (the Montenegro of the Europeans). On the gray granite heights backed against the sheer shore of the Adriatic the mountain Serbs kept their swords and their faith, where monasteries had been turned into forts, priests into warriors, and prelates into diplomats. There they had an active printing press and a legend that Skanderbeg, their defender of old time, walked among them again as a ghost. "Oh, it's no shadow," they said, "the freedom of the Black Mountain. No other than God could banish it, and—who knows—he might tire of trying."

The Turks had tried, by occupying the fertile valleys below, by taking the valley Serbs into the army, and transplanting colonies of Moslem Slavs to the foothills. Cut off from plowable land, the Black Mountain Serbs held out above the cloud level, and in so doing formed a nucleus of resistance.

This isolated group was to move against the Turkish religious expansion long before the courts of Vienna, Naples, or Madrid managed to do so.

The other island of resistance was in reality an island, in the narrows of the Mediterranean, the Malta of the Knights. The Knights, stoically fortifying their rock-ribbed harbor, remained as culturally backward and as indomitable as the feudal Serbs. From that base their squadron of seven red galleys raided the new masters of the Mediterranean. They were very much alone in doing so.

The dreaded Spaniards had been driven back along North Africa to the Gibraltar region by the Turkish sea captains and the expatriated Moors. Far from becoming another New Spain, this continent was astir with the expansion of Islam. Spanish conquistadors returning home with the plate fleet from Mexico and the Indies had to slip past Turkish fleets to gain the guardian rock of Gibraltar.

It was due to Dragut, who bedeviled Philip II as Barbarossa had haunted the memory of Charles. Dragut the Anatolian, impish in his merriment and kindly when not in action, had more than Barbarossa's instinct for battle. His duel with Philip was fought with every weapon, in most unexpected places.

Each summer Dragut called at Naples. His crews overran Sicily, and looked in at Majorca. Slipping past Gibraltar, he hauled in a Spanish treasure convoy from the Atlantic, a few years before the English took to doing so. The English ambassador wrote to his Queen, Elizabeth, "The Moors have despoiled many merchant ships about Seville and Cadiz, and among them three English ships, with a booty of more than 100,000 ducats."

The Moors were on Dragut's ships. Philip II, now King of

Spain, seeking to regain the empire of his father, Charles, found that his commanders were no match for the Turks in seamanship. His first expedition to Africa had been trapped by Dragut in the Yerba lagoon; another twenty-five galleys went down in a storm with their admiral, Juan de Mendoza. For the time being Philip accepted defeat in his duel with Dragut.

Only Malta remained, in 1564, to challenge the Turks.

Dragut believed the stronghold of the Religion too dangerous to attack. When the sea captains from the Golden Horn raided it a dozen years before, he had studied the defenses of its port and had contented himself with capturing the neighboring island of Gozo.

To Suleiman, however, the island of white stone held personal significance. In his youth he had driven those same Knights from Rhodes; they defied not only him but Islam; if they could be swept away again, the paths of the Mediterranean would be cleared. Yet Dragut warned him against attempting it.

So far he had given no order to move against Malta. Embittered now by the execution of Bayazid, and feeling sickness growing upon him, he thought of the capture of Malta as a triumph over the infidels, to mark the end of his life. He was willing now to use all his weapons by land or sea against the Europeans.

Then a slight incident fixed his anger on Malta. The cruising fleet, the seven red galleys, of the truculent Knights took some Turkish merchantmen near at hand in the Aegean, while Dragut and Piali Pasha were off as usual in the west.

Mihrmah seized on the incident to taunt him. Sick herself, in the old palace, she challenged her father. Had he not taken command of the armed forces, to destroy Bayazid? Was he not Protector of the Faithful against these very infidels who had raided within sight of the Dardanelles? What fear kept him from destroying Malta?

How much he was influenced by her taunt there is no telling. Unquestionably there was popular demand for the capture of

Malta. Suleiman ordered it. The new Serasker was to assemble storm troops and siege guns, transports were to be built, and the sea captains recalled from their adventuring to reduce the stronghold of the Knights.

One condition he made. His Serasker and Kaputan Pasha were to undertake nothing on the island until Dragut appeared there and consented to it.

The Dead Men of St Elmo

Perhaps the temperamental Dragut sulked on the way. Perhaps the day of the rendezvous at Malta had not been made clear to him, or he was delayed in assembling the African squadrons. Whatever the reason, he was late. When he sighted the whitish mass of Malta on the sky line, and headed his captain's galley toward the harbor, he heard the thudding of the guns around the point of land on which stood the fort of St. Elmo.

As he rounded the harbor entrance Dragut could see what had happened. The Turkish commanders had not waited for him. Under the haze of smoke their siege lines zigzagged up the height toward the ramparts of St. Elmo. Against those ramparts their batteries were pounding. They had done their work well, at the wrong place. Across the harbor the gray town of the Knights lay like a giant tortoise, its sides armored with forts, unmolested.

When Dragut landed and inspected the small island, which the Turks had overrun easily enough, he realized the strength and the weakness of Malta. Its stone-ridden earth resisted digging—trenches had to be hewn with picks at night; on this barren ground, ceded to them almost contemptuously by the great Emperor, the Knights were waiting behind projecting bastions of solid masonry, shielded by scarp and counterscarp, heavily gunned where cross fire could sweep the approaches.

All these outthrusts of solid stonework had to be shattered by massive gunfire before they could be attacked by fragile human bodies. Against such inanimate strength, mere numbers of attackers availed nothing. Nor were great numbers needed to serve the defenses. The Knights, wise in the ways of sieges, had planned for that. Their galleys were safely ensconced in the basin within the defenses of the town, the Borgo. Across the mouth of this basin a massive chain had been drawn.

(Actually within all the forts there were 500 Knights, 1300 hired soldiery, with 4000 seamen and Maltese. Against these the Turks had brought 4500 veteran janizaris, 7500 dismounted spahis, and 18,000 engineers, sailors, light infantry and others.)

Malta had a weakness, however, and Dragut pointed it out to his commanders. The great harbor sprawled among indentations. The Knights, being few and with little wealth, had been able to fortify only the Borgo itself around the galley basin. Back of the harbor, ridges overlooked this citadel. Batteries placed on these ridges could blast a way into the citadel itself in time.

"Here," said Dragut, on the heights, "should be your cannon."

The commander of the Turks, Mustafa Pasha, the Serasker, had chosen instead to take St. Elmo, isolated across the harbor. St. Elmo was the key to the harbor entrance. Once they had broken into St. Elmo they could bring their fleet into the harbor and come to close grips with the main defenses of the Knights, at the Borgo. Piali, the Kaputan Pasha, did not agree with him, nor did the experienced Dragut. "I see well enough that the fort over there stands in our way to the town," he exclaimed. "But if we take the town itself our work is over, and the fort matters nothing. How much powder and how many lives will you waste at St. Elmo before you order us to do what we must do in any case?"

Still, the advance against St. Elmo had been pushed too far to be abandoned. It had to be carried through, as Malta itself had to be taken. Suleiman had ordered them not to fail. The

Serasker knew, as Dragut and Piali knew, that the three of them could not sail back to the Golden Horn to say to Suleiman that for the first time the Osmanli fleet and army had been defeated.

Moreover, they had to labor against time. Malta was almost within sight of Sicily, which adjoined Italy. Surely in a month, or two at the most, a relief armada would be putting out from the European shores. . . .

The blasting of the Turkish guns cracked and crumbled the solid masonry of St. Elmo. Dragut's driving energy encompassed the doomed fort; his batteries raked it from an opposite height, stopping supplies from crossing the bay to the fort.

It is not by courage and simple hand-to-hand fighting that such segments of earth can be defended. Human endurance weakens under such battering; wearied men surrender themselves or escape if they can, or they fail at the unending labor by which they can keep themselves alive. After the first vicious assault along the broken glacis, the garrison of St. Elmo sent word across to the Grand Master of the Order that they could not beat back another storm.

The Grand Master, Jean de La Valette, was old as Suleiman. He had been spared after the loss of Rhodes and shipped home by the generosity of the Sultan. Devout, he lived out his life in mental armor. Like Dragut, he had been a captive galley slave. He could not conceive of turning his back on the infidel Turks, or of making a truce with them. "Do you wish me, then," he wrote in answer to the survivors in the fort, "to take command at St. Elmo?"

Stung by the Grand Master's scorn, they stood off the next attack. Dragut flung a bridge of spars and canvas across the ditch before the breach. For five hours the Turks attacked across the bridge. Very few of the Knights and mercenaries inside the fort remained unwounded, but they had passed the point where nerves give way. They went on piling broken stones into new barriers.

Dragut had reached Malta the second of June. On the sixteenth, directing an attack along the St. Elmo breaches, he was struck in the head by splintered rock, his skull shattered. Mustafa Pasha hurried to where he lay with physicians, who decided that Dragut could not live. Hearing that, the Serasker put his cloak over the sea captain and stood in his place to take over command of the attack. Piali Pasha was wounded by iron fragments, but not fatally.

While Dragut still lived, conscious of what went on, the unceasing assault thinned down the St. Elmo garrison to the point where the Knights could not muster enough swords to cover all the breaches. Understanding that they could hold out only a limited time, De La Valette sent over a mission of three Knights under cover of darkness, an Englishman, Italian and Frenchman. The three got back to report to him. Two of them gave the opinion that the fort was doomed; the third could not decide, saying that the survivors were of a good mind to man their walls and not to surrender.

The Grand Master decided that they should stay and die at their posts, after taking the final sacrament from each other.

The Turks who broke into St. Elmo on the twenty-fourth of June found wounded men propped up in chairs, sword in hand, to face them. Not one survived. Enraged by their terrible losses, the attackers stripped the bodies, hacking red crosses into the chests and throwing them into the bay to drift across to the citadel.

Dragut remained conscious long enough to hear of the capture of the fort. He had been the most brilliant commander of the Mediterranean, and the only one who had never been known to fail. His loss was to affect the venture of the Turks upon the sea.

No relief fleet appeared on the sky line off Malta. It had been promised by mid-June. At the end of the month a single galley beached on the far side of the island, with less than a hundred

Knights and their followers. They had put off in a vessel of their own, unable to endure the delay of the Viceroy in Sicily, who was assembling a flotilla at Messina.

Aided by a fog and something manifestly like a miracle, this small force found its way through the Turkish lines at night, to report to De La Valette in the Borgo. They told of money given by Pope Pius IV, of promises made by the Spaniards, of ships offered by merchants, and a steady march of volunteers into Messina, where no one embarked because Garcia de Toledo, the Viceroy of Spain in Sicily, would not put to sea without the protection of a battle fleet stronger than the Turks'. The simple truth was that too many people were afraid. The Viceroy now promised that he would cross over to Malta "sometime in July."

His sails were sighted actually on the fifth of September.

For seventy-three days De La Valette's citadel endured the battering that had broken apart St Elmo. From the heights behind the town the Turks kept up a dropping fire that searched the streets, while their engineers drove approaches under the walls. "A battery began," Knolles relates, "in fourteen places with seventy great pieces of artillery amongst which were three most huge basilisks; for the Turks had enclosed all that compass with sundry bulwarks, trenches and mounts, from which they with their thundering shot day and night incessantly battered the towns and castles of St. Michael and St. Angelo, overthrew the walls, beat down the bulwarks, and brake down the houses in such terrible manner that scarce any could be safe therein."

Mustafa Pasha's engineers drove a causeway out to one of the forts. Hassan, the son of Barbarossa—and, like him, Beylerbey of Algiers—contrived to haul galleys overland to launch them in the harbor behind the forts and attack by water. His attempt ended in the total loss of his crews because the vessels were sunk or drifted loose and the attackers were left without means of retreat. The Knights took no prisoners.

Salih Reis, son of the sea captain who had aided Barbarossa,

tried a surprise assault with a small band. They crept forward
during a quiet hour of the day. Five men who had been asleep
in the ruin of a bastion held his party back, until the armored
Knights could come up to defend the post.

Turkish swimmers took axes with them in darkness to reach
and try to destroy the chain across the inner basin. They were
met by Maltese swimmers with knives in their teeth.

The rock-ribbed earth under the walls made tunneling almost
impossible. But the Serasker drove a shaft through and exploded
a mine that shattered the side of a bastion. His immediate attack across the mine crater fell into a trap prepared for it.
Tunneling through rock had made too much noise and the defenders had traced the course of the shaft in time to build new
fortifications at its end.

Still Mustafa Pasha took his losses, knowing that the Knights
were weakened by a little at each clash of the fighting men.
Late in August a series of mines were exploded, and he led a
mass assault himself in his gilded mail. The attack wave could
not penetrate the breaches. The Serasker was pinned down in a
crater with those who had followed him through the outworks.
There they held off the sallies of the Christians until nightfall,
when they could crawl back to their lines.

De La Valette's lieutenants counted their casualties after this
assault. They no longer had sufficient force, they said, to hold
the circle of the forts. They gave their opinion that all holy
relics, personal valuables of the Knights and the remaining
stores should be moved into a part of the citadel still intact, the
Castle of St. Angelo. Thither they should prepare to withdraw.

The Grand Master considered and replied that he understood
their reasoning, but he could not agree to it. Until now the
Maltese and the hired soldiery had stood up well; it would dis-
hearten them if they discovered that the Knights, their leaders,
were making a move to retreat. A soldier will not stand where
his captain withdraws. So—and De La Valette ordered it—they
should move everyone out of the refuge of St. Angelo into the

breaches, except those who must remain to serve the heavy cannon.

Until the end of August the Turks pressed attacks against the breaches. With half his own command casualties or sick in their tents, Mustafa Pasha knew that the strain on the remnant of armored men in the ruins must be unendurable. "Mustafa, the Turks' General," Richard Knolles relates, "now thinking no man so strong who might not with continual labor and watching be wearied and overcome, resolved not to give unto the besieged any time of rest, but commanded his soldiers again to assault the breach at the Castle of Saint Michael."

In those few days the fanatical fury of the attackers failed as at St. Elmo to break the spirit of the defense. For the first time in generations the Turkish *asker* had met a superior fighting force in these men who would not give up an inch of ground until they were killed.

Mustafa Pasha remembered St. Elmo and stopped the wastage of life at the single breach to prepare for a final assault at all points. If that could be launched, some opening would be found unguarded by the mailed Knights. He set a day for it, the seventh of September.

On the fifth of September he heard that the Christian fleet from Sicily had arrived off the north shore. The relief army was landing in his rear.

The Serasker abandoned his works, burning his siege engines and camp. He got his cannon away, except for twenty-four heavy siege pieces. While the Knights displayed their banners on the tower of St. Angelo, the Turks set fire to the forty ships they could no longer man with crews, and put out to sea.

They did not leave Malta without a desperate attempt at final victory. Out of sight of the city they turned back to the eastern shore. There the Serasker disembarked 7000 men still capable of fighting, and led them against the relief column making its way toward the city.

The attack failed against the greater strength of the 10,000 in the army from Sicily. The Turks were driven back to their galleys, losing heavily as they fought their way to their decks and clear of the coast. This time they headed out to Gozo and the east.

Garcia de Toledo, Viceroy of Spain, brought his armada of 70 galleys in toward the scarred harbor of Malta. He displayed his banners. All the remaining guns of Malta fired a salute to the fleet that had ended the siege. Don Garcia answered with a double discharge of all his cannon—and sailed away from the embattled port! A message arrived from him, that he was going back for reinforcements.

His fleet of Sicily did not pursue the crippled Turks. De La Valette sat down to write his report of the action at Malta on behalf of what he still chose to call the Christian Commonwealth.

Mustafa, the Serasker, hove to when he sighted Serai Point. He was not willing to come in to his moorings by the light of day. Waiting until dark, he brought the survivors of the Malta expedition into the harbor of the Golden Horn when they could not be seen from the city streets. Without parade, they dispersed to their barracks and homes.

The loss of Dragut and the military defeat troubled the Serai and the folk of Constantinople sorely. At Malta something unexpected had taken place. Not only had the sickening Sultan demanded its capture. The expedition had been stronger than any other sent out by sea. Yet a small and isolated Christian garrison had prevailed over Turks who had shown no lack of courage. No one could point a finger and say *this* caused it, or it happened by *that* man's incompetence.

No, the disaster at Malta had been written in the book of Fate. Dragut died, because that had been the place and the hour appointed for him. Surely God had willed for them to fail at Malta.

That sense of fatality troubled the Turks deeply, from Ibn

Sa'ud to the boy gardeners. The hammering on the hulls of new vessels in the Arsenal runways across the water did not have the same assurance as before. No new expedition was ordered into the western sea, beyond Malta. Such an expedition would never be sent out again.

Much of the moodiness, especially in the Serai, arose from the restrained anger of Suleiman. After hearing the report of the return of the fleet, the grieving Sultan would not speak of Malta.

Those who sat in the Divan noticed what pains he took to avoid doing so. Mustafa Pasha, who shouldered the burden of blame, came and took his appointed place again in the half circle of the council, as duty required. When Suleiman himself sat with them, he spoke only to Sokolli, now the First Vizir, and to Pertau Pasha, the next in rank. He did not want to speak to Mustafa Pasha, because that would necessitate mention of Malta. So, not to shame the commander, Suleiman refrained from addressing the others seated near him.

All of them, from the sitters in the Divan to the janizaris at the outer gate, wondered what action the Sultan would take in his pain and anger.

No one expected him to do what he did. When the snows melted and the feast of the New Year was at hand—the time of salutations and gifts to the Osmanli Sultan—Suleiman ordered the great drum of conquest to be sounded. He said he had not gone forth at the last setting-out of the *asker* (he did not say, to Malta). This time he would take command and go with them. The result would be good.

They understood that he wanted to compensate for the failure at Malta. But they did not see how, in his sickness, he could go on a march.

MALTA, AND THE LAST MARCH OUT

Change of the Leaders

Odd preparations were made for the march. Suleiman seldom broke his habitual silence now, and never to give explanation of what he meant to do. His eyes gleamed between heavy folds of flesh, as if he judged and condemned those nearest him.

In the small chamber of the Divan they pondered what he had ordered last. The treaty of trade with Florence, giving that free city the same rights as Venice—Ragusa and France to have the silks made in Brusa, for the European markets. His old idea of giving Turkish commerce into European hands impelled him still. Peace treaties with other powers, except the new Emperor, Maximilian—he granted them easily. Forbade Persian pilgrims to journey to Mecca, for fear of disturbance——

He did not send for his son Selim. His letters bade Selim give up wine, "that red mad thing." Confident now, Selim did not cease his debauches, and Suleiman ordered one of his cup companions executed. Then Selim returned to secret drinking.

In silence Suleiman judged his surviving son, finding no worth in him, or his women. Selim must live. He was the only survivor of the Osmanli line, yet he could not rule as the Osmanlis had done. When Murad, Selim's son, insolently asked for a galley to take him home to his father, the Sultan gave him a small ketch instead.

Then he sent for Selim's two daughters, and married them to two men on whom he could depend, Sokolli, and Piali, the Kaputan Pasha. To the tall impassive Croat he gave authority that he had not yielded for thirty years, not since the death of Ibrahim To Sokolli's rank of First Vizir he added that of Serasker. Being united to the blood of the Osmanlis, Sokolli now held all power that Suleiman could give, except the name of Sultan. If he chose to plot for that, he could win it. Yet he would not. This Croat of the mountains did not relish titles. Hard as a granite summit, he found his joy in accomplishment rather than honors. Long years ago in the School he had revealed that, and Suleiman remembered. Neither of them spoke of loyalty.

Before setting out, propped against the pillows of his sleeping place, Suleiman watched the other's face for some trace of indecision or pride, or curiosity as to the failing strength of his master.

His gnarled hands clasped above his knees, Sokolli was thinking out, and repeating details of the march to be made. The mobilization of the Army of Europe——

"And of Asia," Suleiman whispered.

The Vizir's gray eyes turned to him. Not for years had the whole muster been summoned. "Well," he said, and no more.

Carefully Suleiman drank water from a cup. "Ghirei, Khan of the Krım Tatars," he whispered, "to accompany"

A glint of amusement touched Sokolli's bony face. "A parade —a festival, eh? You want that?"

"To have a good feeling, yes." Closing his eyes, Suleiman thought about the march being festive, all the way. "Perhaps even a poem to be read."

"Poets are always glad to read. I will only need to hint, for them to do so."

"Baki."

"Well. Baki will read. The road will have to be made smooth with sand for the Sultan's carriage."

After considering that, Suleiman shook his head. "My horses."

"A litter will be made, then. Your horses will draw it."

Satisfied, Suleiman nodded. If the man before him had protested or tried to persuade him not to undertake the pain and responsibility of the march, he would have been troubled. Now he could go in his litter without misgivings. Leaning forward to replace the gold drinking cup, he felt Sokolli's hand touch his, to take the cup. Suleiman set it down, unaided. Then of his own accord he touched his companion's hand. "I will not go to the Tatars' Meadow," he said forcibly. "I will not go to Adrianople, or even the Danube's bank. I will go all the way. I will be with you in the Land of War. You are not yet the Bearer of the Burden."

He could see well enough from the slits in the litter. The horses could canter over level ground, where the tasseled caps of his runners bobbed beside him . . . the helmets of Sokolli's guards had foxtails tossing, with leopard skins over their cloaks . . . leaving his city for the thirteenth march out.

Past the burnt column of the Roman Caesars his litter sped. The jolting hurt him but it would not do to walk at a funeral pace where throngs of his people watched his passing. By the gray walls of the old palace where Mihrmah no longer waited alone in her room—she lay in her new tomb by the Chamlija, above the Sweet Waters of Asia . . . where he had stolen away to hunt.

Now through the slit he could see the towers of the Suleimaniye, and the small dome of Roxelana's tomb beneath the cypresses. It was a strange feeling, to be passing by. So many times he had merely glanced curiously around, when he rode out, to return again.

Past the cluster of the Seven Towers he sped. Within one he had watched an inscription carved: *The labors of Rustem stored these treasures here.* For whose gain? Turning his head, he caught a glint of blue . . . the lovely breast of Marmora beyond the towers.

It was strange to be passing by in this manner, never to return. Suleiman could not realize that all the others, Ibn Sa'ud, Piali Pasha, and Sokolli, would return without him.

For he was taking them all, part of the way. To the meadow where Baki would come before the pavilion and read rather flamboyant praise of the Osmanli sultans, in the cool of the afternoon, when the horses had been run off to graze and he had had sherbet to drink. All the Divan would gather to listen, and the aghas. . . . He had left behind him only the underlings,

and Selim's court, with which he had no concern. The heads of
the Organization were here, traveling as if on holiday. With
each of them Suleiman managed to have a word about duties
to be shouldered in the future.

At Adrianople the Mufti and the Kaputan Pasha turned back,
to keep the city in order. He told them to watch well his grandson Murad, who had been egged on by women of Selim's harem
to ask for a galley, to be his own.

Climbing into the cold gorges of the mountains, Suleiman
lay back to listen to the familiar beat of rain, waiting to see the
height of Belgrade against the gray of the Danube.

When they ferried him across the flooded river, they told him
that the camels with his pavilion had been lost, and he groped
beside him for the sheets of paper on which he had always made
his daily notes. *Rain: the Sultan's tent was lost in the flood.*
The words formed in his mind, and he did not write.

They found him another tent. On a clear evening he saw
again the lush, swamp-fed green of the field of Mohács. By an
effort he was able to sit in the Divan pavilion when they
brought the son of Zapolya before him, John Sigismund, King
of Hungary, a man grown now. Standing rigid before him, John
Sigismund made complaint of attacks by his enemies from
Austria.

Suleiman assented, liking him. "Well. I will not have our
weapons laid aside until I have made firm your throne of
Hungary."

Sweat dripped from the broad face of the young Hungarian,
as he fought against terror, staring at the gray swollen mask
in which only the eyes of the all-powerful Sultan seemed to be
alive. Helplessly he muttered something in German. Beside
Suleiman, Sokolli's deep voice interpreted quietly, "Something
he wants, he does not say what."

This son of a Polish princess was afraid of him. For an instant
the rigid young face changed, with the smile of his own son

Mustafa, whose dark eyes looked at his father without fear. Suleiman spoke, fighting down the faintness that came with the searing pain in his head. "If he has need of anything make it known, and it will be granted."

They took John Sigismund away, and Suleiman found the arrogant dark face of an officer before him. "Arslan Khan," Sokolli's voice prompted, and Suleiman tried to remember. A brave leader, the Lion Chieftain who spurred himself on with opium and wine, who had disobeyed orders and suffered a defeat. After Malta, there could be no other defeat. Still, only a few hundreds of men and a village had been lost. Arslan Khan smiled at him. "I know what my fate will be."

A spasm of rage shook Suleiman With his hand he made a peculiar sign, and Sokolli whispered to armed men behind the dais. Two of them stepped forward, suddenly twisting a bowstring around the heavy neck of the officer.

Arslan Khan did not struggle until agony seized his body Between them, the executioners held him upright until the head rolled back. Then at a sign from Suleiman, they carried the body out.

The Anniversary at Sziget

At nightfall the boy who had come from the School to the duty of caring for his bedchamber lighted the hanging lamps, and a physician brought in a pungent drink to dull the pain that kept him from sleeping. A reader knelt between two lamps with the Koran outspread on its ivory-inlaid stand before his knees. The voice of the reader began its cadenced call, drawing his thoughts toward it, as swiftly running water draws the eyes . . . he could still see well, and hear.

One evening Sokolli came, wearing his sword, brushing back his scarlet cloak as he made the gesture of stretching his hand toward Suleiman's feet. He had news, not important but affecting the Sultan. There had been a skirmish on the far left of the marching army, an unlucky affair, causing the death of a man known to Suleiman, the First Squire of his household.

It had happened at Sziget, a citadel in the river lands, captured and held by a daring Hapsburg commander, Nicholas Zrinyi by name. It had been, in truth, no more than a skirmish.

Suleiman nodded, and considered it. After a moment he dismissed the bearded reader and the silent page. "We will go to Sziget," he told his commander.

In his turn, Sokolli weighed the order given him. Their line of march had been to the north where a Hapsburg army, breaking the peace, had harried the young John Sigismund. Far to the north the Austrian army could be found at Erlau in the Carpathians. Sokolli could think of no good reason to change the line of march, which would be a difficult undertaking, with the Tatar and Asiatic horsemen so far out on the wings. "Sziget is a small place, water-circled, with a strong citadel, as the Sultan knows. Why should we stoop to pick up a little thing when we can grasp a great one?"

But this place was close to them. Suleiman thought he would be able to see it.

"This Zrinyi has a name for courage," murmured the Serasker.

They had been brave also at Malta, a strong citadel surrounded by water. Suleiman cared little then, or at any time, for the strategy of war. He was more struck by the coincidence that Sziget resembled Malta. He would not fail, at Sziget. "Tomorrow," he ordered, "I will go in my litter with the horses on the road to the west to Sziget. See you to the other matters."

As if touched by cold steel, Sokolli lifted his head. Swiftly he thought of a dozen reasons why tens of thousands of marching men should not be turned aside toward a pile of masonry set into water. As he opened his lips to object, Suleiman spoke, reflectively.

"Mehmed Sokolli, I wish to go there."

The tone more than the words silenced the Serasker. It was

as if his master had said, *Yes, my brother, I know it is neither wise nor profitable and you can give me excellent arguments against doing it, but I do not want to hear them.* For an instant Sokolli wondered if the great Sultan were not really stupid, as many people claimed. Certainly he seemed slow to act for his own advantage——

"I hear it," he acknowledged, bending his head forward. "But a boat will be better than the litter. The galleys are up from the Karadeniz, and you can go almost all the way to Sziget by water."

That he could say for certain, because his home had been near the river, and the mountains to the west.

When he went out to give the necessary orders, the reader came in, raising his voice in the tent. "*Truly thou canst not guide whom thou desirest to guide, but God guideth whom he will . . .*"

Lying back to rest after speaking, Suleiman felt the weight of his failures pressing against his mind. For all of forty and six years he had had to decide for his people, to do this or to leave that undone . . . perhaps he had been foolish to have them destroy the musical instruments, the guitars and especially the flutes that had given him so much pleasure . . . because such pleasure might not be the will of God. Could even Ibn Sa'ud be certain of that?

The boat they gave him on the river Drave was a light yacht, festive in its draping of cloth of gold, with a single gilt crescent. Lying under the stern canopy, he could watch the road by the river. Where the mountains came down on his left, the road was close enough for him to see what people did on it.

Some bullocks dragged a heavy siege cannon more slowly than the yacht moved, upstream. They told him this was the Katzianer cannon, named for the Austrian general who had once fled from his duty to take refuge among the Osmanli people. Suleiman smiled, because they wanted to amuse him. He wondered for a moment what the years would have brought him had there been no cannon or powder, or vessels to carry them across the seas.

On a rock down from the road, a janizary perched with one bare foot soaking in the cool water. Evidently he had hurt his foot and dropped out for a while to rest. The monk's sleeve of his cap hung down over his shoulder, while he devoted all his attention to the flute between his pursed lips. The light wail of the flute could be heard over the soft rush of water.

Sighting the gold drapery of the yacht, the soldier shaded his eyes to stare at it. It seemed to please him because he returned with vigor to his song on the flute, swinging his foot in the water.

Suleiman watched until the little boat entered the shadow of the hills, and the brightness around him became opaque, as if veils had been let down from the sky.

When his litter approached the pavilion made ready for him on the crest overlooking Sziget, the Agha of the Janizaris stepped to the door and begged him to move forward a little to look at what waited for them below.

From the slit in the side he could make out the sweep of a pleasant valley with a road winding through it. The road passed over water to the gray buildings of a town with red roofs and above the roofs a soaring citadel of very strange appearance.

Scarlet cloths draped the summit of the citadel of Sziget. As Suleiman watched, with horsemen crowding around him and the wind stirring the white horsetails of his standard, the citadel began to flash with light. Rays of sunlight shot back from it. People around him said that the Christians had hoisted metal plates, to shine like that in the sun. It looked gay and festive.

A roar burst from the citadel, ending with discharges of single cannon, as smoke drifted up through the flashing rays

"A salute, by God," grunted the Agha, beside Suleiman.

So Nicholas Zrinyi of Sziget had saluted the appearance of

the Sultan who had condemned him and his town to destruction. Suleiman wondered if the castle of Malta had draped itself like that, or if banners had been displayed on the heights of the Black Mountain. There was a stubborn core in such Christians, a way of laughing at fate which he had never understood, although he had tried——

Twenty-four days later the Serasker, Sokolli, entered the sleeping compartment of the pavilion which Suleiman no longer left. This happened to be, as the army well knew, Suleiman's day of luck. On this day he had taken the surrender of Belgrade, and had reined his horse in victory over the field of Mohács, and had entered Buda. The assault that day, through the town and against the massive walls of the citadel, had been savage. It had not ceased until darkness because the officers had wished to tell the Sultan before sunset that this citadel of the Christians also had fallen into his power. They had tried to accomplish that as a gift to the seventy-two-year-old man.

On the bed the Sultan looked up, questioning.

Sokolli wasted no words. "Not yet," he said, showing his empty hands. With the details of a terrible day pressing upon his mind, he made no excuses or promises. "We will have to drive a mine under a section of the walls." Frowning, he reflected. "It will take four days, five—perhaps seven."

While he waited for the Sultan's reply, he felt a stiffening of his muscles, not in fear, but in anticipation of rebuke and different orders.

"Mehmed Sokolli," Suleiman said, "the number of days does not matter."

When he left the tent, Sokolli remembered that for the first time in their talks Suleiman had given him no order.

The mine had not been exploded by the fifth night. It was quiet that night. The physician stretched out asleep, exhausted. Beside the night lamp Sokolli sat, turning over a written message in his powerful fingers.

Beneath the lamp Sultan Suleiman Khan was dead. He, Sokolli, was the Bearer of the Burden

It would not be so difficult at first, he thought. For Suleiman had insisted on this parade of a march. No one else but Sokolli and the physician knew that he was dying. Here in the hills of Hungary, his body could be tended in his tent as if it still lived —no one must discover his secret.

Then, when the mine was exploded and an end made of Nicholas Zrinyi and Sziget, rewards could be given out in the name of Suleiman.

After that the body could ride in the closed horse litter down to Belgrade. It would take three weeks to reach Belgrade, and three weeks for a courier to speed, killing horses on the way to Kutahiya, to fetch Selim the Sot up to Belgrade. After that the secret could be made known.

When he was certain of the count of the days, Sokolli got to his feet. Glancing around the sleeping chamber, he put out the flame in the lamp.

For a moment, in the darkness, Mehmed Sokolli felt something like fear. The step he took from the bedside he would take alone. In the darkness and silence he made himself realize that the master he had known all his life could no longer relieve him of responsibility——

Walking quickly to the entrance curtain, he said casually to the outer guards that the Sultan was sleeping. He asked for a courier to take a message to Selim the son of Suleiman.

VI

Ebb of the Turkish Tide

The Lawgiver

SELIM failed immediately in his first test. Probably he proved to be weaker than even Mehmed Sokolli had anticipated. When he was ferried across from Asia to Constantinople the city had learned Sokolli's secret. Masses of janizaris quartered around the Serai besieged him with their demand for a donation. Frightened, he promised an immense payment, and escaped up the road to Belgrade.

There, encountering the field army in mourning for its Sultan, he took refuge in his tent and ordered Sokolli to lay the tumult of demands. This the First Vizir did, and either because Selim had had a thorough fright, or because he did not lack some shrewd common sense, he retained the grim Croat as the minister of his empire all his life. He survived for only eight years as did Ibn Sa'ud, and Sokolli ruled the Osmanli state for five years more under his son, Murad III.

But the last of the great Osmanli sultans was dead. Selim lacked the courage to attend his burial, beside the tomb of Roxelana in the Suleimaniye. Although some brilliant men reigned in the Serai thereafter and several proved able enough in carrying on wars, the succession of driving personalities from the first Osman and Ertoghrul, through Mehmed the Conqueror, had ended.

This decline of the Osmanli sultans was abrupt as the fall of a curtain, much more abrupt than the deterioration of the Spanish Empire after Philip II. Yet something quite different endured for centuries. It was a nation of great inward strength that survived the degeneration of rulers who often became no more than puppets; this nation outlasted the Serene Republic of Venice, the vast Spanish dominion, and imperial Austria, and it continued to survive with remarkable steadfastness while Poland was partitioned, and Portugal shrank into a segment of the Spanish peninsula.

This spectacular decline of the Osmanlis after Suleiman, and the consequent stubborn endurance of the Turks as a people, has been one of the mysteries of history. Many explorers of the mystery have laid the collapse to the faults of Suleiman; only a few have decided that he was responsible for the strengthening of the nation.

He had so little to say for himself. Secluding himself as he did from visitors, speaking almost always through the mouths of his vizirs, appearing to Europeans throughout his forty-six years of rule as the directing mind of a much-dreaded and highly mobile army, he achieved almost complete obscurity. To that obscurity, prejudice was added, for centuries.

"The longer one studies him," Roger Merriman affirms, "the greater he seems to be."

His actions must help to solve the mystery, when measured against their consequences after his death. For he was a simple Turk, and his story, told only sketchily, as we have certainty of so little of it, is that of the Turkish people in the day when they influenced the destinies of three continents.

Even at his death there was disagreement as to the real Suleiman. Europeans, of course, called him the Magnificent—as he had appeared to them. His people christened him Kanuni, the Lawgiver. Our zealous chronicle, the *Brief World Happenings*, duly noted his death in the year 1566 as that of the tyrant who had been the flail of Christians. Shah Tahmasp said the two stains on his reign were the murders of Ibrahim and Mustafa.

A half century after Suleiman, in Protestant England, good Richard Knolles had this to say of his last days: "*Mahomet Pasha*, after he had placed a Turkish governor in Sziget, called back the dispersed forces, and retired toward Belgrade, carrying *Solyman's* dead body all the way sitting upright in his horse litter, giving it out that he was sick of the gout: which thing the janizaris easily believed, knowing that he had been many years so carried; yet still wishing his presence as always unto them fortunate, although he were able to do nothing." (There is irony in this last ride of the Sultan at the head of the army which he had labored to discipline and suppress.) ". . . he was of stature tall, of feature slender, long necked, his color pale and wan, his nose long and hooked, of nature ambitious and bountiful, more faithful of his word and promise than were for most part the Mahometan kings his progenitors, wanting nothing worthy of so great an empire but that wherein all happiness is contained, faith in Christ Jesus."

The matter-of-fact Englishman is aware of something important. Suleiman in his estimation was worthy of so great an empire. (In the preamble to his voluminous *General Historie of the Turkes* he speaks of "the glorious empire of the Turkes, the present terror of the world.") The Turks were unquestionably dangerous but they were also a great people, and the notable Suleiman had been no isolated personality but one moving in the Turkish tradition.

Baki's lament for his king is eloquent with human grief. He invokes the inevitable phrases of Martyr and Conqueror (Ghazi). Yet he reveals the sense of loss among the people.

Will not the king awake from sleep, when comes the light of day?

Will not he move forth from his tent, bright as high heaven's display?

313

SULEIMAN THE MAGNIFICENT

*Long have our eyes dwelt on the road, and yet no word is come
From that far land. . . .*

Beyond the grieving, there is an unexpected thought:

*Across the face of earth thou hast hurled the right,
From east to west thine armored champions have borne it,
As sweeps a sword. . . .*

This is the culmination of the elegy, and Baki does not use the words "religious faith" or "conquest" here. Suleiman has fought for an intangible thing, the *right*.

Was this intangible thing racial toleration (at a time when minorities were being driven from Spain)? Was it the right of individuals to be protected by law, regardless of religion (when heretics were too often burned at the stake elsewhere)? Was it an actual utopia for human beings (of which Thomas More had written, when beggars in England were maimed or hung)?

Suleiman was not a dreamer. In every case, he worked upward from Turkish tradition; inventing nothing, he tried to adapt that canon of old custom not to the requirements of the age but to something more advanced. It was not that he had modern concepts. He thought as a Turk, in his own day. The intensive schooling for instance was traditional at least from the Conqueror's time; what Suleiman did was to shift the burden of government from the families of hereditary sultans to the best of the School boys.

There was something quite modern in the democratic spirit of his Turkey. Suleiman himself withdrew markedly from personal contact with common folk—Mehmed the Conqueror had spoken face to face with whoever sought him. His impersonal effort had been to protect the individual by economy and by law. Truthfully, his people gave him the title (after his death) of Lawgiver.

Of one of his efforts the evidence survives today. In a sense

Suleiman found a Turkey of encampments and left it one of monasteries and religious schools. (And this at a time when the late Renaissance in the west left an imprint of palatial buildings for the nobility—the gaunt Escorial, the palazzos of the Medicis and D'Estes, the châteaux of the Valois, and the mansions of the Tudors.) The plain mosque centers Suleiman built for his family are among the landmarks of Istanbul today, with those of his fellowship—Barbarossa's small tomb by the Bosphorus adorns a public playground, Piali Pasha's stands by the water channel that he wished, to connect him with the water of the outer seas. The Suleimaniye center is being rebuilt next door to the grounds of the modern university on the crest of the hill. Go to any town in Anatolia, and if you find a mosque of unusual simplicity or a lovely fountain, the people will tell you it is Sinan's work. So is it proved again in Turkey that "what has been, will be."

The Accusers

The collapse of the sultans after Suleiman was so spectacular that Turkish historians sought for reasons in the reign of the Lawgiver. Three generations later Khoja Beg, a very honest man, listed these contributions by Suleiman to the decline and fall of the Osmanlis.

1. He withdrew from the Divan, making himself remote from his counselors in the Asiatic manner.

2. He promoted Ibrahim and Rustem to the vizirate by favor, and not by merit or seniority. And in Rustem's case he named a relative by marriage, which was unlawful.

3. Because of Rustem and Roxelana, women began to intrigue with the ministers of the empire, and in consequence the chief eunuchs came into immense power.

4. The wealth allowed Ibrahim and Rustem was harmful, particularly when stowed away in permanent Wakf (religious) foundations.

315

On all of these counts of Khoja Beg Suleiman was guilty. He did break the Ayin in this manner, and the consequences were bad. Suleiman risked departing from tradition to gain ends of his own.

The celebrated grated window over the seats of the Divan is still there, to be pointed out to visitors and to testify against him. It is a deceptive exhibit, however, because while Suleiman secluded himself from the public parliament, he got around elsewhere to an amazing extent in watching details of government. During an outbreak of plague late in Rustem's life, Ogier Busbecq naturally wanted to move his household from the city for a while. He asked Rustem if he could not reside on one of the islands where he might study the fish and birds of which he was so fond. Agreeing that it could certainly be done, Rustem explained that it must be with Suleiman's consent. If the Sultan, riding through the streets, should miss seeing Busbecq's servitors around, he might ask where they were, and be angered because they had been moved without his knowledge. Busbecq got to his island.

Suleiman experimented, apparently, with letting the government run itself without having him continually as visible head and court of appeal—as he tried to induce the army to function without him.

In the case of the vizirs, he did more than break precedent by selecting them himself. An apt judge of men, he had three great ministers, Ibrahim, Rustem and Sokolli, whose authority for forty-three years impelled the nation strongly forward. Here he tried the immensely daring experiment of taking direction from the hands of the Osmanli family and giving it to the most talented ministers. It is clear that he risked everything to effect this change-over in his last sickness; but he had started to do it with Ibrahim in the first years.

Seemingly he distrusted his own ability and that of his successors to accomplish at the head of an empire, in the changing world of the Renaissance, what the early Osmanlis had achieved at the head of a moving military state. It is said so often that, because Mustafa and Bayazid were killed, the accession of the sottish Selim began the breakdown of the Osmanlis. It may be that, dreading weakness in his sons, Suleiman turned on them with inhuman cruelty at the first sign of disloyalty. Baki termed him "immovable as Fate." And certainly Suleiman's ruthless executions were mainly within his family (Ferhad Pasha and Ibrahim having been brothers-in-law).

Such a precedent was not to be easily followed, lacking a Suleiman and a Sokolli. Personal favorites began to be named to the vizirate, and favorites' favorites to other profitable posts. Yet the rigorous training of the Palace School went on unchanged, and brilliant vizirs like the Kuprulu family were to restore health to the sickening Serai In the test of history subsequent vizirs proved to be better administrators than their imperial masters

After the death of Mehmed Sokolli in 1578, when the struggle for power lay between the vizirate and the harem, there was an unchanging force for stability in the Palace School. Very soon the levy of the tribute children ceased, at least outwardly, and Turks were allowed to enter the privileged School. Education within its narrow walls did not fall behind the times until the eighteenth century, and its tradition remained high until the present century.

"The idea of an education which will develop the individual to the full extent of his capacities is thoroughly modern." Thus Professor Albert Lybyer, who has made a detailed study[1] of the Organization. "In the reign of the great Suleiman no human structure existed which rivalled this . . . in power, simplicity and rapidity of action, and respect at home and abroad."

[1] Titles of these modern authorities are given in the bibliography.

When the Women Ruled

With Suleiman ended the force "immovable as Fate" that had dedicated the family to the rule of the nation. At once Selim II moved into the harem of the Serai with his household of one hundred and fifty women of all degree. Slowly at first but inexorably the Osmanli sultans began to pay the penalty of breeding from slave girls. The women, under lax restraint, fought at first quietly, then savagely for privilege, wealth, and finally for power.

It is commonly said that Roxelana started it. She set a precedent. Roxelana's entrance into the guarded Serai proved to be dangerous, in the crowded corridors and cubicles of the Serai, the women found themselves within whispering distance of the Divan; they lived and slept within yards of their black guardians, who were crowded against the white outer guards. The Treasury was next door to the Throne Room Within.

More than that convenient juxtaposition, however, was the fatal fact that despotic power lay in the spoken word of the Sultan, and accordingly within the reach of women who could influence him. Suleiman himself had been influenced but not led by one woman. Selim, pliable in and out of his cups, still put great affairs in the safekeeping of Sokolli, who was beyond reach of the harem. Yet, as his drunkenness increased, his First Kadin, Nur Banu, gained authority within the harem The mother of Murad, she claimed the title of Sultan Valideh after Selim's death. So for the first time a Queen Mother held court within the Serai itself. Nur Banu was not disposed to yield her primacy to the First Kadin of her son. Her Throne Room Within was to remain a throne room.

Then, with the assassination of the aged Sokolli, the last barrier to the ascendancy of the women was removed. The century that followed was called by the Turks the *Kadinlar Sul-*

tanati, the Reign of the Favored Women. Murad had favored a remarkable Venetian, a girl of the noble Baffo family—known in the harem as Safiye, or the Light One. Blond or redhead, captive of a Turkish sea captain, or secret agent planted in the harem by the astute Venetians, Safiye fought for the interest of Venice and, as Roxelana had done, for the succession of her own son.

Since Murad was addicted to women, his mother Nur Banu made efforts to find girls who would draw him away from the dangerous Safiye. Murad abandoned himself readily enough to such rivalry. He had the precedent of his father for confining himself to the Serai and leaving outer affairs to the Divan. The result in the Osmanli state was good enough. Prestige increased, with Venice joining France in the privilege of the capitulations. But during the procurement of numerous girls from the markets, the power of the Captain of the Girls increased. Safiye, possibly coached by the Venetians, actually had a hand in the movements of the armies and fleets. A Jewish jewel seller named Chiarezza served as her go-between with the Magnifica Comunita.

Under her ascendancy nineteen of Murad's sons by other women were assassinated. Having made herself Sultan Valideh-to-be, she held immense power, fleetingly.

When her son came to the throne as Mehmed III, Safiye found resistance increasing against her. The Venetian Queen Mother might be secluded and inviolate behind the harem gates, yet outside those gates she was held to be a murderess. At the grated window she could overhear the discussions in the Divan; she could never venture beyond the bars.

At the height of the struggle between Safiye and the Organization she turned procuress for her own son, trying to keep Mehmed so obsessed with new girls that he would not take thought for outside matters. Revolt along the northern frontier, however, enabled the army commanders to take Mehmed bodily out of the Serai to march into Hungary as Suleiman had done so often—the first time a sultan had done so in thirty years.

When this absence from the harem did not serve to change his infatuation with the inmates of the harem, Safiye was destroyed in the only possible way. She was strangled in her sleep by eunuchs of other women. This assassination was to be the first of many.

It all centered within the now congested Serai. A son of the Sultan had become an omen of future power, to be kept carefully within walls, subjected to the intrigues of women from the age of puberty. The effect of this harem prisonment showed in the next Sultan, who remained withindoors and under the influence of Kadins and their followings. This in turn served to enhance the powers of the Agha of the Janizaris (who, like a praetorian guard, formed the armed force of the palace, at the outer court). Seldom could individual women be certain of their supremacy without the support of either the kislar (captain) or the agha. To this triangle would be added unexpectedly a fourth factor, in the students across the third court.

So, in spite of the gossip that seeped out of the doorways—one being known now as the Gate of the Shawls and another as the Gate of the Funeral of the Women—and the lurid tales embroidered in Galata across the water, and thence repeated with zest by voyagers, who sought to take back with them the juiciest filth from the "Grand Seraglio" it was only occasionally that a kadin could interfere with the outer government. Usually that happened when, in older age, she struggled to retain her ascendancy over younger women.

It was the disastrous inbreeding of the harem that had sapped the vitality of the Osmanlis. A grandson of Mehmed III was unmistakably insane. Another, Osman, was killed by the janizaris.

A primate of the harem, Kiusem by name, was then trying for the ultimate influence once held by Safiye. Her son, Murad IV, however, threw off the influence of the harem to join the armies in the field. Young as he was, sapped by drink and sickness, he had the neurotic fears of Selim II. It is said that he died of terror during an eclipse of the sun.

There may have been insanity in Murad and in his brother Ibrahim. In any event their weakness under the ruthless scheming of their mother led to a Hamletesque drama of conflict between all the forces now pent up in the Serai.

The young Murad, dying in his sleeping chamber, craved the satisfaction of seeing the hated Ibrahim dead before him. The two brothers were the last male survivors of the Osmanli ruling family, and Murad had named one of his favorites, the Sword-bearer Lord, to succeed him. He ordered the execution of Ibrahim, who was then prisoned in a chamber near him (the forerunner of the "Cage" in which the boys, brothers of the Sultan-to-be, were to be too often immolated, to keep them from active contact with the outer nation). If Murad's command had been carried out it would have put an end to the Osmanli line of sultans and destroyed the Ayin, making an inevitable change in the destiny of the nation.

In this crisis, Murad's personal attendants were too terrified to carry out the command, especially when they were threatened by Kiusem. They reported to the dying man that Ibrahim had been strangled.

It is said that after Murad's death, Ibrahim was so terrified in his prison by the calls of messengers at his door that he tried to barricade himself in. Even when he was girdled with the sword of Osman as Sultan, fear remained latent in him. His dread of his mother and of the endemic conspiracy that surrounded him drove him to insane excesses. More than Ivan the Terrible, who had died two generations before, he seemed to create a world of fantasy close to him, indulging his own cravings and striking at anyone who interfered with him. His brief reign of eight years marked the futile triumph of the harem over the Organization.

Ibrahim put to death his strong Vizir, Kara Mustafa, whose successor rather naturally took pains to allow the Sultan every freedom in his fancies and perverted lusts. Kiusem in her own interest did the same. The half-insane youth who had spent years waiting for an executioner to come to his room with a bowstring avenged himself Caligula-fashion on the other inmates of his harem.

His strange fancies were all indulged—his craving to be saturated with perfumes, especially pungent ambergris, his obsession with furs, particularly sables. (Which led to ransacking the empire for ambergris and furs.) To stimulate his sexual power he filled a room with mirrors, demanded girls from outside untrained in harem tricks, rewarded any follower who conceived of a new stimulant or aphrodisiac. The tale is told that once he had all the women within a room stripped and made to cavort around him on hands and knees like a herd of mares, himself the only stallion.

From perfumes he turned to adorning himself with jewels. His demands for rarities emptied the Treasury, and the women who had to submit to his perversion avenged themselves quite humanly in emptying the outer women's bazaar of jewels and gorgeous attire. Ibrahim had a notion to require the bazaar merchants to keep their stalls open by night as well as by day.

Outside the Serai such mad fancies echoed only faintly. Deftars of the Treasury remarked that never had the Serai wasted so much money as now when the Treasury was empty. Peasants in the streets saw the flash of emeralds in Ibrahim's beard as an evil omen. For these few years, out from the Funeral Gate bodies were carried steadily.

A diver, swimming deep beneath the surface off the small water gate of the Serai, came up with a scream of fright. He said he had sighted throngs of dead women standing on the bottom by him. Swathed from head to foot, they swayed in the strong current. (Inmates of the harem had been done away with secretly; bound, they had been sewn into bags weighted at the foot with stones; they had been dropped from a rowboat at night, and the stones had held their feet to the bottom, while their bodies pulled upward.)

The harem, serving itself by Ibrahim's mad moods, virtually ruled the nation. Against this misrule popular resistance rose steadily, until a deputation from branches of the army and the colleges urged upon the Sultan Valideh, Kiusem, that Ibrahim be deposed and sent back to his cage and his young son Mehmed brought to the throne.

When Ibrahim resisted, the spahis entered the upheaval to demand his death by dictate of the Mufti. So Ibrahim, an Osmanli sultan, was strangled by order of the supreme judge.

The aged Kiusem, however, would not relinquish her power to the new Sultan Valideh, Turkhan Sultan. She still had one card to play, having won over the Agha of the Janizaris. It seemed to be possible, if the janizaris took possession of the Serai, to depose the boy Mehmed and proclaim his younger brother as Sultan.

Meanwhile other forces added themselves to those closing in upon Mehmed and the Divan. Students dismissed from the Enclosed School met with a regiment of spahis likewise dismissed from service, in the Hippodrome, to demand that the murderers of Ibrahim be brought to justice.

Against the supremacy of personalities around the throne a popular reaction was setting in, to restore legal justice and the responsibility of the Sultan himself.

Kiusem played her last card and lost. The grandmother had as co-conspirators the swordbearer, most of the black eunuchs and the janizaris, with their agha. The Sultan Valideh had the support of the Vizir, the Kislar Agha, and the boys of the School.

The ensuing struggle for control of the Serai came to a head one night, when Kiusem persuaded the chief of the gardeners to open the small gates of the inner courts to armed janizaris.

These had the forethought to seize the Vizir himself in his sleep and carry him along as hostage. Their occupation of the Serai seemed assured, when they were tricked by the Vizir, who got away on the excuse that he would summon the Divan to enter the hall and grant their demands. Having escaped from the janizaris, he got in and locked the doors of the third court.

Although it was defended only by boys and servitors, the inner court was held long enough for them to do away with Kiusem. The aged grandmother could not be found in her room. Dragged from a clothing chest, she passed through the hands of her enemies, the heavy jewelry and rich robe torn from her body. Strangled, her body was thrown out one of the garden gates.

A grim punishment followed, with the execution of the leading conspirators, and the removal of the School from its inner court. Turkhan Sultan was wise enough to prefer safety to power, and bowed to the popular resentment. The first of the brilliant Kuprulus became Vizir, and the reign of the women ended, a century after Roxelana had intercepted the messages from Suleiman's son Mustafa, at Amasiya.

(This account of the deterioration of the harem has had to rely upon the stories of resident foreigners who in turn relied on the ceaseless flow of gossip from Serai Point across the water. It is true for the most part, but the results of modern research in Turkey are still to be applied to it. So long has the testimony of foreigners been repeated that legend sometimes takes on the aspect of fact, while fact appears as legend. In dealing with Suleiman's time it was necessary to throw out the often-told tales—from the pages of western history—that Ibrahim, the First Vizir, was a eunuch, that women in the Sultan's family were given away in marriage only to eunuchs so that they might have no children, that Mihrmah and the inmates of her harem demanded the capture of Malta because merchant vessels loaded with clothing and rarities for them had been taken by the galleys of Malta, that Selim ordered the capture of Cyprus because his favorite wines were imported from that island, etc. To their concept of the Grand Turk, and the Terrible Turk, foreigners added very quickly the zestful concept of the Unspeakable Turk. Probably no other nation in history has been viewed by outsiders with such prejudice for so long. Modern scholarship has begun the task of revealing the Turks as they were.)

The Impelling Forces

As for Suleiman himself, we can see more clearly his darker nature, a strong man turning to cruelty; the lighter aspect of the almost unknown man, striving toward something beyond his time, we can hardly glimpse, except in the consequences that followed him. What a vast library we possess of the other great personalities to the west of Constantinople—from Henry VIII to Catherine de' Medici!

Of Suleiman, Sir Charles Oman says: "He fixed the form of the Turkish empire. Its long survival after his death was in a great measure the result of his work, which it took many generations of decadent heirs to undo."

Monsieur de Thévenot a century later (coming from the France of Mazarin) bears witness to the strong agricultural base of the country, the well-being of the peasantry, the abundance of staple foods—and to the pre-eminence of the Organization in government. "All the affairs of the empire rest upon [the Vizir's] shoulders; he discharges the office of the Grand Signior [Mehmed IV, still a youth, seven years after Ibrahim's execution] and only wants the title. This is a very heavy charge."

In foreign affairs Suleiman's policy of fast friendship with France, and accord with the equally enlightened Poland, was continued by Sokolli and subsequent vizirs. Later on it became the mainstay of Turkish policy. By then, however, the evils of the capitulations were manifesting themselves.

His internal policy of tolerance toward the millets and their varied religions broke down rather quickly. Rapacity began to replace tolerance. Patriarchs of the Christian churches, called upon to pay more to their Turkish superiors, drained more money from their own congregations. Their position became anomalous, even intolerable. With ostensible freedom, they were bound to serve almost as tax collectors for the Turks. As early as Suleiman's grandson Murad the Catholic churches in Constantinople were seized and converted into mosques.

At the same time Turkish missionary zeal deteriorated. This may have been coincidence, or due to the growing internal wealth of the nation—the increasing properties of the vast Wakf. The shrewd Busbecq noted at Amasiya that Suleiman was "quite as anxious to extend his faith as to extend his empire." Among modern students, both Temperley and Lybyer believe that the Turkish missionary expansion of Suleiman's time was more dangerous than the military.

As to the staying power of the religious Law, modern opinion is divided. Their intensity of faith impelled the Turks forward for a long time. At some point not yet determined it acted as a retrogressive force. Unchanging in a modern world of change, it created a sense of fatalism, an aversion to new education that made the Turks themselves nostalgic and slow to act—the opposite of the dynamic taskmasters of Suleiman's day. Significantly, the most drastic of Ataturk's reforms, four centuries after Suleiman, was to abolish the Sheyk of Islam and to tear down the fixation of old religious belief. In this last the great modernist did not quite succeed.

The Destructive Forces

Lacking the iron control of a Suleiman or a Sokolli, the accumulation of vendable wealth in the Serai took the rather natural course of pouring out into the hands of grasping officials.

Taxation increased, while fees were wrung from every possible transaction (both Ibrahim and Rustem had paved the way for this). By Knolles's time the imperial revenues had risen to more than 8,000,000 ducats yearly; by Rycaut's time they were 11,000,000. During the century-long Reign of the Favored Women fiefs were sold to the highest bidders, and the coinage was debased, in European fashion.

The naval Arsenal became the spot most privileged in feather-bedding, and unearned pay. Since the Kaputan Pasha drew immense amounts from the Treasury for the building and out-fitting of fleets, his post enriched the holder. Seldom did the fleets that were paid for actually put to sea. (Under the sea conquerors, Barbarossa, Dragut and Piali, the fleets had paid for themselves.) After the chaos of 1640 the galley captains on the pay roll numbered 460, of whom not more than 150 ever rounded Serai Point.

Of late, crews were formed out of the disciplined janizaris, who began to conceive a great dislike for service at sea.

"They man their ships very well with soldiers," Thévenot relates, "and even janizaris; but these blades, who know not what it is to give ground on shore, never go to sea but against their wills; and if they can get off for money, they are sure not to go. All that go for a season to sea are called *Safarlis*, that is makers of a voyage. Three days before the fleet puts out they go along the streets with a hatchet in hand, demanding aspers from all Christians and Jews whom they meet, and sometimes of Turks, too."

Rycaut soon discovered the venality of the Arsenal during the time of troubles. "Through the expense of the naval force, the building gallies and the like—matters not provided for by those who laid the first foundation of this Government—the revenue of the Empire hath been bankrupted, and by the cor-ruption of the Officers, or ill management been sold [i.e., farmed out] for three years to come, until all was redeemed and restored again by the wisdom of the famous Vizir *Kupriuli*."

The worthy English consul touches unconsciously on another drainage of wealth, when he adds that his own countrymen "ought to consider it a blessing that we . . . have tasted of the good and benefit from a free and open trade and friendship with this people . . . begun in the Reign of Queen Elizabeth of blessed memory . . . which, having been improved by the excellent direction of that Right Worshipful Company of the Levant Merchants, hath brought a most considerable benefit to this Kingdom and gives livelihood to many thousands in England, by which also His Majesty without any expense gains a very considerable increase of his Customs."

The capitulations to foreigners, first the merchants, then the governments, had begun.

There is a popular and apparently impregnable belief that the Osmanli Turks in their day of power amused themselves with the women of all the nearer east, that they became the proprietors of oversize harems populated by dancing girls and odalesques—and so deteriorated. This is one of the latter-day legends, at least in Suleiman's time, that appealed so irresistibly to the western imagination.

The reigning sultans did interbreed after a fashion, and the consequences are very easy to observe. Suleiman was an exception. But it is important to realize that the Turkish nation did not follow the example of its sultans. There was little intermarriage from aghas and timariots down to the peasantry. The other, inner peoples kept pretty much to themselves.

The detested slave trade was in the main a business matter—taking profits from captives. The more affluent Osmanlis—few at this time—held slaves only in their households, and under Moslem religious Law the relation of a family slave to the master was different than in Europe proper.

In Suleiman's time the jovial Ayas Pasha had a large harem, and Barbarossa appears to have acquired a wife in every port. But heads of the Organization such as Ibrahim, Rustem, Sokolli,

Piali and the others, after taking a bride from the Serai, were obliged to remain monogamous.

If a balance could be struck, the Organization, from Suleiman down, would be found less bound to, and influenced by, marriage and interbreeding than the European courts of the time. (The Hapsburgs were noted for their manipulation of marriages. Philip wed himself in turn to women of Portugal, England, France and Austria. If the mantle of a Bluebeard is to be bestowed, it must go to the sturdy shoulders of Henry Tudor.)

The Legend of the Warrior

As a military leader, Suleiman remains a remarkable paradox. Tradition required him to play the part of commander of an invincible army engaged in conquest of the Lands of War. What he did about that is revealed in the intimate story of his life.

During his life and after him the great Turkish feudal levies deteriorated as a fighting force. Whether this happened because of Suleiman or simply after him, we cannot say.

On the opposite side of the picture, he strengthened numerically the standing army of the Sultan, the janizaris and spahis. At his death 48,316 soldiers were under Organization pay, and that pay, accordingly, had doubled since he girded on the sword of Osman.

Suleiman may have changed the character of the monkish, poverty-ridden janizaris. He eased the restrictions on the corps by allowing some of them to marry, and allowing some native Turks to enter the corps. Probably the elite fighting force would have deteriorated with time, in any case.

As to his personal leadership, paradoxically, his greatest achievement lies in what he would not do. From Rhodes until Malta, for the space of forty-four years he allowed the *asker* to undertake no punishing campaign or siege At the same time he kept it from being a drain upon the agricultural nation.

Very soon after him, his son Selim II ordered the Don-Volga canal building project in the steppes, which Suleiman had refused to undertake. Although a Turkish fleet came up the Don with supplies to aid it, the expedition fared badly in the dry steppes, being tricked and misled by the Crimea Tatars.

Murad, his grandson, entered upon the great war with Persia, which Suleiman had tried to avoid. It lasted for twelve years—becoming known as "the long war" and accomplishing nothing tangible except to exhaust both Moslem empires in the face of the advancing Russians.

As late as 1683 an ambitious Vizir, Kara Mustafa, attempted the final siege of Vienna, from which Suleiman had withdrawn. The disaster that followed marked the decline of Osmanli military power, in the face of the improved weapons, fighting spirit, and skill at fortification of the Europeans. The man who led the army of relief to Vienna was Jan Sobiesky, a Pole. Suleiman had been careful to preserve amity with the Poles.

In the matter of prestige, Suleiman made no compromise. The prestige of the Osmanli arms remained high, until after the real siege of Vienna.

In actual command, Suleiman accomplished two remarkable feats. Twice he led the army on long retreats out of hostile mountain regions at the coming of winter. He brought it safely down from Vienna to Constantinople, and from Tabriz to Baghdad. Napoleon at Moscow had found such an operation too difficult—at least he left his army during the retreat.

The Turkish army itself offers another paradox. Led by a despot, it was, otherwise, democratic in the modern sense. Most of the officers were graduates of the Organization. No barrier of caste existed within it. A troop commander might change places with a general in the course of a battle.

As the officers, including the Sultan, lived with the troops, so they were also found at the front of the battle lines. Suleiman himself came under fire at Rhodes, Mohács and Vienna. Casualties among the commanders ran very high. Old custom required them to share dangers as well as rewards with the men. In consequence there was a bond of fraternity between men and leaders not found in other armies of the time. Elsewhere in Europe, command derived from noble rank, or favor, as a rule. Leaders seldom saw their armies, and if present at the start of a battle were too often absent at the end. Charles, at Algiers, was an exception, as were the commanders of the Knights

One legend about Suleiman has refused to die until these last few years. It is that he tried to conquer middle Europe, and failed.

A conscientious historian, Roger Merriman, says flatly (1944) that Vienna decided the destiny of modern Europe. "The siege of Vienna appeals strongly to the imagination. Never since the battle of Tours, almost precisely eight centuries before, had Christian Europe been so direfully threatened by Mohammedan Asia and Africa. Had the verdict in either case been reversed, the whole history of the world might have been changed."

It does appeal to the imagination. But Suleiman's objective in 1529 was Buda, at the river end of the great Hungarian plain. There exists no evidence in Turkish sources that he ever planned the occupation of Vienna, and his own statements—which need to be taken seriously in Suleiman's case—say emphatically that he did not.

"This was certainly the most perilous moment for Europe," Sir Charles Oman repeats (1937), "in all the long strife between the House of Hapsburg and the Ottomans. If Vienna had fallen, the Sultan had intended to make it his winter quarters and base of operations for a continued assault on Germany."

But Suleiman did not put a garrison of janizaris into Buda for years after 1529; his troops never occupied the great Hungarian plain, the boulevard to that same "Germany." How the

Turkish horsemen, operating only in the summer months, could have held the German mountain region, snowbound in winter, is hard to imagine.

The legend has simply grown with time—that the victorious Sultan of the east led his horsemen into Europe to wrest it from the mighty Emperor of the west. Since such a decisive battle failed to take place, legend has substituted Vienna for the missing battle. In consequence Charles V soon appeared in legend as the triumphant defender of Vienna (to which he sent only the 700 Spanish caballeros) while Suleiman now appears to be the Asiatic conqueror who was turned back at Vienna.

It makes a good story, easily retold, and the pity is, it is not true.

The Legend of the Pirates, and Lepanto

Somebody long ago began to call the Turkish sea captains pirates and corsairs of the Barbary Coast. It was not in their time, because the words were not in use then, and you will not find them so miscalled even in the massive pages of Richard Knolles.

They were not pirates, nor corsairs of the Barbary Coast, nor Algerine sea lords, nor did they sail from pirates' nests. Yet you will find all these terms in modern histories of the west. You may read, in addition, that Turkish sea power ended with Barbarossa, or at the battle of Lepanto, either one. Neither is true.

Whatever Khair ad-Din Barbarossa's ethics may have been —and he would have made a magnificent pirate—he sailed with only one flag, the Turkish, displayed beside his own ensign; he held admiral's rank, drew his pay from the Turkish Treasury, built his ships at the Arsenal, carried out a plan of operations by one nation against half a dozen enemy principalities or powers.

His great adversary, Andrea Doria, is usually described as the admiral of the Empire. Although Doria changed his flags as he changed his allegiance, had thirteen vessels of his own in the Genoese/French/Imperial fleets, and claimed a percentage of the spoil (as did Barbarossa). Which was the pirate?

These men commanded great fleets that shaped the destiny of nations. The celebrated Spanish armada of 1588 appears on the historical record as the attempt of one nation to invade another, England. Yet its strength of 132 ships, 21,621 troops and 8066 sailors was about the same as the armada of Charles that met disaster at "the pirate's nest" of Algiers, and less than that of Doria at Prevesa, or of either fleet at Lepanto.

As to the equally celebrated battle of Lepanto, the truth is this.

The sea duel begun by Suleiman with Charles continued long after their deaths. After 1568 Philip II, in his endeavor to expand Spain into a western empire, began the extermination of the rebellious Moriscos (converted Moslems) in the Granada region.

In retaliation, or because he desired a conquest of his own, Selim II sent the Turkish fleets to capture Cyprus. Selim the Sot under no circumstances would appear at the head of the army, but he could safely send the fleet on a mission to sea without him. Piali had urged the capture of this last Venetian island isolated beneath the southern bulge of Anatolia—although Mehmed Sokolli took a dim view of the project.

Selim craftily imitated his father in putting the question to Ibn Sa'ud: "When a Moslem country has been conquered by infidels, is it not the duty of a pious prince to recover it for Islam?"

There being only one answer to such a question, the Turkish invasion fleet put to sea in great strength during the early summer of 1570. Lala Mustafa, the former tutor and conniver at the death of Bayazid, commanded it.

(By then young Francis Drake, the disciple in seafaring of John Hawkins, held a commission as privateer from his Queen, and was starting for the Spanish main in a ship named *Pasha*. Presently he would add to Philip's worries by duplicating Dragut's raid upon Cadiz; not yet had an English ambassador requested the aid of the Turks against the "idolators" of Spain.)

The citadel of Cyprus, Famagusta, was defended by its descendants of crusaders, Italian mercenaries, and Greeks against the artillery and mines of Lala Mustafa for eleven months, that is, until August 1571. Then it surrendered upon terms like those once granted by Suleiman to Rhodes—free passage of the garrison to Crete, and guaranty of the lives and rights of the island's inhabitants. But Lala Mustafa was no Suleiman. The garrison, duly embarked on ships, were seized as captives, the commanding officers ruthlessly put to death.

After the invasion of Cyprus a young painter, El Greco, fled from the island to Spain, there to begin the masterpieces that have made his name immortal.

Meanwhile the Serene Republic, which had enjoyed a long and prosperous peace with the Turks since Prevesa, besought the European courts to proclaim a new crusade against the Osmanlis, when its valuable island was endangered. Few responded, and the Venetian fleets prudently kept their distance from the Turkish galleys commanded by Uluj Ali, a former lieutenant of Dragut ("Ochialu" to the Europeans). It did not seem to the Emperor, Maximilian, that the Venetians appeared very convincing in their new role of crusaders.

In any event, aid to Cyprus was delayed until this last stronghold of the crusades was lost, and the Moorish race in Spain ended. Released from this internal war, the forces of Spain, under Philip's half brother Don Juan of Austria—bastard son of Charles—added themselves to the armada gathering in the Adriatic. Some 227 vessels of all types, with 20,000 soldiers, many being arquebusiers of the new model, lay off Corfu with no mission to perform, Cyprus having been lost.

There was much argument among the commanders of this new holy alliance; but Don Juan, a twenty-six-year-old with a penchant for accomplishing tasks, insisted that their armada go to find the Turkish fleet, which was very near in the Gulf of Corinth.

So happened the sea battle of Lepanto, which remains depicted on the walls of the Vatican and the Ducal Palace in Venice.

The triumph, at the moment, was genuine, the defeat of the Turks decisive. They lost almost all their galleys. Experts say that the vast mass of vessels crowded together in the narrow entrance of the gulf, off the town of Lepanto, failed to maneuver, and the advantage lay with the larger galleys, the heavier armor and better firearms of the Europeans. Many commanders of the Organization failed to survive the battle. But the left wing of the Turkish array, under Uluj Ali, not only escaped intact but carried away as trophies a captured Venetian galley and the battle flag of the Grand Master of Malta.

At Lepanto Miguel de Cervantes received the wound that maimed him. His adventures while a captive of the Turks in Africa for five years, after that, must have shaped many of the pages of the matchless *Don Quixote*.

With Lepanto won and Cyprus still lost, the battered armada of Don Juan was repaired during the winter, and the question remained, what was it to do, now that the dreaded Turkish fleet no longer existed to oppose it?

The Venetians failed to agree with Philip, who carried on all negotiations by letter from a distance. There was the project of recapturing the African coast or a part of it, and the project of recapturing the Venetian islands, or some of them.

Into such argumentation came unbelievable news, in the spring. The Turkish fleet that had been sunk, beached or surrendered at Lepanto was putting to sea again, out of the Dardanelles. It was heading for the Europeans, to fight the battle over again.

Seldom has a council of war had to deal with such a shocking surprise.

What happened was this. Uluj Ali had brought back 47 galleys, all told. Piali Pasha, now too old to take to sea, had combed the inland waters for serviceable craft. Above all, Mehmed Sokolli laid down the command that 180 new galleys must be built, launched and equipped between October and April.

Somehow the Golden Horn, by laboring night and day, carried out the order. With janizaris, spahis and timariots drafted to row and fight it, the new fleet sailed, with Uluj Ali as Kaputan Pasha. He had 160 sails following.

This fleet was ill found, the soldiery far from able seamen It was, in fact, the very sort of armada that Barbarossa had dreaded. But it made a fine appearance, and it kept on its course.

What happened then you will not find immortalized in paint on the walls of Italian palaces.

Summer came and the resurrected Turkish fleet held the sea. The new Venetian commander--who had replaced the one that had quarreled with Don Juan about projects--waited for the Spanish fleet, which did not appear. The Turks seemed to be too strong for him to face alone.

When Don Juan of Austria returned with long-delayed orders from Philip, and the European fleet counted some 200 sails, Uluj Ali could no longer be found. He had slipped past the European scouts into the fortified harbor of Modon, south of Lepanto. With his leaky and unhandy ships in port, he called in an army to aid him.

This left Don Juan in a dilemma. He could not undertake a mission at sea leaving the Osmanli battle fleet behind him; nor did even he dare to try to rush the fortified port. It was Prevesa, over again. The Spanish troops landed, under Alessandro Farnese of Parma (who was to become famous as a general in the west), to endeavor to get at Uluj Ali. The Turkish army held off Parma, and when winter came Don Juan in exasperation sailed back to Sicily, the Venetians retreating to their Adriatic.

Then Uluj Ali led his ghost of a fleet, with sick crews, back to the Dardanelles, to refit and make all shipshape for the next sailing season. Probably there was no more thankful man in the Mediterranean than he.

The Barbary Coast

Certainly no bluff in the record of history paid off better than Uluj Ali's. He could not have won another Lepanto. For those two years the Europeans actually held supremacy at sea, but did not manage to accomplish anything. The memory of Barbarossa and the specter of the fleet that *might* be as formidable as ever haunted their councils. As one observing historian puts it: "Lepanto marked the decadence of Spain as well as that of the Turks."

The Spaniards wanted to end the Turkish occupation of the African coast; the Venetians refused to agree to that because the Spaniards would not recover Cyprus for them When Uluj Ali appeared again with a fleet that was at least maneuverable, the Venetians deserted the grand alliance and besought the Serai for new terms of peace. Sokolli gave them little encouragement. His spokesmen laughed—seeing the humor of the situation—telling the ambassador of the Signory, "To lose Cyprus is to you like losing an arm; you cannot get it back. To lose Lepanto, for us, is like shaving off a beard which grows back again."

The Venetians feared for Crete, and accepted the same terms as after Prevesa—they paid the cost of the war and gave up more territory.

The Spanish half of the grand alliance fared little better. Don Juan with a sizable armada captured the fortifications and harbor of Tunis—the African anchor of the Malta-Sicily land bridge to Europe. But Philip, fearing ambition in his young half brother, would send neither supplies nor replacements to Tunis. The following year, 1574, Uluj Ali and Sinan Pasha recaptured the place, sending the usual quota of Spanish commanders to Serai Point in chains.

Philip, occupied now with the Dutch Beggars of the Sea and the Protestant "pirates" of England, abandoned the African coast to the Turks. It was like an arm that he could never get back.

The Gibraltar area he held fast, of necessity—thus bringing Spanish influence and arms in contact with the Moroccan Riff. East of Cape Matapan the Osmanli fleets sailed as before In the middle of the next century they carried out Sokolli's threat to take Crete. The inhabitants of that island preferred Turkish rule to Venetian. One of the greatest of the Vizirs, a Kuprulu accomplished the occupation of Crete, renting Suda Bay there-after to the weakening Venetians.

For one hundred and twenty years after the first plan for naval action was formed between Suleiman and Barbarossa, the Turkish fleets had kept the sea, carrying it out. Against them the Europeans had only managed to send out massive expeditions which—whether successful or not—could not retain Moslem territory for long.

Something was happening, however, to the Turkish ports in the west. Now that the fleets from the Dardanelles no longer appeared there, they were abandoned (in 1659) as provincial holdings, and the Turkish beylerbeys recalled. The heterogeneous reis of the coastal shipping remained. In their comfortable quarters down at the ports, these independent seafarers formed a bizarre maritime aristocracy. Waited upon by slaves, surrounded by luxuries, the reis of Algiers, Bujeya and Tunis lived as their fancy dictated, without masters to enforce discipline.

The tie between them and Serai Point weakened slowly but

steadily. In Algiers particularly, thriving with commerce and the new occupation of piracy, guarded now by the great Fort of Victory raised where Charles had pitched his tent, the brotherhood of the Algerines was reinforced by outcasts and adventurers from the northern shores—Sicilians, Genoese and Neapolitans at first, then Spaniards and even an Englishman or two. These were to become the well-known renegades of the Barbary Coast.

Meanwhile the powerful, broadside-gunned oceangoing man-of-war had been developed, with the first swift two-decked frigates. When such dreadnoughts of the sea, whether English, French or Dutch, cruised the Mediterranean, the African reis could not challenge their strength. In return the Algerines developed their own peculiar corsair craft, swift feluccas able to outsail and close with merchantmen and small vessels. By the 1700s the Moslem battle fleets had almost vanished from Algiers, Tunis and Tripoli, and the swarm of pirate craft had appeared. They were to stay there for some time—until the coming of the first American battle fleet—but they had nothing to do with the Osmanli Turks except to render lip service to later decadent sultans.

About the time of the change-over of the western African coast, the Turkish navy almost disappeared from the eastern half of the Mediterranean. No vessels were built that could stand against the new European ships and cannon. The Turks themselves had a saying that the sea captains had gone into the (women's) workbaskets.

Paul Rycaut was witness to that. "The Turks now despairing of being equal to the Christian forces by sea, and to be able to stand the shock of battle with them, build light vessels for robbing, burning and destroying the Christian coast, and afterwards to secure themselves by flight. Also they serve to transport soldiers, ammunition and provisions for succor of Candia [Crete] and other new conquests . . . the Turks unwillingly apply their minds to maritime affairs, saying, *God hath given the sea to the Christians but the land to them.*"

The spirit of fatalism and the lust for profiteering had settled upon the Golden Horn.

Suleiman and Ivan the Terrible

Something very different was happening to the east of Serai Point.

Suleiman had made himself pretty effectively what his title claimed, Lord of the Two Seas. That on the east was the Karadeniz, the Black Sea, and it had long been a Turkish lake. Suleiman's authority had stretched forth where the steppes began from the mouth of the Danube around the arc of the northern shore with its natural citadel of the Crimea to the great barrier of the Causasus above the clouds.

The river Danube, the peninsula of Crimea and the Caucasus Mountains were all to play very important parts in what followed. That was the endeavor of the Muscovites to take the Black Sea from the Turks.

Suleiman had ridden into the steppes—the province of Yedisan, he called it—with a light rein. These steppes above the Black Sea lay before him fertile and masterless—the "wild lands," the Muscovites named them. At the same time the Muscovite Tsar, Ivan the Terrible in Suleiman's case, was advancing from his stronghold of the Kremlin and his metropolis of Moscow into these same southern steppes.

The Sultan had set bounds to his dominion; behind these boundaries he had formulated laws for the indwelling peoples. Turkish schooling had outdistanced the Muscovite. The Tsar was emerging from the limits of his medieval city-state to subordinate the outer peoples and to create the empire of All the Russias.

Between Suleiman's position and Ivan's there were certain

similarities and certain differences. Both were oriental despots, leaders of only a nucleus of people—the Osmanli Turks and the great Russians—that in turn had mastered many other peoples. Ideologically both the *Kaisar-i-Rum* and the Tsar of a "third Rome" had inherited the role of successor to the late Byzantine emperors, and both had in them the blood of Byzantine princesses. Both tried to educate their marginal people in western ways. The people of both clung firmly to old customs.

As to the differences, Suleiman tried to depart from his traditional role of military leader, while Ivan had been forced by circumstances to act as a war leader, and to militarize his unwarlike Slavs. Of the two, Ivan was more the Asiatic, his ancestors having been under Tatar and eastern influence for two and a half centuries.

As Suleiman held a light rein over the steppe dwellers, the remnants of the once mighty Golden Horde, he had a still lighter tie to the peoples of the eastern steppes—the powerful Nogai, Uzbeks, Kirghiz, and the Volga Tatars. These were all remote kinsmen of the encampments of central Asia, speaking Turkish, and professing Islam.

So on the dry steppes of Yedisan, Suleiman had ventured back to the threshold of the ancient Turkish homelands of the east, from which he had parted but to which he was still attached by sentiment, and religion.

Because Suleiman had this attachment, and this strength upon the Black Sea littoral, Ivan and his Muscovite armies had turned away to thrust at that other sea in the north, the Baltic. The Baltic and the Black Sea outlets were to become the twin objectives of Russian—no longer purely Muscovite—tsars, who often hesitated between them.

Not without a wrench did Suleiman's successors give up hope of redeeming Astrakhan (*At-tarkhan*), the old Turkish town on the outlet of the mighty Volga to the Caspian Sea. This the Russians took easily, and the Volga became the arterial of their trade with the east.

Nothing of the kind happened on the Black Sea. To this the Osmanli Turks held stubbornly. It was part of their heritage; its waters flowed past Serai Point. By holding to its water while slowly relinquishing the northern steppe belt, they reversed their policy of the Mediterranean, for reasons they never explained. It was not pride alone, but something purely Turkish that made them do it.

How they did it is one of the riddles of history.

The Turks Hold to the Black Sea

A century after Suleiman, his Yedisan had become the "Border," the Ukraine, populated by a kaleidoscope of peoples seeking the fertile black-earth steppe, by colonists from Moscow, by "masterless men" fleeing from tsardom and serfdom, by adventurous Poles and even Germans, but chiefly by the remnants of Crimea Tatars, and Nogias, with the strengthening free brotherhoods, or hosts, of the Cossacks. These last centered upon three rivers, the Kuban beneath the heights of the far Caucasus, the Don, and the Dnieper.

Russian peasants fled to the good earth of the wild lands to escape the oppression of labor on the half-barren state lands of the north. Grain and cattle raising transformed the grass steppe.

Offshoots of the human welter upon the Ukraine escaped into the refuge of earlier peoples, the Crimea, or the other refuge of the Caucasus.

The aggressive Don Cossacks claimed that their river lands made another sanctuary. They had a saying, "The Tsar rules in Moscow, the Cossack on the Don." In the melting pot of the Ukraine the Cossack frontiersmen had been half Tatarized, but they held very firmly to their Orthodox religious faith, which was that of Moscow. In the end this brought their allegiance to Moscow.

In their heyday the Cossack hosts put to sea in their caiques, or long boats, to raid Turkish ports and defy the galleys of Constantinople; joining with the Tatars and Ukrainian colonists, they revolted against Russian military rule. The pattern of such revolts of the frontiers against the expanding central power was always the same—a daring Cossack leader gathering the folk along a river to attack the Russian frontier towns. Khmielnitsky ascended the Dnieper, against Polish overlords, while Stenka Razin ruled for a space along the Volga, "sailing down to the blue sea, to the Caspian." The end, also, was the same, when an army from Moscow broke through the ill-disciplined Ukrainians, and purged the area of the revolt savagely.[2]

Often refugees fled from the troops across the Dnieper to Turkish Yedisan. Once the remnant of the Dnieper Cossacks migrated thither in a mass.

Only slowly did the ever-increasing military force of Moscow venture down across the barren steppe to within sight of the Turkish sea. Moscow relied on the armed colonist to penetrate first among the nomadic occupants of the plain. Once blockhouse settlements were built, the troops could advance to hold them. Improvement in firearms aided the agriculturist here against the indigenous horseman, whether Tatar, Cossack or Turk, as elsewhere on prairie frontiers.

On their part the Osmanlis were wary of sending armies into the steppe. They held fast to the river mouths, where slave merchants still dealt in captives from the Russian settlements and the Caucasus. Moscow still feared to challenge Constantinople to a test of war. When Don Cossacks took Azov from its Turkish garrison in 1637, Moscow gave it back to the Turks, much to the disgust of the Cossacks.

Until then the test had been between the two rules, between

[2]Narratives of the expansion outward from Moscow through Asia are given in the writer's two volumes, *The March of Muscovy· Ivan the Terrible* and *The City and the Tsar: Peter the Great*.

Turkish tolerance and order in individual life, and Muscovite aggression in exploitation. And the Turks had gained almost as much by migration of population as the Muscovites had acquired by military conquest. But the balance was shifting along the frontiers. The fire was going out of the Turkish missionary endeavor; leadership of the sultans failed entirely during the anarchy in the Serai; the resistance movement among the Christian minorities of the Balkans—notably the Serbs—gained strength and appealed for Russian aid.

For the first time, by 1670 Russian military power clearly equaled that of the Turks. The grain and the river traffic of the Ukraine turned Moscow's attention thither, instead of toward the less profitable Baltic. Russian armies moved down upon the steppe, only to return badly battered. Intangible enemies, they reported, had beset them; the dry steppe grass had burned, food and water failed, while elusive horsemen harried them.

So it happened that one tsar, Peter Alexeivich (the Great), made his first military experiment at building ships on the Don and assailing Turkish-held Azov. From his first experiment he marched back discomfited. The next year the stubborn Peter sailed down the Don again, and stormed the bastions of Azov with the aid of the Cossacks. Still, he was unable to keep his prize.

How the Turks got Azov back remains one of the muted tales of history. It happened that Charles XII, Peter's great adversary of later years, fled to sanctuary in Turkish territory after his defeat at Poltava. The Turks supplied the noted fugitive with spending money in gold coin and a bodyguard of janizaris.

Very soon after that the Tsar led the victorious army of Poltava across the frontier line of the Dnieper to invade Turkey. Peter managed to cross the Dniester also, but found that armed forces of Christians did not rally to him as he expected. Instead supplies failed, Tatar and Turkish horsemen cut his column off from the rivers. When Osmanli infantry arrived and encircled the Russians with trenches, close to the river

Pruth, Peter capitulated with all his command, women included.

By payment of a massive ransom to the Vizir on the scene, Baltaji Mehmed, he released himself and the army, but he had to pledge the return of Azov to the Turks, the leveling of all Russian fortifications at the river's mouth, and the safe return of Charles to Sweden.

This capitulation has been much criticized as bribe-taking on the part of the Vizir. Yet by it the Turks got rid of one embarrassing refugee monarch and another imperial captive, while regaining their cherished river port. Peter delayed long in carrying out his pledge, but had to do it.

The giant Tsar made a fourth attempt at control of the Black Sea, when he led an army into the land bridge of the Caucasus at the far end. By doing so he hoped to hew a way through Turkish Azerbaijan to rich Persia beyond. An active war with Constantinople seemed in the making. Again the stubborn Peter met with misfortune, in the shipwreck of his supply fleet on the Caspian, in drought and harassing attacks of the Moslem mountaineers, notably the Circassians. He did not get through, and led his army back again. This was the beginning of the century-long siege of the mountain barrier.

"The Russians Stand Firm without Their Heads."

This resistance upon the northern arc of the Black Sea acted to turn the Russians back again to Peter's "window to the west" upon the northern sea, the Baltic. There his new city of Petersburg (now Leningrad) brought the Russian court decisively into the Baltic theater, and Prussian influence.

To free the rivers flowing into the Black Sea, however, remained a major objective with the Russians, and their armies, turning to active invasion, fought for the arc of the steppes. Led by Count Münnich, by Suvarov, a national hero, and Kutusov, the victor over Napoleon, they cleared the rivers from the Kuban to the Dniester. Yet somehow, in spite of official victories, the Turks remained on the shore. Russian soldiers said, "The Turks bowl over like ninepins, yet thank God, our men stand firm, without their heads."

Although they appeared to stand firm on the northern shore, the Russians agreed in the treaty of Belgrade (1739) that no vessel of theirs could enter the Sea of Azov, or the Black Sea.

Although the powerful armies of Catherine the Great occupied the entire Crimea with its port of Sevastopol in 1783, and Potemkin staged his famous triumphal procession through the homeland of the Tatars, Suvarov was still fighting for the mouth of the adjacent Dnieper in 1789. There a Russian fleet, launched upon the river, was led out to battle in the estuary by John Paul Jones, who enlisted under Catherine briefly, to his everlasting regret. Paul Jones won a hard conflict against the Turkish Kaputan Pasha and corsairs from the Barbary Coast. For this victory the Prussian and Russian officers of the imperial court were well rewarded, and Jones recalled to shore duty on the Baltic.

Still the Turks kept the sea.

Potemkin had built one of his made-to-order towns, Kherson, on the Dnieper. Not until 1793 did the first Russian town go up on the coast itself—Odessa, near the Dniester, populated at first with foreigners. Not until the Napoleonic upheaval of eastern Europe did the Russian commands break the line of the Dniester and penetrate to the mouth of the Danube, within the Balkans.

The way through the Caucasus barrier at the far end proved even more impenetrable. The Moslem mountaineers, moved by the spirit of a holy war, made a grim stand there, led for a time by the redoubtable Shamil, and aided constantly by the Turks. The way was literally blasted out with cannon. By 1829 the Russian armies were through to Baku and the Azerbaijan corridor to Persia. They had crossed the land bridge between the inland seas. In 1864 the Circassians who had held the heights migrated to safety in Turkish territory.

By then the Russians, in common with most Europeans, were calling the Turkish sultans the sick men of Europe. The sick men, however, held to the Black Sea. The Turks came back to Sevastopol—with French and English allies, in the Crimean War. The port at the far end, Batum, they held until 1878.

The sea itself is still divided, four centuries after Suleiman, between the Turks and the expanding Soviet Union. The corridor of Azerbaijan, once Turkish, is not yet under Soviet control. The Caucasus heights and the shore of the Ukraine simmered with revolt during the German military invasion of 1943–44. After four centuries Moscow has not been able to wrest the Black Sea from the Turks.

Along the road that Potemkin prepared for Catherine's Black Sea triumph, there was a signpost, "To Constantinople."

The capture of Constantinople on the waterway into the Mediterranean took shape in Russian fancy, joined to the concept of liberating the fellow Slavs in the Balkans. These remained, as Sumner puts it, "schemes and dreams, but pregnant for the future."

During the fabulous nineteenth century tsarist Russia, gripping the Caucasus land bridge at the far end, and with a foothold in the Balkans, argued much about the straits of the Dardanelles, the exit from the sea. "They are the gates of our house."

Russian interest had switched again from the Baltic-and-the-way-out-of-it, to the Black Sea. But Russian policy was rather well satisfied to have the straits neutralized, fortified by the Turks against the approach of war, either way.

"They are the hearth of our house," the Turks explained in answer. The waterways of the Bosphorus, the Marmora Sea and the outer straits form the arterial of their country, as in Suleiman's time.

After the Revolution, the industrial development of the Don

basin and of oilfields in the Caucasus drew the attention of the planners of the USSR away from the Baltic outlet to the Black Sea.

After the climax of the war of 1939–45, the Soviet expansion, following the line of the Molotov-Ribbentrop agreement, pushed swiftly out along the Baltic shores. With the Baltic virtually controlled, Soviet expansion took its course again to the Black Sea.

To the Soviet request for Trebizond and the adjacent mountain frontier, and for the "safeguarding" of the northern shore of the straits by Soviet military posts, the Turks answered in effect, "Then come and take them."

When the Turkish Republic remained immovable on the two vital points of surrendering the Black Sea and the straits, Soviet pressure circled around the inland sea. First it struck tentatively through the Caucasus, at the corridor of Azerbaijan beyond. Turned back from Iran (Persia), it moved west to strike down through the long Greek mountain frontier toward the Aegean and the barrier islands outside the straits.

Turned back from Greece, Soviet expansion moved elsewhere.

The Turks are waiting now (1950) quietly enough for it to return to the Black Sea and the northern shore of the waterways. But the Turks say their straits will not change hands. "What has been, will be."

There are times, like the present, when that is a comforting thought.

In one of the colder winters of the last war, after Christmas of 1944, I visited Istanbul, that had been Constantinople. I wanted a few days' rest from being near the war. So I went to Turkey, as I had done before, to find it.

Rain filled the sky. Some of the small gray ships anchored out from Serai Point up the Bosphorus had the swastika painted broad on their sides, because the Nazis then held the adjacent

Aegean islands. Few people were in the Covered Market where I browsed, looking for a stray Koran or an Armenian manuscript.

Mist lay like a veil out from Barbarossa's tomb. The day that I took one of the small trams up the hill to the university and went into Suleiman's mosque for a farewell look around, it rained hard.

No one else had come into the mosque. Yet out in the courtyard a company of boys waited, in their gray uniforms of cadets. They had overcoats, and they waited cheerfully enough for something.

Then a trivial thing happened. Two schoolgirls came in out of the rain. At the entrance, according to old custom, they slipped off their shoes. They went to a carpeted window embrasure and opened their books as if to study between classes. They looked like any American girls, and they behaved in the same way because, after curling up on the carpet, instead of studying they began to chatter, very softly, because, after all, they had come into a mosque.

Watching them, apparently unheeding the cadets outside, I wondered what the story of their lives might be. We knew so little of the Turks. As a people they have been silent, and Americans can find little of their history to read.

It seemed absurd that the modern schoolgirls across the dim space of the mosque should be like creatures of an unknown people. I wondered why I kept coming back to this particular place, and why this mosque had been built, and who Suleiman had been, who built it.

Acknowledgment

In this effort to tell the life story of the first Suleiman for the general reader, I am deeply indebted to the masterly study of the economy of the Sultan and his time by Professor Lybyer: *The Government of the Ottoman Empire in the Time of Suleiman the Magnificent*, Albert Howe Lybyer, Harvard University Press, 1913. (Notable for its clear exposition of the ruling institution—the Organization—and a superb bibliography.)

I am indebted to Professor Barnette Miller for details of the Enderun from her *The Palace School of Muhammad the Conqueror*, Harvard University Press, 1941. I have made use of several reports of the various Italians from the chronological biography of the noted historian of Spain, Professor Roger Merriman, *Suleiman the Magnificent, 1520–1566*, Harvard University Press, 1944.

In her Introduction, Professor Miller warns us that "The knowledge of the Turks which has existed in the Occident until recently has been very limited. It has been confined almost wholly to their past military glory, the fanatical aspect of their religion, a magnificence so great that Europeans—not Turks—bestowed the epithet of 'Magnificent' upon Suleiman in the magnificent age of the Renaissance, and certain sensational features such as massacres and the harem system—generally viewed through the perspective of the Crusades and the modern Protestant missionary movement. As a consequence the Turkish nation has for centuries been viewed with an ignorant prejudice almost unparalleled in history."

I think both the ignorance and the prejudice are without any parallel in history.

ACKNOWLEDGMENT

The Turkish way of life in the sixteenth century is strange to us. Of it Hester Jenkins says, "it is very difficult to place soberly before occidental readers. . . . But our only chance of understanding it is to banish from our minds western conceptions and accept as facts what seem like wild imaginings."

So this book has been written from the Turkish viewpoint, as I could understand it, against the background of their country as it could be reconstructed. All the people existed as they are shown; the events took place; at times thoughts and words have been conjectured from some known fact.

I have been aided by material generously given by Dr. Adnan Erzi of the Historical Library, Ankara. Lewis V. Thomas of Princeton University gave me wise advice that no textbook could supply, when we met last summer in Istanbul.

The three titles cited above are all that curious Americans may find in libraries in this country. No modern history of the Turks, from their early migration to their splendor and decline and subsequent recovery today at the threshold of Europe, can be found, because it does not exist. There is no account of them, both modern and accurate, in English. As Richard Knolles said more than three centuries ago, there is nothing more strange or wonderful in the empire of the Turks "as that it is not well known unto themselves, or agreed upon even among the best writers of their Histories."

Turkish scholarship in the last generation has made a good beginning at establishing the realities of the past. Among its publications, the sixteenth volume of the *Dunya Tarihi—Osmanli Tarihi* (*History of the Osmanlis*), II *Cilt*, Ankara, 1949, has 115 pages dealing with the reign of Suleiman. It is a chronological outline, with emphasis on military achievement.

This book is based on the ten volumes of Joseph von Hammer-Purgstall, the monumental and detailed *Geschichte des Osmanischen Reiches*, Pesth, 1827–35. (French translation, *Histoire de l'Empire Ottoman depuis son origine jusqu'à nos jours*, J. de Hammer, Paris, 1836.) Von Hammer worked from manifold Turkish sources, some of them not utilized since his day. Time has served to lay bare his errors but not to better his achievement.

351

ACKNOWLEDGMENT

I have made use chiefly of the following:

Alberi, Eugenio, *Relazione degli ambasciatori Veneti al Senato*, 15 vols., Florence, 1839-63. (The remarkable accounts of Venetian envoys who served also as polite spies.)

Charrière, Ernest, *Negociations de la France dans le Levant*, 4 vols., Paris, 1848-60. (The documents, often startling, of the French dealings with the Turks.)

Gibb, E. J. W., *A History of Ottoman Poetry*, 6 vols., London, 1900-9. (The poetical efforts of the sultans, with sketches of Yahya and Baki.)

Postel, Guillaume, *De la répablique des Turcs*, Poitiers, 1560.

Rustem Pasha. *Die osmanische Chronik des Rustem Pasha* by Ludwig Forrer, Leipzig, 1923. (Partial translation of Rustem's memoirs.)

ACCOUNTS OF THE VISITING OBSERVERS

Aramon. *Le voyage de Monsieur D'Aramon—par Jean Chesneau*, ed. by Charles Schéfer, Paris, 1897. (The experience of the French envoy who first dealt with Barbarossa, by his secretary.)

Busbecq. *Life and Letters of Ogier Ghiselin de Busbecq* by Charles T. Forster and E. H. Blackburne, 2 vols., London, 1881. (The best narrative of the last years of Suleiman, in frank letters to a friend.)

Navagero, Bernardo, *Relazione*, 1553.

Rycaut, Paul, *The Present State of the Ottoman Empire*, London, 1668. (View of a realistic Englishman, a century after Suleiman.)

Thévenot, *The Travels of Monsieur de Thévenot into the Levant*, London, 1687. (Most valuable for its details of ordinary life.)

ACKNOWLEDGMENT

TESTIMONY FROM THE OUTSIDE

Bourbon, Jacques de, *La grande et merveilleuse et très cruelle oppugnation de la noble cité de Rhodes*, Paris, 1527. (The best eyewitness account of the siege.)

Commentarius Brevis Rerum in Orbe Gestarum, Cologne, 1567. (This *Brief World Happenings* written by Catholic Germans far from the scene still mentions Suleiman and his doings only less often than Luther and Charles V. With other chronicles, it reminds us how vitally Suleiman affected the interests of Europeans in his day.)

Hippolyto, Sanz, *La Maltea en que se trata la famosa defensa de sant Joan en la isla de Maltea*, Valencia, 1582.

Jovius, Paulus, *Turcicarum Rerum Commentarius*, Paris, 1538.

Knolles, Richard, *The Generall Historie of the Turks*, 4th ed., Adam Islip, 1631. (Written in 1603 and continued after him to 1621, this full-bodied narrative of the Turks from outer testimony reflects the fear and the admiration they aroused.)

Luther, Martin, *De Bello Turcica*, 1530.

Pantaleon, Henrico, *Militaris Ordinis Johannitarum, Rhodiorum aut Melitensium Equitum Rerum Memorabilium*, Basle, 1581. (One of the many histories of the Knights, and their defense of Malta.)

THE SEA, AND ITS STORYTELLERS

Haji Khalifa, *The History of the Maritime Wars of the Turks*, translated from the Turkish by James Mitchell, London, 1831.

Piri Reis, *Bir Turk Amirali*, Istanbul, 1937. (Sketch of the career of Piri Reis as a geographer, admiral, and finder of a portion of the lost map of Christopher Columbus.)

ACKNOWLEDGMENT

Sidi Ali Reis, *The Travels and Adventures of the Turkish Admiral Sidi Ali Reis*, translated by A. Vambéry, London, 1899.

De La Gravière, Jurien, *Doria et Barberousse*, Paris, 1886. (The only western narrative of the Turks in the Mediterranean that is not biased, misleading, or misinformed. A notable work by a man of the sea.)

Mercier, Ernest, *Histoire de L'Afrique Septentrionale (Berbérie)*, Paris, 1891. (The only adequate account of medieval North Africa, its conflicts and its peoples. Like the Turks themselves, this coast has been dropped from the course of western history. It disappears from Roman times to colonial French.)

Oz, Tahsin, *Barbarosun*, Istanbul, 1936. (A new appreciation of the first Turkish admiral.)

THE MEETING WITH THE RUSSIANS IN THE STEPPES AND THE BEGINNING OF THE STRUGGLE FOR THE BLACK SEA

Howorth, Sir Henry, *History of the Mongols* (Part II, the So-Called Tartars of Russia), London, 1880. (Dealings of the Krim khans with Moscow.)

Inalcik, Halil, *The Origin of the Ottoman-Russian Rivalry, and the Don-Volga Canal*, 1569.

Lamb, Harold, *The March of Muscovy*, New York, 1948.

———, *The City and the Tsar*, New York, 1948.

Sumner, B. H., *Survey of Russian History*, London, 1944. (Contains a study of the Russian expansion toward the two outlet seas, the Baltic and Black Sea.)

FOR GENERAL READING

Colorful accounts of the Serai, with good maps and photographs, are to be found in *Beyond the Sublime Porte* by Barnette

354

ACKNOWLEDGMENT

Miller, Yale University Press, 1931, and in *The Harēm* by N. M. Penzer, London, 1936.

Two brief German volumes—*Konstantinopel unter Suleiman dem Grossen, aufgenommen im Jahre 1559* by E Oberhummer, München, 1902; and Franz Babinger's *Die Geschichtsschreiber der Osmanen und ihre Werke*, Leipzig, 1927—give a description of the city at that time, and Turkish sources.

One of the most understanding appraisals of Turkish character lies in *Turkey in Europe* by Sir Charles Elliot. *The Bektash Order of Dervishes* by the master of Turkish lore, J K. Birge, sheds light on the great influence of that little-known order.

Sir Charles Oman's fine *A History of the Art of War in the Sixteenth Century* is imbued with the Victorian conviction that the Turks were attacking Christendom. This distinguished scholar did not understand the Turkish character or objectives, but his description of the European efforts is painstaking.

Index

Abu Hanifa, grave found, 217
Aden, seized by Turks, 237
Adriatic Sea, 162; sea campaigns under Barbarossa in, 179, 183–87, 193–98
Aegean Sea, 162; Turkish control won by Barbarossa, 186
Aegina raided by Barbarossa, 186
Africa, North, attempt of Spain to control, 234–36; conflict with Europe, 162–64
Ahmed, Vizir, 252
Ahmed Pasha, 87
Akbar, Emperor of Hindustan, 268
Alexander the Great, Suleiman influenced by, 24
Algiers, besieged by Charles V, 201–6, piracy developed in, 339; seized by Barbarossa, 164; Spanish fleet captured at, 166
Ali Pasha, 275–76
Alva, Duke of, 202
Alvaro de Sande, Don, 270
America, early map of, 176
Anatolia, Turkoman outbreak in, 111
Anne of Bohemia and Hungary, wife of Ferdinand I, 111
Arabs, in Constantinople, 84

Ardibil, raided by Turks, 219
Armenians, in Constantinople, 84; trade concessions under Turks, 112
Army, Turkish, 330–31; in camp, 210–11; importance of, in Osmanli rule, 31, 154; on march, 40–41; plundering as economic necessity for, 101–2; in Suleiman's old age, 281–83
Army of Asia, 41
Army of Europe, 41
Arslan Khan, 305
Arta, Gulf of, sea battle between Turks and Holy League in, 193–98
Artillery, at siege of Rhodes, 60
Asia, Suleiman's turn to, 156–67, 170, 207–9; Turkish campaign in, 211–19
Asker. See Army, Turkish
Astrakhan, seized by Ivan the Terrible, 262–63; Suleiman's plan for retaking, 264; Turkish supervision of, 227
Austria, first Turkish campaign against, 125–33; second Turkish campaign against, 151–56; Suleiman's intentions toward, 153–55

357

Avlona, landing of Turkish troops at, 183

Aya Sophia (Santa Sophia), 82–83

Ayas Pasha, 61; as First Vizir, 220–21, 238

Ayın (old custom), 26–27, 31–32, 316

Azov, Crimea, conquests of, 343–45

Azov, Sea of, 161

Baden, Turkish seizure of, 132

Baghdad, retaken by Turks, 216; seized by Persians, 212

Bairam, feast of, described by Ogier Busbecq, 209–10

Bajazet *See* Bayazid

Baki, poet, 287, 302; quoted, 313–14, 317

Bali Agha, 42–43

Balbus, Hieronymus, 93–94

Baltajı Mehmed, 345

Barbaro, Marcantonio, quoted, 76

Barbarossa, Khair ad-Din, 161, 164–206, battle of Prevesa, 193–98, campaign in Adriatic, 179, 183–87; campaign in western Mediterranean, 200–1, 206; capture and loss of Tunis, 170–74; expedition to France, 227–31; honored by Sultan Selim, 165; made commander of Turkish fleet, 166–70; negotiations with Christian powers, 180–82, 201

Barbary Coast, development of, 338–40

Bavaria, Reformation in, 134

Bayazid, son of Suleiman, 118, 141, 243, 249; death of, 284–85; favored as heir to Suleiman, 251, 257; rivalry with brother Selim for right of succession, 277–79; treachery of, 271, 279–84

Bayazid II, 7–8

Beat-the-Devil, lieutenant of Barbarossa, 165, 171, 173, 194

Beaufort, Henry of, expedition to Africa, 234

Belgrade, campaign against, 37–42; conquest of, 42–43; treaty of (1739), between Turks and Russians, 346

Berbers, in Constantinople, 84

Biths, seized by Persians, 212

Bizerta, as hideaway for Barbarossa, 171, 174

Black Mountain (Montenegro), 289–90

Black Sea, 161, 222–23; conflict between Turks and Russians for, 340–48; peoples of, 223–27

Bohemia, Suleiman's intentions toward, 153; in Turkish campaign against Hungary, 95–96

Bologna, Charles V crowned emperor at, 134

Books of library in Suleimaniye, 255

Bosnia, advance of Austrian army through, 188–89

Bourbon, Duc de, expedition to Africa, 234

Bragadino, Venetian Bailo, *quoted*, 119

Brief World Happenings, 312–13; *quoted*, 132, 175, 188, 205

Brotherhood, Suleiman's concept of, 69

Brunn, Turkish seizure of, 132

Brusa, 249–50

Buda, after death of John Zapolya, 199–200; held by Turks for John Zapolya, 134–35; occupied by Ferdinand, 119–20; retaken by Turks, 124–25; Turkish conquest of, 102–4

Buildings ordered by Suleiman, 254–58

Bujeya, captured by Turks, 234; retreat of Charles V to, after defeat at Algiers, 205

Bulgars, 113

Busbecq, Ogier, Austrian ambassador to Turks, 209, 261, 265, 274, 289, 316; *quoted*, 53–54, 209–11, 212, 253, 270–71, 274–76, 277, 278

Byzantine influence on Osmanlis, 83–84

Cacca-diabolo. *See* Beat-the-Devil

Cambrai, League of, 192*n.*, peace of, between France and Charles V, 125

Caravels, 172

Cartier, Jacques, 182

Castro, captured by Turks, 183

Catherine of Aragon, 18

Catherine the Great of Russia, 346

Cephalonia raided by Barbarossa, 186

Cervantes, Miguel de, 335, *quoted*, 206

Charles V of Holy Roman Empire, 17–18, 92–94, in campaign to defend Vienna against Turks, 150–53; conflict at sea with Turks, 165–66, 171–76, 180–81, 200–6; in defense of Hungary against Turks, 95; in defense of Vienna, 126; land force sent down Drave River against Turks, 187–89; and Lutheran uprisings, 94–95, 150; as member of Holy League, 189–98; Peace of Crépy with Francis I, 231; peace mission to Suleiman, 133–35; peace treaty of 1547 with Suleiman, 240; peace treaty with Francis I, 125; relationships with European powers, 110–12; retreat to monastery, 272; sea and land attack of French and Turks against, 228; second peace mission to Suleiman, 157–60; ten-year truce with Francis I during invasion of

Italy, 184; treaty of Madrid with Francis I, 108; after Turkish conquest of Rhodes, 67; and uprising of Lutherans, 94–95; war with Francis I, 56

Charles XII of Sweden, 344

Chiarezza, 319

Christianity, attitude of Suleiman toward, 68–69, 115–16, 149, 261; resistance of, within Suleiman's dominion, 289–90

Christians, Turkish treatment of, 7, 68, 76, 116, 255

City of God, by St. Augustine, 162

Civita Vecchia, threatened by Barbarossa, 228–29

Clement VII, Pope, 95, 96; held prisoner by Charles V, 111

Colombo, Cristoforo, 163

Commentary on Turkish Affairs, by Paolo Giovio, 239

Constantinople, 9–10, 82–85; bodies of water surrounding, 161–62, conquest of, by Turks, 3, 6, 30; festivals in Hippodrome, 86–87, 136–41; religious center built by Suleiman in, 254–56; Suleiman's ambitions for, 145–46

Contarini, Bartolomeo, *quoted*, 16–17

Conversion of Christians to Islam, 288–89

Corfu, Turkish siege of, 184–85

Cornaro, Mark Antony, 190–91

Cortez, Hernando, 202, 204

Cossacks, 224–25, 342–43

Crépy, Peace of, between Charles V and Francis I, 231

Crete, captured by Turks, 338; raided by Barbarossa, 186

Crimea, 225–27; Tatar khans of, 116, 262–63

Croats, 113; as allies of Suleiman, 123

INDEX

Crusades, retreat of Knights to Rhodes, 56

Cyprus, rental paid Turks by Venice for, 47; retreat of Knights to, 56; Turkish invasion of, 333–34

Danube River, first Turkish campaign to break European defense of, 37–44, second campaign against, 90–92, 94–104; third campaign against, 123–33; Turkish missionaries along, 113

Dardanelles, 162, 347–48

De Bello Turcica, by Martin Luther, 133

De la Forêt, Jean, 181–82

Diet of Spires, 95

Diet of Worms, 92–93

Diu, attacked by Turks, 237

Divan, 75; harem influence exerted over, 241–53, withdrawal of Suleiman from, 114–15

Diyarbekr, Rustem appointed Beylerbey of, 244

Don Cossacks, 225, 342–43

Don River, canal to Volga, attempt at, 330, plans for, 264

Donini, Marcantonio, *quoted*, 288

Doria, Andrea, negotiations with Francis I, 231; sea campaigns against Turks, 166–67, 171, 174–75, 179–81, 192–98, 202–5, 233–34, 236

Doria, Giovanetto, 232

Doria, Giovanni, 236

Dragut (Torgut), Turkish admiral, 194–95, 202, 231, campaign against Malta, 291–95; in command of Turkish fleet, 232–36, 240, 264–65, 270, 290–91

Drake, Francis, 334

Drave River, Austrian advance against Turks down, 187–89

Dürer, Albrecht, 239

Education, 7; at Enclosed School, 48–54; schools in new Suleimaniye, 255

Egypt, France given trade concessions by Turks, 110–11; under Turkish rule, 87, 146, 147, 259

Elba, plundered by Barbarossa, 167–68, 231

Enclosed School *See* School

Enghien, François Bourbon, Duc d', 229

Enzersdorf, Turkish seizure of, 132

Ertoghrul, ancestor of House of Osman, 29–30

Erzerum, seized by Persians, 247

Eszék, rout of Austrian army by Turks at, 188–89

Europe, conflict with North Africa, 162–64; disunity after defeat of Rhodes, 67; fear of Suleiman, 144–45; first campaign of Suleiman against, 36–44; fourth campaign of Suleiman against, 150–56; knowledge of Suleiman, 239, last campaign of Suleiman against, 301–10; middle, under control of Hapsburgs, 112; muster of armies at Vienna for expected Turkish attack, 150–56, peace treaty of 1547 with Suleiman, 239–41; second campaign of Suleiman against, 90–92, 94–105; third campaign of Suleiman against, 123–33

European rulers, Suleiman's efforts toward friendship with, 69–71; *see also* Suleiman I, diplomatic relations with European powers

Extraterritoriality, principle of, established between Turks and French, 182

Farming as basis of Osmanli civilization, 33

Farnese, Alessandro, of Parma, 336

INDEX

Ferdinand I of Holy Roman Empire, 95; advance along Drave River against Turks, 187–89; effort to regain Hungary by truce with Suleiman, 134–35, effort to seize Hungary after death of John Zapolya, 199; elected emperor, 235, 272; envoys sent to Suleiman by, 119–23, 240; as member of Holy League, 189–98; peace treaty of 1547 with Suleiman, 239–41; re-entry into Hungary, 150; second effort to achieve truce with Suleiman, 157–60; during second Turkish invasion of Austria, 155; six months' truce with Turks, 276; during Turkish siege of Vienna, 126

Ferdinand V of Castile, 163

Ferhad Pasha, 47, 62, 77–78

Floating castles. See Galleons

Florence, trade treaty with Turks, 301

Flower of Spring. See Gulbehar

Fondi, plundered by Barbarossa, 170

Foreign birth of government officials, 49–50, 53

Foscari, Francis, 191–92

France, Barbarossa's expedition to, 227–31; given trade concessions in Egypt by Turks, 110–11; trade privileges ceded by Turks, 182–83; Turkish desire for friendship with, 106; see also Francis I; Henry II

Francis I of France, 17, 93, 137; aided by Suleiman, 105–8; as ally of Suleiman in sea campaign against Charles V, 179, 181–84, breaking of truce with Charles V, 206, as host to Barbarossa, 227–31; Peace of Crépy with Charles V, 231; peace treaty of 1547 with Suleiman, 239–41; peace treaty with Charles V, 125; as prisoner of Charles V, 94; support of Reformation, 134; ten-year truce with Charles V during campaign in Italy, 184; treaty of Madrid with Charles V, 108; war with Charles V, 56

Franciscans, quarters of, in Jerusalem, moved by Suleiman, 256–57

Frangipani, Count, 91, 105–7, 112, 113

Fratricide as Law of Osmanlis, 78, 117–18, effort to change, 243–44

Fugger, Jakob, 17, 110

Galleons, 192, 195, 196

Galley slaves, 171–72, 232

Genoa, relations with Turks, 45; in sea battle against Barbarossa, 193; sea power of, 163

General Historie of the Turkes, by Richard Knolles, *cited*, 313

Georgians, 282, 283

Germany, uprising of Lutherans in, 93, 94–95, 134; *see also* Charles V

Ghazali, 47

Ghirei, Krim Khan, 226, 262–63, 302

Gibraltar, raided by Barbarossa, 201

Giglio, Isle of, captured by Barbarossa, 231

Giovio, Paolo, 239, *quoted*, 17, 18, 44, 113

Goa, Turkish efforts to dislodge Portuguese from, 266, 269–70

Gonzaga, Giulia, flight from Barbarossa, 170

Gonzaga, Viceroy of Sicily, 180

Government, Turkish, foreign birth of officials, 49–50, 53; *see also* Organization

Gozo, captured by Turks, 291

Gran, Turkish occupation of, 124

Granada, Spanish conquest of, 163

Greece, islands raided by Barbarossa, 186; under Turkish rule, 112, 146

Gritti, Andrea, Doge of Venice, 46, 137; as member of Holy League, 189–98

Gritti, Luigi, 46–48, 54–56, 113, 137–40, 146, 160; as envoy from Hungary, 123, 132; as liaison officer for foreign affairs, 74, 91–92, 110

Gulbehar, mother of Suleiman's first son, 18–21, 22, 80, 82, 118–19, 142, 242

Guns, siege of, 152, 155

Hafiza, Sultan Valideh (Queen Mother), 21–22, 79–80, 118–19, 141–42

Hajji Khalifa, 186, 187

Hannibal, Suleiman influenced by, 24

Hapsburg, House of. See Charles V; Ferdinand I, Philip II

Haram (Sanctuary) in Jerusalem, 256–57

Harem of Sultan, 18–22; customs of, 79–81, 118–19; hierarchy of, 119; influence exerted over government affairs, 241–53; misconceptions about, 328–29; rule of, after Suleiman, 318–25

Hassan, son of Barbarossa, 296

Hassan Agha, 176, 201–6

Henry II of France, 272

Henry VIII of England, 18, 44; allegiance to Charles V, 227; in defense of Hungary against Turks, 94, 96

Herberstein, Sigismund, Baron von, 240

Hereditary rights of dependents of government officials, 116–17

Hippodrome, Constantinople, first festival in, 86–87; second festival in, 136–41

Hobordanacz, envoy from Hapsburgs to Suleiman, 120–23

Holy League, formation of, 189–92; sea campaign against Turks, 192–98

Holy Roman Empire, Charles V elected emperor of, 17–18

Hospitals in Suleimaniye, 255

Hostels in Suleimaniye, 255

Hungary, as divided by Suleiman after death of Zapolya, 200; Ferdinand proclaimed king of, 111; first campaign of Suleiman against, 37–44; last campaign of Suleiman in, 304–10; march of Turks through, in support of Francis I, 228; second campaign against, 91–92, 94–105, third campaign against, 123–25; torn between Hapsburgs and Zapolya, 119–23; tribute paid to Turks by Ferdinand I for holdings in, 240–41; Zapolya crowned king of, 112

Huss, John, 95–96

Ibn Sa'ud, Mufti, 238–39, 248, 261, 264, 283, 286, 304, 311, 333

Ibrahim, 5, 7–9; accused of treason, 217–18; on campaign into Asia, 213, 216; as Captain of Inner Palace, 23–25, 70–71; execution of, 219–20; increasing luxuries of, 89, 138; increasing self-importance of, 148–49, 159–60, 208; made Serasker (Marshal of Army), 124; named First Vizir, 73–74, 76–77; overstepping of authority, 213, 218; as Vizir, 87, 110–11, 120–22, 135, 158–59, 168

Ibrahim, Sultan, 321–23

Ibrahim the Drunken, stained-glass windows by, 256

Idiger Khan, 262

India, journey of wrecked Turkish seamen through, 266–68; relations with Turks, 212, Turkish sea expedition to, 237–38

Indian Ocean, Turkish expedition in, 237–38

Inn River, Turkish campaign reaching to, 132

Irene, Empress, 84

Isabella of Castile, 163

Isabella of Poland, Queen of Hungary, 199–200, 272

Iskander Chelebi, 74, 150, 159-60, 217–18

Islam, conversion of Europeans to, 288–89

Ismail I, Shah of Persia, 72, 211–12, 213

Istanbul. See Constantinople

Italy, campaign against, 179, 183–85

Ivan the Terrible, Tsar of Russia, 227, 262–63; efforts to control Black Sea, 340–41

Jahangir, son of Suleiman, 142, 243, 249

Jallal ad-Din Rumi, tomb of, 214

Janizaris, 10–11, 15, 88–89, camp life of, 210–11; family rights of, 117, number increased, 221, organization of, 38–40; in rivalry between sons of Suleiman, 278–83; uprising of, 89–90

Jerusalem, building done by Suleiman in, 256–57; French protectorate over Holy Places in, 183, Turkish control of, 115–16

Jews, in Constantinople, 84, Turkish treatment of, 68, 76, 104

Joanna of Aragon, 170

John I and II of Hungary. See Zapolya

Jones, John Paul, 346

Juan of Austria, Don, 334–38

Julius II, Pope, 192n.

Justinian, 82

Kabiz, trial of, 149

Kaffa, Crimea, 223

Kaikhosru, Sultan, 29–30

Kairouan, 163

Kara Mustafa, 322, 330

Kasım Pasha, 74–75

Katzianer, John, 188–89

Kazan, capture of, by Ivan the Terrible, 262–63; Suleiman's plan for retaking, 264; Turkish supervision of, 227

Kemal, Mufti (Sheyk of Islam), 74

Kemal Pasha Zade, quoted, 104, 105

Khair ad-Din. See Barbarossa

Khasseki Khurrem (Favorite Laughing One). See Roxelana

Kherson, 346

Khmielnitsky, 343

Khoja Beg, 315–16

Khurrem. See Roxelana

Kiusem, mother of Murad IV, 320–24

Klosterneuburg, Turkish seizure of, 132

Knights of Malta, in battles against Barbarossa, 173, 192–93, 195, 202–4, 229; campaign against, 290–99

Knights of Rhodes, 56–57; defeated by Turks, 58–67; see also Knights of Malta

Knights of St. John. See Knights of Malta; Knights of Rhodes

Knolles, Richard, quoted, 63–64, 151, 189, 296, 298, 313

Kossovo (Field of Crows), 40

Krim Khan, 116, 154, 225–27; see also Crimea, Ghirei; Tatars

INDEX

Kuprulu family, 317, 323
Kurds, 282, 283
Kutusov, Mikhail Ilarionovich, 345

La Valette, Jean de, Grand Master of Knights of Malta, 232, 294–99
Lala Mustafa, 279–81, 333, 334
Lands of War, Osmanli duty to march against, 72
Laughing One. *See* Roxelana
Law, as administered by Divan and Sultan, 114–17; conflict between religious and civil, 149, 221–22, 257; of foreigners in Constantinople, 85; judges of, 76; Suleiman's emphasis on, 32, 147
Law of Egypt, Book of, revision of, 147
League of Cambrai, 192n.
Leo X, Pope, 17
Lepanto, sea battle of, 333–37
Library in Suleimaniye, 255
Lipari Islands raided by Barbarossa, 231
Lodron, Ludwig, 188–89
Louis II of Hungary, 95–99
Louis XII of France, 192n
Louise of Savoy, Queen Mother of France, 105–8
Louvre, Paris, building of, 254
Ludovisi, Daniello de', *quoted,* 207–8
Lull, Raymond, 145
Lutfi Pasha, 178, 180, 183, 184, 186, 194
Luther, Martin, 18, 93, 95, 133
Lutherans, Book of Regensburg, 202; religious truce of Nuremberg with Charles V, 150; uprising of, in Germany, 94–95
Lybyer, Albert, 326, *quoted,* 317

Machiavelli, *quoted,* 51
Madrid, treaty of, between France and Spain, 108

Magnisiya, Mustafa given government of, 142
Magyars, Hungarian state to be ruled by, 123
Mahdiya, captured by Sicilians, 233, captured by Turks, 234
Mahon, Port, plundered by Barbarossa, 174–75
Malta, 237, 290; attack on, 291–99, given to Knights, 67; *see also* Knights of Malta
Malvasia, besieged by Turks, 186
Mamelukes, rule of Egypt by, 87
Marmora, Sea of, 161
Marriage of Suleiman and Roxelana, 144
Martinengo, Gabriel, 60, 65
Mary Hapsburg, Queen of Hungary, 95, 103
Massawa, seized by Turks, 237
Matthias Corvinus, 103
Maximilian I of Holy Roman Empire, 192n.
Maximilian II of Holy Roman Empire, 301, 334
Mecca, aqueduct to, 238; removal of Mantle of Prophet from, 115
Medici, Catherine de', 228, 254
Medici, Giovanni de'. *See* Leo X
Medina-Celi, Duke of, 236
Mediterranean Sea, conflict across, between Europe and North Africa, 162–64; control of, 162–64; failure of Spain to control, 234; western, Turkish power weakened in, 338–40
Mehmed II. *See* Mehmed Fatih
Mehmed III, 319
Mehmed IV, 323–24, 325
Mehmed Fatih (the Conqueror), 6–7, 28, 49; law of fratricide established by, 78
Memmo, Messer Marco, 45–48, 54–56, 90–92
Mendoza, Juan de, 291

Merriman, Roger, *quoted*, 312, 331

Mesopotamia, conflict between Turks and Persians in, 212–16

Mevlevi dervishes, 14

Michelangelo, and dome of St. Peter's, 254

Middle Sea. *See* Mediterranean Sea

Mihrmah, daughter of Suleiman, 238–39, 243, 252, 271, 286, 291, 303

Minorca, plundered by Barbarossa, 174–75

Mirror of Many Countries, The, by Sidi Ali, 269

Mocenigo, envoy from Doge, 137–40

Mohács, battle of, 94–99

Mohammed. *See* Mehmed

Montenegro. *See* Black Mountain

Moors, in Constantinople, 84, 112; driven out of Spain, 145, 165; resistance of, in Spain, 92–93

More, Thomas, 314

Morgan, John, *quoted*, 200–1

Morosov, Ivan, envoy from Moscow, 116

Moscow, envoys to Turks from, 72; relations with Tatars and Turks, 116, 154, 224, 226–27; *see also* Muscovites

Moslem tradition, importance of, 149

Mosque of Suleiman, 255–56

Mufti (Sheyk of Islam), authority of, 77, 221, 246; *see also* Ibn Sa'ud

Muley Hassan, 173–74

Münnich, Count, 345

Murad I, 26–27, 31

Murad III, 301, 304, 311, 318–19, 330

Murad IV, 320–21

Muscat, seized by Turks, 246

Muscovites, campaign toward Crimea, 262–63, relations with

Turks, 212; struggle for control of Black Sea, 340–48; *see also* Moscow

Mustafa, eldest son of Suleiman, 18, 118–19; accused of rebellion, 247–48, efforts of Roxelana to dispose of, 244–45; execution of, 249–50; popularity of, 141–42, 244; as recognized heir to Suleiman, 221, 243

Mustafa Pasha, Serasker, 293–300

Naples, attacked by Barbarossa, 231; conflict with papacy, 273; proposed campaign against, 181

Nauplia, besieged by Turks, 186

Navagero, *quoted*, 239

Nepotism, laws against, 117

Nice, besieged by Barbarossa, 206, 229

Nicopolis, 40

North Africa. *See* Africa

Nur Banu, First Kadin of Selim II, 318–19

Nuremberg, religious truce of, between Luther and Charles V, 150

Ocean, The, treatise by Sidi Ali, 266

Ochialu. *See* Uluj Ali

Odessa, 346

Oman, Sir Charles, *quoted*, 325, 331

On the Liberty of a Christian Man, tract by Martin Luther, 18

Organization (Turkish government), balance of, with religious Law, 221–22, 257; bribery and dishonesty in, 259–60; changes made by Suleiman in, 72–75, 76; law against appointment of relatives, 117; nature of, 75–77; property rights of officials, 116–17; training for, 48–54

Osman, 29, 30; tomb of, 216

Osman, House of, 6–7, 14, 29–31, 311

Osmanli Empire, extent of, under Suleiman, 157; after Suleiman, 312, 317–47

Osmanli Turks, history of, 29–32

Palace of Sultan, 18–22

Palatine, Count, 97–98, 126–27, 131

Papacy, as member of Holy League, 189–98; peace treaty of 1547 with Suleiman, 239–41; *see also* Clement VII; Julius II; Leo X, Paul III; Paul IV; Pius IV

Paul III, Pope, as member of Holy League, 189–98

Paul IV, Pope, 272–73

Pax Turcica See Turkish peace

Peace, effected by Suleiman. *See* Turkish peace

Pereny, Peter, 123

Persia, campaign into, 212–13, 215–19; Erzerum captured by, 247; first envoys to Turks from, 72; peace treaty with Turks, 274–76, relations with Turks, 211–12, religious faith of, 213–14, retreat of Bayazıd, son of Suleiman, to, 284–85; second expedition to, 245–46; war with, under Murad III, 330

Pertau Pasha, 300

Peter the Great of Russia, 157, 344–45

Petersburg (Leningrad), 345

Philip II of Spain, 234–35, 338; battle of Lepanto, 333–37, driven from Mediterranean by Turks, 290–91; expedition against North Africa, 235–37

Piali Pasha, sea commander, 176–77, 232, 236, 270, 293–95, 301, 304, 315, 333, 336

Piracy on Barbary Coast, 338–40

Piri Pasha, 137, 156; at accession of Suleiman, 12–15; advice against Rhodes campaign, 58, at death of Selim I, 1–4, dislike for European campaign, 34–36; retirement of, 73

Piri Reis, 237, 246

Pisa, sea power of, 163

Pius IV, Pope, 296

Plundering of Turkish army, 100–2

Poland, relations with Turks, 45, 224; treaty with Turks, 91

Pope, Turkish attitude toward, 69

Popes. *See* Clement VII; Julius II, Leo X; Paul III; Paul IV; Pius IV

Port Mahon. *See* Mahon

Porto Ercole, plundered by Barbarossa, 231

Portuguese, efforts of Turks to dislodge from Goa, 266, 269–70; opposition to Charles V, 110; sea trade of, 237

Potemkin, 346

Prevesa, sea battle between Holy League and Turks at, 193–98

Prisoners of war, treatment of, 41, 42, 65–67, 99, 130–31, 200

Property rights of government officials, 116–17

Ragusa, relations with Turks, 43, 45

Ramberti, Benedetto, *quoted*, 88–89

Razin, Stenka, 343

Red Sea, Turkish fleet on, 237

Reformation in Europe, 93, 94–95, 134

Regensburg, Book of, 202

Reggio, plundered by Barbarossa, 170, 228

Reign of the Favored Women, after Suleiman, 319–25

Relatives, law against employment of, by government officials, 117

Serbia, advance of Austrian army through, 188–89

Serbs, 113, 282, 289–90, 344; in Constantinople, 84

Shi'ites, 212, 213–14, 245–46

Ships, types of, 171–72, 192, 339

Sicily, conflict with papacy, 273

Sidi Ali, admiral and poet, 265–69

Sinan, lieutenant of Barbarossa, 165, 171–73, 177, 194, 232, 235

Sinan Agha, the Architect, 238, 247; buildings by, 256–57; Suleimaniye built by, 254–56, 315

Sinan Pasha, 338

Sinan Reis, 265

Slavery, Turkish traffic in, 276

Sobiesky, Jan, 330

Sokolli, Mehmed, 264, 280–84, 286; as First Vizir, 300, 301–2, 304–11, 313, 317, 318, 333, 336–37; rise in Organization of, 74, 247; as student at School, 52–53

Spahis, 38, 148, number increased, 221

Spain, attempt to control North Africa, 234–36; claims to western Mediterranean, 162, invasion of, by Arabs, 163; invasion of North Africa under Ferdinand and Isabella, 163–64; Moors driven from, 145, 165; resistance of Moors in, 92–93; see also Charles V; Philip II

Spires, Diet of, 95, 126–27

Stambul. See Constantinople

Starhemberg, John, 132

Stuhlweissenburg, Turkish occupation of, 124

Styrian mountains, Turkish devastation of, 132

Suez isthmus, Turkish fleet taken over, 237

Suleiman I (the Magnificent), accession to sultanate, 3–17, Barbarossa given command of Turkish fleet by, 166–70; brotherhood concept of, 69–71, 140; campaign against Italy, 179–85; campaign against Malta, 290–99; campaign against Rhodes, 56–67; decision to end European campaigns, 156–57; diplomatic relations with European powers, 45–48, 105–9, 119–23, 134–35, 156–60, 179, 272–73, 276; evaluation of, 312–17, 325–26, 329–32; family intrigues over succession, 241–53, 257; fourth European campaign of, 150–56; and Hungarian succession, 199–200; journey into Asia, 170, 207–19; last march into Europe, 300–10; life of citizens under, 145–48; marriage to Roxelana, 140–44; official life of, 25–33, 114–17; peace treaty of 1547 with European powers, 239–241; personal life of, 18–25, 79–82, 118–19; second European campaign of, 90–92, 94–105; third European campaign (siege of Vienna), 123–33; and treachery of son Bayazid, 271, 277–85

Suleiman Pasha, 237–38; as First Vizir, 244

Suleimaniye, religious center, built by Suleiman, 254–55, 315; mosque of, 255–56; plans for, 246–47

Sultan, hereditary rights of blood relations and descendants, 117–18

Sumner, B. H., quoted, 347

Suvarov, Field Marshal Aleksandr Vasilievich, 345–46

Syria, under Turkish rule, 146

Szegedin, Turkish occupation of, 124

Sziget, siege of, by Turks, 306–10

Tabriz, raided by Turks, 219; re-captured by Persians, 219; Turkish siege of, 213, 218

Tahmasp I, Shah of Persia, 212, 245, 269, 284–85, 313

Tatars, in invasion of Austria, 151–52, 154–55, relations with Turks, 116, 225–27, 262–63, 282; warfare with Russians, 262–63

Taxation of citizens by Turks, 68, 76, 84–85, 146, 259–60; war levies discontinued, 150

Theodora, Empress, 84

Thévenot, Monsieur de, 162; *quoted*, 325, 327

Titian, Suleiman painted by, 239

Toledo, Garcia de, 233, 296, 299

Tomori, Archbishop Paul, 91, 97–100

Torgut. *See* Dragut

Toulon, Barbarossa and Turkish fleet at, 206, 229–31

Transylvania, 112, 224

Treasury of Osmanlis, 28–31, revenues and expenditures of, 146–47, 259–60

Treaties, Turkish: with France, 105–8, 182–83; with Holy Roman Empire, 240; with Poland, 91; with Venice, 45–48

Treaty of Cambrai between France and Charles V, 125

Treaty of Madrid between France and Charles V, 108

Trebizond, 223

Tripoli, captured by Turks, 235, 265

Tuileries, Palais des, Paris, 254

Tunis, captured by Barbarossa, 170; captured by Spain, recaptured by Turks, 338; recaptured by Charles V, 171–74; under Spanish rule, 174

Turkhan Sultan, mother of Mehmed IV, 323–24

Turkish culture, desire of Suleiman for, 145–46

Turkish fleet, Barbarossa given command of, 166–70; *see also* Sea campaigns, Turkish

Turkish peace (*pax Turcica*), 112–13; first plans for, 70–71, 157; treaty of 1547, 239–41

Turkish Republic, 348

Turkish revenues, 146–47

Turkomans, 282

Turks, history of, 29–32; internal strength of, 312, and struggle with Russians for Black Sea, 340–48

Ukraine, 342–48

Uluj Ali, sea captain, 334–38

Uzbeks, 268, 285

Valideh, Sultan (Queen Mother), position of, 21–22

Valois, House of. *See* Francis I; Henry II

Valpo, rout of, 188–89

Varazdin, Bishop of, 96–97

Vasily, Grand Prince of Moscow, 226

Venice, effort to regain sea power after Suleiman, 333–38; peace treaty of 1547 with Suleiman, 230–41; relations with Turks, 43–48, 90–92, 110–11, 139–40, 146, 223; sea empire ended by peace of Prevesa, 198; sea power of, 162, 163; sea warfare with Turks, 177–87; *see also* Holy League

Verday, Paul, 124

Vermeyen, Jan Cornelis, painting of siege of Tunis by, 174

Veronese, Paolo, Suleiman painted by, 239

Vienna, European army mobilization at, for expected Turkish siege, 150–56; legend of Turkish defeat at, 331–32; siege of, after Suleiman, 330, Turkish siege of, 125–31

Villiers de L'Isle Adam, Philippe, Grand Master of Knights of Rhodes, 57, 64–66

Volga River, canal to Don River, attempt at, 330; plans for, 264

Wallachia, 222–25
Wallachians, 113, 223–24, 282
War galleys, 171–72
Warfare, economic necessity of plundering, 101–2; Osmanli duty to wage, 72
Weixelberger, envoy from Hapsburgs to Suleiman, 120–23
White City. See Belgrade
White Sea. See Marmora
Women of Sultan's household, 18–22, 79–82, 118–19, see also Harem of Sultan
Worms, Diet of, 92–93

Ximenes, Cardinal, 92–93, 163

Yahya, poet of Constantinople, 250, 251–52
Yavuz Sultan Selim. See Selim I
Yerba, captured and lost by Spaniards, 236; sea battles of, 233–34, 236
Young Troops. See Janizaris
Yunis Bey, 146, 184

Zante, rental paid Turks by Venice for, 47
Zapolya, John, 96, 103, 112; conflict over succession after death of, 198–200; defeated by Hapsburgs, 119–20, supported by Suleiman, 123–25, 132–35
Zapolya, John Sigismund, King of Hungary, 199–200, 272, 304–5
Zrıngi, Nicholas, 306, 308
Zuñiga y Requeséns, Luıs de, 270

CPSIA information can be obtained
at www.ICGtesting.com
Printed in the USA
LVOW03s2304301116

515236LV00008B/36/P